June Cleaver
Was a Feminist!

D1273830

ALSO BY CARY O'DELL

Women Pioneers in Television:
Biographies of Fifteen Industry Leaders
(McFarland, 1997; paperback 2009)

June Cleaver Was a Feminist!

Reconsidering the Female Characters of Early Television

CARY O'DELL

Foreword by Yvonne Craig

McFarland & Company, Inc., Publishers
Jefferson, North Carolina, and London

Portions of this book are based on works by the author
previously published in *Television Quarterly* and *Nostalgia Digest*,
and on the websites TVparty.com and TVobscurities.com.

LIBRARY OF CONGRESS CATALOGUING-IN-PUBLICATION DATA

O'Dell, Cary, 1968–
June Cleaver was a feminist! : reconsidering the female characters of
early television / Cary O'Dell ; foreword by Yvonne Craig.
p.   cm.
Includes bibliographical references and index.

ISBN 978-0-7864-7177-5
softcover : acid free paper ∞

1. Women on television.   2. Situation comedies
(Television programs)—United States.   I. Title.
PN1992.8.W65O325 2013   791.45'652042—dc23   2013014207

BRITISH LIBRARY CATALOGUING DATA ARE AVAILABLE

On the cover: Barbara Billingsley as June Cleaver in *Leave It to Beaver*
(Photofest/CBS/ABC); sign element © 2012 Shutterstock

Manufactured in the United States of America

*McFarland & Company, Inc., Publishers
Box 611, Jefferson, North Carolina 28640
www.mcfarlandpub.com*

Table of Contents

Acknowledgments vi

Foreword by Yvonne Craig 1

Introduction — "I'll Be Your Mirror" 3

1. "Here, There and Everywhere": Television's Big Picture 11

2. "Mama Said": Television's Wives and Moms 23

3. "She's a Rebel": Lucy and Her Kind 73

4. "Bewitched, Bothered and Bewildered": The Rise of the
   "Magicom" and the Women Who Dominated It 88

5. "She Works Hard for the Money": TV's Women at Work 98

6. "Sisters Are Doin' It for Themselves": Single in the City 162

7. "Femme Fatale": Television's Secret Agents and Super Heroines . . . 176

8. "Voices Carry": A Conclusion 204

Appendix — The Myths of a Medium 207

Chapter Notes 213

Bibliography 224

Index 229

Acknowledgments

Thank you to my friend, the esteemed media historian Dr. Mary Ann Watson, for her insight and advice.

Thank you also to my friends Karmon Runquist and Mike Heintz who proved remarkably patient with me whenever I espoused the underlying symbolism of *The Flying Nun* and *I Dream of Jeannie*.

Foreword by Yvonne Craig

When some time ago Cary mentioned to me that he was writing a book, I knew — based on the kind of person he is — it would be well-crafted and well-researched. However, until I received the manuscript for *June Cleaver Was a Feminist!*, I had no idea how expansive the coverage would be nor how well-founded and logical his conclusions. With the exception of some of the early '50s television shows, I watched as a viewing adult most of the examples he cites. But because I felt independent and free to make choices on my own from the time I was seven years old, it never occurred to me to question whether my personal view of womanhood was being replicated accurately in the visual medium of television.

In reading this book, I became very aware of the degree to which some writers have chosen to misread and therefore mislead us into believing that until recently (and perhaps not even then), women have been ciphers in the realm of television characters. Unfortunately, in many cases the proponents of this view were female writers and critics themselves. All too often it's simply easier to perpetuate an invalid conclusion or misperception than to re-examine it without bias.

This brings to mind a sad but true event. In the heat of the "feminist movement," in which every action seemed to be fraught with motives of female oppression, I worked with a hyper-sensitive female attorney who daily pointed out that it was incumbent upon each of us to ferret out inequities against women and bring them to the fore. One day we got the news of a devastating air crash killing everyone on the plane; we all took bets on how soon she would arrive and ask why more women were not aboard!

Time and time again as I read *June Cleaver Was a Feminist!*, I was amazed at Cary's depth of perception as well as the amount of viewing time it had to have taken to cover this vast subject properly. I'm glad to find someone who holds women in such high regard and who was willing to go deeply into the subject of women's roles in television. I think this book will be an eye-opener for many. Ultimately, I hope it will rightly be considered the definitive book on women in television.

Beyond its being very informative it will bring back floods of memories of the shows some of us remember and inspire those who missed them to take a look.

Thanks, Cary. I'm exceedingly proud to have been a part of this history and prouder still to have been asked to write this Foreword.

Originally a dancer with the Ballet Ruse, Yvonne Craig made her film debut in 1957 and would go on to appear in more than 80 film and television productions. She is best known for her role as Batgirl on the 1960s TV series Batman. *She maintains her own website at Yvonnecraig.com.*

— Introduction —

"I'll Be Your Mirror"

There is more in heaven and earth, Horatio,
than is dreamt of in your philosophy.— Hamlet

In June of 1998, *Time* magazine made some news of its own when they put the disembodied head of TV character Ally McBeal (actress Calista Flockhart) on its cover and asked the question "Is Feminism Dead?"[1]

It was an odd overall statement not only in terms of real-life women at the time but also in regard to the women who were co-existing on TV with Ally at that time. In 1998, *Ally McBeal* was far from the only (or the most popular) leading lady on the small screen. Consider these others from '98: *Buffy, the Vampire Slayer, Xena: Warrior Princess,* Captain Janeway of *Star Trek: Voyager,* Agent Scully of *The X-Files, Profiler,* Helen Hunt in *Mad About You,* Helen Mirren in *Prime Suspect,* and Patricia Richardson of *Home Improvement,* not to mention such other far-from-retiring females as Judge Judy, Barbara Walters, and Oprah.

Unfortunately, this *Time* article was not the first — or last — time that the fictional images of women on television have been admonished for what they supposedly "represent" about the lives of real-life women.

For example, in her 1991 book *Backlash,* Susan Faludi takes to task television of the 1980s and its depictions of women. But her critique is (not surprisingly) one-sided. Faludi picks apart the female characters of *thirtysomething* (unfulfilled working woman Ellyn and unfulfilled housewife Hope), failing to note that the male characters of that same series (self-involved Elliot, immature Gary) were far from "positive" role models either.[2]

Faludi also slams what she calls "the only good mother is a dead mother" genre of sitcom where families are overseen by widowed males. This sort of *Mr. Mom* genre has long been a TV staple (*Bachelor Father,* etc.) and while in evidence in the 1980s, in *Full House*

Though her name and character has long been misappropriated, Barbara Billingsley's June Cleaver on *Leave It to Beaver* (1957–1963), on closer examination, reveals a woman competent, caring, and highly individualistic.

and *My Two Dads*, etc., Faludi fails to mention series of the time that depicted single mothers where dad was dead, gone, or obsolete: *Grace Under Fire*, *Who's the Boss?* and *Baby Boom* as well as the similar shows *The Facts of Life* and *My Sister Sam*.[3]

Despite evidence to the contrary, many of Faludi's opinions have been accepted as fact. The phrase "'80s backlash" repeatedly appears in works as shorthand for something that might not have happened as many of Faludi's "findings," even beyond TV, have since been debunked by *The New York Times* and others.[4]

Faludi isn't alone when dispersing misinformation about women on TV. In 1995, *Working Woman* magazine put Cybill Shepherd on its cover and praised her and other TV actresses for "finally" offering a "realistic" view of working women.[5] Inside, along with the article, was a pictorial showing such classic working women as Mary Richards and Murphy Brown but ignoring any working women prior to 1959, erasing a decade of television programming and its female participants. Interviewed for the article was David Poltrack, VP of research and planning for CBS, who stated, "In the '50s and '60s, working women [on TV] were housewives."[6] But that's not true. What about the teacher of *Our Miss Brooks*, Susie McNamara of *Private Secretary*, Lois Lane, magazine writer Doris Martin on *The Doris Day Show*, TV writer Sally Rogers on *The Dick Van Dyke Show*, and entire programs like *The Nurses*?

Still earlier, in 1989, *TV Guide* stated:

[*I Love Lucy* and *The Honeymooners*] were wonderful shows, and the women were brilliantly funny, but the jokes had to do with how dumb Lucy was and how long-suffering Alice was. And other women: June Cleaver on *Leave It to Beaver*, Donna Stone on *The Donna Reed Show* and the whole page-boyed sisterhood whose repertoire ran from fussing to fainting to cooking.[7]

The above statement is, quite simply, wrong: Lucy wasn't "dumb"; Alice didn't "suffer" (or suffer fools), and of TV's classic moms — Mrs. Cleaver, Margaret Anderson, Donna Stone, and Harriet Nelson — only Mrs. Stone sported a page-boy. And in *none* of their series did any of them faint.[8]

According to Susan J. Douglas' *Where the Girls Are: Growing Up Female with the Mass Media*, not a single uplifting image of American womanhood has ever appeared on television. She dismisses *The Bionic Woman* as Bionic Bimbo and labels *The Gale Storm Show* and *Our Miss Brooks* as "sexist" but fails to give any reason as to why.[9] As with Faludi, Douglas' statements have since been widely referenced in other works without question to their validity, again proving the adage "Don't believe everything you read."

In another frequently cited work, Linda Meehan's *Ladies of the Evening: Women Characters of Prime-Time Television* (1983), the author undertakes a quasi-qualitative analysis of fictional females — and finds them all wanting.[10] Unfortunately, Meehan only viewed — literally — a handful of series, thus creating skewed "findings." She further handicaps the characters she studied by forcing them into her categories of "Harpy," "Decoy," and "Bitch." Nevertheless, Meehan's declarative statements are often used as "proof" about women on TV.[11]

Despite the fact that with just a little thought or a flip of the TV's on-off switch, many of these statements can be disproved, they still make it into print and, from there, become "truth." Why?

Perhaps they endure because in trying to write about television, one is undertaking a monumental task. Though TV is a young medium — just over 60 years old — it has nevertheless already showcased an extraordinary amount of images. It is impossible for anyone to have seen them all and, because of this, time and space, people are simply unable — or unwilling—to immerse themselves fully into the scholarship necessary before making pronouncements. Instead, they rely on the writings of others or on their own assumptions. And, as we've seen, often these are wrong.

Sometimes these incorrect generalizations thrive because, believe it or not, they are well-intentioned. Many writers, in order to praise a *Roseanne* or *Xena*, state that some new program is "the first!" without taking into account TV's full history. As celebratory and seemingly feminist as many of these statements are meant to be, ultimately they end up doing greater disservice. Certainly it is not the objective of feminism to carelessly ignore its female forebears.

It is also common for fictional women of early TV[12] to get short shrift when approached en masse, that is, in a "macro" rather than "micro" sense. The housewives of early TV (like *Donna Reed*) usually get stamped as Stepford Wives when they are addressed as a group. But, interestingly, once a researcher takes to exploring just one series, suddenly there are "exceptions" to this "norm." For example, few TV stars have been more reviled than Ozzie and Harriet Nelson, whose televised picture-perfect-ness has supposedly done more harm than the A-bomb, with Harriet often held up for special contempt. Yet in her essay on *The Adventures of Ozzie and Harriet* in *The Encyclopedia of Television* (2001), Dakota Weisblat has to concede, "Although she may have seemed something of a cipher to viewers, [on closer examination] Harriet represented the voice of reason, rescuing Ozzie—and occasionally David and Ricky—from the consequences of over-impulsive behavior."[13]

———✦———

It is my hope that this book will bring about similar reassessments and that female fictional characters in television history—from Lucy to Mrs. Cleaver and beyond—will be rescued from such simplistic readings and unjust presumptions which often get them labeled "oppressed," "dumb," or "sexist."

This is not to say that *all* images of women on television have been of strong, liberated women. We can no more say that than we can say that current or recent TV images (*The Bachelor*, *Weeds*, *Desperate Housewives*, and those late night ads for *Girls Gone Wild* videos) are always of positive, inspiring women.

Rather, it is the goal of this work to prove that there are no absolutes. As they are today, the images of women on early TV are complicated.

But most were empowering.

In order to make this point, I'm going to let female TV characters, via their dialogue and actions, defend themselves. For simply by watching episodes of various series, one quickly discovers just how far off Faludi, etc., have been.

Of course, I haven't seen every episode of every television series ever. To do so would exhaust any number of decades. So, instead, I have viewed a sampling of episodes from different series (in no particular order), across all genres and, from there, gathered the necessary data.

Though much of the dialogue from shows that I cite is straightforward (when Alice Kramden tells Ralph "Ah, shut up," there's no gray area), I understand that others watching the same program could come away with different interpretations. Therefore, I have attempted to further support my findings, my "take," with the conclusions of other researchers, writers, and historians who have also taken a "micro" approach to the subject. Even then we must concede that drawing ironclad conclusions about fictional TV is tenuous.

Unlike a book or film, television's sheer volume of images, even from one series, almost always makes 100 percent irrefutable proof of anything difficult to support (or, conversely, discredit). The average script for a half-hour show is 80 pages long. At a conservative 26 episodes per season, even a show that lasts only one year would generate 2,080 pages of text, twice the length of *War & Peace*. An hour-long drama of 26 episodes means that if each episode was shown consecutively, they would be four times the length of the average movie. To add to the sheer volume of televised product, many of the series discussed in this book lasted for years: *Father Knows Best* ran for six seasons; *Donna Reed* for eight; *Gunsmoke* for 20.

That said, even a show that did not last years — like many of the shows discussed herein — could still have a broad impact. It must be remembered that TV of the 1950s through the 1970s was not the 100-channel universe of today. Back then, you were lucky if you got a half-dozen stations. Therefore your viewing options were less and audience sizes inherently larger.

Furthermore, the big three networks of the era, since they did not have other competition, could be more patient with struggling series. Today shows frequently get canceled after one airing. In contrast, throughout the 1950s and '60s, low-rated shows were often kept on for a full year. *The Girl from UNCLE* was one of the lowest rated of the 1966–1967 season but it still lasted 29 episodes.

Another factor unique to television is that if a series runs for multiple years, characters can change. A character that starts out shallow can grow, making fool-proof declarations about them dicey. Some who evolved: Sandra of *227* and Suzanne of *Designing Women*.

It is also difficult to impose messages — including messages of gender politics — onto TV shows. This is true today (shall we deconstruct *Whitney*?) and it is especially true of shows from the 1950s and '60s, as they were usually quite innocuous in subject matter (i.e., a major plotline is Beaver won't eat his Brussels sprouts). The 1950s and '60s were the pre–Lear era of television, where TV comedy was to amuse you, not engage you in political discourse. Note how the Ricardos never discussed immigration and the Mertzes never went for couples therapy.

Perhaps the biggest difficulty in analyzing TV is simply trying to define the terms we are trafficking in. If we all agree that images of women on TV should be positive, what is "positive"? And, conversely, what is "negative"?

If "positive" (or, at least, not "negative") characters should be smart, independent, and non-subservient in their behavior, what is "smart" in terms of a TV character? Unfortunately, characters seldom take IQ tests so there's no way to prove that Mrs. Brady was smarter than Mr. Brady.

Additionally, some characters generally considered "smart" can sometimes (like most of us in real life) say or do "dumb" things, but that doesn't make them (or us) "stupid."

Even some characters generally considered pretty dim, like Gilligan, Gracie Allen, and Ted Baxter from *Mary Tyler Moore* (who thought Albania was the capital of New York state) can have their moments of insight and brilliance.

Consider Gracie Allen. In watching the comedy team of Burns and Allen, most people would agree it is Gracie who is the dim bulb of this duo. But that assessment is not without its counter-opinions. Scholar David Marc has said, "[Allen's] 'stupidity' reveals itself as a deep intelligence; her humor is based on a foundation of complex language play, Elizabethan in proportion and style."[14] In her book *Sexual Personae*, Camille Paglia labels Allen "sibylline."[15]

Additionally, in many series, who is "right," "wrong," "strong" or "weak" is not easy to determine, or delineate along male/female lines. Sometimes characters "positive" in one scene can be "negative" in the next. Case in point: In a *Donna Reed* from 1958, Donna's daughter, Mary, can't decide which of two boys to go to a dance with. Rather than choose, she coquettishly strings both of them along. Observing all this is another boy, a nice, not-so-popular one who walks Mary to school and carries her books. We know this last boy is the one Mary should *really* go to the dance with but it takes Mary all episode to figure it out. In the program's final scene, Mary has finally come around: She is at the dance with boy #3. While there, boys #1 and #2 come up and ask her to dance. Mary tells them, "Only if my date will let me."

Viewed on its own, this denouement makes Mary appear highly deferential. But Mary is actually, finally, showing the boy some respect, especially since her treatment of him (actually, all three) throughout the episode had been so self-centered.

—◊◊◊—

These quandaries are not the only ones that come up when taking on the topic of gender on television.

For example, if, just for argument, we decide Lucy was dumb and Gracie was spacey, shouldn't we also ask, "So what?"

The character of Sally Rogers (played by Rose Marie) on *The Dick Van Dyke Show* was, without question, man-hungry and husband-hunting; nearly every line out of her mouth was a wisecrack about her unmarried status. But at what point is a character just a character and not an indictment of a gender?

And why do we apply a standard to some series but not others? In 1989, while *Ally McBeal* was being attacked, the Brit-import *Absolutely Fabulous*, with its two shallow female boozers, was airing concurrently but never found itself held up to ridicule.

And that's not the only double standard. If the characters played by Lucille Ball and Gracie Allen are detrimental to women, why are male actors never taken to task for their roles? Despite the long history of sitcom men who have been "scatterbrained," no one has labeled Ralph Kramden or Herman Munster as injurious to men and boys. Nor have various male comics from Bob Hope to Jack Benny been vilified for portraying characters that could be considered cheap, cowardly, or dumb.

In the end we must ask ourselves just how "politically correct" we want our entertainment. And what are we willing to sacrifice? Do we rob from the world the gifts of Lucille Ball because a viewer somewhere might get the wrong idea? Is that fair to female performers? Is it fair to us?

To continue this thought, if characters like Lucy, etc., are bad role models for young girls, then why do little boys not seem to suffer problems due to, say, Gomer Pyle? Do we give the benefit of the doubt to boys but not the same to girls and, if we don't, who is sexist now?

We also tend to impose another Catch-22 on female characters, one seldom applied to men. If female TV characters like June Cleaver are "too perfect," we hate them. But if a female character is too flawed, say like Ms. McBeal, they end up a decapitated head on *Time* magazine. Women on TV, it seems, just can't win.

—◊◊◊—

There's another hard truth in all this talk of images: Ultimately, it is not the job of any entertainment medium to present us with accurate portrayals. As Donna McCrohan states in her book *Prime Time, Our Time*, while one might be able to see an image of oneself in the surface of a plate, that is not the *purpose* of the plate. Just like TV, that's not what it's for.[16]

As crass as it sounds, the primary goal of television is to sell you stuff—from cars to shampoo. In simplest terms, your TV (PBS notwithstanding) is just a conduit for commercials. And television programming (from sitcoms to sports) is just there as window dressing, a carnival barker of sorts, to entice you in for a sales pitch. Providing accurate and "positive" images is not TV's top priority.

Nor is it the job of theater or movies, yet for some reason it is always TV (the "idiot box," the "boob tube") that gets our contempt. (When in doubt, blame Donna Reed?) Why isn't blame—if there is blame—shared equally among other types of entertainment?

Though some of the movies of the late '40s, '50s and '60s showcased vital, vibrant women (Katharine Hepburn in *Adam's Rib*, Rosalind Russell in *Auntie Mame*, etc.), others were questionable. Consider: Margo Channing from *All About Eve*; Norma Desmond from *Sunset Blvd.*; the trio of *How to Marry a Millionaire*.

Many of the female characters on Broadway in the 1950s and '60s were a surly lot too. Think of the women of *I Am a Camera* (the precursor of *Cabaret*), *Who's Afraid of Virginia Woolf?* and *Sweet Bird of Youth*. Were these women "positive"? Were they good "role models"?

And what about the rarefied world of books? While characters like Jo from *Little Women*, Scout from *To Kill a Mockingbird*, and Alice (the one in *Wonderland*) are literary heroines, what about other fictive females? What about Holly Golightly? Two of the biggest-selling books during the era of June Cleaver and Donna Stone were *Peyton Place* and *Valley of the Dolls*. Were these books' female characters empowering and "positive"?

—⁕⁕⁕—

Not only has actress Donna Reed often found herself diminished, but her entire era of television often finds itself diminished too. From reading various "histories," one could easily think that television of the 1950s consisted of only *I Love Lucy* and *Leave It to Beaver* as opposed to the hundreds of programs which actually made up primetime.

If the '50s is usually thought of only in terms of *Leave It to Beaver*, then the 1960s is usually capsulated into just *Bewitched* and *I Dream of Jeannie*. This manages to ignore Barbara Stanwyck in *The Big Valley*, *Honey West*, *The Nurses*, and *Julia*, along with dozens more.

The 1970s is often remembered only as the decade of *Mary Tyler Moore*. But Mary was far from alone. Also on that decade: Maude, Alice, Ann Romano of *One Day at a Time*, and Olivia Walton, not to mention *The Bionic Woman* and *Wonder Woman*.

Finally, the 1980s, the decade of alleged "backlash" on the small screen, was actually the era of *Cagney & Lacey*, *Murphy Brown*, *Designing Women*, and *LA Law*, not to mention the formidable women of nighttime soaps like Joan Collins on *Dynasty*.[17]

Again, this is a phenomenon unique to television. Motion picture history is never reduced to just one or two films. And it's absurd to sum up American literature in just a handful of books.

—⁕⁕⁕—

Further, while TV is many things, it's not a time machine.

Odd then that so many seem to have such expectations of the television shows of yore.

Again, it seems to be a demand exclusive to TV: When reading newspapers from 1955, we don't expect them to be up-to-date in language, attitudes, and matters of gender. But, for some reason, many expect TV from decades ago (despite the presence of items like rotary phones, etc.) to, magically, be modern in terms of attitudes and mores.

Case in point: In 1993, actress, producer, and multiple Emmy winner Betty White, along with actress Gale Storm, the top-billed star of two hit series, sat down with a female interviewer to discuss the images of women on the small screen. The interviewer began by asking her guests, "Did it ever occur to you the harm you women were doing, portraying these stereotypes?"

As White related about the interview in her autobiography: "My back teeth ... clenched." She continued:

> Without treading on any feminist toes, I tried to indicate that [the era of our shows] was another time and place, and it is specious to overlay today's values on where the world was forty years ago. I couldn't help wondering out loud how our contemporary television shows and lifestyles and attitudes would be perceived by some future group of young women, say forty years in the future.[18]

One also has to wonder just how many episodes of Ms. White's and Ms. Storm's shows this interviewer had seen lately ... if ever.

Madeline Davis, one of the writers of *I Love Lucy*, once said:

> Ricky saying, "I want you to stay home and cook my meals and have my children." I would never write that today. It was a long time ago. People say, "Has comedy changed?" Well, life has changed. So if you write, if you're going to be funny, you write about the funny problems today, which are a little different from the funny problems then.[19]

Yes, art imitates life. But it can only imitate the life and times in which it was created. Television isn't a crystal ball. And even as a *de facto* mirror of a society (and an era), the best TV will ever be is a Dali-esque interpretation of reality, a funhouse mirror, in which some parts are reflected as they are, while others are distorted due to TV's need to entertain. As scholar Mary Ann Watson put it, "[A] thoroughly realistic depiction [of life] is limited by the narrative conventions of drama and comedy."[20]

All this begs another question: Who are these images for anyway? Are they for men to learn what "real" women are like? Are they for adult women so that they can see themselves "mirrored"? Or are "positive" TV images needed for girls so they can have female role models?

And how much "damage" was done anyway? If, for the sake of argument, the images of women on television in earlier years were harmful and stereotypic, then why didn't real-life women revolt? I have yet to hear of any woman of 1950s or '60s America kicking in her Zenith when Donna Reed popped up on it. Do we believe that women weren't "empowered" enough? Don't we have to give our mothers, grandmothers, aunts, and big sisters more credit than that? Lest we forget, many of the women of this era grew up with Rosie the Riveter or had been or known members of the WACs. It's not as if American women underwent a collective lobotomy the minute World War II came to an end and TV came in.

If nothing else, the women of the time certainly had the ability to write letters of complaint to networks or boycott sponsors. If enough found *Father Knows Best* unacceptable, they could easily have protested with their pocketbooks.

But they didn't.

Furthermore, if the girls and women of that era were so crippled by June Cleaver, et al. (like that Chicago radio interviewer suggested), then how did this generation of women go on to become the largest group of women in history to attend college, found businesses, and be elected to government office, not to mention spearhead the modern feminist movement?

And what of the women who worked in broadcasting at that time, both those in front of and behind the cameras?[21] Do we believe that not one female actor, director, writer, or producer was ever able to take pride in her work and in the images they were creating?

And what of the men who worked behind the scenes? Do we buy the all-out misogyny that some authors suggest? Can we not fathom at least one male producer, director or writer who wanted to project "positive" images of women if only to inspire his daughters or appease his wife? As we owe more respect to our mothers and grandmothers, we too owe more than that simplistic stance to our fathers and grandfathers.

———❧———

If, in the end, television is all these things (difficult to analyze, innocuous, etc.), then why (and how) do we need a book like this at all?

Because we need to be liberated from misconceptions.

And the women who worked to bring these early images to the screen need to be vindicated. In the past few decades there has been a concerted effort to unearth the contributions of women (and other minorities) in the sciences, literature, music and the visual arts. But, so far, TV has been omitted. Therefore, it's been misunderstood. It's a misrepresentation that skews our view of history. For a full reassessment of female TV images not only changes how we remember these characters and the actresses who played them, but, ultimately, how we think of the real-life women who watched them.

— 1 —

"Here, There and Everywhere"
Television's Big Picture

Many women are singing together of this....—Anne Sexton

As mentioned, though the history of primetime television isn't very long, it is wide. From its fuzzy beginnings, television has always been more than just dramas and sitcoms, more than just *I Love Lucy* and *Donna Reed*. Odd then that so much television "history" attempts to reduce TV's formative years to just a handful of programs, when in actuality there were all sorts of shows — from music to game shows, anthologies, talk programs, and even primetime sports coverage — to be seen. In fact, network television was a far more diverse place in *types* of shows on the air in previous decades than it is today since some genres — like anthologies and variety — have all but vanished from primetime. But before these programs disappeared, they thrived and often showcased some of the greatest female talents of the 20th century.

Therefore, if, for argument, *Donna Reed*, et al. did unprecedented damage to American women, could the presence of these other women — headlining their own shows or displaying their artistry — counter any ill effects? Could these women be considered "positive" images?

One of primetime TV's most important early genres — since they were relatively easy and inexpensive to produce — were talk shows.[1] And throughout the 1950s, many of these primetime and late night chats were hosted by women like Wendy Barrie, Maggie McNellis, Faye Emerson (often referred to as "Mrs. Television" for her early omnipresence), Arlene Francis (who has the distinction of being the first woman to guest-host *The Tonight Show*), and Ilka Chase. These women's nightly 15- to 30-minute programs were usually Carson-esque in their formats, with their hostesses sitting down with celebrities or "regular folk."

In 1952, radio's Dorothy Gordon brought her well-received *Youth Forums* to television, stating, "When we encourage a flow of ideas between the young ... we are planting the seeds of democracy."[2]

Another notable primetime talk show was *Power of Women* (1952), hosted by Vivien Kellems, then president of the Liberty Belles. It examined topics from a "woman's point of view."

Other early female talkers included Helen Sioussat, long-time director of talks for CBS radio, who hosted one of television's earliest (if not *the* earliest) roundtable discussions in 1945; radio newswoman Mary Margaret McBride, who brought her folksy interview style to TV in 1948; and Virginia Graham, who made her first appearance in 1952. Even screen diva Gloria Swanson headed her own talk show for a time.

Meanwhile, long before *Deal or No Deal*, primetime also featured highly rated game,

11

Faye Emerson (seen here in a circa 1953 shot) is often referred to as Mrs. Television because of her high visibility during the medium's early days. She authoritatively hosted talk shows and game shows and served on TV quiz panels during her small-screen career.

quiz and panel shows[3] with two of the most enduring being *To Tell the Truth* and *What's My Line?* On these two shows, and others, various female panelists often took part ... and shone brightly. In fact, Faye Emerson was such a consistent presence that *Cue* magazine labeled her TV's "peripatetic panelist."[4] Emerson had made her quiz show debut, with then husband Elliott Roosevelt, son of FDR, in 1948 on *Who Said That?* Legend has it that Emerson showed up her husband so much, she apologized for him on air.[5]

Emerson would stay with *Who Said That?* for years and, on it, she maintained the highest rate of accuracy among her fellow panelists which included newsmen and radio commentators.[6] Later, Emerson was a panel member on the quiz shows *Quick as a Flash* and *Masquerade Party.*

Other notable female primetime panelists included Kitty Carlisle, Arlene Francis, Dorothy Kilgallen, Betsy Palmer, and Peggy Cass. *TV Guide* called the classic four-person panel of *What's My Line?*, which included Kilgallen and Francis, "the wittiest lineup of celebrities in game-show history."[7]

Furthermore, even though it was (and is) rare, a few women have even occasionally gotten to act as MC (or "femcee") of game shows, taking their place in the authoritative role of host (as opposed to being seen in more Vanna White capacities). Arlene Francis hosted *Blind Date* (1949) and later *Who's There?* (1952) and *Talent Patrol* (1954). Kay Westfall co-hosted *Sit or Miss* in 1950, and Denise Darcel hosted *Gamble on Love* in 1954.

If not as panelists or hosts, women were often legitimate winners on some of TV's earliest quiz programs, in the process becoming nationally known and, arguably, the first stars of what we now call "reality TV." Before finding fame as an on-air psychiatrist, Dr. Joyce Brothers won the full $64,000 on the subject of boxing on *The $64,000 Question.*[8] And before *Get Smart*, Barbara Feldon, in 1957, also won the show's top prize on the topic of Shakespeare.[9]

Other winners: Catherine Kreitzer, a typist from Pennsylvania who had an expert's knowledge of the Bible; and Gloria Lockerman, a 12-year-old African American girl from Baltimore, whose spelling skills won her $32,000.[10] Meanwhile, on *Twenty-One*, 32-year-old Elfrida Von Nardroff from Brooklyn Heights won a staggering $225,000 on the subject of history.[11] And on *The Quiz Kids* (the *Are You Smarter Than a 5th Grader?* of its day), at least two of that show's prodigies were always girls, including regulars Joan Bishop, who had an IQ of 157, and Vanessa Brown, whose IQ was 169.[12]

As popular as any genres during early TV were anthology programs.[13] These weekly series told a different story each week, sometimes original to the medium, sometimes adapted from the stage or a book. Often the only unifying thread each week was that series' host — and many of these name-in-the-title presenters were women.

June Allyson, Jane Wyman, Loretta Young and Barbara Stanwyck all helmed their own anthologies and quite often took on starring roles in that week's presentation. Each of these actresses, having come from movie stardom, had no intention of taking a backseat on their shows or in the types of roles they played.

On her anthology, Stanwyck appeared several times as a character named Josephine Little, an American who ran an export business in Hong Kong. On her program, Wyman once played an army nurse described as "sensitive, intelligent, mature [and] who did a lot of good for her patients."[14] On her long-running show, Young played a variety of professional women including an art director, doctor, and judge.

Many legendary film actresses brought their talents to television in the 1950s and 60s. Here, Ingrid Bergman plays the lead opposite Hayward Morse in a production of *The Turn of the Screw* in 1959.

If not in the role of hostess, the existence of anthology programs also allowed some famous actresses to shine: *Philco Television Playhouse* presented "Dinner at Eight" with Peggy Wood in 1948; *Prudential Family Theater* did "Over 21," written by and starring Ruth Gordon, in 1950 as well as "The Barretts of Wimpole Street" with Helen Hayes that same year. *Omnibus* presented Eartha Kitt in "Salome" in 1955.

Playhouse 90 gave viewers one of the medium's first classics with "Requiem for a Heavyweight" in 1956; it featured Kim Hunter as a compassionate social worker. *Playhouse 90* later brought viewers Teresa Wright and Patty McCormack in "The Miracle Worker" (1956) and Maria Schell in "For Whom the Bells Tolls" (1958).

In 1956, on *Four Star Jubilee*, there was "Blithe Spirit" with Lauren Bacall and "The Day Lincoln Was Shot" with Lillian Gish. In 1959, on *Ford Startime*, Ingrid Bergman starred in "The Turn of the Screw."

Bette Davis appeared on *GE Theater* in 1954 and '57, on *Schlitz Playhouse of Stars*, in 1957, and on *The Dupont Show* in 1959. Tallulah Bankhead appeared twice on *The United States Steel Hour*, once as Hedda Gabler. And Joan Crawford had roles in episodes of *GE Theater* and *Zane Grey Theater*. Other actresses who made multiple anthology appearances during the genre's heyday: Claire Bloom, Ruth Chatterton, Jessica Tandy, Eva Marie Saint, Kim Stanley, Katharine Cornell, Margaret Leighton, and Eva LeGallienne.[15] By the end of the 1960s, anthologies gave way to made-for-TV movies and miniseries.[16]

The 1970s are usually considered the "golden age" of the TV movie. Certainly that decade gave some actresses career-defining roles. Some of them: *The Autobiography of Miss Jane Pittman* starring Cicely Tyson in 1974; *A Case of Rape* with Elizabeth Montgomery in 1974; Susan Clark as Babe Didrickson in *Babe* in 1975 and the following year in the title role in *Amelia Earhart. Sybil* starring Sally Field and Joanne Woodward and *Eleanor & Franklin* starring Jane Alexander both aired in 1976. *Roots* aired in 1977; it featured Cicely Tyson and Lillian Randolph. *Friendly Fire* with Carol Burnett, in a dramatic role, aired in 1979.

In the 1980s, the decade of alleged "backlash" on TV, films for television continued to impress. Vanessa Redgrave led an all-female cast in the Holocaust drama *Playing for Time* in 1980; Joanne Woodward was a courageous teacher in *Crisis at Central High* and Faye Dunaway appeared in the title role in *Evita Peron*, both in 1981. Nineteen eighty-two brought *A Woman Called Golda* with Ingrid Bergman; *Sister, Sister* with Diahann Carroll; and *Who Will Love My Children?* starring Ann-Margret. In 1985, the AIDS drama *An Early Frost* featured Gena Rowlands. That same year Lucille Ball was in *Stone Pillow*.

Vanessa Redgrave was back on TV, playing Dr. Renee Richards, in *Second Serve* in 1986, while the following year Ann-Margret co-starred with Claudette Colbert in *The Two Mrs. Grenvilles*. Ann Jillian played herself in a dramatization of her breast cancer battle in *The Ann Jillian Story* in 1988, the same year that Julie Christie appeared in *Dadda Is Death*. In 1989, NBC aired *Roe vs. Wade* starring Amy Madigan and Holly Hunter.

Just as anthologies have all but disappeared, so too has the variety show.[17] But, in the dawning days of television up through the 1970s, variety shows were a popular format and, often, these shows were headlined by women.

The very first regularly scheduled TV variety show was NBC's *Hour Glass* in 1946. It was hosted by Evelyn Eaton before Helen Parrish took over. Parrish is often considered to be the first "star" created solely by being on TV.[18]

The Kate Smith Show ran from 1951 to '52 and then again in 1960. Patti Page headlined her own program during the 1950s as did Jo Stafford, Joan Edwards and Rosemary Clooney. *The Ina Ray Hutton Show* starring Hutton and her all-girl band debuted in 1956; *Here's Edie* starring Edie Adams was on in 1963 and 1964; *The Leslie Uggams Show* ran in 1969; *The Pearl Bailey Show* in 1971; and *The Diahann Carroll Show* in the summer of 1976. The most popular star on the long-running *Your Hit Parade* was Gisele MacKenzie, who had a solo show in 1957 and 1958.

In 1963, CBS premiered *The Judy Garland Show*. As author Michael McWilliams wrote of Garland's hour, "Through sheer naked tenacity Garland pulled off some of the most electrifying moments of her career."[19]

Perhaps the woman most identified with musical variety is Dinah Shore, whose shows aired in various incarnations from 1951 to 1962.

In the 1970s, Cher starred opposite then husband Sonny (frequently making jokes about his nose and height) on *The Sonny & Cher Show* and in her own program, *Cher*. That same sort of "Bickersons" repartee was echoed in Tony Orlando's sparring with Telma Hopkins, one half of Dawn, on *Tony Orlando & Dawn* (1974–1976). (Hopkins would later star in *Family Matters*.)

TV's last truly successful variety show was probably *The Carol Burnett Show* which aired from 1967 to 1978. (Another female comic, Martha Raye, headlined her own comedy-variety show from 1954 to 1956.) Many of the last few attempts to bring variety back has been built around women: Tracey Ullman in her *tour de force* on FOX and Dolly Parton and Barbara Mandrell with their country music hours, all in the 1980s.

One of the greatest variety shows ever was *Your Show of Shows*. Among its cast of players, which included Sid Caesar and Carl Reiner, was Imogene Coca. Coca has been acknowledged as an influence by everyone from Carol Burnett to Lily Tomlin. Upon Coca's death in 2001, *Entertainment Weekly* said: "While she played everything from a tremulous wifey to a cuckoo-clock figurine, it was easy to take for granted how powerfully equal she was on a show whose writers included Mel Brooks, Neil Simon and Woody Allen."[20]

The variety format also gave innumerable female performers — singers, dancers, comics, etc. — a chance to perform, often to their largest audiences ever.

For most people, TV variety is defined by *The Ed Sullivan Show*[21]; it was *the* television showcase for some of the world's greatest performers during its run (1948–1971). Some of the women who appeared: Maria Callas in 1956; Ella Fitzgerald in 1957; Sophie Tucker and Odetta in 1960; Leotyne Price in 1961; Joan Sutherland in 1964; Margot Fonteyn in 1965; Dame Judith Anderson, performing a scene from *Elizabeth the Queen*, in 1966; Ethel Merman, also in 1966, in an excerpt from *Annie Get Your Gun*; Miriam Makeba in 1967; Janis Joplin and Beverly Sills in 1969; and Tina Turner in 1970. The Supremes appeared on *Ed Sullivan* 16 times.

Other women who made regular appearances on variety programs: Maria Tallchief, Lena Horne, Roberta Peters, Ann Miller, Della Reese, Mahalia Jackson, and Ethel Barrymore.[22]

Popular vocalists also guested on the airwaves during the variety era.[23] These included Julie London (who told her ex to "Cry Me a River" in 1955); Gale Storm, who scored with "I Hear You Knockin' (But You Can't Come In)" that same year; and Dinah Shore, who had a hit with "Whatever Lola Wants (Lola Gets)" in 1953.

Via series like *Ed Sullivan* and *Shindig*, rock began to creep onto the airwaves. And while Elvis and other men may have dominated, female artists were always around and on

TV. Connie Francis could be found circa 1958 doing her revenge hit "Who's Sorry Now?" Wanda Jackson and the Shirelles both had hits in 1959.

In 1962, Peggy Lee sang "I'm a Woman." Lesley Gore declared "It's My Party" and that she'd cry if she wanted to in 1963. Her anthem "You Don't Own Me" appeared in 1964.

In '63, Little Peggy March stood up to everyone by declaring "I Will Follow Him." The 15-year-old March was a favorite of Perry Como's and often appeared on his program. The following year, the Shangri-Las sang "The Leader of the Pack" while the Supremes said "Stop! In the Name of Love" in 1965.

Nineteen sixty-six saw Nancy Sinatra say "These Boots Were Made for Walkin'" while Aretha Franklin demanded "Respect" in 1967.

Nineteen sixty-eight brought Linda Ronstadt on *The Johnny Cash Show*. Cash's show also featured one of Joni Mitchell's rare TV appearances. Helen Reddy's manifesto "I Am Woman" arrived in 1972; she headlined her own summer replacement series the following year.

The succeeding years brought Gloria Gaynor's "I Will Survive"; Marianne Faithfull's "Broken English" (she performed the title track on *Saturday Night Live* in 1980); and the "punk" movement which included Patti Smith.

Famous female singers from every genre of music were featured regularly on the variety shows of the 1950s and 1960s. The Supremes appeared on *The Ed Sullivan Show* over 16 times during their long career.

Live Aid aired worldwide in 1985. It featured, among others, Tina Turner, Madonna, and Patti LaBelle.

A myriad of important funny ladies also proved popular on variety shows. They included Jean Carroll who appeared over 20 times on *Ed Sullivan* and, later, Phyllis Diller. Diller appeared on *Jack Paar* over 30 times.[24] Mae West appeared on *Red Skelton*, Joan Rivers on *The Flip Wilson Show* and Minnie Pearl on *Jonathan Winters*.

Elaine May, with partner Mike Nichols, was a favorite of Jack Paar's. Jackie "Moms" Mabley appeared on the shows of Merv Griffin, Bill Cosby, Flip Wilson, and the Smothers Brothers.[25] Anne Meara, with husband-partner Jerry Stiller, was also a frequent guest on a number of variety programs from the '50s up through the '70s.

━━◦∞◦━━

Another genre where women dominated were one-off TV "spectaculars" now referred to as "specials." These high-profile presentations ran the gamut from specially produced adaptations to hour-long concerts.

As today, the *Hallmark Hall of Fame* has always been a bastion of well-produced productions — and women have often starred. Ruth Chatteron co-starred in 1953's "Hamlet." Greer Garson was in "The Little Foxes" in 1956. Other stars in other *Halls*: Eva LaGallienne in "The Corn Is Green" and Lilli Palmer in "The Taming of the Shrew," both in 1956. In 1957, Julie Harris starred as Joan of Arc in "The Lark." Harris would also play the title role in "Johnny Belinda" in 1958 and starred in "A Doll's House" in 1959. Helen Hayes headed "Ah, Wilderness!" in 1959, the same year that Dame Judith Anderson starred in "Medea." Ruth Gordon, Rosemary Harris and Rachel Roberts were in "Blithe Spirit" in 1966.[26]

Prestige was also obtained in non–*Hallmark* programs, many of them also showcasing the talents of women.[27]

In 1953, both NBC and CBS aired "The Ford Fiftieth Anniversary Show" with Mary Martin and Ethel Merman. Martin revived her stage hit *Annie Get Your Gun* in 1957 and then *Peter Pan* in 1960. In 1957, CBS aired "The Lady from Philadelphia" detailing Marian Anderson's tour of Asia.

Nineteen fifty-eight offered a remake of *Little Women* featuring Florence Henderson and Margaret O'Brien. Later, Maureen O'Hara starred in a 1960 remake of *Mrs. Miniver*. And a young Mariette Hartley gave an electrifying performance as Joan of Arc in "Saint Joan" in 1961.

Julie Andrews and Carol Burnett paired for a special, *Julie and Carol at Carnegie Hall*, in 1962. Two years later, Burnett appeared in *Once Upon a Mattress*. Wendy Hiller played Anne Hutchinson in a 1964 *Profiles in Courage*. In 1965, Dinah Shore saluted the Peace Corps in an hour-long special. That same year Barbra Streisand headlined *My Name Is Barbra*. In 1966, *ABC Stage '67* aired Capote's "A Christmas Memory" starring Geraldine Page.

In 1967, on a *Bell Telephone Hour* special, divas Joan Sutherland, Leotyne Price, Renata Tebaldi and Birgit Nilsson gathered. In 1969, *An Evening with Julie Andrews and Harry Belafonte* aired on NBC; Belafonte teamed with Lena Horne for *Harry and Lena* the year after. A Supreme-less Diana Ross had *Diana!* in 1971. The following year, Liza Minnelli starred in *Liza with a "Z."*

Marlene Dietrich brought her one-woman show "I Wish You Love" to the airwaves in 1972; Lily Tomlin's first special appeared in 1973; Marlo Thomas bowed in *Marlo Thomas and Friends in Free to Be ... You and Me* in 1974; Ann-Margret tore up the stage of her 1975 special by dueting with Tina Turner; and Bette Midler filled an hour in 1978. Into the mid–1980s, yearly specials were presented by Shirley MacLaine, Mitzi Gaynor, and Lynda Carter.

—◦◇◦—

Even the "old boys' club" of TV news was not without women.[28]

As early as 1946, Chicago's WBKB (now WLS) featured Ann Hunter as a news reader.[29] In 1949, Pauline Frederick became the first female journalist to work full-time for an American TV network. In 1976, she became the first woman to moderate a televised presidential debate.[30] Nancy Dickerson was the first woman to report from the floor of a national political convention. At the time of Dickerson's death in 1997, Lesley Stahl called her "the ultimate pioneer."[31]

ABC's Lisa Howard scored on-air interviews with both Castro and Khrushchev in the early 1960s. Liz Trotta was a foreign correspondent covering Vietnam in the '60s and '70s. Marlene Sanders, beginning in 1964, was an on-air reporter and a documentary film producer for ABC. In 1976, Sanders gained the distinction of being the first female vice-president of a network news division. Barbara Walters began her career in 1963.

—◦◇◦—

Women were featured prominently in early TV sports coverage. Circa 1960, Joanie Weston (right), a.k.a. "The Blonde Bomber," was a superstar of TV's coverage of roller derby.

Early sports coverage often provided powerful female images.[32] The first TV broadcast of the Olympic games was in 1960. U.S. swimmers Lynn Burke and Chris Von Saltza both medaled and sprinter Wilma Rudolph won the gold. At the 1976 Olympics, gymnast Nadia Commenici scored a perfect 10. That same year, in the winter games, Dorothy Hamill skated her way to victory.

In 1973, quite famously, Billie Jean King beat "male chauvinist" Bobby Riggs in a highly hyped televised battle-of-the-sexes tennis match.

Absent from the airwaves today but hugely popular in its time was TV's coverage of roller derby. Consisting of all-male, all-female, and co-ed teams, it was a fast-moving game of roller skating, hitting and "jamming." In 1949 and '50, roller derby was the most watched program on ABC, airing three nights a week. Some of the top female stars of the game included Judy Arnold and Marge Laszlo. Its biggest star was Joanie Weston a.k.a. "The Blonde Bomber," a lady who skated fast and hit hard. Over six feet tall when in skates, Weston was named to the derby all-star team a record 19 times. Upon Weston's death in 1997, *TV Guide* recognized her as "one of TV's first female sports stars."[33]

Nearly as popular as roller derby was professional wrestling. Long before the WWF and WWE, the matches of Gorgeous George and other colorful wrestlers intrigued audiences. Though most wrestling was done by men, some women's matches, featuring the likes of Mildred Burke, were also televised.[34]

Today, we can say what we want about both roller derby and wrestling as "sport" and spectacle but for years both were popular and their female stars far removed from housewife archetypes.

〰〰〰

Here is another persistent myth: Women's fictionalized roles during TV's early days were, supposedly, inherently unrealistic since few (or no!) women worked behind the scenes. In fact, this assumption is so accepted that in 1989 *Newsweek* ran a story which celebrated the achievements of female TV producer-writers Diane English (*Murphy Brown*) and Linda Bloodworth-Thomason (*Designing Women*) and the magazine treated these latter-day women as the first of their kind, even though they weren't.[35]

Gertrude Berg created, wrote, produced and starred in TV's *The Goldbergs*. It ran from 1949 to 1954.[36]

Peggy (Peg) Lynch brought her creation *Ethel and Albert* (in which she also starred) to television in 1953. Around this same time, actress Joan Davis created, produced and was the owner of *I Married Joan*; and Marge Greene starred in and wrote *Marge and Jeff* which aired over Dumont.

Betty White began her television career as the star, producer and owner of her first two series *Life with Elizabeth* and *A Date with the Angels*. In her autobiography, White related, "For four separate series of shows, I worked not only as a performer, but as a producing partner with two strong men, and if I was treated as a second-class citizen, I admit I was too dumb to know it."[37]

Lucille Ball co-created and co-owned *I Love Lucy* with husband Desi Arnaz.[38] In 1962, Edie Adams had her own half-hour variety show, *Here's Edie*, produced by her company Ediad.[39]

As mentioned earlier, one of the most popular genres in the 1950s and '60s were anthologies. Jane Wyman had the title of producer on her program.[40] Though Barbara Stanwyck did not have a producer credit, she did, according to biographies, have full script and cast approval.[41] Meanwhile, in Judy Lewis' biography of her mother Loretta Young, Lewis said about her mother's role behind the scenes of *The Loretta Young Show*:

> [H]er workdays ran from early morning to late at night. She attended all the story meetings, production meetings, and casting sessions. She even viewed the dailies ... instructing her editors about which takes to use and which to eliminate. She was not only an actress but an executive and part owner as well. There wasn't one small element of *The Loretta Young Show* that she didn't oversee.[42]

Not all women did double duty in front of and behind the camera but they still wielded power. For example, Carol Irwin was the producer of *Mama*. And according to Robin

Morgan (the actress who played daughter Dagmar), Irwin held all the strings behind the scenes.[43]

Bonita Granville Wrather was the producer of TV's *Lassie*. Gail Patrick Jackson did the same for *Perry Mason*, and Joan Harrison oversaw *Alfred Hitchcock Presents*.[44]

Mildred Freed Alberg was the founding producer of TV's *Hallmark Hall of Fame*. Mary Ahern was producer of *Omnibus*. Beginning in the 1960s, Lucy Jarvis produced landmark documentaries on the Kremlin and the Louvre for NBC. Rachel Stevenson produced *The Quiz Kids*; and while Burr Tillstrom might have animated the puppets Kukla and Ollie, he and co-star Fran Allison answered to their producer Beulah Zachary.

Geraldine Toohey was producer of *To Tell the Truth*; Jacqueline Babbin produced *Armstrong Circle Theatre*; Jean Hollander, produced *Beat the Clock*; and Jean Kennedy produced *Open End*.

Olga Druce was a producer of *Captain Video*. Producer Phyllis Adams Jenkins produced the *Home* program as well as *What's the Problem?* and *Author Meets the Critics*. Vivian Cox was a producer of *The Kraft Mystery Theatre*; Jacqueline Bobbin of *The DuPont Show of the Month*; and Leotine Klein on *Your Show of Shows*.

Sometimes women could even be found in the director's chair. Frances Buss Buch directed her first program in 1941. She went on to direct early programs like *The CBS Television Quiz* and *Mike and Buff*. Betty Turbiville directed episodes of *Life with Elizabeth*. Lela Swift directed installments of *Studio One*. Barbara Schultz directed episodes of *CBS Playhouse*. And one of the most employed directors of episodic television in the '50s and '60s was former film actress Ida Lupino. She helmed many TV productions including *The Twilight Zone*, *The Untouchables*, and *Gilligan's Island*.

Women writers were there too. Madelyn Pugh Davis was one of the primary writers for *I Love Lucy* and followed Lucy to her later series. Lucille Kallen was one of the writers for *Your Show of Shows*. Anne Bailey Howard composed scripts for *Kraft Television Theatre*, *Robert Montgomery Presents*, and *Armstrong Circle Theatre*. Catherine Turney contributed to *Lux Video Theatre*. Dorothy Fontana (under the name D.C. Fontana) wrote for *The Tall Man*, *High Chaparral*, *Ben Casey* and *Star Trek*.

Lois Peyser, Joanna Lee and Joan Maples all wrote episodes of *Gilligan's Island*. Selma Diamond (later to become famous as one of the bailiffs on *Night Court*) won an Emmy in 1954 as a writer on *Caesar's Hour*. Barbara Avedon, who went on to co-create *Cagney & Lacey*, began her TV career writing *Father Knows Best*, *The Donna Reed Show*, *Gidget*, and *Bewitched*. Mary Orr wrote for *Mr. and Mrs. North*. Mona Kent contributed to *Captain Video and His Video Rangers*. Marianne Mosner wrote for *Rocky Jones, Space Ranger*. Margaret Armen for *The Rifleman*. Pauline Stone for *Ironside* and *Lassie*. Ellen M. Violett contributed scripts to *The Defenders*, *The United States Steel Hour* and *Cameo Theatre*. Elaine Leslie wrote for *A Date with Judy*. Brenda Blackmore for *The Invisible Man*; Irma Kalish for *My Three Sons*, *F Troop*, and *Nanny and the Professor*; Charlotte Brown for *The Doris Day Show*; Treva Silverman for *Room 222* and *The Monkees*; Juanita Bartlett for *Little House on the Prairie*, *Bonanza*, and *Alias Smith and Jones*; Wanda Duncan for *Bonanza*, *Land of the Giants*, and *Lost in Space*; Cynthia Lindsay for *My Three Sons* and *Bachelor Father*; Ruth Brooks Flippen for *The Odd Couple* and *Gidget*; and Peggy Chantler for *Dennis the Menace*, *Hazel*, *Donna Reed*, *The Adventures of Superman*, *The Farmer's Daughter*, *Bewitched* and *The Mothers-in-Law*.

Meanwhile, Ruth Woodman wrote almost every episode of *Death Valley Days* and the entire genre of daytime drama owes its origins to one woman: Irna Phillips. Having created and written serials for radio, Phillips later brought her hugely successful *The Guiding Light* to TV and later added to the air *As the World Turns, Days of Our Lives* and *Another World*. One of her apprentices, Agnes Nixon, went on to create *All My Children*.

⁓⁓⁓

But wait ... there's more! The creator and original host for television's longest-running program, *Meet the Press*, was female. She was Martha Rountree.

Mili Bonsignori was an innovative film editor whose credits included *See It Now*. Judith Cary Waller was the first station manager (male or female) of Chicago's WMAQ and brought to TV's its first educational program for children, *Ding Dong School*. Starring Miss Frances (a.k.a. Dr. Frances Horwich); that series began in 1952.

If most accounts are to be believed, Faye Emerson held enormous control over her programs. The same for Arlene Francis on her daily *Home* show. Donna Reed, on her sitcom *The Donna Reed Show*, had enough say to install her husband as one of its producers. And Joan Ganz Cooney founded the Children's Television Workshop (now Sesame Workshop) in 1968; the CTW went on to create *Sesame Street*.

Perhaps the ultimate female TV pioneer was Elma "Pem" Farnsworth, the wife of Philo T. Farnsworth, the inventor of all-electronic television. According to Mrs. Farnsworth, on her wedding night Philo confessed to his 19-year-old bride, "You know, there's another woman in my life. Her name is 'Television,' and in order to have enough time together, I want you to work with me."[45] She did. Pem Farnsworth has the distinction of being the first woman *ever* shown over the medium of television.

Frieda Hennock was the FCC's first female member and served on the Commission from 1948 to 1955. In 1948, the very first Emmy ever presented went to a woman: Shirley Dinsdale, a talented ventriloquist, won in the category Most Outstanding Television Personality.

Meanwhile, the puppeteer who pulled Howdy Doody's strings was Rhoda Mann-Winkler. TV's most famous salesperson was also female — Betty Furness for Westinghouse!

In 1962, Julia Child debuted in *The French Chef*, in the process reclaiming the kitchen, transforming it from a place of pseudo-servitude for women into one of creativity and fulfillment.

It can also be argued that televi-

Martha Rountree (seen here circa 1950) was the co-creator and original host of televisions longest-running program *Meet the Press*. She served as moderator from 1947 to 1953.

sion has done more than any other medium to showcase examples of non-performing but important women of accomplishment. Thanks to TV news and shows like *Person to Person*, some of the 20th century's most admired women were seen and heard like never before.

Eleanor Roosevelt appeared in *The Four Freedoms Awards* over CBS in 1950. Others who made repeated TV appearances: Grandma Moses, Golda Meir, Margaret Mead, Georgia O'Keeffe, Clare Boothe Luce, and Margaret Chase Smith.

From 1952 to 1961, Ralph Edwards regularly paid tribute to women via his *This Is Your Life* program. While many featured famous woman, many focused on notable "everyday" people, including the former Allied spy Yvonne Files Kennedy and renowned newspaperwoman Virginia Marmaduke.

In 1952, one of the biggest stories of the decade airing on television had a woman at its center — Queen Elizabeth II's coronation.

A decade later, in 1962, audiences watched as First Lady Jacqueline Kennedy led viewers on a tour of the White House. Subsequent First Ladies have also been frequently on air — from the ever-candid Betty Ford in her famous 1975 *60 Minutes* interview to Nancy Reagan promoting "Just Say No" in the 1980s.

With this galaxy of talented, diverse, and influential women, visible on the screen or active behind the scenes, why is there still so much misinformation about women, fictional and non, in early TV?

Perhaps because, unlike *I Love Lucy* or *The Honeymooners*, anthology programs and variety shows and other genres have not proved popular in rerun. Hence, when something is out of sight, it's out of mind. While almost all of us can easily conjure up an image of Lucy setting fire to her putty nose, few of us have had the opportunity to see an Arlene Francis or a Joanie Weston. But just because something isn't around any more, doesn't mean that it didn't exist at all. And to state otherwise is to engage in revisionism, in the process obscuring an honest picture of the TV medium and ignoring entire generations of pioneering women.

— 2 —

"Mama Said"
Television's Wives and Moms

Wally, I wasn't born a mother!—*June Cleaver on* Leave It to Beaver

Television programs about married couples have been on the air since real-life married couple Johnny and Mary Kay Stearns debuted in *Mary Kay and Johnny* in 1947. The Stearns also have the corner on being one of the medium's first family sitcoms since their son, Christopher, made his appearance on his parents' show before he was even a month old.[1]

If over the years the dominant images of women on television has been as somebody's wife or somebody's mother, then there's a good reason for it—because in real life, wives and mothers dominate as well. Every single one of us got here by way of a mother, probably a married one. And art gains its power by being relatable: While few of us can identify with being an ER doctor, we can identify with some sort of family.

Furthermore, if television of the 1950s, '60s, and '70s tended to primarily show us women who were married moms not working outside the home, then in this way too, television reflected reality. Many historians believe there was a concerted effort after World War II to remove women from jobs and return them to the home (the domestic sphere), or into traditional female occupations, so that returning servicemen could get jobs stateside.[2]

Then, after the war, came the baby boom and soon America's women found plenty to be done with the raising of America's next generation. Some women, even if they wanted to work, couldn't due to the shortage of proper daycare, while other factors—including the GI bill—allowed many women to be stay-at-home mothers, i.e., Mrs. Cleaver.

Statistics back this up. According to the Department of Labor, in 1955, only 31 percent of American women worked *outside the home*. While this is a significant chunk, it is still the minority.[3] Hence if less than one-third of all women were in the workforce, that means that well over half of American women were working *inside* the home. If that's the case, it stands to reason that women's TV counterparts would be too.

And what about TV's tendency to show families consisting of married couples raising the proverbial 2.5 children? In the era of Ozzie and Harriet, this type of family unit too was the norm. According to the U.S. Census, in 1945, just as TV was gearing up, 80 percent of American children were being raised within nuclear families. Even by 1960 the traditional family unit remained the standard with 75 percent of all households being nuclear in form.

Other particulars of Mrs. Cleaver et al. also have historical foundation. As McCrohan points out, the women of postwar America really did "dress up for afternoon club meetings, and they did attempt to raise money for projects."[4] In the postwar years, the female sex channeled the energies they had previously utilized on the home front into peace-time concerns. All of TV's classic moms were seen in their series as active in PTA or fund drives. This disproves then what Betty Friedan wrote in a 1964 article where she asked, "Why is there no image [of women on TV] acting to solve more complex problems of their own lives and society?"[5]

But even if TV moms didn't engage in community issues, their concern for home and hearth — i.e., the role of "mother" — was a noble one. For as one author has noted, "The family, religion, shaping the hearts and minds of the next generation ... can't be reduced to just shining floors and wiping noses."[6]

To this point, many episodes of sitcoms from the 1950s and '60s were built around the premise of mom pursuing an outside interest usually with the early support of her family. But, inevitably, by episode's end, everyone has come to discover that Mom's work with her family matters as much as any so-called "public" cause. Consider a 1963 episode of *Donna Reed* in which Donna's women's club suggests that Donna run for city council. The idea catches fire and Donna returns home that evening mulling it over. Her husband and kids are supportive and soon Donna is hitting the campaign trail. But, soon, the Stone household is in disarray: the kids are fighting, Dad can't sew on a button, and they all burn their breakfasts. But, trying to be supportive, Mr. Stone and the kids pretend all is fine, encouraging Donna with rallying cries that the city needs her!

The campaign wears on until one night Dr. Stone has a dream about Donna's political career. Will he become obsolete? Will he never see her again? Will he become "First Gentleman"? It's a sacrifice he's not willing to make. He awakes, wakes up his wife and implores her to end her burgeoning political career, stating that while the city might need her, her family needs her too.

Donna agrees and withdraws from the race, returning to her earlier job — looking after her family. (*Father Knows Best* covered similar ground with its 1958 episode "A Medal for Margaret.")

What do we make of this episode? Is this a case of women suppressed by the patriarchy? Or, since Donna is considered a viable candidate, is this episode about the choices women often have to make in balancing work with family?

Many critics will view this episode as an attempt to reinforce patriarchal structure, to keep women in their "rightful" place. But I would argue that these episodes, rather than undermining women, actually do their best to show appreciation for them. Donna Stone's brief foray into politics serves to remind her — and her husband and children — that the work she does as "just" a housewife is valid. With the majority of real-life women, according to statistics, working within the home during the series, the message conveyed no doubt resonated with many female viewers who probably too seldom got a "thank you."

Another twist on this type of episode is the "gender switch." Their plots go like this: The "guys" decide that the "girls" don't know how rough they have it. Meanwhile, the women don't think the men know how tough *they* have it. So, each decides to adopt the other's roles for a time. In *I Love Lucy*'s "Job Switching," Lucy and Ethel square off against Ricky and Fred about which sex has it worse. In order for the ladies to prove themselves right, they have to "bring home the bacon" while the men have to cook it. (This episode features the "Lucy at the candy factory" sequence.) In the end, both sides fail miserably and everyone returns to their old roles.

Almost twenty years later, the Bradys engaged in this. Before you can say "cliché,"

Mrs. Brady has to teach the boys baseball while Mr. Brady has to teach the girls cooking. Carol proves herself no whiz at baseball and her attempt to slide into a base results in an injury. In the kitchen, Mr. Brady creates havoc by turning the mixer too high, dropping eggs and slipping on the yolks, resulting in his own injury.

That night, as Mr. and Mrs. Brady sorely climb into bed, each admits defeat. They then promise that, come morning, they will both return to what each knows best.

It's doubtful that these episodes were an attempt to make a socio-gender statement. They are just tried-and-true sitcom tradition. In "switching roles" episodes, the plot is pre-constructed and most of the laughs can be delivered with slapstick.

Since these episodes all end with neither gender "winning," they seem to be less about pointing out what women and men supposedly can't do than they are about discovering respect for the others' skills. Just as the Stone family discovered the importance of Mom's contributions, so too do husband and wives emerge at the end of these episodes with new-found appreciation for their significant other's important, albeit traditional role.

—◊◊◊—

Most charges lobbed at *Donna Reed* et al. regard the excessive idealism with which they portrayed life. Despite the fact that (as Stephanie Coontz states in *The Way We Never Were*), "Contrary to popular opinion, *Leave It to Beaver* was not a documentary,"[7] but that hasn't stopped these shows from being used as yardsticks against which to measure "reality." As David Marc said of TV's ideal towns like Springfield, "In the fifties and sixties, the sitcom ... offered the Depression-born post–World War II adult group a vision of peaceful, prosperous suburban life centered on the stable nuclear family."[8]

But by the time television arrived, such quaint hamlets were nothing new; consider the locales of the Andy Hardy movies. Furthermore, since the 1950s, the American appetite for these Main Street utopias has not diminished. As one author said of *Leave It to Beaver's* setting, "[It is] the primetime equivalent of John Cheever's sunlit lawns and the immediate ancestor of Steven Spielberg's split-levels."[9]

If their make-believe communities aren't being ridiculed, the mothers of classic TV are usually being derided. Though these characters are more than their clothes, perhaps the greatest criticism these women get concerns their wardrobes. The accepted image of Mrs. Cleaver et al. is that of a woman vacuuming while in high heels, pearls and house dress. But this isn't accurate. Often throughout each of their series, June Cleaver and TV's other classic moms could be seen in practical attire. In one episode of *Father Knows Best*, Margaret Anderson is seen doing her spring cleaning in jeans and work shirt. Once, when daughter Kathy spilled paint, Margaret was seen in a sweatshirt with a kerchief around her head. Donna Stone was always in jeans when in the garden.

Along with her charming performance as June Cleaver, Barbara Billingsley is perhaps best remembered for her character's high heels and pearls. But as Billingsley endlessly explained, her clothing for the show had more to do with television production necessity than with sociological statement: "When we started [the show] I wore flats but as the boys grew I had to too." Hence, the heels. Meanwhile, Billingsley said of her trademark necklace, "I have a 'hollow' around my neck and it was difficult to light without getting a shadow. The pearls filled in the hollow and made it easier to photograph."[10]

Even if these women were over-dressed, there are still things that should be pointed out in regard to their appearance:

- Female TV characters were not the first who never looked less than stunning. *Mrs. Miniver*'s Greer Garson endured the Blitz without losing any glamour. And though Scarlett O'Hara got dirty during *Gone with the Wind*, never did a bruise form on Vivien Leigh's flawless face.
- The times were more formal. Well into the 1960s, men still sported hats and women wore white gloves. When Jacqueline Kennedy became First Lady in 1961, women all over America upped their wardrobes with pairs of white kid and pill box hats. "Casual Friday" had yet to arrive.
- Television was still new when *Beaver* et al. began. An attitude was still afoot that people coming into your home via TV were akin to invited guests. And when guests came calling, they had to dress appropriately. Note the gowns of Loretta Young and Faye Emerson. Today it's common to see actors on *The Tonight Show* in Dockers and T-shirts, but not back then. Even the Beatles wore suits in their first American TV appearance.
- Finally, these women were not alone in their formalized fashions. Their husbands were seldom seen in anything but their gray-flannel best. Ward Cleaver and Dr. Stone are almost always at the dinner table still in their suit, their ties still knotted.

On the issue of women's TV dress in earlier eras, the book *Prime Time, Our Time* proposes an interesting theory: that the visual perfection that TV housewives maintained was not an edict to women but instead a sales pitch for modern technology and the efficiency of the various household appliances.[11] The well-turned-out lady on TV conveyed that if you wanted to look like June Cleaver, then you better make your next purchase a Westinghouse.

This sort of logic makes sense during an era when single sponsorship of TV was normal and held enormous power. After all, if you were a coffee manufacturer underwriting a series (like Sanka did with *The Goldbergs*), you wanted the show's characters to drink coffee. If you were a cleaning product company, you wouldn't sponsor a show where "your" characters lived in filth.

—◦∕◦∕◦—

Beyond wardrobe, TV's most legendary moms are also known for their sunny dispositions and fresh-baked cookies.

Ultimately, the high standard of homemaking exhibited by these ladies is, of course, impossible to attain. But, once again, if sitcoms did contain unrealistic women images, they did the same with men: Jim Anderson never got down-sized, Ward never lost his temper. Similarly, the kids of TV at the time didn't do drugs, run away (not for real) or commit high crimes.

These whole families were, thanks to television, wholly removed from reality, even from their own time. During the 1950s and '60s, none of them ever spoke of the Cold War or built a bomb shelter, nor were they ever touched by racial unrest.

In the end, the only thing TV housewives can be accused of is being good — gifted — at their chosen profession, that of homemaker. They were accomplished in running their households and caring for their families. None was portrayed as incompetent while, simultaneously, none was shown to be obsessive-compulsive either. Would female viewers of the era (the majority of which were homemakers themselves) have been happier if these housewives were shown to be sloppy housekeepers and uninvolved mothers? Is that "positive"?

Discussion of these mothers reveals a double standard, suggesting we have yet to truly value full-time homemakers. Had Donna Stone been a skilled businesswoman, she would today be held up as one of TV's great women. But because she excelled in home economics, she has been decried for it, labeled everything from sell-out to cipher.

In the end, programs like *The Donna Reed Show* never purported to be true-life reflections. And American viewers, deep down, knew they weren't either. After all, even though they suspended belief for the 30 minutes, viewers knew that Donna Stone was really Donna Reed, an actress playing a character.

And, yes, in the end, these shows were idealized but, in the end, was that so bad?

Though they presented to America an unattainable standard, weren't the positive values that these series promoted — like respect from child to parent and spouse to spouse — better than if they had, in terms of "realism," attempted to appeal to the lowest of humanity? Like the novelist or musician who defends elements of racism, violence or misogyny in their work by stating it reflects "real life," society must ultimately ask: to what end? To what degree do we want the media to "reflect" rather than, perhaps, lead by example?

The Originals

Actually, TV's first notable mothers were not the idealized images like the women discussed above. These earlier mothers were older and more matronly and, because they belonged to a lower economic class, their wardrobes more Woolworth's than Bloomingdale's.

The Goldbergs (1949–1954) was already a legendary radio series when its creator, producer, writer and star Gertrude Berg brought it to television. In the show, Berg starred as Molly Goldberg with Phillip Loeb originally co-starring as her husband, Jake, and Larry Robinson and Arlene McQuade as the Goldberg children, Sammy and Rosalie.

Mr. and Mrs. Goldberg were immigrants and lived in the Bronx. There was no attempt to assimilate the family into a middle–American milieu. The elder Goldbergs spoke with heavy accents and the family was both proudly Jewish (in one episode the missus wins over some new neighbors with her gefilte fish) and working class.

The Goldbergs was not very "sitcom-y" either. Its pacing was more daytime serial (as it had once been on radio) than that of a slap-happy comedy and many of the jokes were meant to be more endearing than laugh-out-loud funny. Much of the series' humor was from Molly's misuse of English i.e., "I'm putting on my robe and condescending the stairs." Though language misuse could be considered slurring, Berg said of Molly, "[Her] humor comes out of life. Ours was never a show that made jokes about people. The humor came from the love and warmth of the characters. Molly was never a joke."[12]

Furthermore, for every mixed-up "Molly-ism" that came from Molly's mouth, there were bits of wisdom, like when Molly said, "Better a crust of bread and enjoy it than a cake that gives you indigestion."[13] Such charm endeared Berg's program to legions of fans; an estimated 13 million watched *The Goldbergs* every week.[14]

Berg and Molly were also popular with various organizations for the image they projected. During the show, Berg received citations from the Girls Clubs of America and the National Conference of Christian and Jews.[15] As one author wrote about the show, "The differences between traditional values and middle–American values are consistently exposed as merely stylistic."[16]

In the final years of TV's *The Goldbergs*, the family left the city for the fictional suburban

Haverville, mirroring the life of many American families. (The program subsequently began to look like *Father Knows Best*.) The Goldbergs were moving up and living up to the show's original radio title, *The Rise of the Goldbergs*. The closing credits now even stated "House decorated by Macy's New York."

Nevertheless, a yenta in the city is one in the country. In one later-day episode, two crooks break into the Goldbergs' house. Molly, alone reading *Anthony Adverse*, gets taken hostage. One by one, the other members of the family come home and are also taken hostage. Though her husband "forbids" Molly from making any attempt to disarm the crooks, she tries anyway. And though her first attempt fails, Molly ultimately saves everyone by getting her son on the phone and delivering a "coded" message that gets him to summon police.

Far-fetched, yes, but this episode nevertheless is indicative of the smarts and strength that was central to Molly.

In both her radio and TV versions, Molly has been assessed as "patient, wise and resourceful"[17] and as "an image of a wise, humorous matriarch, charmingly mangling the language, directing her family with care and determination. Molly was the family authority, a multidimensional character who assumed control."[18]

In her persona as Molly Goldberg, Berg fashioned an enduring image of the Jewish mother. And while some might view her as "stereotype," others see "icon." Since then, other TV characters have been "Molly-esque": *Mama Malone* was a 1984 sitcom about a Brooklyn-living Italian mama who hosts her own cooking show, and *Frannie's Turn* (1992–1993) was a sitcom which *TV Guide* described as being about "an overworked seamstress — who's about to become a feminist."[19] It's certainly the persona that Marion Ross channeled for *Brooklyn Bridge* (1991–1993).[20]

—◈—

Concurrent with *The Goldbergs* was the early sitcom *Mama* (1949–1956), which usually aired live. Derived from the play and film *I Remember Mama*, which itself came from a book, the series starred Peggy Wood in the title role of Marta (Mama) Hansen. Marta was the matriarch of the Hansen family which consisted of her, husband Lars, eldest daughter Katrine, son Nels, and littlest daughter Dagmar, as well as Aunt Jenny, Uncle Chris and Uncle Gunnar.

Mama bears similarities to

TV's first successful sitcom *Mama* (1949–1957) focused on the strong but loving Marta Hansen. She was played by Peggy Wood.

The Goldbergs. Both shows were gentle comedies about human foibles; both centered on immigrants (the Hansens were Norwegian); and both were non-glamorized depictions of the working class. The Hansens' clothes and household, though not as bare bones as the Kramdens', were realistic and utilitarian. Furthermore, both of the lead actresses on these series, Wood and Berg, were over 40 and neither could be considered svelte. And as with Molly, Mama was the soul of the show. Even the show's opening mentions that: "But, most of all, I remember Mama."

The Great TV Sitcom Book calls the series *Mother Knows Best* and says, "It was always Mama with her down-to-earthiness and her good humor who would put things back together.... Mama held her family together through hard times with love, compassion and common sense."[21]

Among the responsibilities that Mama had was overseeing the family budget. In one episode, she is shown having to come up with enough cash to put aside for Nels to eventually attend college. In order to save, Mama begins cutting back on what few luxuries she enjoys. Thanks to Mama's good example, soon all the family is cutting back.

This is not to say that Mama's life was nothing but basking in her family. In "Mama's Bad Day," Mama experiences a series of discouragements including finding cigarettes in Nels' room. Mama's sister Jenny tells her she must talk to Nels and make him mind. This causes Mama to wonder, "Why do I have to *make* everyone do everything?" Mama's day doesn't get better when, at dinner, a special meatloaf goes unnoticed by her brood. Earlier, Mama confided to Jenny, "Sometimes I wish I was an old maid. What does a family mean? Work. And nobody appreciates it." Media writer Mary Desjardins notes about the series, "It was not uncommon for Papa and the Hansen children to have to come to terms with the value of Mama's work."[22]

In another episode, this one addressing gender roles and the immigrant experience, Papa wants to become a U.S. citizen but is too proud to take classes. Mama, though she thinks his pride foolish, takes the course for him, then tutors him.[23]

Mama was a slice of early television Americana and the medium's first true hit not sprung from radio.

But its importance is not what kept it on the air for so long. Rather, as one author has written, "The success of *Mama* was due in large measure to the broad appeal of sympathetic, well-cast characters brought home by the excellent writing, direction and acting."[24] Others have celebrated the series' "complex characterizations" and its "treatment of cultural tensions," and have described it as a "deservedly admired" television achievement.[25]

Speaking of history, it's notable that with *Mama* and *The Goldbergs*, television's first two successful sitcoms both focused on matriarchal figures. Robin Morgan, who played Dagmar on *Mama* from 1950 to 1956, and later become a founder of *Ms.*, has spoken well of the program's enduring images: "I was glad much of [my career] had at least been spent on a program with a female lead, strong women characters and an immigrant, working class setting...."[26]

The Classic Four

Mama and *The Goldbergs* were successful, but since they were usually done live, they have not been seen nearly as much as such cultural touchstones as *Father Knows Best, The Donna Reed Show, Leave It to Beaver,* and *The Adventures of Ozzie and Harriet.* Hence it is this foursome which have come to epitomize not only all television of the era but also 1950s America — even to ridiculous degrees. For example, there are two books about *real-life* women who take issue with Beaver's mom. One is titled *Not June Cleaver*, the other *I Killed June Cleaver*. Among the things these tomes ascribe to June, they obviously assign a lot of influence — a lot of power for a fictional portrayal aired one half-hour per week for a handful of years.[27]

As noted earlier, the actresses of these classic four have long been the subject (or victim) of some devastating criticism. One book says, "The wives in *Father Knows Best* and *Life of Riley* [were] essentially reduced to the role of decorative nonentities."[28] Another author says, "Mrs. Dad was always trim, erect, loyal, like a well-bred whippet; but even she sometimes made trouble and had to be reminded how to roll over and play dead."[29]

But June, Donna, Margaret and Harriet weren't dogs and weren't those women just described. They are regularly seen in their programs as smart, funny, logical, and level-headed; in other words, fully developed characters, real, inspiring women.

—◆◇◆—

The longest running of the classic four was *The Adventures of Ozzie and Harriet* (1952–1966). More than the others, *Ozzie and Harriet* truly blurred the lines between real and TV. Not only did the elder Nelsons play "themselves" on the show, so too did their real-life sons.

Much has been made about the program's self-reflexiveness: Where did the real Nelsons end and the TV Nelsons begin? It was hard to determine and was not something patriarch Ozzie Nelson (who also produced and directed the show) attempted to explain. Perhaps that is why this series, more than any other, gets cited as setting up impossible standards. Despite the neo-realism of *Leave It to Beaver*, deep down audiences knew that the series consisted of actors playing roles. But on *Ozzie and Harriet*, the lack of fictional names and relationships suggested, yes, this is how this family really lives.

Regardless, *Ozzie and Harriet* still gets a bad rap. As one author put it, "Nowadays *Ozzie and Harriet* has become easy shorthand for a world that is passé — the old-fashioned world of fifties clichés. But this is unfair. The show is certainly a product of its era, but it is hardly a fairy tale, and it is full of humanity and humor."[30]

The leading lady was the former Harriet Hilliard, a film actress and 1930s big band vocalist who, in contrast to her later prim image, in her youth often sang torchy love songs wearing clinging satin dresses.

In her second incarnation, that of Harriet Nelson, she has been called "the most steadfast of all Mother Figures."[31] And indeed she had to be. Far more than any of the other three classic TV dads, *Ozzie and Harriet* as a series falls into the blundering dad/man subgenre of sitcom, that group epitomized by *The Honeymooners* and *Home Improvement*. As one author assessed:

> The genial, bumbling Ozzie was the narrative lynchpin of *Ozzie and Harriet*, attempting to steer his young sons into proper paths (usually rather ineffectually) and attempting to assert his ego in a household in which he was often ill at ease.... That ego, and that household, were held together by wise homemaker Harriet.[32]

Father Ozzie's role was rather peculiar. Will Miller says Ozzie is the "prototype lost American male" who, having been made more or less obsolete by the industrial revolution and suddenly directionless after World War II, is "superfluous to the family except as a figurehead."[33] Among other things, we were never clear what — if anything — Ozzie did for a living. Did he just

With Ozzie Nelson often portrayed as a bumbler, it usually fell to his wife, Harriet Nelson, to keep tabs on him on *The Adventures of Ozzie and Harriet* (1952–1966).

hang around the house all day? So it seemed. It is this lack of direction which often fueled some of the family's odder adventures, like when Ozzie insists that the family stage *Hamlet* in their living room.

Some of Ozzie's other ideas also fail miserably. In a Halloween episode, Ozzie decides that the neighborhood's annual party needs to be run with more "masculine efficiency." He sets down a minute-by-minute schedule for the adults, from apple-bobbing to eating. Unfortunately, for all his planning, Ozzie forgets to arrange a venue for the party. Fortunately,

Harriet has thought of this "minor" detail. By evening, she's informed all the guests where the party will be. Later, at the party, Harriet inquires about refreshments. Ozzie's shocked that she didn't prepare something until she reminds him that he was supposed to do it.

Throughout the series, Mrs. Nelson kept a cool head and understanding demeanor. And like many of her TV mother contemporaries, it often fell to her to save the day and speak the truth. Consider this exchange about Ricky's decision to go to a dance instead of sports practice:

> OZZIE: I would think you'd rather be out playing football than attending some dance with a bunch of girls.
> HARRIET: Oh, fiddle sticks! I think it's a very nice idea.
> OZZIE: Well, maybe you're right.
> HARRIET: After all, he's not going to be playing football all of his life but he will be meeting and associating with people. And girls are people.

Harriet Nelson is probably the most underappreciated comedienne in TV. She's got a great deadpan. She's always ready with a witty comment and her blunt, slightly sarcastic delivery often keeps the series from turning into mush.

With that going for her, Harriet therefore often functions as the great truth-teller who, like Alice Kramden, is the only thing that can keep her husband's ego in check.

Mr. and Mrs. Nelson never had any all-out fights a la the Kramdens (who did?) but, like Alice, in nearly all marital discussions, it's usually Harriet who has the last word. In one episode when Ozzie expounds on what fools men often make of themselves over women, Harriet responds, "Yes, but I married him anyway."

—◦◦◦—

Premiering two years after *Ozzie and Harriet*, the long-running *Father Knows Best* (1954–1963) has been subjected to almost as much conjecture as the Nelsons due, mostly, to its title. But *Father Knows Best* is not synonymous with "Mother Knows Nothing."

Actually, the program's title has an interesting history. Like many other early TV hits (*Amos 'n' Andy*, etc.), it came from radio where the title had a question mark—*Father Knows Best?*—which changes its tone. For whatever reason, when the show came to TV, it lost any sense of doubt. But that didn't mean that the title wasn't ironic. As Michael B. Kassel noted:

> [C]areful viewing of each of the series' 203 episodes reveals that the title was more figurative than literal…. Jim Anderson could not only lose his temper, but occasionally be wrong….[34]

In one episode, Jim has two tickets to a big football game. Since he only has two tickets means that only one family member can accompany him. He decides to take daughter Betty (played by Elinor Donahue). Later, though, at the office, Jim's newest client hints that he'd like to attend. So what's a father to do? Jim decides he has to put work before family and attempts to disinvite Betty … much to Betty's dismay. How does all of this resolve itself? Via wife Margaret. She tells her husband that the only *right* thing to do is send Betty with the businessman. Dad (reluctantly) agrees. But then Jim fumbles again: He manages to misplace the tickets. Margaret—again—saves the day: She finds the tickets on top of the dresser, right where he left them, and gives them to Betty and the businessman.

As further evidence of times where Mrs. Anderson outdistanced her husband:

• Bud is failing a class in school so Jim strikes a deal: If Bud gets his grades up, Dad will buy him a new boat! Bud jumps at the chance but Margaret questions her husband's logic. She points out that Bud will only study to get rewards, not because it's important. Then Betty wants in on this deal. She asks her mother, "If Bud gets a boat, why can't I get a new dress?" Margaret replies, "Because your father can't go fishing in a new dress."

- Betty starts dating a new boy but Dad thinks "Princess" is too young to get serious. He lets his imagination get the best of him and concludes that Betty's about to elope! Margaret tries to settle her husband. "Jim, when are you going to stop being a comic strip father?" Jim doesn't listen and attempts to prevent the "elopement."

- At the close of an episode, Jim is laughing about how bowled-over Bud is by a new girl. He laments how easily boys are made to run amok by women. After Jim finishes, Margaret appeals to him to get her a pillow and then some tea. Jim obliges. After he leaves, Margaret looks at us and gives us a knowing wink. (This is a "decorative non-entity"?)

Co-starring with Robert Young, who played Jim, was Jane Wyatt. The descent of one of America's oldest families and a graduate of Barnard, Wyatt's well-breeding and elegance veiled a steely core. As a girl, Wyatt's choice of a theatrical career got her old-money family expelled from the social register. Years later, Wyatt was one of the few stars to take a vocal stand against Senator McCarthy.[35]

On *Father Knows Best*, Wyatt possessed too much poise and dignity to come across as subservient. If anything, her Margaret is the stabilizing influence against her husband's occasional over-zealousness. In his book *TV Sirens*, author Michael McWilliams says of Wyatt's performance, "Her Margaret Anderson is at once unbelievable (i.e., perfect) and instantly immediate (i.e., human). She's the most determinedly unflappable Mother Figure in all of television...."[36]

Wyatt won three Emmy Awards for her performance.[37] Her success had to do with the way she exerted control without emasculating her husband. Wyatt said in a 1993 interview, "On *Father Knows Best*, Dad made all the decisions.... [H]e didn't realize that I put it in his head to begin with."[38]

To some, *Father Knows Best* represents how white bread TV once was. (This was a family so middle-of-the-road, their last name was Anderson, they lived in Springfield, Dad worked for the General Life Insurance Company, and their Hispanic gardener was named Frank Smith!) But, for some reason, the family still resonates today as ideal, unattainable but meaningful in that the family unit was not treated as a joke. Despite the father's foibles, as Brooks and Marsh categorized them, "Jim and his wife Margaret were portrayed as thoughtful, responsible adults."[39] *The New York Times* said of the series when it debuted, "Robert Young and Jane Wyatt have restored parental prestige on TV."[40] And, as late as 1993, in a study of "healthy" fictional TV families, *Father Knows Best* ranked near the top, alongside the more modern families like those on *Life Goes On*.[41]

—◦◦◦—

Just as misunderstood as Margaret Anderson is June Cleaver on *Leave It to Beaver* (1957–1963). Barbara Billingsley, who embodied June with poise, once said about her, "I know people think that June had no brain but in my opinion she was not a dishrag."[42]

Yes, as mentioned earlier, Mrs. Cleaver was almost always wearing pearls. But attire aside, what was June Cleaver really like?

She wasn't dumb. She never fell for Eddie Haskell's sucking-up. And she was not a "dishrag."[43] In one episode, June rushes in to break up a fight between the boys, then lectures them on how lucky they are to have each other.

June Cleaver was also not a subordinate partner. In fact, the marriage of Mr. and Mrs. Cleaver is portrayed as very equal. There is a constant channel of communication between the couple. June's line "Ward, I'm worried about the Beaver" is not a woman forfeiting authority but initiating a discussion. Granted, it is often Ward who takes the lead in correcting the boys but such communication in families is often along gender lines. After all, only a father and son can have "man-to-man" talks.

All in all, the Cleavers were a very functional family, even within their own sitcom. As author Gerard Jones points out about Beaver's friends: Larry's father was always away on business, while his mother was ineffectual and his sister a brat; Lumpy's father, Fred Rutherford, held too-high expectations for his son; and Whitey Whitney often commented about his family's constant yelling.[44]

Despite Mrs. Cleaver's respect for her husband (and family), June (like Harriet Nelson before her) could take her husband down a peg when necessary:

WARD: I used to read three books a week when I was his age.
JUNE: Uh-huh, you and Abe Lincoln.

And when her husband grows nostalgic and long-winded:

WARD: I remember when I was a boy —
JUNE: Dear, won't you be late for the office?

June was also not always the happy homemaker: In one episode she informs Ward that she's worn out from household work. So, sympathetic to his wife's plight, Ward springs for a part-time maid.

Mrs. Cleaver wasn't panicky or helpless either. Billingsley, like Jane Wyatt, brought great dignity to her role. McWilliams calls Mrs. Cleaver the "coolest and sharpest of Mother Figures."[45] With unruffled grace, she weathered all of Beaver's crises with a quiet calm. It was a calm she called on often, considering how nearly delinquent her sons were. Over the course of the series, Beaver and Wally just never seemed to learn their lesson. Consider: When Beaver gets a ticket from a policeman for using his "real racin' car" on the street, Wally acts as Beaver's guardian in court so their parents won't find out; when the duo breaks the window in Ward's car, they try to fix it without 'fessing up; and when Beaver puts a tear in his new suit because Eddie was "horsin' around," he lies, saying a dog did it.

Actually, as a parent, June was often better than Ward. Sometimes he was overly emotional and agitated; other times he was far too forgiving, getting lost in nostalgia. In regard to this latter tendency, the author of the official *Leave It to Beaver* guide labels Ward "recidivist."[46] And it's true: Repeatedly, Ward refuses to take seriously some of Beaver's behavior, such as fistfighting. In the episode that introduced bully Lumpy Rutherford, Ward actually tells the boys about how he once got back at a bully by placing barrel hoops outside his house. In another episode, Ward gets carried away "helping" the Beav with his homework; June has to chide him about doing his son's work for him.

In contrast to Ward, June has neither the hardcore standards of her husband or his Wordsworthian view of childhood. She is compassionate, yet practical. As Applebaum points out, "June—especially in the early shows—proves to be the more flexible and inventive voice of parental reason."[47] This is true in "The Haircut" which, along with disproving June's subordinate status, shows her to be the more understanding parent. Consider:

WARD: I just cannot understand it. I have tried so hard to win their confidence, to prove to them that I'm on their side. Why should they lie to me? It's certainly not my fault.

JUNE: It certainly is!

WARD: No man has ever tried harder to be a buddy to.... What did you say?

JUNE: It certainly is your fault and mine. Why don't you realize what a spot we put him on? Put yourself in his place. He loses his lunch money three days in a row and after being warned that this is his last chance, he loses his haircut money. Naturally he's afraid to tell us.

WARD: What's so "natural" about it? Are we monsters? Do we hit him? Do we beat him?

JUNE: Ward! The only guide the little guy has is the love and approval of his parents. If he thinks he's lost that, it's worse than a beating.

WARD: Well ... I don't know.

JUNE: Look, he was afraid to tell us the truth, wasn't he? Whose frightening him if it isn't you and me?

In another episode, June chastises Ward, "If something's bothering you at the office, you certainly shouldn't take it out on the Beaver."

Like Mrs. Goldberg, June has a deep wisdom about life. In one episode she tells Beaver, "Girls today are becoming doctors and lawyers. They are just as ambitious as boys."[48] In another, "The Silent Treatment," Beaver (on Eddie's advice) decides to give his mom the cold shoulder. Ward wants to talk to the boy but June talks him out of it, believing Beaver will eventually come around. And he does. In another episode, Beaver tells his mom, "You know, Mom, when we're in a mess, you kinda make things seem not so messy."

To which June replies, "Well, isn't that sort of what mothers are for?"

———◆◆◆———

No TV mom — or actress — has been more defamed than Donna Reed, star of *The Donna Reed Show* (1958–1966). As one author put it, "In the media 'Donna Reed' is Donna Stone distorted..., a cultural icon, loved and scorned."[49] Indeed, Reed's name has become an adjective, one that supposedly sums up an era, as when *Time* magazine once spoke of "Donna Reed time, when things seemed simpler."[50]

But Donna Reed wasn't an era, she was a real-life woman, a wife and a mother and a gifted actress capable of playing opposite Jimmy Stewart in *It's a Wonderful Life* or playing a prostitute, her Oscar-winning role in *From Here to Eternity*. She was also a humanitarian who, in her post–Donna Reed life, helped found the anti–Vietnam organization Another Mother for Peace.

Mickey Rooney said of her, "Donna was sweet and demure. Inside, she was a tough dame."[51] And Barbara Avedon, who wrote scripts for *Donna Reed* and would later co-create *Cagney & Lacey*, said of Reed, "[She was] a feminist before there was a feminist vocabulary."[52]

And when one views *The Donna Reed Show*, one finds that Donna Reed and her TV character have a few things in common.

Rather than a fairy tale, Reed considered her series "honest and unpretentious."[53] When it premiered, *Variety* said the show's plots, rather than being broadly played, were consistently "somber, sensible and plausible"[54]; and *TV Guide* celebrated the series when it debuted, stating, "[S]he actually acts like a mother, an impersonation that hasn't been successfully perpetuated on television since Peggy Wood [of *Mama*] left."[55]

The series concerned the Stone Family headed by husband-father Alex (played by Carl Betz), a physician, and wife-mom Donna, a former nurse, now a full-time homemaker. They had two children: daughter Mary (played by Shelley Fabares) and son Jeff (played by

Paul Petersen). (Later, the Stones adopted a little girl named Trisha, played by Patty Petersen.) The relationship between the kids was portrayed pretty realistically: They fuss. Other things in the series that are also true to life (i.e., not "perfect") is the fact that in one episode we learn that son Jeff gets mostly C's in school, low for the son of such high-achieving parents.

The marriage of Dr. and Mrs. Stone (like that of the Cleavers and Andersons) was portrayed realistically (despite the twin beds in their bedroom) and quite positively. This is a couple who respected one another. Their respectful dialogue is a startling contrast to more recent TV portrayals of marriage on *Married ... with Children* and *Lucky Louie* where domestic discourse seems just this side of warfare.

But the Stones were not immune from disagreements. At these times, Donna is far from a complacent, long-suffering wife. In one episode, where Dr. Stone is grumpy in the morning, Donna asks him, "Do you want a dog biscuit with your coffee? You're barking at everyone." (Another time, Donna accused her husband of being both "smug" and "ever so faintly patronizing."[56]) Reed once said, "My TV series certainly aggravated men. Hollywood producers were infuriated that Mom was equal and capable."[57]

Not surprisingly, most episodes prominently featured Mother Donna and depicted her as smart and loving. Reed believed that such an image was hungered for by audiences, that they wanted to see "a healthy woman, not a girl, not a neurotic, not a sexpot."[58]

In an episode that proves this, 1958's "The Foundling," the Stones find the proverbial baby on the doorstep. Thanks to Donna and her husband's medical training, the baby is in good hands. But Donna of course can't keep it, so she does detective work to find out who it belongs to. The note attached to the baby says his name is Willy. When Donna learns that Willy might be the Americanized version of the Italian "Guillermo," she has a theory. Isn't the Stones' milkman an Italian immigrant?

Donna solves another problem — and perhaps saves a few lives — in an episode when her father-in-law (co-star Betz under makeup) comes to visit. Dad's a bad driver but won't admit it. That is, until Donna hatches a plan to show him.

Interestingly, *Donna Reed* often addressed some of the show's criticisms. In one episode, Donna learns that she's considered the ideal mom ... and she doesn't like it! Another episode has Donna fed up with being called "sweet." She tells Alex, "[People] were trying to say I'm a goody-goody brought up on Pollyanna and Florence Nightingale!" So, the next day, Donna decides to incorporate "no" into her vocabulary. A delivery man who takes advantage of her is told, "I have been used, victimized, and exploited by my children and husband!"[59] In another installment, Donna is in the supermarket and straightens out a radio man interviewing "little housewives." She explains what "housewife" entails: "nurse, psychologist, diplomat, philosopher." She informs the man, "We are not part of a herd!"

Contrary to popular belief, Donna was not portrayed without faults. In one episode, she tells a woman's group that the biggest gift they can give their children is trust. She says that their offspring are more responsible than they think and that they should be allowed to make their own mistakes. Donna wins over the crowd and believes her own message until Mary begins dating a boy Donna doesn't like.

During its eight-year run, *Donna Reed* often played to an audience of over 35 million (with young black women the program's biggest fans).[60] The series was also showered with awards from women's, youth and educational organizations. The president of the AMA once even cameoed.[61]

In watching just a few episodes, it's hard to comprehend how Donna Reed–Donna

Stone has been so stereotyped. This was Reed's show, named after her, starring her, and with her getting top billing. The series itself was produced by Reed and her then-husband Tony Owen's TODON Productions. Co-star Shelley Fabares has stated that besides being the lead, Reed was involved in every aspect of the series — writing, casting and production.[62] A co-worker says of Reed, "She wasn't overseeing everything. She *knew* everything. She had the best sense of a set of anyone I ever worked with."[63]

Despite on-air evidence, Reed herself (actress, producer, activist) has been largely forgotten as people prefer to hang onto a myth, sometimes disturbingly so: In 1992, author Dalma Heyn wrote that women's fulfillment depended on "the murder of Donna Reed."[64]

But as Reed's biographer points out, "Donna Stone was not a plaster-perfect woman-manqué, smiling vapidly and cleaning the house. Yet that image of her — of Donna Reed — is perpetuated by commentators and analysts of American popular culture."[65]

Today, while it's nice to see that Donna Reed and Stone are remembered, it's unfortunate that both are usually remembered as something neither of them ever were.

Father Knows Least?

Ironically, considering all the flack Donna Stone et al. have received, at the time of their airing it was not these women but their male counterparts which got the most criticism.

Due to shows like *The Trouble with Father*, *The Honeymooners*, and even *Father Knows Best*, various critics wondered if TV wasn't waging a war on American men.

In 1953, *TV Guide* asked, "Whatever happened to men? … Once upon a time a girl thought of her boyfriend or husband as her Prince Charming. Now having watched the antics of Ozzie Nelson and Chester A. Riley [of *The Life of Riley*], she thinks of her man, and any other man, as a Prime Idiot."[66] A year later, *Time* magazine stated, "In television's stable of 35 home-life comedies, it is a rare show that treats Father as anything more than the mouse of the house — a bumbling, well-meaning idiot who is putty in the hands of his wife and family."[67]

Evidence of this sort of stereotyping was evident well into the 1960s and '70s. Consider Oliver Douglas of *Green Acres*; the dueling hysterical Darrins of *Bewitched*; man-child Herman Munster; and the neurotic Bob of *The Bob Newhart Show*.

The 1950s sentiment was replicated in a *Washington Post* article by Dick Dabney in 1981 titled "How Men Sold Out Their Manhood,"[68] and again in the 1990s and early 2000s, by various (mostly male) critics like Joe Queenan, who wrote in *Men's Health* in '03, "Look at virtually any sitcom, drama or animated feature on television today and you will find a dope, a dork, or a doofus vainly trying to run the family...."[69]

Also in 2003, on PopMatters.com, critic Michael Abernethy wrote, "Where television used to feature wise and wonderful fathers and husbands, today's comedies … often feature bumbling husbands and inept, uninvolved fathers."[70] Similar concerns were echoed in 2004 on AmericanPopularCulture.com.[71]

The doofus-dad sitcoms of recent vintage include *Malcolm in the Middle*, *Everybody Loves Raymond*, and *Modern Family*. The trend has spread to "reality" TV, where celebrity dads are usually the butt of the jokes. (Consider: *The Osbournes* and Bruce Jenner on *Keeping Up with the Kardashians*.) Perhaps as disturbing as the trend of dumb dads was the early 2000s phenomenon of fathers as monsters. Consider the angry, often abusive dads in *Titus* and *That '70s Show*, and Peter Boyle on *Everybody Loves Raymond*.

In terms of men, we must also acknowledge the enduring subgenre of sitcoms built around Mr. Mom failing miserably: *Family Affair, Bachelor Father,* and *Full House.*

If the dad-as-dunce genre has a torchbearer, it was probably *The Life of Riley* (1949–1950; 1953–1958). Described by TV historian Les Brown as the "prototypical Bumbling Father comedy" featuring a "likable but stupid working-class head of family who managed always to muddle through mild trouble,"[72] *Riley* first aired in 1949 with Jackie Gleason in the lead. Despite being slimmer than in later years, Gleason's Riley bore resemblance to Ralph Kramden as he too stormed his way through his household causing trouble.

Like Ralph, Riley was blessed with a level-headed wife, Peg, played by Rosemary DeCamp. This was good since Riley was prone to jump to conclusions as in the episode where $5 is missing and Dad suspects his son Junior. Trying to figure out how to discipline Junior, Mr. Riley discusses it with Mrs. Riley. Dad's inclination is towards corporal punishment. But Peg resists, reminding her husband that Junior's "as much my son as yours!"

The Gleason version of *Riley* aired from 1949 to 1950. In 1953, *Riley* was relaunched with William Bendix in the lead and Marjorie Reynolds as Peg. Little else changed. As one author notes, "Most of the problems in the Riley household occurred when the private and public realms merged, usually when Riley interfered with Peg's responsibilities," thereby causing Peg to try "to keep the family in order despite her husband's calamitous blunders."[73] And blunders were plentiful:

- Riley's idea for lowering the family's food budget is to tell everyone to stop eating.
- Riley's over-involvement in his daughter's college election nearly gets her thrown out of school.

It was not just critics that knew Riley was ineffectual, everyone in his household did too. At one point Peg says to him, "I've been the anchor of this house since we moved in." In another, when Riley states that the "head of the house" needs to get a second job, his son exclaims, "Mom has to get another job?!" Throughout the series we also learn that Mrs. Riley metes out most of the punishments in the house, pays the monthly bills and even speaks French.

Similar to *The Life of Riley* was *The Trouble with Father* (a.k.a. *The Stu Erwin Show*) (1950–1955). Like the Nelsons, Stu Erwin played himself on his series and his wife was played by his real-life wife, June Collyer.

Erwin had built a career on playing bumbling characters, in film and on radio, before coming to TV in what's been called "TV's leading bumbling-father sitcom in the 1950s."[74] Author Rick Mitz said of Erwin:

> He was the king of the incompetents. He always had good intentions—he wanted to fix something, he wanted to surprise someone, he wanted to help his kids. But it never worked. Thankfully, there was the required levelheaded, sensible, down-to-earth Mom ... who'd come to the rescue.[75]

And if Mom wasn't around, the Erwins had two daughters, Joyce and Jackie, who watched out for Dad. As one book states, "It was often Jackie who attempted to rescue her hapless dad"[76] from one of his endless errors, like the time he decided to make money by raising chickens ... in the backyard.

Another TV wife of the era who was also no pushover was Margaret Williams (played by Jean Hagen) on *The Danny Thomas Show* (a.k.a. *Make Room for Daddy*) (1953–1964). Based — supposedly — on the real life of comedian Danny Thomas, the show starred Thomas as entertainer Danny Williams. He was often on the road; when he came home, the whole family had to rearrange their lives to "make room for Daddy."

Just as Lucy had to contend with Ricky's show biz ego and Latin machismo, Margaret had to contend with her husband's show biz ego and his Old World traditions, not to mention his sometimes condescending nature. She resented Danny's assumption that she wasn't autonomous, especially considering how often he was absent.

But, like Alice of *The Honeymooners*, Margaret didn't take any guff. As one author said, "Margaret, played by the sharp-tongued comedienne Jean Hagan, never hesitated to cut her husband down to size."[77]

Margaret's many retorts are evident throughout the series. In one episode, after Margaret has taken the children to see *Peter Pan*, Danny objects to her taking them to such a play. Margaret responds, "What did you want me to take them to? *Death of a Salesman?*"

Even after Williams changed wives, he never quite learned. After the show's first three seasons, Hagen left. Since divorce was not widespread — at least not on TV — Hagen's character was killed off.

Danny was single for a while before meeting Kathy Clancey (played by Marjorie Lord). Kathy and Danny were married by the 1957 season. As can be expected, some of the same gender-based fireworks that Danny experienced with Margaret he experienced with Kathy. In one episode, Kathy decides she wants to secure a job in show business (shades of Lucy?). Danny dares her to try to "make it" so that she will finally "learn a lesson." Danny even goes so far as to try to sabotage one of her auditions. Of course, Kathy eventually learns the truth and there's hell to pay for Danny.[78]

Yet one more befuddled father could be found on the sitcom *Professional Father* (1955). Its set-up is one that TV has revived often. (In fact, it bears a resemblance to *Growing Pains*.)

In *Father*, Steve Dunne played Dr. Thomas Wilson, a well-respected child psychologist who, though skilled with young patients, had less luck with his own family.

Co-starring as Dunne's wife, Helen, was Barbara Billingsley, who two years later achieved greater fame — nay, immortality — on *Leave It to Beaver*. (Though June remained her definitive role, Billingsley proved again that she was not a one-trick pony; note her cameo as the jive-talking grandma in *Airplane!*)

Billingsley's Helen Wilson was a bit more cynical than June Cleaver. She was not above pointing out to her absent-minded professor of a husband that her biological and hands-on experience outdistanced his diplomas. Her manner circumvents the patriarchy. In one episode, when the doctor realizes he's been hoodwinked again, he asks his wife, "How'd you think of something like this?"

Helen replies, "Darling, you're a psychologist, I'm a woman."

Other dim-bulb dads could be found on *The Tom Ewell Show* (1960–1961) and even *Jack Benny* (1950–1965).

The Stalwarts

The dim dad shows are only slightly removed from another sitcom subgenre: the wacky husband-staid wife formula. It's been a staple for decades, all the way up to such series as *Home Improvement* and *Everybody Loves Raymond*.

In fact, almost all domestic sitcoms (i.e., those built around married couples) are based around the concept of one "normal" spouse paired with one, well, less conventional one

Audrey Meadows, pictured with Jackie Gleason, always gave as good as she got without resorting to empty threats when playing Alice Kramden on *The Honeymooners* (1951–1956).

(consider *I Love Lucy* and *I Married Joan*). But sometimes the genders are reversed, with the wife portrayed common-sensibly and the husband as madcap and prone to outrageous plans.

No show better embodies this than *The Honeymooners* (1955–1956). In the Kramden apartment, it is husband Ralph (Jackie Gleason) who is always losing his cool, embarrassing himself and coming up with "get rich quick" schemes. (During the show's run Ralph invested in everything from glow-in-the-dark wallpaper to low-cal pizza to make money.)

By contrast, his wife Alice (played by Audrey Meadows) is sensible and stoic. Said one author about her, "[She] was practical, plainspoken and deeply rooted in reality. She could never join her husband in, let alone help devise, the harebrained schemes that allowed Gleason and [co-star Art] Carney to glow."[79]

Ralph and Alice had a great love between them and that allowed them to have the biggest fights in TV history. Much has been made about Ralph's threats of "To the moon, Alice!" when sparring with his spouse. Some believe that Alice was an abused wife. But, by definition, she was not. He never laid a hand on her. In an article on battered women in 1998, Kathleen Waits dismisses the batterer argument: "Ralph is certainly a jerk, and there is an assertion of male privilege in his statement. But, as portrayed in the show, I think he presents no credible threat of violence to Alice."[80] Certainly Alice's on-air reaction to her husband supports this: never did Alice indicate fear. She never shook in her sensible shoes and never cowered by the ice box. Alice was never afraid.

To remember only Ralph's "threats" without placing them in context, that is, partnered with Alice's tough resilience, is wrong. Along with Alice's retorts, her physical stance is unforgettable: lips pursed, arms folded, eyes forward and standing as solid as the Berlin Wall.

Ron Powers said in his book that Audrey Meadows "could stand still better than anyone in the business."[81] Meadows wisely played Alice during her fights with Ralph as if she were the calm center of a hurricane. It was a conscious choice. Meadows wrote in her memoir, "Since Jackie and Art were both so physical in their characters, I decided to keep Alice very still in contrast."[82]

Ralph's "threats" to Alice were cartoonish. In a book, Donna McCrohan suggests that Ralph references violence only because stronger language could not be aired.[83] I would also suggest that Ralph's "threat" was because he was less witty than his wife. Alice had excellent comebacks, often leaving her husband speechless, forced to utter his "to the moon" reference. Consider some of Alice's zingers:

RALPH: This place ain't big enough for you and me!
ALICE: This place ain't big enough for you and *any*body!

Once, when faced again with Ralph's famous line, Alice responded:

RALPH: Do you wanna go to the moon?
ALICE: It'd be an improvement.

Sometimes Alice couldn't even be bothered with a comeback. Just as Ralph could fall back on his "to the moon," Alice sometimes just used her own too often unremembered "Ahhhhh, shaddup!" In and of itself, how about this? A 1950s American woman telling her husband to zip it!

Carl Reiner said of Meadows' delivery, "She had as much power as Gleason without matching his volume." And *People* said that Meadows' "tart-tongued realist" could make "grown men squirm with an acid skepticism that could etch glass."[84] Michael McWilliams says of Meadows:

> Because Gleason hated rehearsal and often resorted to hammy overstatement on camera, Audrey was forced to pounce on every one of her cues as if it were the last meal on Earth. Her speed, her electricity — her real brilliance, I think — came from her instinct to pull her weight in a sitcom top-heavy with locker-room grubbiness and vaudevillian mugging. At the same time she needed to suggest levels of bitterness over Alice's childlessness.
>
> That she expressed her character's personality without seeming monstrous is the truest testament to her professionalism.[85]

Said Meadows about her character, "I loved Alice because she was strong and she was tender."[86]

Alice was no fool either. In an episode focusing on an upcoming election, there's this exchange:

RALPH: When we go down to the polls tonight, I want you to wear that button.
ALICE: I can't wear this button, Ralph.
RALPH: Why not?
ALICE: I'm not voting for Pinrose, I'm for Harper.
RALPH: You can't be for Harper. I'm for Pinrose and I'm your husband. Everybody knows that a wife has to vote the same way her husband votes, it's been going on for years.
ALICE: Oh, that's absolutely ridiculous, Ralph. A woman votes the way she wants to vote, not the way her husband tells her to.
RALPH: How come all of a sudden you're for Harper? I know why you want to vote for him. I know why you want to vote for him. 'Cause he's handsome, that's why. 'Cause he's got a mustache. That's all you women ever vote for — mustaches! It's a good thing Jerry Colonna isn't running for office. Boy, it proves what I've always said: Women know nothing about politics!

ALICE: They know a lot more than you think, Ralph. It took me a long time before I made up my mind. I'm voting for Harper because he has promised to build a recreation area by floating a bond issue, he's for decentralization of the budget authority and he's also for broadening the anti-trust laws.

RALPH: That proves it! Women know nothin' about politics!

There are similarities between *The Honeymooners* and *I Love Lucy* inasmuch as both focus on issues of male ego versus female empowerment. For example, repeatedly, Alice is forbidden by Ralph from getting a job. Though they lived with few luxuries, one of Ralph's few ego-boosters is that his wife doesn't (i.e., doesn't have to) work. Similarly, Lucy is also career-deprived. In her memoir, Meadows gives thought to Alice's at-home status:

> The younger the journalist who interviews me, the more often I get the question, politely or provocatively, depending on the mien of the reporter, "Why didn't Alice get a job and be her own person instead of just being a wife to Ralph?" Alice did have three jobs in five years, as a babysitter, a secretary and her old job in the bakery.
>
> In the mid-fifties, a man with an average job owned a home and a car, supported wife and family, saved for his kids' education, and had many times more leisure hours available than he does today.... Women customarily worked until a year or two after they were married.... Ralph would have been considered distinctly usual if his wife worked when the spouses of all the other city drivers were housewives.[87]

Alice is a feminist icon. She was "the greatest." Whether standing stoically or holding her own against Ralph's latest tantrum, or embracing Ralph at the end of an episode, Meadows represents a fully integrated mix of vulnerability and impregnable feminine strength.

—◦◦◦—

Economically higher than *The Honeymooners*, but within the "wacky husband-staid wife" mold, is *The Dick Van Dyke Show* (1961–1966).

In this series, wife Laura (played by Mary Tyler Moore) usually comes across as far more grounded than her husband Rob. Perhaps because Van Dyke, like Lucy, was such a superb physical comedian, his Rob often found himself in unfortunate predicaments. Lest we forget, it's not Laura who falls over the ottoman!

Said Moore about her role, "I wanted to establish her as a woman who had her own point of view and who would fight with her husband — a good fight, if necessary. She wasn't a 'yes' wife, nor did she focus everything on him."[88]

In one episode, Laura implores her husband not to go skiing; she's afraid he'll get hurt. Not heeding his wife's Cassandra-like prediction, Rob goes anyway and ends up with a "sprained body." In another, Laura accuses Rob of attempting to buy his friends' acceptance after he grabs the check in a high-end restaurant. At first, Rob dismisses his wife's criticisms but, later, when he observes his son Ritchie engaged in a similar display, he realizes that Laura's right.[89]

Laura was always good at standing up for herself. In one episode we learn she maintains a "secret" bank account. In another, we learn that she opposes buying a toy gun for her son. Consider also this exchange, which took place after Rob was unable to defend Laura against a letch:

ROB: How come you never dress like a girl?

LAURA: What?!

ROB: Shirts and slacks, shirts and slacks, shirts and slacks, that's all I ever see you in when I come home.

LAURA: You love me in slacks.

ROB: Yeah, but whatever happened to dresses?

LAURA: I wear dresses ... Rob this is about the stupidest conversation we've ever had. I mean, just because your male ego took a beating today is no reason to attack my femininity.

Speaking of clothes, Laura Petrie is often cited as the first TV homemaker to don a pair of pants. But, to be fair, Lucy was often seen in pants and, as mentioned, both Donna Stone and Margaret Anderson sometimes appeared in trousers.

If Laura can't take credit for that fashion sea-change, it doesn't matter: There are certainly other areas where she can. Several times throughout the series, we are informed that Laura once had a viable career as a dancer, which she gave up for marriage and motherhood. This is in contrast to some of her wife and mother predecessors whose pre-marriage careers (if any) were unknown.

Thanks to these elements, and others, there was also always something strikingly modern about the Petries — perhaps because they were younger than the Nelsons, etc., perhaps because Rob had an up-to-date career (he wrote for a TV show in contrast to Jim Anderson's old-timey selling insurance). The Petries even lived in the suburbs.

A popular theory regarding the success of *Dick Van Dyke* has to do with it arriving when it did. In some ways, the Petries could be mistaken for the Kennedys, the stylish couple who moved into the White House the same year that the Petries debuted. There was something "Jackie" about Moore's wardrobe and easy coiffure. Certainly the Petries did seem to represent everything a modern American family could be. If Mary Tyler Moore in her next TV incarnation as Mary Richards became a feminist heroine, she could only become one thanks to Laura Petrie.

⚡

This staid woman with a manic man could even be found in *The Munsters* (1964–1966).

In this case, Herman Munster, though seven feet tall and built like a wall, is nevertheless extraordinarily immature. He whines and throws tantrums, yelling "Darn! Darn! Darn!" He stomps his feet until the house shakes and its cobwebs flutter to the floor.

Perhaps Herman's arrested development is understandable: He hasn't really "grown up" at all. Stitched together out of body parts, Herman came into the world fully formed, never learning to control his temper.

Of course, Grandpa, despite being (almost) human, is little better. Though supposedly ancient (300+ years old), he too acts like a little boy, frequently following Herman's lead in ill-advised schemes as in an episode where he and his son-in-law aren't getting along and decide to divide the house in half by painting a white line down the center of every room. Later, the duo drag boulders in and begin to build a dividing wall. Herman's levelheaded wife Lily — no shrinking violet — eventually steps in to scold them.

As played by Yvonne DeCarlo, Mrs. Munster has an iron will and a direct attitude perhaps acquired from own hundred years of life, many of them spent trying to keep Herman from tearing the house down or Grandpa from blowing it up.

Lily repeatedly demonstrated strength. One episode concerns Lily suspecting Herman of cheating. It's a misunderstanding but when Lily finds her husband at the home of the "other woman," she doesn't hold back. When Herman claims that it's all a mistake, Lily responds, "And I'm Sonny Liston!" and she fells him with a punch. Not to encourage domestic violence, but it was quite the punch. And shouldn't Herman have known better? In another episode, Lily banished Herman to the sofa after he stayed out all night.

Sometimes Lily took on the role of savior-rescuer. Once, on a camping trip, Grandpa turned into a wolf and ended up caught by forest rangers. It's Lily to the rescue. In another episode, an unconscious Herman is mistaken for a mummy; Lily has to collect him from a museum.

In her role as Lily, DeCarlo came into her own. She previously played exotics in "B" movies; it was via *The Munsters* and some film roles that audiences discovered an adept comedienne. (Later, Broadway would learn how good she was when she introduced the survivor's song "I'm Still Here" in *Follies*.)

Ultimately what makes Lily work is that DeCarlo plays her as straight as Donna Reed played Donna Stone. (In fact, the opening credits of *The Munsters* was a parody of *Donna Reed*'s.) Though Lily looked a lot like Vampira, underneath her coffin-lining coat she was just your average mom. As McWilliams said of DeCarlo's role, "Her vampish Lily is the sanest character she ever played — a hardworking homemaker with a sweet smile."[90]

The Glamour Gals

A long way from *Mama* were a group of sophisticates who brought to the airwaves a *savior faire* that turned TV domesticity on its ear.

Spun off from 1930s movies, *Topper* (1953–1956) told of two happy-go-lucky ghosts. Husband and wife George and Marion Kerby had lost their lives skiing but death didn't dampen their spirits. In the show, they had become the paranormal houseguests of a stuffy businessman, Cosmo Topper. Topper, though he liked the Kerbys, was often frustrated by them, especially since only he could see them.

They were played by real-life husband-and-wife Robert Sterling and Anne Jeffreys, and death did nothing to dull this couple's witty interaction, especially Marion's slicing tongue which was often used to deflate her husband's ego. In one episode, George and Marion learn of a dinner that Topper's about to attend. George is especially interested when he learns that an old flame of his will be there. George waxes nostalgic about his long-ago love, a woman so completely smitten with him — or so he says — that, even now, she's probably still broken-hearted. Marion isn't buying it. She's not convinced that this long-ago relationship was nearly as intense as George believes. Still, George continues down Memory Lane, eventually wondering, "I wonder if she knows I'm dead?"

To which Marion replies, "If you ask me, she never knew you were alive."

—◦◦◦—

Besides Sterling and Jeffreys (and Lucy and Desi), there was another pair of married former movie stars on early TV. In *Mr. Adams and Eve* (1957–1958), Ida Lupino and Howard Duff, starred in a show that was an inverse of *I Love Lucy*. While Lucy and Ricky were East Coast working class, the Adamses were West Coast and wealthy.

Lupino and Duff played married movie stars, Howard Adams and Eve Drake. Unlike

Lucy, Eve didn't have to fight to be in show business, she already was and was successful. Hence, this couple's problems were less about stretching a dollar than finding Oscar-worthy scripts. Allegedly many of the sitcom's plots were based upon real-life incidents from the Lupino-Duff household ... or so the producers wanted us to believe.[91]

Still, rich or poor, famous or unknown, the plots were pretty universal in dealing with various aspects of married life and the "war of the sexes," a topic as old as the show's Garden of Eden title.

In one episode, Eve feels ignored when her husband seems more interested in boxing on TV than he does in her. With the aid of her agent — the Ethel to Lupino's Lucy — Eve comes up with a scheme to get her husband to notice her again.

Since little new ground was being broken in terms of subject matter, what lingers about this series is the image of Eve Drake as an autonomous entity. Famous and successful before marriage, she is not dependent upon her husband for his name, her self-worth, status or money. In her Dior dresses and furs, Lupino's Eve is self-defined and every bit the Major Movie Star, one not likely to defrost the fridge.

One year after *Our Miss Brooks* ended, Eve Arden returned in a second sitcom, *The Eve Arden Show* (1957–1958). Arden played Liza Hammond, a successful author who was also a widow raising twin teenage daughters.

But unlike, say, the widowed mother of *Lassie* (discussed later), whose work kept her close to home, Liza had to earn her living by giving speeches and going on book tours. Since she was often away from home, she was forced to be dependent on pretty much the only childcare available at the time: a relative, in this case, her own mother. Frances Bavier (pre–Aunt Bee on *The Andy Griffith Show*) co-starred as the girls' grandmother who lived alongside Liza in a high-rise New York apartment.

As millions of working mothers knew or would learn, having a family and a career was not easy. Liza's work was glamourous to an extent but it did not allay her guilt during long absences. In one episode, when one of her daughters is sick, Liza contemplates canceling an upcoming engagement but her agent says that if she wants to pay the rent, then she has to go. On the plane, she falls asleep and has a vivid dream fueled by mother's guilt. In it are her sick daughter, her exhausted mother and an evil landlord ready to toss both into the cold.

This episode from the 1950s, with its unique and honest examination of "working mother's guilt," seems almost apocalyptical. But there it is, literally, in black and white.

Perhaps no TV spouse has ever been as much of a glamour puss as Lisa Douglas of *Green Acres* (1965–1971).

Created by Paul Henning as one of his country-themed sitcoms (*The Beverly Hillbillies* and *Petticoat Junction*), *Green Acres* was an inverse of *Hillbillies*: Instead of transplanting a family of "hillbillies" to a metropolis, a pair of city slickers go rural.

But while the Hillbillies came to California with wide-eyed innocence, *Acres*' Oliver (played by Eddie Albert) arrives in Hooterville with crazy idealism. Armed with farming textbooks, Oliver wants to drag his new wife Lisa to the sticks in order to take farming by storm. But Lisa isn't eager. The show's well-remembered opening theme recounts the his/her city vs. country debate, eventually ending with Oliver pulling rank and demanding his wife accompany him to the sticks.

Based upon the opening, it seems that Lisa has been denied her freedom. Much like the caveman dragging his mate by the hair, Oliver seems to be forcing Lisa to trade SoHo for silos. However, what is seldom mentioned is that there was a deal struck between Lisa and Oliver in the premiere which puts Lisa's acquiescence into perspective: Lisa agrees to try the country for six months and, if she doesn't come around, Oliver agrees that they will return to Gotham. Six months later, Lisa is ready to return to her "penthouse view" until she learns that in the Douglases' absence their existing livestock will be killed. Choosing humanity over the Hudson, Lisa remains in Hooterville.

Despite the possibility of Lisa being a fish out of water, it's she who best adapts to their new environment. While Oliver encounters frustration as he attempts to impose "logic" (what some might consider male thinking anyway) onto Hooterville customs, Lisa has no such trouble and takes to "the simple life" in a way that, years later, another rich blond socialite, Paris Hilton, never would.

Marc proposes that Lisa (played by Eva Gabor) being foreign-born, with a background "in a traditional, preindustrial European feudal system," is better equipped to take on a new environment especially one built around agriculture.[92] I also believe that Lisa, as an immigrant, has already experienced adapting to new cultures and this allows her to better function within the borders, mental and physical, of the Hooterville universe.

But Lisa's abilities are the result of more than just her foreign birth. Here again, womanly influence outdistances male force. This can be seen when Oliver phones the Hooterville fire department and gets no response. Later, when Lisa phones, they arrive immediately. When Oliver asks why, Lisa replies, "I'm sexier than you are."

As with Gracie Allen, Lisa's logic makes sense to her and, for that matter, to the other citizens of Hooterville. Within this Dali-esque environment, it alarms no one but Oliver that a local couple would raise a hog as their "son."

Lisa even proves herself more adept at farming than her husband. In one episode, when a group of city kids visit the farm, Lisa imparts to them an "old country" way of getting seeds to sprout overnight: sleep with some of the soil under your pillow. Oliver scoffs but, come morning, each of the children's plants have sprouted.

Repeatedly, Lisa comes across as an alluring Mother Earth, in tune with the elements. Along with her plant-growing knowledge, Lisa is able to request a specific number of eggs from the chickens each morning and get that number. She also has a rapport with Eleanor the cow who always produces just the right amount of milk.[93] As Michael McWilliams said, "Despite her ritzy appearance, [Lisa's] an indomitable force of nature."[94]

In many incidences, Lisa, rather than adapting to Hooterville, bends Hooterville to her. In one episode, she brings a symphony conductor to town and, in another, transforms Sam's general store into a beauty salon.

From Lisa's oversize bed to her silk housecoats, we see that while you can take the girl away from glamour, you cannot take the glamour from the girl. Via such means as clothes, hair and makeup, Lisa openly defies her mundane surroundings. As Smith has noted, "[S]he displays, in her costumes and demeanor, pride and confidence in herself as a woman. She dresses not for her husband but for herself."[95]

Though her *Eve Arden Show* only lasted a season, a force like Arden couldn't be kept down long.

For *The Mothers-in-Laws* (1967–1969) the premise was as old as *Romeo and Juliet*: Two wildly different families — one upper-class, one working class — are united by the marriage of their children. Produced by Desilu, it bore all the marks of Desi Arnaz: class conflicts and the battle of the sexes.

Arden played Eve Hubbard, who was upper-class but down-to-earth. Mrs. Hubbard was a great cook, a former champion golfer, and an expert gardener. Playing opposite Arden was brassy Kaye Ballard. The actresses couldn't have been more different in both looks and performing style. If throughout the series Arden maintained the same sort of sophisticated in-control quality that Miss Brooks always had, Ballard as Kaye Buell was the other extreme. Loud and proudly blue-collar, Mrs. Buell is possibly the only TV parent that *Roseanne* can claim.

As the title suggests, this was a show about the women, which allowed Eve and Kaye to be a latter-day Lucy and Ethel.

Actually, many of the show's plots seemed as old as *Lucy* but were nevertheless made passable by the go-for-broke styles of the leading ladies. Some of the situations: Eve and Kaye get locked in a store overnight; both couples arrive at the same winter cabin for the weekend.

One interesting installment sums up the broad humor and female resolve of this series. In this episode, an escaped convict (*F Troop*'s Larry Storch) breaks into Eve's house and takes her and Kaye hostage. When the husbands arrive, they discover the crook and attempt to rescue their wives … and fail. All four end up locked in a closet.

Later, Eve's daughter Suzie comes over to pick up a cake from Eve. The convict hides behind a curtain and orders Eve to hand over the cake and get her daughter out fast. But just before Eve hands it over, she scrawls "HELP CALL POLICE" into the icing. When Suzie discovers the message, she contacts the cops, who storm the house.

It's a sitcom situation for sure but, nevertheless, it's still Eve who saves everyone.

On Her Own

Portrayals of fractured families, ones upturned by divorce or death, debuted on television long before such series as *Grace Under Fire*. They date back to TV's first days. Their early debut makes a certain sense; World War II created many widows and, with that, single-parent families.

TV's first single mother was probably on the drama *The O'Neills* (1949–1950). Based upon the radio serial, it told of Peggy O'Neill (played by Vera Allen), a dress designer and mother to two boys.

TV's next significant single mother could be found, perhaps surprisingly, on *Lassie* (1954–1971). Actress Jan Clayton enacted the role of Ellen Miller, widow, farm woman, mother to Jeff and owner of Lassie. (More about Mrs. Miller later.) What began with Mrs. O'Neill and Mrs. Miller soon spread.

The mid-'50s sitcom *It's Always Jan* (1955–1956) starred singer-actress Janis Paige as Jan Stewart, a war widow with a young daughter. Besides raising her daughter, Jan also pursued her singing career. She worked regularly, if not too glamourously, in various New York nightclubs. The singer-nightclub angle of the show allowed Paige (previously of Broadway's *Pajama Game*) to sing once per episode. Her daughter's sole provider, Jan had to pursue her career seriously; she couldn't use work as a pathway to marriage.

Though every episode showed us what a good singer and mother Jan was, one episode also gave us an example of what a good person she was. In the episode, after a performance, Jan is approached by a well-connected agent anxious to sign her to his agency. But signing with him would mean Jan would have to fire her old agent, a man who has stood beside her during the highs and lows and become a close friend.

As the episode plays out, there's some comedic hemming as Jan wavers on her decision: Should she go for the "big time" even if it means sacrificing friendship? In the end, Jan decides that loyalty matters to her more than a few extra bucks. She sticks by her ethics and in the process sets an example for her daughter.

—⁂—

Another series with an early single mom jumped various media on its way to TV— *The Ghost and Mrs. Muir* (1968–1970). It was originally a successful novel, then a film; it seemed inevitable that this haunting romance would eventually come to television.

And it did. When *Ghost* arrived, it was updated from the Victorian era to modern times. Edward Mulhare starred as the sea captain ghost of the title while Hope Lange played Mrs. Carolyn Muir, a widowed mother of two.

To support her family, Mrs. Muir worked as a writer. The idea of having Mom work as a writer was a great boon to the world of domestic comedy: Mom could have a career but still be at home. Later, TV would expand this work-at-home scenario. Elyse Keaton, the mom of *Family Ties*, was an architect but always able to work from the kitchen table.

What was refreshing about Mrs. Muir's work was that we sometimes saw her struggling—rubbing her forehead while starring at blank paper or admonishing her kids, "Be quiet when Mommy's working."

As the series began, the Muirs had just had just moved into Gull Cottage, a house on the New England coastline. Unfortunately, the cottage had one drawback: a ghost. The ghost, Captain Daniel Gregg, had died over 100 years before but haunted the hallways and had successfully scared off anyone who dared to dwell in "his" home.

But that was before he met Mrs. Muir. After exhausting all his tricks to get Mrs. Muir to flee, the captain finally materializes in hopes that he can frighten her out. But, instead, it only makes her determined to stay.

At its core, *Mrs. Muir* was basically a love story with about as much time per episode devoted to romantic interludes as jokes. Eventually Captain Gregg would become visible not only to Mrs. Muir but to her children.

Captain Gregg was a persnickety ghost often infuriated by modern manners and the role women played in the 20th century. He was also quite selfish, always demanding attention from Mrs. Muir and always making demands about "his" house and possessions. In one episode, he's up in arms when a tree in "his" yard is about to be cut down. Another episode was about the captain's old tea set. This was one high-maintenance ghost.

By contrast, Mrs. Muir was "unflappable."[96] She was always able to handle both parenting and poltergeists, even lecturing her unwanted houseguest in one episode:

> MRS. MUIR: You don't understand about car batteries and picking children up at school and tidal floods in the kitchen. You don't understand and you don't care to understand.

CAPTAIN GREGG: It's regrettable that our attitudes towards life are at such odds as you have certain qualities that I could admire.
MRS. MUIR: Speaking up is not one of them?
CAPTAIN GREGG: Bickering is not one of them.
MRS. MUIR: You have no awareness of anyone else's needs. You think the woman's role is to cater to the male's ego and knit foot-warmers. Well, thanks for the bolt of silk from the Indians!
CAPTAIN GREGG: I assume that that last remark had some significance?
MRS. MUIR: It means that women are free! Totally free! Do you understand?

───────

Though much of the success of *The Partridge Family* (1970–1974) can be ascribed to David Cassidy, other theories have also emerged.

By the early 1970s, with divorce becoming more commonplace, even families in the suburbs were being increasingly turned into single-parent households. Hence, *Partridge* struck a chord. Series star Shirley Jones, though a widow on the show, has recalled some of the fan mail she got: "A lot of the letters [were] from broken homes, troubled teens, and kids who wanted me to be their mother."[97] As one TV writer noted, the message of *The Partridge Family* was that "even a family that has been diminished by death ... can maintain a very structured family life."[98]

The Partridge Family's success has also been attributed to its merging of certain fringe elements, thus making them palpable to mainstream America.[99] Though rock 'n' roll had in its early years a somewhat sanitized image (Pat Boone, etc.), by the 1970s rock was no longer so innocent. In the post–Woodstock era, rock had gotten darker, fueled by decadence and drugs. When the Partridges came along, they set rock (or pop) within the context of the all–American family, returning some paternal friendliness to the genre.

The series might also have served as something of a connector between older and younger, retro and futuristic. As Jones once put it, "Somehow, [*The Partridge Family*] seemed to bridge the big bad generation gap with the simple elixir of music."[100] Even the family's vehicle was a melding of small-town school system with psychedelic colors.

Like other TV moms, Mrs. Partridge, despite the stresses of family life and the music industry, always maintained a calm, reasonable stance. Co-star Susan Dey, who played daughter Laurie, once praised Jones' "almost regal ladylikeness."[101] Jones herself has said she was drawn to Mrs. Partridge "for her warmth and her brains."[102] One writer said the character "embodies common sense."[103] Certainly all of these traits came in handy when dealing with her son Danny and with Reuben, the family's screw-up manager.

From her shag hairdo to her Mondrian-painted bus, Mrs. Partridge was a thoroughly modern woman. And while she possessed many of the tenets of a traditional mother (as far as TV was concerned) in that she vacuumed and cooked, she was at the same time a single working mom in a highly non-traditional career (she played in a band). Even during its original run, audiences seemed to recognize this deviating from normal. In a letter to *The New York Times* in 1973, a viewer wrote, "Shirley Jones in *The Partridge Family* is perhaps the most liberated woman being portrayed on any television program this season."[104]

As the program continued, Mrs. Partridge became even more modern. In the episode "The Undergraduate," she went shopping and tried on hot pants; in another episode, she explained the facts of life to her two youngest children.

Also of note is the episode "Hel-l-l-l-p" in which she and eldest daughter Laurie go camping while "the guys" (sons Keith and Danny, along with Reuben) secretly follow. They are sure the women will fail when they rough it. The women prove themselves excellent survivalists while the men get lost and go hungry.

Far from being a hausfrau, Mrs. Partridge was also portrayed as a highly desirable woman with an active — but responsible — dating life. Over the course of the series, she had several evenings out and even once said to her kids:

> Let me explain something to you. I'm your mother, and in that way I'll always belong to all of you. But I'm also a woman. And even with five children whom I love very, very much, and who I know love me, there are times when I still feel lonely.

Besides being a smart and reassuring mother figure, Shirley also worked to instill values in her children. In one episode, she admonished her kids, "Instead of sitting here complaining about the way things are, why don't you do something about it?"

But she just didn't talk the talk. Though a family of five could always use a few extra bucks — even if they were recording artists — Mrs. Partridge refused to let money corrupt her family. Along with remaining in their simple suburban home, she often infuriated both Reuben and Danny with her largesse. In one episode, after recording a song featuring whale sounds, Shirley donates all the profits to the New York Zoological Society.

She is also the voice of reason in one of the most dissected episodes of the series, "My Son the Feminist." In this installment, Keith's new girlfriend, Tina, heads a local feminist group, and when she asks the Partridges to perform at an upcoming rally, they accept. Controversy arises when another local group, the Morality Watchdogs, threaten a boycott of all Partridge music if the band plays. Mrs. Partridge refuses to be strong-armed and is determined to make good on her promise to perform.

The day of the concert, Tina tells Keith that some of the lyrics of some of the songs need to be changed due to what she views as sexism. Keith, on artistic principle, refuses. Then he refuses to perform at all. Only a stern lecture from Shirley keeps the political from being personal. The show goes on.

Throughout this episode, Reuben is useless and Keith wavers. Not Mrs. Partridge. She simply refuses to take edicts from anyone. Her approach to these warring viewpoints is one of common sense and First Amendment freedoms. Hers is also the lone non-judgmental, non-extremist voice in either direction.

In this same episode there is another interesting scene. Several days before the concert, Tina comes to dinner and expresses her opinions. Here again, Shirley cuts through jargon, focusing instead on knowledge from her own experience:

> TINA: Women are discouraged from having careers. We're supposed to get married, become a housewife and wait for the babies to come.
> MRS. PARTRIDGE: I think it's a little more than just waiting.
> TINA: The family unit is decadent. It's only pleasurable and beneficial to the husband.
> MRS. PARTRIDGE: Don't you think you should have a husband and a family before you make that statement?

Return to Rural

While Lisa from *Green Acres* started urban and went rural, other TV wives-moms stayed in the country, making sure that heartiness and liberation reached beyond city limits.

As mentioned earlier, *Lassie* (1954–1971) can lay claim to featuring one of TV's first single mothers, Ellen Miller. Mrs. Miller was TV's first family to own Lassie on TV. She lived on a farm with her father and her son Jeff. Orphan Timmy was later added to the household.

Broadway vet Jan Clayton played Ellen. She was described in the book *Lassie: A Dog's Life* as "a full business partner in the farm with Gramps, she was independent, made her own decisions, dealt with men on their level and was both a father and mother to her son. She camped out with Jeff and his friends, she fished, played softball...."[105]

Clayton brought a grittiness to her role. She was believable as a country woman, unafraid of the dirt. In one episode, out hunting for a missing boy, she trips and falls alongside the road. In true pioneer fashion, she picks herself up, dusts herself off, and goes on with her search.

When Clayton left in 1957, Cloris Leachman became the new woman in Lassie's life. After Leachman's season, Lassie's most famous mistress arrived: June Lockhart. Lockhart played Ruth Martin from 1958 until 1964. Said Lockhart (who received top billing in the program):

> It's a lovely part, and a dignified role.... She was educated, literate, she had a sense of community spirit, she was really a very well-rounded character, and it was written that way, more and more, the longer I played it....[106]

Collins concurs that Ruth Martin was remarkably adept:

> [S]he often ran the farm while her husband, Paul, was away, making the decisions about purchases, crops, and livestock, and she once took a job as a fire watcher in a forestry tower. She could shoot a rifle, pitch a tent, and make a camp, and she drove all over the country without a man at her side, just like any real farm woman....[107]

Ruth Martin's strength and vitality was never more on display than in one classic *Lassie* episode where, driving alone in the country, Ruth's pick-up gets a flat. When she pulls the spare from the back of the truck (she doesn't think twice about changing it herself), it accidentally rolls down hill. When she climbs down to get it, she steps in a bear trap. And the timing couldn't be worse! Earlier, we learned that there was a hungry cougar loose in the woods. Well, wouldn't you know, only minutes after getting trapped, Ruth hears the cougar and then sees it in the distance. Repeatedly she tries to free herself from the trap ... but to no avail. Instead, she begins to gather nearby rocks to use as weapons. Eventually, Lassie comes along and Ruth is able to communicate to her to run home and get her a C-clamp. Lassie runs off and returns with the clamp. Mrs. Martin uses it to free herself just seconds before the cougar lunges.

In this episode, though Lassie of course comes to the rescue, not once is Ruth tempted to give up. Nor does she break down into sobs or scream for a man to come to her aid. Instead, she's resourceful, resilient, and fearless, especially as she prepares to take on the rabid animal.

Other aspects of Ruth are also interesting. In one episode, we learn that Ruth once worked for the U.S. Park Service. Frequently as well, Ruth's on-air wardrobe consisted not of frilly dresses but practical clothes in keeping with farm life.

—⁂—

If country girl Ruth Martin looked like she belonged, another TV farm wife was surprising.

Though on the big screen she often played urban sophisticates, Doris Day came to TV, in *The Doris Day Show* (1968–1973), playing a woman living in the country.[108] Day played Doris Martin, a widow with two young sons, who, after her husband's death, returned to her father's ranch.

In her season of rural episodes, it seemed Doris was always helping someone. When platonic friend Leroy (played by James Hampton) got a crush on the new librarian, Doris helps him woo her. And when her father, Buck (played by Denver Pyle), and his life-long friend have a falling-out, Doris finagles a plan to get the men to make up.

Finally, in one fascinating episode, Doris' old city life returns to the fore. It seems that before moving to the country, Doris was a senior writer for a national magazine. When a story that Doris once wrote needs an update, her former editor tries to get Doris to return to the magazine ... at least for a while.

It takes coaxing to get Doris to swap her Levis for a business suit, but Doris does eventually return. When the editor presses her to stay on, it causes Doris to do some soul-searching.

Surprisingly, this episode is very *un*-cut-and-dried. Rather than making a quick decision, Doris is tempted to return to her old job. Her father and her sons will support whatever Doris decides. Eventually Doris determines that life in the country suits her — and her family — just fine.

So what are we to make of this episode? Does it support the stereotype that the big city is bad while country life is good? More importantly, does it support the idea that career women are inherently unfulfilled? While both assumptions might be evident, Doris' serious consideration of the offer speaks to the choices many American women were going to have to make in regard to "having it all." It also echoes the rash of real-life women who often opt out of the rat race in order to devote themselves full-time to their children.

—◦◦◦—

For years *Lassie* was the primary source for rural family drama, but that changed in the 1970s. Perhaps it was in reaction to the 1960s or maybe the looming Bicentennial had just gotten Americans thinking about history. Whichever, in the early '70s two series successfully mined the past.

The Waltons (1972–1980) told the story of an expansive, proud but poor family during the Depression. The series launched a variety of imitators and one famous catch-phrase, "Good night, John-Boy."

While eldest son John-Boy was (until the exit of actor Richard Thomas in 1977) the show's central character, various female members of the Walton household were nevertheless able to make their presence felt.

The matriarch was Olivia Walton. Olivia was deglamourised, plain-spoken and played by Michael Learned with a weariness that was understandable for a woman raising seven children. Learned's multifaceted performance (for which she won three Emmys) was loving but also a little melancholy and revolutionary in that it was more Ma Joad than Susie Home-maker.

Learned worked to push realism into her character. Episodes that dealt with Olivia suffering a miscarriage and facing the onset of menopause were based on her suggestions.[109] Sometimes Learned's reach for realism was minor but meaningful. In one episode, she's scrubbing the floor and mutters, "I hate washing this floor!" (Learned had asked producer Earl Hamner if she could interject the word "damn"; he requested she not).[110]

In Olivia's marriage, we never got any sense that she was anything but his equal and a full co-parent; she was as likely to discipline the boys as the girls and was regularly sought out for advice and comfort from both.

Mary McDonough, who played daughter Erin, said of Learned, "She brought an amazing grace and dignity to [the portrayal of] motherhood...."[111]

Since ending in 1980, *The Waltons* has been adopted as a touchstone for "family values." Unfortunately, those who co-opt the show are overlooking the heavy realism it trafficked in. The Depression was not sugarcoated. In fact, perhaps one of the reasons that *The Waltons* struck such a chord was because the hard times of the 1930s often reflected the economic lean times of the 1970s.

The unexpected success of *The Waltons* soon ignited a trend towards other historic family dramas. *Little House on the Prairie* (1974–1982) seemed like a natural for this epoch. Based on the Laura Ingalls Wilder books, the series had the benefit of arriving with a built-in fan base. Toss in TV fave Michael Landon and gifted child actress Melissa Gilbert and a hit seemed assured.

And while Landon and Gilbert dominated the show, Karen Grassle, in her role as Caroline Ingalls, wife and mother, shed light onto the role women played during westward expansion. Along with the work needed to take care of a family, there were also episodes featuring Caroline laboring in the fields and chopping wood. Whatever it took, she did. But Caroline was not all muscle. In one episode, when the schoolteacher becomes incapacitated, it is Caroline who takes over the school.

The success of *Little House* and *The Waltons* inspired imitators, each with Willa Cather-like leads. *The Family Holvak* (1975–1977) featured preacher the Reverend Tom Holvak, his wife Elizabeth, and their children, who resided in the South in the 1930s. Glenn Ford starred as the devout reverend and the role of Elizabeth was played by Julie Harris.

Meanwhile, disaster master Irwin Allen reworked *The Swiss Family Robinson* into a TV series (1975–1976). Though it was based upon the old novel, it had many similarities to *The Waltons* et al.: set in the past, the story of a family attempting to survive the unknown while finding their greatest strength in each other. Pat Delaney was Mrs. Robinson and a young Helen Hunt was featured as Helga, a girl who had survived the same shipwreck as the Robinsons. Each week these two resilient women, along with the menfolk, took on hardships, from tidal waves to pirates.

The Eccentrics

Few programs have become the phenomenon that *The Beverly Hillbillies* (1962–1971) became when it debuted. Even now, the series remains one of the most watched programs in history.[112]

Hillbillies was the story of some stereotypical backwood folk who get rich and move to California to interact with some equally stereotypical bourgeois. The series was an exaggerated farce with deeper undertones. It was, as one author put it, "a refreshingly zany satire on American class society, a meaningful absurdity that illustrated the pretentious phoniness and shallow snobbery of the monied upper crust."[113] In the show, the Hillbillies come across better than their superficial, egotistical new neighbors.

Jed Clampett, who had brought the family to the world of movie stars, was the patriarch of the show, but even he was no match for his vibrant mother-in-law, a woman known as Granny. Granny (played by Irene Ryan) was probably TV's most imposing mother figure before the formable Mama of *Mama's Family* and, of course, *Roseanne*.

A "senior citizen" in society's eyes, Granny doesn't buy into "little old lady"-dom. She is active to the point of being manic; "a feisty hellcat whose character was the exact opposite of that of Aunt Bee of *The Andy Griffith Show*,"[114] according to one source. Granny does not go gently anywhere; she only reluctantly came to California.

Once there, like her other family members, she refuses to be corrupted by *nouveau riche* society or modern technology. In his book *Demographic Vistas*, Marc compares the entire Clampett clan to the then-rising hippie movement.[115] Like flower children, the Hillbillies refuse to be assimilated. Though their home is equipped with a state-of-the-art laundry room, Granny prefers her wash tub. She also rejects consumerism. Though the stores carry soap, Granny prefers to make her own lye.

Also similar to the hippies, the Clampetts are diehard environmentalists. Though they live urban, overbuilt to the point of a "cement pond," the family remains in touch with nature: There's Elly Mae's "critters," and the family's food comes from their backyard, not from some grocery store. Granny also has disregard for modern medicine, preferring her own herbal remedies. Medically speaking, Granny must have known what she was doing; in a later cross-over with *Petticoat Junction*, Granny goes to Hooterville to assist Bradley daughter Betty Jo when she has her baby.

The Clampetts are also Calvinists in their dedication to work. They reject all attempts to supply them with servants and luxuries. Though Jed liked to whittle and Granny liked to rock in her chair, the Clampetts seem to have little comprehension of leisure. In their eyes, even items in their mansion meant for relaxation take on practical uses — pool cues are just sticks for passing hot dishes.

While all the Clampetts display traditional qualities, it's to varying degrees. Jethro is most easily swayed by "high livin'" while Granny is the most resistant — often in the extreme. When strangers, even chefs, enter Granny's kitchen, they get chased out with a cleaver.

Granny has a short fuse. She reaches for her shotgun whenever she feels threatened. She's not above tackling her neighbor, Mrs. Drysdale, when Granny views her as an interloper. In one classic installment Granny even boxes a "giant jackrabbit" (actually a kangaroo) that has wandered into the backyard.

Granny's equally quick with her tongue. If she's got something to say, she says it. Consider such comments as "You can throw her in the river and skim ugly for two days." Her opinionated nature prefigured the bluntness of Sophia on *Golden Girls* and, again, *Roseanne*.

Speaking of *Golden Girls*, Granny is a significant bridge along that continuum that began with *December Bride* (to be discussed later) and then marches to those four Miami ladies. Like them, Granny brings to TV an image of an "elderly" woman who is vibrant and active.

—◦◦◦—

As Erik Barnow has pointed out, like their equally creepy neighbors, the Munsters, the Addams Family (in the 1964–1965 same-name series) were basically "wholesome and lovable."[116] A book on the series goes even further about the family, stating, "For all their inherent bizarreness, they were probably the nicest family in all of sixties TV."[117]

Certainly, the Addamses were a liberal, non-judgmental bunch. Like the Munsters house, the Addams home is inclusive to multiple generations. But here the family stretches their benevolence beyond blood in order to include others whom society also views as "grotesque." For example, tall and gruesome butler Lurch would have a tough time finding employment had the Addamses not hired him. Furthermore, the lineage of Thing, the hand who delivered the daily mail (among other five-fingered tasks), is never explained. But since he is referred to as just "Thing," as opposed to say *Cousin* Itt, it seems safe to assume that Thing is a non-relation and that this disembodied hand has also been welcomed into this family. The Addamses would allow into their home others who have been labeled deviant, from beatniks to Iron Curtain dignitaries.

The family is anchored by Mr. and Mrs. Addams, Gomez and Morticia, played by John Astin and Carolyn Jones. Jones' casting has been described as "perfect" as it did play to the actress' comic gifts and unique femme fatale qualities.[118]

At the time of the show, Mr. and Mrs. Addams had perhaps the most equitable marriage on TV. There was never a quarrel between them and neither was portrayed as necessarily smarter than the other. (Though Morticia did once correct Gomez on his Shakespeare.) *Addams Family* producer Nat Perrin said, "Of a thousand shows with husbands and wives, there was always bickering or misunderstandings. I didn't want to do another version of *The Bickersons*, because I thought it would look like every other show."[119]

Additionally, the Addamses also had the most romantic, overtly sexual relationship then on air. Gomez wrote poems to his wife and their dialogue was filled with innuendo. Gomez was also powerless whenever Morticia uttered a word in French; one "merci" from Morticia would cause Gomez to seize her arm and kiss it uncontrollably. Even the couple's living room swordfights seemed like foreplay. Since the couple, like the entire family, was pretty cartoonish, the censors no doubt allowed greater leeway.

While Morticia sometimes indulged in traditional "womanly" activities—she liked to knit and tend to her African strangler plant—most of the time her life was as non-traditional as everything else in the household. In one episode she wrote a children's book after deciding that most of them were "corrupted" with their negative portrayals of witches. In another, she takes up sculpting; and still later she offers dancing and fencing lessons to the public. Throughout all her endeavors, Morticia retains a calm self-assuredness. She is remarkably self-possessed, often holding court from her wide-backed wicker chair, her at-home throne.

Morticia Addams is also a fashion icon. Siouxsie Sioux once said, "My role model, inspiration and heroine is Morticia Addams."[120] Indeed, Morticia's "out there" tastes and non-traditional personality (she's the "anti-chirpy") prefigured a generation of punk girls and goth chicks. Her wardrobe, the long slim skirt with its cloth tentacled hem, has gone on to inspire everyone from Elvira to Angelina Jolie at the 1999 Oscars.

In her garb, Morticia shows she is above fashion. Her form-fitting black sheath is not, according to popular thought, appropriate attire for household duties, yet it's what Morticia wears. Why? Because it suits her. Her dress is a reflection of her and, like Lisa Douglas, she uses it to express her individuality.

In *Where the Girls Are*, Susan Douglas takes issue with Morticia's sexual persona, stating that female sexuality at that time on TV could only be depicted if it were "totally unrealistic" and tempered by Morticia's "ghoulishness."[121] But Morticia was far from the first time we saw sexual women in the media. If this statement were true, then what about the "vamps" of the silent screen? Or the love goddesses of Hollywood's postwar period, like Rita Hayworth and Lana Turner? What of Bettie Page? And on TV, from Faye Emerson's notorious cleavage to Edie Adams' smoldering cigarette commercials, innumerable female TV personalities were powerful and sexy but never "monstrous."

If Mrs. Addams was an unusual mom, then what about one reincarnated as a car?

In *My Mother the Car* (1965–1966), Jerry Van Dyke starred as Dave, a son who one day bought a 1928 Porter, only to discover that the jalopy possessed the soul of his long-dead mother! His mother, the car, communicated to her son via the car's radio. Ann Sothern provided the voice of the vehicle.

Besides the oddness of finding out that one's parent is now a buggy, the program is fraught with Freudianism. What does it mean when you rotate "Mom's" tires or crawl under "her" to change the oil? In fact, actual episodes were based on the son worrying about "Mom's" high oil pressure. In one episode, like any good son, he took Mom out for a drive on her birthday.[122] But Mom was good to have around. In one episode, she foils some hoods when they try to use her as a getaway car.

Despite the program's reputation as one of TV's worst, viewed today, it's no funnier nor less funny than other comedies of the era. *My Mother* sticks in memory because of its strange premise. Though, to be fair, it was not much more far-fetched than a group stranded on an island.

Besides, as a mother image, *My Mother the Car* could be considered good. Though Dave does suffer in some ways due to this in*car*nation of his mother (mainly because she talks only to him), he is not angry over her reappearance. Throughout the series, no matter how many times Mom smacks her son with "her" door, he never attempts to "unload" her. In this regard, *My Mother the Car* could be viewed as social statement, a metaphor for how often society "ditches" its elderly like so many broken-down Buicks.

The honoring of elders is a primary tenet of many Eastern philosophies and *My Mother* might only be bizarre when viewed through Western eyes. There is something Buddhist-like in the message of *My Mother* as it ultimately is about life after death. As Mom says in the series' first episode about her rebirth, "It was the only way I could find to bring me back." Ultimately what *My Mother the Car* says is that, in any form, TV moms are forever still loving, loved and needed by their children.

As radical as *Roseanne* was, many other earlier TV moms were also loudly, proudly "domestic goddesses." One of those was "Mama" Harper of *Mama's Family* (1983–1990).

When the character of Mama (real name: Thelma) began on *The Carol Burnett Show* and Vicki Lawrence transformed herself into the blue-haired old lady, she engineered a most startling metamorphosis. Lawrence's is a *tour de force* performance of a *tour de force* character.

After *Burnett* ended in 1979, Mama would later rise again via her own sitcom. Now with a half-hour, the producers could delve deeper into the Mama character and get behind her bluster.

With time, we learn how smart Mama was. She was a contestant on *Jeopardy!* in one episode and, in another, proved herself a skillful poker player. She was also a community activist; in one episode she pickets a mini-mart to make them remove adult magazines.

Mama on the sitcom has been described as the only sane person among insane people, i.e., her nutty family. On the series she certainly stands above her dull-normal son Vinton (played by Ken Berry) and her trashy daughter-in-law Naomi (Dorothy Lyman). Note these exchanges:

> VINT: Just think, Mama, you made a total jackass out of yourself just because I asked you.
> MAMA: Well, that's all right, Vint. You've always done the same for me and I never even had to ask.

> VINT: Mama, you never could throw anything out, no matter how useless it is.
> MAMA: It's lucky for you.

Like Maude before, and Roseanne after, Mama refuses to be silenced.

But, as with real families, Mama won't tolerate anyone else making disparaging remarks about her brood. As *Entertainment Weekly* said of her, "Mama remains a fierce defender of her nincompoop-infested family, and when she's forced to reveal her true feelings, the lips quiver, the voice cracks, and the dollops of down-home wisdom come spilling forth."[123]

No-nonsense mothers like Thelma laid the groundwork for other non-traditional TV moms. While *Roseanne* would be the best example, she would be followed by Lois on *Malcolm in the Middle* and even Sharon Osbourne on *The Osbournes*.

The Lear Years

Its importance in broadcasting — and American — history should not be diminished. Norman Lear's *All in the Family* (1971–1983) marked a seismic change in situation comedy.

Prior to the Bunkers, most sitcoms had restricted any message to little moral lessons (tell the truth, etc.). *All in the Family* ushered in a new era of issue-led comedy as well as a frankness with which these issues were discussed.

Furthermore, before *All in the Family*, few sitcoms ever dared to feature characters with such fervently held political opinions or, for that matter, who dared be so outwardly unlikable.

The premise of *All in the Family* was a microcosm of the American political debate. Ultra-conservative Archie Bunker every week faced off against his liberal-minded son-in-law Michael (a.k.a. "Meathead"), thus making the Bunker household a constant battlefield of political ideologies.

They were originally conceived more as mouthpieces than people; in the beginning, all four main characters (Archie, wife Edith, daughter Gloria and Michael) were caricatures. Archie was bigoted to the point of buffoonery. And Michael, despite good debating skills, was something of, well, a meathead and sometimes a hypocrite as well (he once balked at the idea of a woman surgeon). Meanwhile, Gloria (Sally Struthers) was whiny and immature and Edith (Jean Stapleton) was either histrionic or inconsequential.

As the series progressed, the characters developed. Archie became less hateful, Michael morphed into bourgeoisie and Gloria grew up.

But no one changed like Edith. In the beginning, saddled with the nickname "Dingbat" by her husband, and overshadowed by two warring males, Edith was eager to avoid conflict and often got lost in the din. As one author put it, Edith was the "compassionate dingbat who saw everybody's side of everything, but took years to realize that she was entitled to her own opinions."[124]

With time, Edith came out of her shell. She would come to stand up to her husband (once famously telling him to "stifle"), join a women's group, and battle a local bank when they refused to give her a loan without her husband's signature. She would also go on to stare down breast cancer and even defend herself against a rapist.

Edith also often served as this show's moral center, its voice of reason. As one author noted, "[W]e frequently see her deep sense of compassion or her common sense approach winning out over Archie's incredible boisterousness."[125]

Despite a sometimes scattered demeanor, Edith's unique way of seeing the truth allowed her to successfully put up with — and see through — her husband's obnoxiousness. Consider what she once told Michael:

> Do you wanna know why Archie yells at you? Archie yells at you because Archie is jealous of you. You're going to college. Archie had to quit school to support his family. He ain't never going to be any more than he is right now. Now you think that over.[126]

The success of *All in the Family* soon allowed Lear to spin off other series. In regard to *Maude* (1972–1978), it might be risky to include her in a chapter on wives and mothers; if Ms. Findley were real, she probably wouldn't be pleased. Yet, despite the lead's frequent politicking, most *Maude* episodes took place within the Findley household and dealt with issues personal, not political. Moreover, though Maude might have had more volume, there's only a matter of degrees between her and two other TV housewives, Alice Kramden and Lucy Ricardo.

Maude was first introduced in an episode of *All in the Family*. She was a cousin of Edith's who was "the perfect liberal counterpart to Archie's conservatism."[127]

Beatrice Arthur was full-on on *All in the Family*. Her on-screen sparring with Carroll O'Connor's Archie seemed to resemble classic gladiator games. So, because she earned it, Maude eventually got her own show.

Premiering in 1972, the same year that Congress approved the ERA, Maude was probably TV's first self-proclaimed feminist. Her theme song described her as "anything but compromising."

Maude was also what almost no other character had ever been before: totally unapologetic. She was three times divorced and didn't seem to care. She was also an older woman (who had an adult daughter and grandson who lived with her) at a time when Mary Richards and her many clones were populating primetime. And, more importantly, Maude dared to look her age: wrinkles and gray hair. Maude was also openly confrontational. She took no guff, carrying on a tradition of wisecracks begat

Unbullied and overshadowed by no one, Beatrice Arthur played TVs first self-described feminist on *Maude* (1972–1978).

by *Our Miss Brooks*. Maude first battled with Archie, then, on her own show, she often took on her neighbor Arthur, and, when he wasn't around, she dueled with her husband Walter. Said author Michael McWilliams, "Whenever Maude went up against a legion of men ... it was like watching a sitcom version of *The Little Foxes*."[128] Even when Walter got the upper hand, Maude still had the last word by uttering, "God will get you for that, Walter."

In her bombast Maude was to neo-liberalism what Archie was to neo-conservatism. Opposites in gender and political viewpoints, the two are mirror images of each other, sharing mutual extremism. Noted Newcomb, "She, too, is a parody, and her weaknesses demonstrate the real bite of the show."[129]

There were chinks in Maude's leftist armor. Sometimes her opinions worked better in theory. When daughter Carol's boyfriend spends the night, Maude — surprisingly — thinks they should have separate rooms. Later, Maude's grandson Phillip introduces her to his special male "friend" and Maude has to adjust.

But in terms of being issue-oriented, episodes like these two were only the start. During its run, *Maude* had as much drama as a daytime soap, with no episode more notable than the one in which Maude underwent an abortion.[130] Other lighting rods: Maude discovered she was manic-depressive and later would go through menopause. In a 1974 episode, the Findlays got audited and their tax man turned out to be the man who raped Maude 31 years ago. Walter wants his wife to try to forget about it. Maude replies, "Nothing has changed, you men don't give a damn about how women feel."

During the course of the show's run, Walter's business went bankrupt, he was treated for alcoholism, and he suffered a breakdown. As a character, Walter could be viewed as pathetic. Despite occasional displays of backbone, mostly Walter existed in his wife's shadow. As Philip Wander put it, "[Maude] was bigger, brighter and more articulate than her husband."[131] Indeed, Walter's resonating image is one of him nursing a cocktail while walking around in his boxer shorts; literally and figuratively not wearing the pants in this household. It's fascinating to consider what would be said about this less than empowering male character if *he* had been a *she*. Portrayed as a poor businessperson with a proclivity for alcohol, a "female Walter" would be a constant for criticism; but since he is male, Walter's seldom cited in TV gender studies.

Despite *Maude*'s success — it was seldom out of the top ten during its run — and Maude's pioneering traits, she and her show aren't talked about much. Numerous articles on women on the TV skip her as they bounce from *That Girl* to *Mary Tyler Moore* to *Murphy Brown*. Perhaps it's because, as strong as she was, Maude also embodied many stereotypes of "women's libbers": she was loud, overbearing, mannish in appearance and voice. It's not surprising therefore that many prefer to remember the stylish Murphy Brown as opposed to Maude in terms of pioneering women. Murphy mixed her political views with a savvy sensibility that seemed to make her message more digestible, less abrasive than Maude's.

—⦿⦿⦿—

But if that's the case with *Maude*, then why do so many articles also ignore Ann Romano of *One Day at a Time*?

Though created by Whitney Blake (the mom on the first incarnation of *Hazel*), *One Day at a Time* (1975–1984) bore all the hallmarks of being a Norman Lear program (as it was) as it mixed its humor with melodrama.

Though TV moms from the "golden age" were far more "real" than they are usually considered, we must credit Ann Romano (played by Bonnie Franklin) for being one of television's realest moms ever.

Ann was not TV's first divorcee; Vivian Vance on *The Lucy Show* and Diana Rigg on *Diana* preceded her. But Ann was the first to take back her maiden name ("because I want to be a liberated woman") and to insist on "Ms." She was also the first to truly convey the economic uncertainty that often arises when one is female, divorced and raising children. Creator-producer Blake said of Ann, "[S]he is not a chicly turned-out woman of the world … she is vulnerable and scared — like a woman stepping off a high diving board and suddenly realizing she doesn't know how to swim."[132]

Ann was depicted as tired, worried, and, sometimes, at loose ends. Why shouldn't she be? Married at 17, divorced at 36, with teen daughters Julie and Barbara, she had no college education and little work experience. Ann's plight as a "displaced homemaker" reflected a growing segment of American women.

But Ann didn't play the victim to obtain more child support or a better job. (In fact, in one episode, Ann runs the risk of losing an advertising client because she refuses to flirt like a rival female does.)

Though most of *One Day* took place on the domestic front, the series frequently focused on the reality of work. Ann would eventually rise up the ladder in advertising, but it wasn't easy. She was seen as embarrassed by her lack of a college degree. Later, she battled her male boss over whether a woman could do the same job as a man. Once she battled a lecherous client.

While Maude was a card-carrying feminist, she dealt more in the movement's philosophy than practical applications. By contrast, Ann was on the front lines like when it came to equal pay and respect. *Ms.* magazine said of the show, "*One Day at a Time* comes closer than anything … in sitcom [to] portraying a feminist point of view."[133]

Even with Ann's tough work life, it wasn't as complicated as her home one. Life in the Romano-Cooper[134] household was not glamorized. Ann's wardrobe was off the rack and the family's apartment, though pleasant, wasn't palatial. Money was an issue since her ex-husband only begrudgingly paid child support.

Furthermore, Ann's eldest, Julie, was rebellious. The hijinks of Dennis the Menace were nothing compared to Julie who staged pranks (like going through a car wash *sans* car in one episode), took up with a man twice her age, and had a short-lived religious conversion (which saw her bring home a homeless man). Finally, in one three-episode story arc, Julie ran away with her boyfriend Chuck. In the penultimate scene, after Ann tracks Julie down, the two have an intense mother-daughter conversation. In it, Julie attempts to bargain her return home by laying out new rules she and Chuck want. Then, in what was probably TV's first example of "tough love," Ann tells her daughter, "Fine. Don't come home."

Even after this crisis, mother and daughter continued to have problems, often played out in multiple episodes. Though these multiple episodes could be self-important, they did buck the TV cliché "All problems must be solved in 30 minutes."

As bad as Julie was, she was balanced by Barbara, played by Valerie Bertinelli. Barbara was a "good girl" — though not a sickening one. Bertinelli was the program's breakout star as she transformed from a tomboyish teen into a stunning young woman and an effective comedienne able to hold her own opposite Franklin and Nanette Fabray. (The latter eventually joined the show as Ann's mother.)

With the addition of Fabray, *One Day* became, even more than before, a female-centric series, one built around three generations of women. This is notable since male offspring have traditionally dominated TV families. Consider *Leave It to Beaver* and *My Three Sons* where there were no girls. Or *The Waltons* and *The Partridge Family* where girls are outnumbered.

Nevertheless, even in this women's world, on *One Day at a Time* there was a quasi–"man of the house": the apartment building's superintendent Dwayne Schneider (Pat Harrington, Jr.). During the course of the series, Schneider became more integrated into the lives of Ann and her children. Author Ella Taylor holds Schneider up for ridicule, saying that he "takes his place in a long line of castrated males in television entertainment, men who make themselves absurd with tough macho talk, who are safe because they have been stripped of the sexual challenge that complicates relations between men and women...."[135] This author's criticism begs questions: Would she have preferred, rather than "castrated," Schneider was portrayed as lecherous?

On the series, Schneider acts respectfully toward the girls and their mother and often functions as a father figure. Like Elden, the live-in painter on *Murphy Brown* later, Schneider's straightforward blue-collar approach often spoke the ultimate truth while also adding comic relief.

In time, the Romano-Coopers became less a "broken family" than a blended one due to Schneider's unofficial role and due to later developments. In season five, Ann became engaged to a man with a young son. When the series returned in the fall of 1981, the audience learned that Ann's fiancé had died. But since Ann and her soon-to-be stepson had become close, he moved in anyway. Later still, Julie, her husband Max and their baby returned to live with Ann. In the show's final season, Barbara married Mark, a dental student, and Ann got engaged to Mark's divorced dad, Sam.

The Romano-Coopers were complicated. But as step-, blended and eventually gay families emerged, what was being played out on *One Day* may very well have helped educate many viewers about new definitions of "family."

Though *One Day* was on for nine seasons, like *Maude* it seldom gets remembered in retrospectives of women on TV. Douglas makes no mention of it in *Where the Girls Are*,[136] and though *One Day*'s run extended into the 1980s, Faludi doesn't cite it in *Backlash*.[137]

—✧✧✧—

There's a similar silence for Florida Evans who, after leaving *Maude*, got her own series, *Good Times* (1974–1979).

The Evans family consisted of Florida, her husband James, eldest son James, Jr. (J.J.), daughter Thelma and youngest son Michael. Before its debut, star Esther Rolle had insisted that she be married on the show, as opposed to *Julia*'s widowhood. Remarkably, this was the first time that series TV had presented an intact African American family.

The title *Good Times* was ironic as the show's family faced many more "hard times." The series built many of its stories around timely politics — the failures of the Carter administration and runaway inflation. But while other TV families of the era talked about them, the Evans lived them, as in the time James got laid off.

The series also, like *Maude*, tackled a wide spectrum of issues: alcoholism, drugs, and child abuse.

Good Times presented to audiences an unvarnished view of the working poor. For the Evanses, "home" was subsidized housing where the elevator seldom worked and the walls were ugly cinder blocks. The program's opening credits continued the show's neo-realism.

Shot in Chicago where the series was set, it showed the world outside the Evanses' window: cracking sidewalks, graffiti-covered concrete, rusted swing sets. The fact that the family lived in an apartment at all is notable, since most TV families tended to dwell in homes with well-manicured lawns.

The only concession made to TV fantasy was that Florida didn't (at first) work outside the home. And surely this family could have used extra money. But Florida's status as a stay-at-home wife was explained via an old staple: Florida's husband James wouldn't allow it. And like Alice Kramden before her, Florida stayed at home. Neither logic or economics could surmount male ego when it came to the idea of "the little woman" having a job.

This did not mean that Florida was dominated. Throughout the series, Florida was the voice of reason. In one episode, her set of principles stops James from signing on to a shady business deal.

Repeatedly Florida refuses to sell out. She turned down a part in a TV commercial when she realized the product was shoddy. In another, she throws J.J. out when she learns he's working in a little "gambling business."

Besides being of high morals, Florida's smart and capable. In one episode, she starts night school to get her GED. In another, when she begins work as a school bus driver, she's labeled a hero for her quick thinking during a snowstorm.

In the series' most clearly feminist episode, the stress of living near poverty with three kids begins to get to Florida. After an early morning filled with household mishaps, a complaining James and a bickering J.J. and Thelma, Florida snaps, eventually slapping Michael. Reduced to tears, Florida runs to her bedroom, emerging later only with the assistance of her friend Willona, and Willona's invitation to attend a "women's awareness" meeting.

The women's meeting is portrayed in the manner in which TV has treated (or continues to treat) feminism: as a group of complaining extremists. At her "consciousness-raising," Florida soon realizes that her family respects her more than many of the other women there.

But Florida's newfound contentment doesn't last. She arrives home to find a fuming James, who lectures her that "a woman's place is in the kitchen and the bedroom!" But Florida has measured out the extremes she's experienced and informs her husband that she doesn't want to walk ahead of him or behind him but beside him. She goes on to inform her family that she's more than just "James' wife" and "J.J. and Thelma's mother," that she's her own person and would like to be treated as such.

Though this episode is loaded with dogma, it's not that far from the under-appreciated mom episodes of *Mama* et al. While some will choose to see this episode's resolution as sell-out, it is nevertheless in keeping with the general tendency for TV, when addressing social and political movements, to seek out and support a common ground. What Florida finds in this episode is her own "women's lib," one that's satisfying to her.

Though Rolle was a formidable actress, when the series began, the breakout star of the series was Jimmy Walker who played J.J. Walker's physical comedy made the show a hit and his trademark shout of "Dy-no-mite!" a catchphrase. Originally *Good Times* was to focus on the entire family, but the popularity of J.J. turned it into "The Jimmy Walker Show."

But the more successful J.J. became, the more the show was criticized. The skinny, rubbery-faced Walker, and the character he played, was called an updated minstrel character.

In retrospect, the criticism aimed at J.J. may have been overkill. J.J. was a "good kid." He didn't steal, do drugs, or hang with gangs. Meanwhile, the sort of physical comedy that got Walker into trouble would later make mega-stars of John Ritter on *Three's Company* and Michael Richards on *Seinfeld*, and launch Jim Carrey.

Nevertheless, the emphasis on J.J., and what Rolle perceived as his stereotyped behavior, caused the actress to exit the series at the end of 1977: "I did not agree to do a clown show for you to degrade young black men."[138] In her exit, Rolle became one of the few TV performers ever to leave a series over matters of principle.

Florida's husband James had already been written out (killed off, in fact) when actor John Amos left the series in a similar dispute and now Florida would also exit quickly (if not permanently). The plot line that explained Florida's absence had Florida remarrying and relocating to the southwest for her new husband's health. This explanation did not sit well with Rolle. "A mother just wouldn't do that, abandon her children in that way," she said.[139]

When *Good Times* returned in the fall, Florida's vanishing was explained and the character of neighbor Willona (played by Ja'net DuBois) began to take on a more maternal role, with her eventually becoming an adoptive parent to a little girl, Penny (played by a young Janet Jackson).[140]

Willona's wasn't the only character that changed. Ironically, it took the departure of Amos and Rolle to finally achieve what they wanted — greater depth for J.J. With his father's death and mother's absence, J.J. now had to take on more responsibility.

Eventually, pleased with the changes, Rolle returned to the show in fall 1978. Though *Good Times* was no longer huge in the ratings, Rolle's comeback brought back its gravitas. While in her absence, the kids had been all right, they were still kids. Florida's return restored a level of realism to the family dynamic.

On screen, or off, nobody could take the place of Rolle. Upon the actress' death in 1998, Norman Lear said of her, "I think through all the years of television she was *the* black matriarch."[141]

—◦◦◦—

At the other end of the economic spectrum from the Evanses was the Jeffersons, TV's other notable black family of the 1970s.

The Jeffersons (1975–1985), another Norman Lear series, was spun off from *All in the Family*. George Jefferson (played by Sherman Hemsley) was a successful dry cleaner with a chain of stores. Before he and his wife Louise moved uptown, he often clashed with his neighbor Archie Bunker — not so much because they were opposites but because they were similar. Both Archie and George were wildly opinionated and bigoted (note George's frequent "zebra" insults regarding interracial neighbors Tom and Helen Willis) and both tended to dish out more than they could take.

As opposed to Archie's wife Edith, however, Louise (played by Isabel Sanford) was less tolerant of her husband. And if Louise was more vocal, she had a reason to be. Mr. Jefferson had far greater delusions of grandeur than Archie. Hence, it often fell to Louise (and tart-tongued maid Florence) to keep him grounded.

Despite her *nouveau riche*-ness, Louise refused to become a "lady of leisure." In one episode, she tells George she's bored at home all day. She wants a job and a life. George, ever proud, doesn't like the idea of his wife working. After an argument, Louise decides to teach George a lesson and gets back at him in a profound way: She goes out and gets a job — with one of George's rivals!

That rebellion aside, however, Louise eventually finds her contentment in giving back to the community from which she and her husband emerged. She, with friend Helen, devote countless hours to an inner-city Help Center.

But Louise's humanitarianism is on display even when she's not at the Center. Louise — again — is the show's moral center and voice of reason. Said one author, Louise is "an expansive, tolerant lady ... trying to remain friends with the white neighbors and the black domestic [Florence] helper who George consistently alienated."[142] (Louise, we learn later, comes by her respect for Florence naturally; she too once worked as a housekeeper.) In one episode, after two youths are arrested for vandalizing George's store, Louise persuades him not to press charges but to let her rehabilitate them.

Like the Kramdens, George and "Weezy" (as he affectionately called her) had a lot of arguments but (also like Ralph and Alice) there was a strong current of love beneath their shouting. There was another constant in all these fights as well: As Jannette Dates wrote, "The humor and warmth of the show often came from Louise's methods of controlling George and the problems he caused.... [N]o matter what the conflict, George was never right."[143]

Case in point: In one episode, George prepares his will, leaving everything to Louise. However, he also stipulates that Louise will forfeit everything should she remarry. While Louise states she can't imagine ever remarrying, she does take issue with this clause, telling George, "I won't have you run my life now and I won't let you run it after you're dead."

Louise never had a problem putting George in his place:

GEORGE: You don't need any more bad luck.
LOUISE: I know. I already got you.

Or:

GEORGE: I wear the pants.
LOUISE: And when you zip them up, include your mouth!

As with Alice, Louise's comebacks are evidence of a quick-thinking mind. Even the actor who played George eventually had to concede his co-star's authority. Upon her death in 2004, Hemsley said of Sanford, "We called her 'the Queen'.... We bowed to her.... She had that air."[144]

Sanford's "royal air" was recognized at least one other time. In 1981 she won an Emmy for lead actress in a comedy. To date, she's the only African American woman ever so honored.[145]

Thoroughly Modern Moms

Please Don't Eat the Daisies (1965–1967), the sitcom inspired by the Doris Day movie and Jean Kerr's book, isn't widely syndicated today. That's too bad as its lead character, Joan Nash, even now, is strikingly modern.

Though married to a professor and the mother of four, Joan, played by Pat Crowley, was not "just" a wife and mother but also a successful freelance writer. Furthermore, Mrs. Nash almost always wore pants and made no bones about her preference to work at her typewriter rather than at cleaning.

As if all this wasn't progressive enough, the Nashes also have the distinction of being TV's first "realistic" (read: not *The Munsters*) couple seen regularly sharing a bed.

As a writer, Joan published under the name Joan Holliday — literally creating an identity outside of marriage and motherhood. Sometimes Joan's writing caused conflicts within her family, yet they never resulted in the family thinking Mom shouldn't work. Instead, most "complications" were "sitcom-y." When Joan authored a piece on offering second chances to ex-cons, she's forced to hire a former felon to act as a butler; when Joan writes about her kids, they demand a residual.

Sometimes, though, Joan's writings did result in episodes that flirted with larger issues. In "My Mother's Name Is Fred," Joan adopts a male *nom de plume* to write about lacrosse in the men's magazine *Romp*. She tells her friend Marge the magazine won't accept articles by women, to which Marge points out, "If they didn't accept photos of women, they'd be out of business." Once the article appears, *Romp* wants to do a writer's profile. When the magazine editors arrive at the Nashes, mistaken identity run rampant. Even husband Jim isn't sure what's going on. Referring to his wife, he tells the magazine guys, "She can't be [the writer], she doesn't know anything about lacrosse." (Which only shows how little he knows about Joan!)

Throughout *Daisies*, Joan enjoyed success in her career — enough to cause Jim to feel inadequate. In the premiere, Joan writes a newspaper article about the foibles of her husband. Everyone finds it funny — except for Jim. In "A Matter of Concentration," Joan uses a recent paycheck to buy gifts for everyone, but this causes yet another inferiority complex in her husband.

The marital problem of a wife overshadowing her husband is the progression of what was hinted at in *I Love Lucy*. Had Lucy ever been able to work outside the home, her marriage would have to address the issues with which Jim and Joan wrestled.

—⁕—

As iconic as Mrs. Stone and Cleaver are, perhaps no TV mom has left a bigger impression than Carol Brady.

Though not a giant hit during its original run, *The Brady Bunch* (1969–1974) has gone on to become a staple of syndication and revival. *The Brady Bunch* is the series that will not die.

Many theories abound as to why the Bradys just won't — or can't — stay away. One is that despite the ample camp aspects of the show, there remains something very modern about this family. Its morality lessons are still relevant. And the joys and difficulties of blending a family made up of his kids and her kids is even more topical now than it was during the show's original run. And, even more prophetic, the Bradys were the medium's first family to be a truly melded one, a family conjoined more by emotional ties than DNA.

The series' overall cast/gender symmetry seems to have something to do with its longevity. With three kids of each sex making up the family, it appealed equally to boys and girls. And with every birth position — oldest, youngest, middle — all represented, the show's appeal was broadened.

One is also struck by what a modern mom Mrs. Brady was. Carol's fondness for pants, her latter easy hairdo (a sort of early mullet), her '70s style which has since come back into fashion, keep her contemporary, as do other aspects. Though the series begins with her marriage to Mike, prior to that Carol must have been a working mother earning enough to support three girls. And though Carol became a full-time wife and mom, she let it be known working at home was hard. Daughter Marcia, after seeing her mother's golf clubs in the garage, asks her, "Why don't you play golf any more?"

Carol replies, "Six children, a husband, a house and a dog and you ask me 'How come?'"

Brady modernism (compared to *Roseanne*'s post-modernism) is further underscored by Mr. and Mrs. Brady's co-parenting dynamic. In the 1950s, TV parenting often broke down along gender lines. By contrast, the Brady parents are often seen discussing whatever problem a youngster is having.

Unfortunately, such understanding between the sexes didn't always trickle down. More than almost any other series, *The Brady Bunch* delved into gender politics. Consider:

- The boys object when they learn that the girls (and Carol and housekeeper Alice) are coming on their camping trip. But once they arrive at camp, the girls do a better job "roughing it."
- Marcia joins the all-boy Frontier Scouts much to the consternation of Greg, Peter and Bobby. Quid pro quo, the guys force Peter to become the world's first male Sunflower Girl. Humiliated, Peter quits. But Marcia stays the course as a Scout and aces her initiation.
- After numerous comments about "women drivers," Greg and Marcia challenge each other to a driving test. Greg's ego won't let him practice or look at the track. In the end, Marcia is the victor.

This is not to say that the series was flawless in its gender treatment. Remember the episode where Carol and the girls' attempt to build a clubhouse ends in disaster? Mike and the boys have to come to their rescue and the "lady folk" are sent to fetch lemonade!

Despite that misstep, the women usually held their own. Consider the time the girls got back at the boys with fake ghosts.

Furthermore, Mrs. Brady was depicted as highly accomplished. She's a skilled sculptor. (Her bust of Mr. Brady's head was so real, Alice mistook it for an intruder.) In one episode, Mrs. Brady published a magazine article. She's also a good photographer, adept at turning the bathroom into a darkroom. From being dragged into court on a bogus whiplash complaint to facing Greg's orange hair, Carol always kept an exceeding self-possession.

Mrs. Brady's abilities reflected those of the lady who played her. Florence Henderson began her career as a singer on *Jack Paar* and was one of the original *Today Show Girls*, doing news and interviews. Since hanging up her polyester, Henderson has emerged as a witty raconteur whether she's making jokes about once "dating" Barry (Greg Brady) Williams or holding her own when grilled by Joan Rivers. She even proved herself a sultry competitor on *Dancing with the Stars*.

—◦◦◦—

Despite the opinion that the 1980s was the era of TV "backlash," when the decade began, a group of interesting TV wives and moms arrived with it. One came via Maggie Weston of the sitcom *Maggie* (1981–1982).

While *Maggie* could be considered just another family sitcom from the era that saw the rebirth of the genre with *The Cosby Show*, what differentiates it is that it was created and produced by Erma Bombeck, the longtime patron saint of the American mom.

Bombeck's program focused on Len and Maggie Weston (played by James Hampton and Miriam Flynn), a middle-class couple in Dayton, Ohio (not coincidentally the town where Bombeck grew up). Len was a public school vice principal–teacher and Maggie was a stay-at-home mom (though we learn in a later episode that, in shades of Bombeck, she harbored an interest in writing). The Westons had three children: Christian, 8, Mark, 12, and L.J., 16, who, in a running gag, was never seen since he was supposedly always in the bathroom.

Bombeck's knack for making the mundane funny, infused the series with realism. Maggie was no "supermom" and hence represented the second wave of TV motherhood which includes *Roseanne* and *The Middle*'s Frankie.

While Maggie was not as loud as Roseanne, she did wield a mean wit. In one episode she says about her oven, "I was going to clean it on Wednesday, but then I decided to wait 'til the kids were grown." In another she echoes the thoughts of many moms when she says, "I don't have time for a time-management seminar!"

But despite these asides, Maggie liked her life. In a twist, in one episode, Maggie's mother downplays her daughter's life and chastises her daughter for not "making more of herself." But Maggie points out that her choices were hers to make and the fact that her mother might have made different ones is irrelevant. In another episode Maggie says about motherhood, "It's my job and there's no security or paid vacations or retirement plans or stock options but I show up for it everyday because I happen to think what I do is important."

The Weston house was strictly middle-class, a simple, cluttered ranch style. (Ironically, the house's layout resembles the Bundys' on *Married ... With Children*). Though livable, the house was not a showplace. Instead, it reflected a typical house of one working-class family.

The Westons often worried about money, like when they learned that Mark needed braces. Determined her kids won't have teeth "like the front of a '52 Buick," Maggie gets a part-time job. In this episode, for Maggie, once her "day job" was done, she then got to return home and take care of her own family, beginning the second half of a constant double-shift that many working mothers could relate to.

Maggie's one respite was the beauty parlor owned by her friend Loretta (played by Doris Roberts). As in *Steel Magnolias*, the beauty parlor functioned as a women's sanctuary, one where Maggie was free to voice complaints about how she often felt overwhelmed.

Maggie, despite its good pedigree and relatability, only lasted a few episodes; it was the first cancellation of the 1981–1982 season. What went wrong? Perhaps the time slots the show had during its tenure — on Fridays, then Saturdays — were not the best for a show geared towards real-life moms.

Whatever, it's unfortunate it didn't last. Had it, Bombeck's *Maggie* would no doubt have become one of TV's most memorable mother figures.

—◦◦◦—

While Miriam Flynn–Erma Bombeck might have seemed like perfect envoys for TV motherhood, actress Susan Clark would seem, at first, like an unusual choice.

When Clark came to weekly television she had already earned Emmys for TV movies where she played Babe Didrickson and Amelia Earhart. In other roles, Clark often excelled by playing efficient and calculating characters, including a clever murderess on *Columbo*.

But a sitcom mom Clark became when she teamed with real-life husband Alex Karras and pint-sized child star Emmanuel Lewis for *Webster* (1983–1987).

Clark starred as Katherine Calder-Young Papadapolis, a consumer advocate and newly-wed. When the series began, she had just married George Papadapolis, an ex-footballer turned sportscaster. No sooner had the couple tied the knot than they found themselves parents.

George had, years ago, promised a teammate that if anything ever happened to him and his wife, he'd take care of their child. While George and Katherine were honeymooning, the couple died in a car accident and George received legal custody of Webster, a seven-year-old African American boy.

George was a Teddy bear beneath his grizzled facade and transitioned easily into parenthood. In contrast, Katherine didn't take quickly to her new responsibilities.

Katherine's awkward early days as "Mom" could be viewed as cliché — an example of the career-minded woman depicted as incompetent in domestic situations. But, before anyone yells "backlash!," Clark's approach to her character was deliberate. She related:

> I had a lot of input into my character. I didn't want a mother who was traditional. I wanted a non-traditional [image] of someone who was loving and supportive and aware....
> You don't have to be good at cooking and housekeeping to be a good mother.[146]

Thanks to the uber-cuteness of Lewis, *Webster* was a hit. But there was more to this series than just "awww" moments. It often tackled true-life situations. Over its run, *Webster* explored explaining death to children (Webster had originally only been told that his parents "went away") and sexism, as in the episode where Katherine becomes a scout leader for Webster's all-boy ranger troop.

In that episode, Katherine's ascension to leader doesn't happen easily. You see, Woody, a male leader, doesn't like the idea of women being added to the group. He only begrudgingly admits Katherine when he learns he has no right not to. Still, Katherine's induction doesn't stop the other boys from being tainted by Woody's attitude. As soon as Katherine is put in charge, the other scouts quit.

Later in this same episode, Katherine laments how some things haven't changed: "We have a woman Supreme Court justice but Woody can't handle a woman ranger leader."

Undeterred, Webster and his friend Norman form a troop of their own with Katherine as their "lady troop leader." At the big ranger competition the next day, Katherine's troop is clearly outnumbered by Woody's. But Webster and Norman really know their stuff, from building birdhouses to putting up tents. Then ... things go bad for Woody when he falls and twists his ankle! It's a sprain and none of his troop know what to do ("You said 'Skip it, it's not in the competition'"). But Webster and Norman, thanks to Mrs. P., know to set the leg in a splint and call 911. As Woody is carried away, he and his troop realize that women can be good leaders.

Though she was shown to be a savvy leader and a respected career woman, Clark, as she had intended, wasn't a "Super Mom." Her Katherine was a "good mom," based upon her own terms. Thanks to Clark, TV not only got a "mother of another color" but also a new type of mother image.

So Many Moms (and Wives)

One of the great comedic creations in history is the comedy creature inhabited by Gracie Allen, the better half of comedy duo Burns and Allen as seen on *The George Burns and Gracie Allen Show* (1950–1958).

Like some of her so-called "scatterbrained" sisters, Allen has often found her persona described, if not as "stupid," then at least as ditzy or dim. But, on inspection, Gracie's so-called "stupidity" is actually not caused by a lack of knowledge. Rather, what is viewed as "stupid" is actually Gracie's unique approach to processing language. For Allen, the crux of her comedy comes from the duality of certain words and gathers momentum from the sloppy syntax of those around her. For example, in one episode, after Gracie comes from visiting a friend in the hospital, George asks, "Did you take her flowers?"

Gracie replies, "Yes, when she wasn't looking."

Levels of duality, not only of language but of everything else, was essential to the comedy of Allen. In the series, it is often hard to tell who is outwitting who. In one episode, Gracie finds herself taken hostage by a group of goomba gangsters. However it's never clear if Gracie actually knows she's been kidnapped. By the end — shades of O. Henry — the kidnappers let her go since they have become worried about their own sanity. Of course, it's open to debate just what really transpired here: Was Gracie just oblivious or did she skillfully "play" the kidnappers until she beat them at their own game?

For all of Gracie's alleged daffiness, she nevertheless exhibits a wisdom. In one episode, when meeting with the tax man, Gracie asks if her taxes will go to pay the salary of all the representatives. When he assures her yes, Gracie wants to know why then she can't declare them as dependents.

Along with often being surprisingly insightful, there is also something subtly feminist about Gracie. As one author puts it, Gracie repeatedly "took symbolic pot shots at the gender order by subverting her husband's logical, masculine world."[147] Gracie's thinking and logic makes perfect sense to *her*; if others don't get it, well, that's their problem.

In the end, Gracie is the most "at ease" of any of the characters who populate this program, even George. Her ability to transgress this universe says less about her "intelligence" than it does about the perceived intelligence of those around her.

―――⟨ʘ⟩―――

Even today, some fifty years later, it's still a firebrand. And rightly so. It's difficult to put a positive spin on radio's long-running *Amos 'n' Andy*, a program on which two white men portrayed black characters by adopting "black" dialects and, in photos, were often shown in blackface.

But then in the early 1950s, when *Amos 'n' Andy* moved to TV, things got even more complicated. *Amos 'n' Andy* was the creation of Freeman Gosden and Charles Correll (the aforementioned white men). Set in Harlem, the series (on radio and TV) centered on George "Kingfish" Stevens and his friend Andrew "Andy" Hogg Brown. Among other traits, Andy was portrayed as pretty gullible, always falling into whatever far-fetched plan Kingfish attempts to hatch. Also featured on the series was Kingfish's wife Sapphire and Sapphire's mother, referred to as "Mama."

On radio, Gosden and Correll played the leads but once *Amos 'n' Andy* came to television (from 1951 to 1953), it necessitated hiring black actors.

Interestingly, the two female roles on the radio show had always been played by black performers. Ernestine Wade played Sapphire and Amanda Randolph[148] played Mama. These two performers would also be the only two to (understandably) carry their roles over to television.For the African American actors playing these roles, it was a Catch-22. While in many ways their roles were stereotypical, these roles nevertheless gave them work. Hattie McDaniel once said that she would rather play a maid than be one; Wade stated that for black actors to turn down these roles would not only allow white performers to take them but also steal from the media potent images of African Americans.[149]

Over the years, Wade was often called upon to defend the series and her work. She said once:

I don't think people tune into a comedy show for an education. If [the show] had been a documentary, it would have been a different thing. All people will scream about things they don't enjoy. You take *The Grapes of Wrath* and *Tobacco Road*. There was a lot of static about those. But people like that really exist; their names might not be the same, but their proto-types exist.[150]

In defending the series, Wade had her work cut out for her as many viewed her role as Kingfish's tough, straight-talking wife as a negative image, one that reinforced assumptions about black women as harridans. In fact, for a time Sapphire became slang in the black community for any shrill and complaining woman.[151]

Now, no one ever stated that Sapphire was a perfect character (what TV character is?). But perhaps she does deserve, now with historical distance, a second look. Writer Melvin Patrick Ely states:

Sapphire was strong-willed and decisive. Her stage dialect was never exaggerated as that of Andy and the Kingfish, and she often spoke cultivated English.... Ernestine Wade portrayed Sapphire as a bright woman, much of whose scolding of her husband was understandable in view of his laziness and dishonesty.[152]

Due to the reasons stated above, a consensus about the program has never been achieved. In fact, in 1951, while many African Americans were calling for the show's cancellation, a black-owned newspaper in Pittsburgh defended it.[153] Furthermore, at the time and since, many authors have pointed out that the program often featured African Americans seen as doctors, lawyers and affluent business owners.[154]

Years later, actress Marla Gibbs said of the series, "Personally, I don't think it reflected the *wrong* images of black people; I think that it was the fact that it was the *only* image of black people on TV at the time."[155]

In 1997, scholar Pamela S. Deane had to concede, "Contemporary television viewers might find it difficult to understand what all the clamor was about."[156]

So what are we to make of this?

Though more is still needed, with the greater number and diversity of African American images on air today — and now a few generations removed — for *Amos 'n' Andy*, it seems that while the controversy has faded, the artistry has remained.

—❧❧❧—

There's no way to describe savvy senior Lily Ruskin of *December Bride* (1954–1961) other than as the "Golden Girl" of her day.

Played by Spring Byington, Lily was a thriving woman "of a certain age." A widow, she lived with her daughter Ruth and son-in-law Matt, both of whom welcomed her. (Lily and her family's attitude towards her stands in contrast to a current elder persona — Cloris Leachman's demented "Maw Maw" on *Raising Hope*.)

Rick Mitz described Lily: "She was self-sufficient. She was always cheerful. She was more open-minded than her children and she loved trying new things. She adored a good adventure. Lily was a young kid in old person's drag. She was never a burden."[157] In fact, in one episode, Lily becomes (erroneously) convinced that her family no longer loves her. To get herself thrown out, she cooks badly and ruins the laundry. But to no avail. Matt and Ruth can't imagine any reason why they'd ever want Lily to leave.

Along with various stereotypes about the elderly — and mothers-in-law — that *Bride* didn't support was that the gray-haired set was asexual. In fact, the show's title says Lily's still able to be a bride again. Moreover, Lily's daughter and son-in-law are always playing matchmaker for Mom. Their view that Lily is a "great catch" is presented without sarcasm; in one episode, when Lily announces a new beau, Matt replies, "Who's the lucky guy?"

Moreover, Lily is not presented as an anomaly. Her friend Hilda (played by Verna Felton) was just as spry and salty. Hilda once laid down her dating perimeters: "I never go out with boy scouts or Civil War veterans."

Lily was active. Often with Hilda, she found herself caught up in "hijinks." In one episode, Lily and Hilda attempted to retrieve an accidently mailed letter. In another, Lily becomes the manager for a wrestler. Though exaggerated for comedy, Lily's adventures illustrate that this is a woman not content to sit and knit.

Lily also served as the voice of reason. In one episode, when Matt and Ruth are considering separate vacations, Lily states, "Well, once I knew a couple that decided to take separate vacations from each other and they're happily married now ... but not to each other."

Actress Spring Byington was 68 when she took on the role of Lily, disproving assumptions about the supposed lack of roles available for actress over 30 even "way back when."

Byington said of her character, "Lily hasn't lost her appetite for life and is now free to do ridiculous things. She can play with life much more because she is mature of heart. She isn't stopped because other people are not doing it."[158]

—◦◦◦—

For many, 1970s TV is summarized by the Bradys or Mary Tyler Moore; but for six years during that decade, another fully realized woman also existed.

Emily Hartley, wife of psychologist Dr. Bob Hartley of *The Bob Newhart Show* (1972–1978), has been described as "smart, funny, sexy" by one author[159] and as "beautiful, affectionate, sophisticated, and [a] vivacious pillar of strength"[160] by another.

Suzanne Pleshette played Mrs. Hartley. She said of her character, "I think she was bright, funny, loving, kind, nurturing, sensual."[161]

Certainly Emily has a range of qualities that distanced her from her neurotic husband. As they say today, Dr. Bob had "issues." In various episodes we learn he has a fear of zoos; of horses; of wearing birthday hats, and of elevators. He also has a range of phobias regarding emotional and physical intimacy. In regard to the latter, consider this husband-wife exchange:

EMILY: Bob, I know the morning didn't start off too well, so why don't we go out to dinner tonight? It'll be fun.
BOB: Nah.
EMILY: Well, why don't we go to the movies?
BOB: Nah.
EMILY: Well, why don't we just go to bed early?
BOB: Hey, the movies aren't a bad idea.

As if Dr. Bob didn't already have enough problems, he compounded them by marrying a woman as accomplished as Emily. In one episode, we learn that Emily has a higher IQ than her husband; it's a discovery that sends Bob into a tailspin. In another, when Emily takes a fulltime job as a third-grade teacher, Bob feels emasculated.

One almost wonders why, with all of her husband's eccentricities, a woman as dynamic as Emily would stay with him. It is to Pleshette's credit that Emily always came across as even-keeled, never a "woman who loves too much." She said:

I think it was a very equal marriage. She was there because she wanted to be.... Bob and I created a very loving marriage of two independent people who seemed to love each other for their idiosyncrasies as well as their wonderful qualities.[162]

—◦◦◦—

Over the years, there have been many other magnificent moms.

By the final seasons of *My Three Sons*, women had stormed the all-male Douglas home. They were lead by Beverly Garland playing schoolteacher Barbara Harper beginning in 1969.

The series *What's Happening!* (1976–1979) has drawn praise for Mabel King's motherly but "all-business" character Mama Thomas.[163]

The drama *Family* (1976–1980), once described as "too good for television,"[164] boasted Sada Thompson as Kate Lawrence. Kate was the middle-aged mother of three. Described as "quiet and steadfast," during the show's run Kate faced a variety of challenges including whether to abort a late-in-life pregnancy and whether to re-enter the workforce.[165]

Two years later, a very different but similarly stoic mother figure debuted. *Dallas* (1978–1991) presented a resonating maternal image via Barbara Bel Geddes, whose interpretation of a Southern matriarch was Earth Mother, not Scarlett O'Hara. Her Miss Ellie was not a flouncy rich lady but a determined woman who, like the men around her, had pulled herself up by her bootstraps. Bel Geddes brought a great sincerity to her work. This was never more noticeable than in season two when Miss Ellie underwent a mastectomy. Her performance won her an Emmy.

The premise of *Kate & Allie* (1984–1989) mirrored *The Lucy Show* as two smart but suddenly single moms, both divorcees, pooled their resources and skill sets (Allie in home-keeping, Kate in business) to forge a new hybrid family. As one author has noted about them, "They needed each other to survive."[166] Kate and Allie's domestic dynamic is as much about emotional support as it is economic survival. Said one critic, "[B]oth women are smart, but smart enough to know that a good brain is hardly impenetrable defense against the infinite assortment of wounds and hurts that are waiting out there."[167]

Conclusion

As we've seen, since the beginning of television, there have been a myriad of ways to spell M-O-T-H-E-R. Whether from the past or the present, on their own or in traditional families, TV's wives and mothers have repeatedly proved that though they are often being seen as somebody's wife or somebody's mother, that doesn't mean they're anybody's fool.

— 3 —

"She's a Rebel"
Lucy and Her Kind

Well-behaved women seldom make history.— a recently seen bumper sticker,
credited to historian Laurel Thatcher Ulrich

Without question TV's greatest icon is comic supreme Lucille Ball. Even sixty-some years after her debut, Lucy remains as popular as ever. It seems that everyone knows — and loves — Lucy.

How well do we know her? In 1974, *TV Guide* put forth a staggering claim: Due to omnipresent reruns, the editors theorized that Lucy had been seen by more people more often than anyone else in history.[1]

But despite her fame and the fact that many *I Love Lucy* plots are now cultural touchstones, there exist a lot of misconceptions about both "Lucy" and Lucy.

For example, the author of a 2001 essay in *Electronic Media* stated that though she liked Lucy for not being a "good girl" (i.e., always doing what's expected), she finds fault with Lucy's methods, her "manipulative" dishonesty and "trickery."[2] Granted, Lucy did often, well, lie: She attempted to pass off her clay-covered head as a sculpture and she once switched real tulips with fake ones hoping no one noticed.[3] But to state that dishonesty was what *I Love Lucy* (1951–1957) was about is to ignore some of the series' most beloved episodes and misinterpret the character.

In fact, often it is Lucy who is lied to. Consider the time Ricky made Lucy think that a burlap sack was *haute couture* or when he tricked her into believing she'd won new furniture.

Sometimes trickery is shared, as in the episode "Deep Sea Fishing," where the Ricardos and the Mertzes engage in a fishing contest and all four resort to buying fish and trying to pass it off as their catch.

But even with Ricky's frequent duplicity, many episodes end with Lucy getting the last word. For example, in "The Gossip," the "boys" bet the "girls" that they can't stop gossiping. When the girls hold fast and it appears they'll win, Ricky and Fred have to devise a scheme to make them lose. In "Lucy's Schedule," Ricky gets fed up with Lucy's lateness and puts her on a tight regimen. When Ricky later brags to his boss that his wife is as well-trained as a seal(!), Lucy invites the boss over to show him what living on a schedule means. With Ethel's help, Lucy stages a lightning-fast dinner party that embarrasses Ricky. (This episode contains the scene of Lucy in a baseball mitt as she yells into the kitchen, "Okay, Ethel, let's have those biscuits!") In "Equal Rights" (a loaded title) the boys attempt to make a point to the girls by refusing to pay for their wives' dinner, resulting in Lucy and Ethel having to wash dishes. Lucy and Ethel laugh last when the guys later pretend to be robbers in order to scare the ladies. But the guys get arrested. A line of Ricky's from this episode, "I'm not arguing about women's rights. I agree that women should have all the rights they want, as long as they stay in their place," if taken out of context, seems like the lead to an article declaring the "sexism" of early TV until you consider the episode's ending.

Ask most people what *Lucy* is usually about and they'll say Lucy's "schemes." And, yes, Lucy does often find herself in some unique situations as in "Lucy Gets Ricky on the Radio" (where Lucy swipes the answers for her and Ricky's quiz show appearance ... unfortunately they changed all the questions) or "The Handcuffs" (where Lucy links herself to Ricky so he won't leave home). But as Horace Newcomb points out:

> [Lucy] has no such sense of probability—not because she is stupid, for her schemes demonstrate exactly the opposite, but because she is innocent. Gilligan and Ann Marie are similar examples. They are without malice, and if their actions precipitate a chain of events that weighs heavily on other characters, it is not because they are cruel, for just as often they suffer the consequences themselves.[4]

Most of the time, Lucy's troubles aren't her own making. It's not her fault that the candy conveyer belt zipped by at hyper speed, or that the woman she was stomping grapes with turned homicidal, or that Vitameatavegamin was 90 proof.

Sometimes episodes aren't about "schemes" at all. In "Lucy Gets Homesick in Italy," the comedy comes out of elevators, hard hotel beds and Lucy's attempt to talk transcontinentally with Little Ricky. In "Little Ricky Gets a Dog," trouble arises when the Ricardos' new pet might get forced out of their "no pets" building. In "Lucy Hires a Maid," the comedy is based on the hiring of an overbearing housekeeper.

Sometimes the plots are organized around Ricky's own "schemes." In the episode "Inferiority Complex," Ricky hatches a plan to make Lucy feel better about herself. He invites a psychologist over but throws the doctor out when the man's flattery of Lucy makes him jealous. In "The Courtroom," Ricky and Fred's male egos clash over a television set.

At one time or another, that sitcom staple of jumping to conclusions ensnared everyone in *I Love Lucy*—not just Lucy. Though the redhead does do her share of jumping—as in the time she thought Ricky was a murderer—no one's immune. It's Ricky who jumps to conclusions in "The Kleptomaniac" when he's convinced Lucy is stealing. It's Ricky and Fred who jump when, in one episode, they both believe their wives are "expecting." Meanwhile, the episode "Ricky Thinks He's Getting Bald" speaks for itself.

Even the Mertzes sometimes get into the act. In the episode "The Black Eye," the Mertzes think that Lucy's shiner means Ricky is abusive only to find out that it was accidental. Then, sometimes, *everyone* jumps as in "Too Many Crooks" when a cat burglar named Madame X makes everyone suspicious of each other.

Of course a great many *I Love Lucy* episodes are based on the premise "Lucy wants to get into the show." This is the plot of "Lucy Does a TV Commercial" (which contains the classic Vitameatavegamin bit), "The Ballet," and others. Lucy's attempts to enter entertainment almost (*almost*) always end up in disaster. Nevertheless, despite Lucy's repeated failures, she's never deterred. Lucy does not suffer from "low self-esteem." Throughout the series, she remains convinced she has talent if only Ricky (and the world) would give her a chance.

What is seldom noted is that for every time Lucy fails in show business, there are episodes where, in grand tradition, Lucy saves the day by stealing the show. In "Lucy and the Dummy," Lucy tries to pass off a life-size dummy of Ricky as the real one for some executives. Of course, the dance number Lucy stages is a bomb but the suits find her so funny they offer her a contract. In "Ricky Loses His Voice," Lucy performs at the Tropicana's reopening when Ricky has laryngitis. With Fred and Ethel's help, Lucy is a hit and the club is saved!

Many of Lucy's other so-called "wild schemes" frequently pan out in the end. In the episode "Ricky Asks for a Raise," Ricky is canned from the Tropicana. To get his job back, Lucy and the Mertzes pose as customers who immediately leave the club when they learn that Ricky's no longer there. Lucy's plan works and Ricky gets his job back.

Far from being hare-brained, Lucy is at times almost ingenious. Consider the episode where she smuggles Italian cheese through customs first by disguising it as a baby and then later by shoving pieces of it inside Ricky's band's instruments. ("The trombone was easy, but that piccolo....")

—⟋⟍⟍⟋—

Whatever the plots were, Lucy was always breaking the rules — trying to spend the night with her son in the hospital, trying to win a contest against the odds, or just trying to get out of the house. In her attempts to do these things, she's always demanding greater choice within her life.

And why wouldn't Lucy want to rebel, especially when she has a husband who reads her the riot act all the time, as in one episode when he tells her, "I don't want my wife in show business ... all you got to do is clean the house for me, hand me my pipe when I come home at night, cook for me, and be the mother for my children."[5]

But no matter what Ricky said, Lucy would always ignore his lectures. In her era, Lucy rejected the rules of her husband the way Murphy Brown would later reject the edicts of a vice-president. And, hence, Lucy embodies all the tenets of modern feminism. While we might sometimes blanch at the *means* by which Lucy attempts to reach her goals, we have to appreciate her reasons. Critic John Javna once said, "[Lucy] couldn't just sit home and watch soap operas, and she couldn't get a job. She was trapped somewhere between."[6] And as was pointed out in the PBS *American Masters* episode "Finding Lucy," "Lucy was not a feminist [?], but the show demonstrated why we need feminism."[7]

Cult director John Waters has labeled Lucy a classic "outsider": "As an eight-year-old voyeur, looking ahead to my teenage years was a lot easier because of *Lucy*. I knew you could break the rules."[8]

Lucille Ball as Lucy Ricardo was always boldly or symbolically circumventing the patriarchy as represented by her traditionally minded husband Ricky (played by Desi Arnaz) on *I Love Lucy* (1951–1960).

Meanwhile, another voice praises Lucy's "never-give-up" attitude by saying, "Instead of sitting around waiting for things to happen, [Lucy] *makes* things happen."[9]

TV scholar David Marc says, "Lucy refuses to allow bourgeois role destiny to stifle her organic desires" and "On *I Love Lucy*, Ricky's moral, economic and intellectual superiority is relentlessly questioned by Lucy."[10]

⸻ ❧ ⸻

No examination of *Lucy* would be complete without discussion of the handful of times (four out of 180 episodes) that Ricky put Lucy over his knee and spanked her. Some have had a field day with these incidences; Lynn Spangler gets a lot of mileage out it in her book *Television Women from Lucy to Friends*.[11]

But as shocking as these occurrences might be to modern viewers, it is equally surprising that, at the time, it didn't seem to raise any eyebrows; nowhere is there any record of protests or letters of complaint. Does this lack of controversy suggest that such actions between a husband and wife were typical of the time? But, if so, then why did no other shows of the era feature intermarital spanking? This dynamic seems unique to the Ricardos.

What then explains Ricky's behavior? Perhaps Ricky, so often distraught over his wife's "shenanigans," too quickly morphs into a parent, regressing to primitive methods of behavioral modification. (He tells her in one of the episodes, "If you are going to act like a child, I will have to treat you like a child.") Or perhaps it's something cultural, born out of Ricky's Latin heritage; he lacks the cool — some might say "uptight" — reserve of *Father Knows Best*'s Jim Anderson.

Of course, this doesn't explain why Lucy doesn't fight back. Was this sort of physicality the norm for this couple?

For all the attention these "spanking" incidents get, it's surprising that more is not made of the times that Lucy is physical with Ricky, as in the time she attacked him with a rolled-up newspaper.

⸻ ❧ ⸻

Much has also been made about how Desi Arnaz had top billing in "Lucy's show." He's the "I" in *I Love Lucy*. With time, however, that changed. By the time the series entered its seventh season and became a series of hour-long specials, the title morphed from *I Love Lucy* into *The Ford Lucille Ball-Desi Arnaz Show* and, later, into *The Westinghouse Desilu Playhouse Presents the Lucille Ball-Desi Arnaz Show*. Finally, these installments were syndicated under the title *The Lucy-Desi Comedy Hour*.

Lucy's progress didn't stop here. In many ways, Lucy's later incarnations reflected women's growing independence. In her next series, *The Lucy Show*, she was a single mom. After that she was a working woman. Finally she was a business owner.

Additionally, after *I Love Lucy*, Ball never again played a married woman. Rather, she was always a widow, on her own. She also was always paired with women: First, in *The Lucy Show*, with Vivian Vance, then, at other times, with Ann Sothern, Carol Burnett, and finally, in *Here's Lucy*, with her daughter Lucie Arnaz. Her latter husband-less series were always female-centered, with female friendships taking precedence over men.[12]

The female friendship of Lucy and Ethel (and later Lucy and Viv et al.) added a feminine twist to the cannon of great comedy teams like Laurel and Hardy, and laid the groundwork for *Laverne & Shirley* and *Absolutely Fabulous*. In fact, in an episode of *The Lucy Show*, where Lucy and "The Countess" (Sothern) go wine-tasting on an empty stomach, their drunken antics resemble *Ab Fab*.

Perhaps it can even be argued that, as McWilliams has stated about Lucy and Ethel, since "to this day their bonding hasn't been surpassed,"[13] the duo of Ricardo and Mertz even helped pave the way for *Cagney & Lacey* and *Thelma & Louise*.

—◊◊◊—

As mentioned, after *I Love Lucy*, Ball's return to TV came via *The Lucy Show* (1962–1968). In its first incarnation, the series was like *Kate & Allie*: Lucy's character, Lucy Carmichael, had been widowed (making her one of TV's first single mothers) and left with two children to raise and a meager trust fund (set up by her deceased husband) to do it with. To make ends meet, Lucy invites her friend Vivian Bagley (Vivian Vance), a divorcee (quite possibly TV's first in a major role), and Viv's son to move in with her brood.[14]

For comedy, Lucy had to have reasons to get into scrapes. Since show biz plots wouldn't do, some plots instead centered on money. Whether Lucy was trying to earn some or save some, her attempts to be more financially independent were the basis of many episodes. Most of Lucy and Viv's classic adventures are based on attempts to try to make do with little. An absence of funds necessitates the two installing their own TV antenna or shower. Lucy and Viv would also try an endless stream of short-term jobs and even get-rich-quick schemes when they found themselves cash-short. But as authors Andrews and Watson have pointed out, "At no time, however, were Lucy's shenanigans ever presented in a vein detrimental to her role as a mother."[15] In fact, almost every time Lucy and Viv were shown to be in need of money, it was not for themselves but for basic upkeep of their home or for their kids. As Warren G. Harris says in his book of Lucy's second incarnation, "[She's] a widow who worried more about her children than about finding another husband."[16]

Although jokes are often made in the series about Lucy's "wild" spending, we never find out if Lucy is a spendthrift or not. Is it possible that her monthly "allowance" from the bank is too small for a family of three? All we ever really know is that Lucy's always short of money and must constantly appeal to miserly bank president Mr. Mooney for a loan or advance. Lucy's repeated attempts to extract money from Mooney prefigures a generation of women who'd later struggle to get child support from deadbeat dads.

It has been said of *The Lucy Show*, "[I]n essence, [it's about] survival in modern times with [Lucy and Viv] trying to handle the normally masculine details of running a house and, at the same time, attempting to retain enough femininity to attract male companionship."[17]

Lucy and Viv's dating lives — or lack thereof— were also popular plotlines on *The Lucy Show*. At one time or another, Lucy would date, on screen, such actors as Dick Martin, Clint Walker, and William Windom. Perhaps because Lucy is so associated with Ricky, mention is seldom made of the image Ball projected later as a single woman over 40 (Ball was 51 when *The Lucy Show* began) with a healthy interest in the opposite sex and one with the opposite sex healthily interested in her.

But Lucy in *The Lucy Show* did more than just showcase an attractive, vibrant woman "of a certain age." For a woman who is often remembered only for her funny physical antics, it's noteworthy how socially aware Lucy could be. As authors Andrews and Watson state, at the time of *The Lucy Show*, "American society was in a state of flux..., and not the least

An early example of both single motherhood and even a "blended" family could be found on *The Lucy Show* (1962–1968). Left to right, Ralph Hart, Vivian Vance, Lucille Ball, Jimmy Garrett and Candy Moore.

of the nation's problems was a serious breakdown in communication between parent and child.... The new Lucille Ball series attempted to bridge and satirize the 'generation gap'— Lucy style."[18] In *The Lucy Show* (and later *Here's Lucy*), both parent and children were portrayed as multi-dimensional. For example, in one episode, Lucy trusts teen daughter Chris to throw a New Year's Eve party without her present. In another, when Chris wants a new band uniform, instead of hitting up Mom for the money, she gets a job.

Most profoundly, in "Lucy Gets Her Diploma" (from the sixth season when Lucy lived in California and worked for Mr. Mooney), a new bank policy says all employees must have high school diplomas. This causes Lucy Carmichael to disclose that, due to illness, she never took her final exam and hence never technically graduated. So it's back to school!

As a student, Lucy councils a troubled young man about finishing his education. She's then asked to give the school's commencement address. In the final scene, Lucy points out what her generation was famous for: swallowing goldfish and crowding into phone booths. She adds:

> You know, recently I ran across a statement which said: "I'm very worried about the younger generation. The youth of today is ill-mannered, ill-bred and shows little respect for their elders. I fear to trust them with the future." Now this statement was made by Socrates more than two thousand years ago. Well, I agree with Socrates, I too am worried about trusting the future to the younger generation. I'm worried they will do a far better job than we did.[19]

The power of this speech about "those kids today" is not only in what is said but who says it. To have an individual as iconic as Lucy speak as eloquently as she does about the next generation very well might have changed some attitudes on both sides.

But Lucy's depth didn't end there; she might have also helped promote the idea of the blended family. In the *Lucy Show* episode "Together for Christmas," the merged families of Lucy and Viv at first butt heads in their varying family traditions before learning understanding of each other's beliefs. Geoffrey Mark Fidelman in his *The Lucy Book* calls this installment "insightful," noting that at the time, images of Christmas on TV were "almost always homogenized."[20]

Lucy had great largess too. In an episode from *Here's Lucy*, she learns of a waitress who has been fired because of ageism. Anxious to fight youth-obsession, Lucy schemes to get the woman her job back. In another *Here's Lucy*, guest star Wally Cox appears as a down-on-his-luck detective on the receiving end of Lucy's help.

As with *I Love Lucy*, often in her later series Lucy ends up, again, saving the day. In "Lucy the Sheriff," from *Here's Lucy*, Lucy Carter learns that she's the great-granddaughter of a Montana town's first female sheriff. The town invites her to visit. Once there, Lucy ultimately apprehends some bank robbers.

—⁊⁊⁊—

Lucille Ball once said that the key to her longevity was that her basic character always stayed the same.[21] But Lucy gives herself short shrift. Her character did change over the years; one could hardly imagine Lucy Ricardo speaking on behalf of America's youth.

The constantly shifting details of Lucy's life, especially on *The Lucy Show*, is interesting: One week she's a policewoman, the next she's a flight attendant. By plan or accident, Lucy often took on careers that were, at that time, not considered "appropriate" for women: astronaut, firefighter, and boxing manager, piercing the "male sphere."

Other details about Lucy Carmichael's life and history are also always in flux. Sometimes she's a high school dropout, later, she's a college graduate. Such wavering "facts" can be frustrating as Geoffrey Mark Fidelman learned in his episode-by-episode breakdown of Ball's TV career in his *The Lucy Book*. But "Lucy's" shifting histories can be viewed as an attempt to make Lucy a master of all personas, an across-the-board "everywoman." Like the mythical White Goddess, another shape-shifting legend, Lucy's encompasses all. Lucy on *The Lucy Show* (and later *Here's Lucy*) seems to exist in neither time nor place and without a linear history. And why not? As was once noted, "the zany comedian has defied every other law of nature."[22]

Her Kind

Lucy did not originate the "wacky wife" comedy genre. Gracie Allen had been portraying that sort of role for years. Meanwhile, madcap characters like Mame (a character Ball later played) had already been featured in book form. But Lucy did take this formula to such artistic heights that it inspired imitators. All of them, from *My Little Margie* to *Oh, Madeline*, are attempts to replicate the *Lucy* formula. "Lucy," and Lucy, has always been the goal, the road map, the alpha and omega of TV comedy. As *TV Guide* has noted, "Lucy is the medium's DNA. Her uncanny and exuberant instincts for slapstick shaped everything that followed."[23]

But Lucy did more than just set the bar for future comedy, she also laid the groundwork for generations of rebellious women.

In a typical publicity pose for their program, actress Gale Storm shows the spunk that often stressed out the men around her, especially her father (played by Charles Farrell), on *My Little Margie* (1952–1955).

Consider *My Little Margie* (1952–1955), which told the story of widowed advertising exec Vernon Albright (played by Charles Farrell) and his spunky 21-year-old daughter Margie, who lived in a plush penthouse in New York. In her autobiography, star Gale Storm sums up the premise of the show and, indeed, many of the era's female-led sitcoms: "In those days…, the woman was always the clever one who could get the big, good-natured guy to do anything she wanted, one way or another."[24]

As mentioned, the program's title role was played by Storm and at the risk of a bad pun, Storm was a force of nature. In her role, she is as unstoppable as a tornado.

Margie had a habit of getting herself into unusual situations and engaging in outlandish antics, despite her father's stringent objections. Here again, the supposedly "in charge" household member (father Vernon) is at his wit's end, unable to control the female in his life. The overall tone of the series was communicated in the show's opening credits where side-by-side photos of stars Farrell and Storm speak to the camera. Dad said:

> I've been both mother and father to her since she was born. She's grown up now. When she was a little girl, I could spank her and make her mind me. I had control over her. What can you do when a girl reaches this age? She's completely out of hand. I've got a problem, believe me, I've got a problem.

Most of the program's publicity shots featuring the two stars echo this theme with Storm beaming and Farrell looking frazzled. Interestingly, though Margie — supposedly 21 years old — was of marrying age, she never pined to settle down. And father Vernon, despite his occasional exasperation, never seemed to push her. Margie was no "husband-hunter."

Margie's weekly plots, sometimes cartoonish, sometimes contrived, nevertheless did serve as evidence of an intelligent (Margie's last name Albright seemed appropriate) woman as well as (in the words of Rick Mitz) "a nice kid from a nice family who knew how to have fun."[25]

In contrast to Lucy, most of Margie's schemes did not involve show business; in fact, most had nothing to do with *her*. Instead, Margie's always looking out for others. In one episode, she takes to the TV airwaves to stick up for a cereal company that's about to be swallowed up by a giant conglomerate. At the studio, a company exec (in fact Margie's father's boss, Mr. Honeywell, from the firm of Honeywell & Todd) doesn't want her to say anything but he doesn't stand a chance:

> MARGIE: Well, gentlemen, you may keep Dad from taking part in the show but you certainly can't stop me!
> MR. HONEYWELL: Now you listen to me, Margie Albright!
> MARGIE: No, you listen to me! I'm not under contract to Honeywell & Todd and I'm going on the air alone. So there! [*She moves in front of the camera.*] Good evening, Stratosphere Scouts, wherever you are. Instead of the program you expected, I have an announcement to make to the parents of America because it is you parents who buy the products we adver-tise and thus make our programs possible. So you have a right to know the truth as to why Vernon Albright will not be appearing tonight. It's because of the selfish interest of one man who resorted to legal trickery to keep my father off the air! The president of a rival company. Calvin Burns!
> MR. HONEYWELL [*running into frame*]: Margie Albright get away from that microphone!
> MARGIE: Ladies and gentlemen, this is Mr. Honeywell, Mr. Burns' accomplice...

Other episodes dealt with Margie taking equally radical measures to defend her father either from gold diggers or unscrupulous associates.

Much has been made over the years of the close relationship between Margie and her father. Ultimately, though, the show is simply a gender and generational reversal: Instead of a father compulsively attempting to protect his daughter, we have a daughter shielding her dad from various bad apples. In one episode, Margie has to end her father's engagement when Vern gets carried away and proposes to a woman he hardly knows.

Margie's motives were a little more personal in another episode. In it, Margie exhibits her "have fun" mentality and ends up gaining — again — the upper hand over the men around her. On a trip out west, Vern's plan to keep Margie and her friend Mrs. Odettes occupied by having them hunt gold in a phony mine backfires when the ladies learn the truth and turn the tables. Soon, Margie and Mrs. Odettes have Vern believing that there really is gold in them thar hills. When Vern takes the bait and rushes off to the mine, he's taken hostage by a group of "Indians" (actually actors whom Margie has hired). In the end, the whole episode plays like Margie's revenge against the white man.

Though Margie's zesty personality often caused heartburn for her father, he was not above turning to her when he was in a jam. Such is the case in "Hillbilly Margie," where Vern calls upon his daughter to help him win over some "backwoods folk."

In 1993, Professor Mary Ann Watson compared Margie with later TV icon Murphy Brown, believing that these two women, at opposite ends of the TV continuum, were cut from the same cloth. She said, "Margie Albright and Murphy Brown would have been whopping good pals. Had they been, say, college roommates, heaven only knows to what dizzying heights they might have taken the art of practical jokery."[26]

But Gale Storm, whose Margie was the original "girl who wanted to have fun," has the final word. She said, "Margie was liberated. She would try anything. Her father didn't always like it, but she made herself free."[27]

—⁂—

Very much in the Lucy mold was fellow '50s sitcom *I Married Joan* (1952–1955) starring Joan Davis. Davis had been in show business since childhood and settled in Hollywood in 1934. Described by one author as "a gangling, loose-jointed, raucous comedienne, who would punch herself in the jaw to produce laughs,"[28] she was previously used on the big screen in both "A" and "B" pictures. In the 1940s, she began a successful career on radio as the star of *Leave It to Joanie*, and in 1952 Davis came into her own as the star (and owner-producer) of *I Married Joan*.

Davis starred as housewife Joan Stevens, the wife of Bradley Stevens, a county judge (played by Jim Backus, pre–*Gilligan's Island*). Heavy on slapstick and outlandish situations, most episodes of *Joan*, like *I Love Lucy*, explored male-female dynamics.

Nearly every episode opened with Judge Stevens in his chambers counseling a young husband. There he gave no-holds-barred advice on how to "figure out" a woman or properly "control" her. All of his theories were drawn from his marriage to Joan. When the judge began his story, there would be a flashback, returning to the incident.

These preambles, taken on their own, have a belittling tone. But as each episode plays out, viewers quickly learn that Joan always has the power and that Judge Stevens' "expertise" was always anything but.

Consider this episode: Brad has worked out a wager with Joan. If she can keep a "perfect" house for six months, he'll buy her a new diamond bracelet. But when the six months are up and Joan has passed her "test," Brad reneges, stating that proving that she could be a better housekeeper should be reward enough. In order to teach her husband a lesson, Joan turns their house into a pigsty with up-turned cushions, ashes on the floor and a line of laundry bisecting the living room. Of course the day that Joan does this is also the day Mr. Stevens brings home two dinner guests, Superior Court Judge Anderson and his elegant wife. Upon entering, Brad is aghast, but Joan just smiles as she peels potatoes in the living room. Later, when the men retreat to the kitchen, Mrs. Anderson inquires, "As one gal to another, what's going on here?"

Joan responds, "To tell you the truth, I'm doing this to teach my husband a lesson."

Mrs. Anderson replies, "Well, I'm always in favor of teaching a husband a lesson." After Mrs. Anderson has been brought up to speed, Joan keeps up the charade and finally gets Bradley to admit that he was wrong.

In another episode, Joan and Bradley have had such a tiff that Bradley moves out. But, wouldn't you know it?, a day later there's a call from a superior court judge: Bradley is up for a promotion to the domestic court. The judge states he wants Bradley on that bench because he knows the Stevenses home life is one of such bliss. Hanging up, Joan realizes that a power shift has occurred. Her husband's career is now in her hands. Thinking to herself, she moves over to the sofa and picks up some walnuts from a dish on the coffee table. "My wandering rooster will be coming back to the henhouse," Joan says. And then, for emphasis, she crushes the nuts in her fist.

Most of Joan's misadventures, like Lucy's, revolved around her breaking out of her role as "the little woman." Attempts by her husband to regulate her behavior always backfired. Joan's frequent usurping of her husband's power is made all the more significant considering her husband's career. As a member of the predominantly male judiciary, he is not only (supposedly) the imposer of law and order but also the representative of all that is logical and dispassionate. And yet, in his home, his authority is constantly undermined by his wife. Literally, she is inverting the structure of "traditional" marriage and, symbolically, striking out against vestments of male power.

I Married Joan ended in 1955, after 98 episodes. Despite various attempts to return to TV—including a comedy pilot where she would play a female astronaut—Davis never reclaimed her earlier fame. She died in 1961.

I Married Joan remained popular in syndication. Even Davis seemed to see the series as her greatest achievement, saying near the end of her life, "The [shows] have to be good. They are my legacy both as a comedienne and as a businesswoman. The pictures will be playing when I'm in a wheelchair and after that it'll be great for my daughter. I'll leave her with a cracked voice and a lot of [film] negatives."[29]

—⁕—

Though most know Betty White for her work on *Mary Tyler Moore* and *The Golden Girls*, White's TV career dates back to the medium's earliest years. After working as a TV deejay in early LA television, White, in the early 1950s, created and starred in the first of what would prove to be many TV endeavors.[30]

In the sitcom *Life with Elizabeth* (1953–1954), White played Elizabeth while Del Moore played her husband Alvin. (The show never gave them a last name.) One distinguishing feature of the series was that each half-hour episode was divided into three different segments, each unrelated to the others, each illustrating a different "incident in life with Elizabeth."

Though often considered with other "wacky wife" sitcoms of the era, *Elizabeth* was more dialogue-driven than the physical comedy–prone shows of Ball et al. That did not mean that female rebellion was not evident. Perhaps more than any other show of the era—even *The Honeymooners*—Elizabeth and Alvin are the spouses who most regularly play a game of one-upsmanship via comic banter, usually with Elizabeth uttering the last word. Consider the time that Alvin returns from the dentist with a mouth full of Novocain. He says to his wife, "I'm just dead from the neck up."

To which Elizabeth replies, "I know that but what happened to your face?" (Of course, White delivers this line while wearing one of her trademark apple-pie smiles.)

In another, Alvin implores his wife to not "talk like an idiot." Elizabeth replies, "I have to talk like an idiot so you'll understand me." It's a comeback that would make White's later Sue Ann proud.

Besides her wit, Elizabeth's most distinguishing trait is her desire to have fun. She is quite the cut-up and will make a corny joke if she wants. Her hunger for fun often gets on the nerves of her husband. Alvin's always demanding that Elizabeth be "serious." But Elizabeth could never hold her tongue for long; she refuses to be silenced.

But just because Elizabeth is full of fun doesn't mean she isn't smart. In one installment, Alvin and Elizabeth are out for a ride with an old buddy of Alvin's when they get a flat tire. The guys are clueless about changing it but that doesn't stop them from turning the experience into a macho exercise. First they demand that Elizabeth stay in the car. Luckily for them, though, she doesn't follow orders; she's the only one with any tire know-how. Throughout the scene, unbeknownst to them but visible to us, Elizabeth is giving them the right tools, loosening the lug nuts and placing the jack. All the time she's also letting loose with her witticisms. When a patronizing Alvin tells Elizabeth that the spare tire is heavy, Elizabeth replies, "I just don't understand how something filled with air can be so heavy ... then again, you weigh 180 pounds."

As each segment of the show came to its close, always with Elizabeth triumphant, the show's off-screen male narrator would break the fourth wall and ask, "Elizabeth, aren't you ashamed?" To which Elizabeth would always squarely face the audience and shake her head "Nope!" This "Nope" may not be in the same league as "I am woman!" but it does show a woman of 1950s TV unapologetic and guilt-free over her actions.

—◦◦◦—

The torch of the rebellious woman on TV flamed anew in 1969 via Debbie Reynolds in *The Debbie Reynolds Show* (1969–1970).

Reynolds had been film's first "Tammy" as well as the star of *Singin' in the Rain* and *The Unsinkable Molly Brown*. Like the characters she often played, Reynolds would herself prove to be unsinkable too. Saddled at various points with everything from scandal to bankruptcy, she has survived them all and gone on to sing and dance another day.[31]

In her series, Reynolds played Debbie Thompson, stay-at-home wife of successful sportswriter Jim Thompson (played by Don Chastain). In the show, Debbie yearned to be a reporter like her husband and she often got in odd adventures as she attempted to get herself away from the house and kids and into a career.

If *Debbie* sounds like *I Love Lucy* (the wife seeking to break into her husband's line of work), then it came by its style honestly: Former *Lucy* producer Jess Oppenheimer created the series.

Though the show never recycled any *Lucy* scripts per se, it's easy to see how Debbie Thompson and Lucy Ricardo could have often switched places. In one episode, Debbie learns that hidden cameras have been installed at her local grocery to film real-life testimonials about a soup. Determined to be on TV, Debbie goes into the store and loads her cart with soup cans. She proceeds to perform for the "secret" cameras in order to snare the starring role in the ad. Though Debbie gets the commercial, she later learns that her husband's recently launched sports show is being sponsored by a *rival* soup brand.

In another episode, Debbie finally snags an assignment as a sportswriter but she ends up in the middle of a wrestling ring with a grappler named Terrible Tessie. It's sort of like when Lucy went grape-stomping and it's a scene that would later be largely replicated in *Oh, Madeline!* with Madeline Kahn.

Like Lucy before her, Debbie never sat on the sidelines. In one episode, Jim, his brother, his brother's wife, and a world-famous football star all fall under the mind control of a bogus guru. Eventually, it's up to Debbie to de-program everyone—especially the football player as he has to compete in a playoff game. In the end, Debbie debunks the guru and then, in a Knute Rockne moment, she storms the men's locker room (talk about infiltrating the "male sphere"!) and gives the kicker the pep talk he needs to win!

Despite its good pedigree and likability, *Debbie* only lasted one year. Though Reynolds and NBC had a contract that guaranteed her two seasons, Reynolds would later balk when she found out that—against her wishes—her show would be sponsored by a cigarette manufacturer. In order to obtain new sponsorship, the network forced Reynolds to cancel her second-year clause. Reynolds' tough stance (and so-so ratings) convinced the network not to renew. So, ultimately, though Reynolds might have lost her series, she hung onto her principles. Now that's a rebel.[32]

—◦◦◦—

TV's most obvious (and successful) descendents of Lucy and Ethel arrived with *Laverne & Shirley* (1976–1983).

Laverne DeFazio and Shirley Feeney (played by Penny Marshall and Cindy Williams, respectively) made their first appearance on *Happy Days* in late 1975. The Fonz-centered sitcom was then at the top of the ratings. The first incarnation of Laverne and Shirley, in their *Happy Days* appearances, is different from the Laverne and Shirley America would come to love. Originally, the duo were portrayed as "bad girls," the type who had shady reputations ... and didn't care. In and of itself, their origin as "loose" women bespeaks of their rebellion: existing outside of social (male) norms, of the era in which the program was set, the 1950s, and in which the series aired, the 1970s.

When Laverne and Shirley got their own series, they underwent some alterations. Their bad girl personas disappeared. Replacing them was a Shirley who was prim and proper and wore virtue as a badge; and a Laverne, who, though more predatory with men, was still determined not to be a "fun date."

This watering-down of Laverne and Shirley did not undermine them. Nor was their characters' alteration gender-specific. Over on *Happy Days*, the Fonz also underwent a major revision. Originally meant to be a James Dean type, Arthur Fonzarelli "evolved" morally when he became that show's breakout character.

Laverne and Shirley were eventually able to move beyond stereotypical good girl-bad girl roles, and away from stigmatizing labels like "brain" and "brawn." As one author noted, "Laverne appears to be tough, [but] has a soft center, while Shirley appears to be soft-centered, she is tough."[33]

In terms of their representations of real-life women, Nill puts it succinctly: "If on the surface [Laverne and Shirley] appeared to be longing to fulfill the stereotypical 1950s role of women, their true actions and attitudes cast them as two of television's first liberated women."[34] This point is well-taken. For all the talk the two ladies engaged in about finding boyfriends and husbands, they are most often on their own and content. In fact, repeatedly, they choose friendship over romance. In one episode, they go so far as to make a pact that no man will ever come between them. On *Laverne & Shirley*, sisterhood prevailed.

If anything, boyfriends usually caused more trouble than they were worth, as in the time their dates turned out to be bank robbers or when the "boyfriend" of one had the nerve to ask out the other!

Furthermore, neither Laverne nor Shirley appeared in any rush marriage-wise. Laverne "plays the field," and Shirley, though she has a good guy in casual boyfriend Carmine, chooses not to marry him, fearful that he's not "the one."

Perhaps Laverne and Shirley just aren't that interested in husbands after all. They can take care of themselves. In various episodes, when the ladies find that their weekly bottle-capping wages aren't enough, they don't hunt wealthy suitors. Instead, they take on any number of odd jobs — from working in a shoe store to volunteering to be "guinea pigs" for scientific research — in order to make extra money.

For many of these jobs, the ladies engaged in a wide assortment of activities that were not and are not considered traditionally female (they joined the police force and the army).

Additionally, Laverne and Shirley were activists. In various episodes they express their dislike for fur; stage a sit-in at the power company; and even handcuff themselves to a dog at the pound.

No matter what they were doing, when the chips were down, they were there for each other. As one author put it, "[Their] system of mutual support demonstrate[d] that women could compete in the world of work as well as in the world of ideas."[35]

Despite the show's success, criticism abounds. One critic called it "eminently forgettable."[36] But, if so, why was it so popular? One critic takes issue with the cursive "L" with which Laverne always adorned her blouses; the author states "it had all the charm of the

Scarlet Letter."[37] But Laverne's "L" could just as easily be interpreted as akin to Superman's "S." She is after all branding herself, declaring her individuality.

Other authors' takes on the series have been more upbeat. Said one, "[*Laverne & Shirley*] painted a picture of the 1950s from the single, independent woman's point of view. The plots of the episodes reflected concerns about holding a factory job, making it as an independent woman, and dealing with friends and relatives in the process of developing a life of one's own."[38]

If Laverne and Shirley were an update of Lucy and Ethel, then they're also a bridge to Roseanne. Like Roseanne, they were blue collar workers who worked in factories before moving into less grimy positions in department stores and restaurants. Like Roseanne, they depended on each other just as Roseanne frequently turned to sister Jackie, or vice versa. And like that "domestic goddess," these two

Cindy Williams (left) and Penny Marshall as Shirley Fenney and Laverne DeFazio, respectively, on *Laverne & Shirley* (1976–1983) continued the long-standing TV trend of female rebellion well into the 1970s and '80s.

working class queens saw no reason to take orders from men if it meant they wouldn't get what they wanted.

——◦/◦◦—

Sung with conviction by Jeannie C. Riley, the song "Harper Valley PTA" was a hit in 1968, reaching number one on the charts. Written by tunesmith Tom T. Hall, it told of a young widow with a taste for mini-skirts and good times who one day dared to stand up to her small Southern town.

Ten years after its release, the song inspired a feature film of the same name starring Barbara Eden. A few years after that, it became a TV series. Again starring Eden, *Harper Valley PTA* (1981–1982) told of Stella Johnson (she had no first name in the song) who, like some sort of small-town Joan of Arc (another persecuted woman), was always rallying against hypocrisy, double-standards, and ignorance.

Most of the accusations aimed at Stella came from her chief nemesis Flora Simpton Reilly, a high-ranking PTA member and goody-two-shoes. Over the course of the series, Flora spread endless rumors about Stella: that she had a drinking problem, that she was practicing the "world's oldest profession," that she was involved with a married man. Each was untrue and in the end Stella always proved her innocence while Flora ended up with egg (among other things) on her face.

When not defending her honor, Stella was often seen defending others from runaway Puritanism, city corruption, even violent crime. In various episodes she chains herself to a tree to protest it being chopped; storms into a meeting of the city council to point out the inefficiency of the fire department; and once even foiled a bank robbery.

Author Rick Mitz described *Harper Valley* as "*Green Acres* meets Norman Lear"[39] in that, via its broadly drawn characters and situations, issues of bigotry, hypocrisy and faulty small-town romanticism were all challenged within the framework of the TV sitcom.

Conclusion

Though their influence can be seen up to modern day — the two "fash mag slags" of *Absolutely Fabulous* and 2011's *2 Broke Girls*— the rebellious woman of TV is still best characterized by Lucy.

Lucy would continue with her *Lucy* character — with Gale Gordon as a substitute Ricky — up until 1986 when her final series *Life with Lucy* ended. And though one could consider some later TV characters — like Jeannie in *I Dream of Jeannie* and of course *Roseanne*— to be decedents of Ball's rebel persona, the majority of Lucy-esque characters would decline over the years.

One theory is that producers could never replace the original. Lucy was one of a kind. Without a talent like hers to pull it off, a replacement *Lucy* would probably end up just silly. A second theory is that as feminism blossomed in America, the cathartic need for such on-air rebels gradually lessened.

Which is not to say that Lucy and her sisters are now "passé." If anything, they are as good an example today as ever. After all, if modern-day practical feminism is defined as "outrageous acts and everyday rebellions," then certainly nothing fits that more than Lucy and her kind.

— 4 —

"Bewitched, Bothered and Bewildered"
The Rise of the "Magicom"
and the Women Who Dominated It

Bottled, But Not Contained....—ad copy for Uninhibited perfume

They are two series forever intertwined. And, granted, *Bewitched* and *I Dream of Jeannie* do have many things in common: They premiered within a year of each other; both had their lead female characters endowed with supernatural powers; and both revolved primarily around male-female relationships.

They have something else in common: long-standing bad reputations in our post-feminist world.

They premiered not long after Betty Friedan's 1963 *The Feminine Mystique* appeared; many television scholars have since pointed to these programs as evidence of a persistent, even unconscious sexism in TV (and society) at the time.[1] *Bewitched* and *I Dream of Jeannie*, they say, feature men "forbidding" women from utilizing their natural gifts, be it genie magic or witchcraft. Both shows, therefore, were — supposedly — a metaphor for the women's movement, with the powers of Samantha of *Bewitched* and Jeannie of *Jeannie* representing the emerging independent woman and its threat to America's status quo. One writer so subscribes to this theory he called *Bewitched* the "most sexist program of all time."[2] Another writer, more bluntly, called *Bewitched* "as anti-feminist, anti-sexual, and procentrist as a sitcom can be."[3]

But such summation (dismissal?) of both shows is a superficial reading, the TV equivalent of judging a book by its cover. While labeling the programs "sexist" might be borne out by the shows' general premises, it is not evident in actual episodes. In fact, in the end, *Bewitched* and *Jeannie* are both further steps along the *I Love Lucy* continuum as both were, in the end, about female power in conflict with male "authority."

Witch's Way

The overall power structure of *Bewitched* (1964–1972) is communicated by the program's title — it's Darrin, not Samantha, who's "bewitched" (not to mention bothered and bewildered). This dynamic is underscored by the program's animated opening where a slightly bemused Samantha (Elizabeth Montgomery) flies through the sky, eventually landing in the middle of her kitchen. There she is joined by husband Darrin (Dick York, later Dick Sargent), who is depicted as haggard and utterly overwhelmed.

This mode of behavior would continue throughout the series. Almost every episode of *Bewitched* contains at least one scene of Darrin yelling and slowly losing his grip (usually in the Dick Sargent episodes; he was great with his Kramden-esque lunacy) or yelling and losing his cool (mostly in the Dick York episodes; York was better with the slow burn). One critic has described Darrin as "pop-eyed, confused, sweaty."[4] Said *Entertainment Weekly* about the series, "Samantha was much smarter than goofy, grinning Darrin."[5] And scholar David Marc has said about him, "Darrin can be seen as a transitional figure from the paternal omniscience and omnipotence of Jim Anderson in the fifties to the powerlessness and stupidity of Archie Bunker in the seventies."[6]

Darrin's catchphrase in the series said it all: a desperate shout of "Saaaaaam!" Meanwhile, the most hysterical Samantha ever got was a soft "Well...." or a far-from-shocking "Oh, my stars."

On *Bewitched* (1964–1972), Elizabeth Montgomery played Samantha Stephens, a modern-day witch who made her own choices.

Writer Jess Cagle breaks with the norm and calls *Bewitched* "the most subversively feminist series of its era."[7] Another writer notes, "Elizabeth Montgomery brought a sparkling intelligence to the role of Samantha Stephens."[8] (How smart was Sam? Among other talents, she was fluent in Spanish, Italian, French, and most animal languages.) Ken Tucker also defends the series by saying, "Elizabeth Montgomery's luminous presence [shined] in the context of a suburbia populated by grotesques both human and supernatural...."[9]

In the pilot of *Bewitched*, Darrin learns about his wife's witchcraft and asks her to abstain. Much has been made over the years of Darrin's request. But, before passing judgment, Darrin's request should be contextualized.

Episode one of *Bewitched* quickly recaps the courtship of Darrin and Samantha. They meet "cute" — they keep bumping into each other around town, almost like they were destined to be together (a device that would be copied later on *Dharma & Greg*). But, for however long their romance is, it is not until their wedding night that Samantha discloses to her husband that she's a card-carrying witch.

Why, pray tell, did Samantha, an otherwise seemingly level-headed woman, wait until her wedding night to disclose to her husband this *Jerry Springer*–worthy confession? Had a chance never come up before? And what did she tell Darrin (first as boyfriend, then as fiancé) about her parents? With her mother Endora's series-long dislike for Darrin, is it perhaps not surprising that Samantha kept her mother away?

Taking into account Samantha's less-than-honest approach to marriage, Darrin's request for her to be an "ordinary" housewife sounds less inconsiderate. With few exceptions, the popular image of witches — Darrin's frame of reference — are of evil, poison apple–carrying crones. Shouldn't Darrin have been a little afraid?

Despite the brouhaha regarding Darrin's stance on his wife's witchcraft, the majority of *Bewitched* episodes don't concern "suppression" of his wife's abilities at all. As Williams Kuhn states, "Samantha's spooky powers are usually only incidental."[10] The majority of *Bewitched*'s episodes focus not on Sam, but on various spells that Endora inflicts on her son-in-law (she turned him into a parrot, a goat, a mule, a toad...) or on some strange disease that Samantha falls prey to and which requires the attention of Dr. Bombay ("Dr. Bombay, Dr. Bombay, come right away!"). Some of the ailments that Sam suffered: square green spots, metaphysical molecular disturbance, and something called gravitutis inflammatitus.

Still other episodes focus on Sam's relatives causing problems via mischievousness (like any time Sam's sister Serena stopped by) or via incompetence (as when Sam's Aunt Clara popped in). When the Stephens had children, many episodes were devoted to problems caused by the little witch and warlock slowing discovering the power, but not the responsibility, of their magic.

Despite whatever disturbance factored into an episode, each had at least one thing in common (besides a meltdown by Darrin): how Sam's witchcraft, combined with her quick thinking, always ends up saving the day. As Darrin fumes and his boss Larry becomes crazed, Samantha, with either a spell in iambic pentameter or a twitch of her nose, rights wrongs, cures the sick, or saves Darrin's latest big account at work. This happens in the episodes "Instant Courtesy," "Samantha the Bard," and "A Bum Raps," among others.

Sometimes Samantha's magic even saves a life — like Darrin's. This happens in "Samantha's Thanksgiving to Remember" (where the family gets zapped back to the Salem witch trials and Darrin's accused of witchcraft) and in "Many Happy Turns" (where Sam saves him from burglars).

Considering all the havoc that the witchcraft of others inflicted on her household, is it any wonder that Sam, too, was usually willing to forgo it? The very fact that Samantha marries a mortal suggests that she is not only a "rebel" but that she is also not averse to living without magic. She knew beforehand that marrying a mortal would mean a different life. In marrying Darrin, Samantha chose to give up certain aspects of her witchcraft-led life and settle for a simpler sort of existence. There is a quasi–Amish aspect to Sam's choice. Just as the Amish (like Wicca, another aged religion) could ease their lives by employing modern technology but don't, Samantha, whose life could be streamlined via magic, also resists.

David Marc, in *Comic Visions*, likens Samantha's magic to the tranquilizers ("mother's little helpers") that were over-prescribed at the time.[11] In Sam's refusal to indulge in shortcuts and easy outs, Samantha is, basically, "just saying no." In this scenario, Darrin functions as something akin to his wife's sponsor in assisting her resistance.

Throughout the series, Samantha always insists on doing things the right way — that is, without magic. For example, in "It's Magic," Samantha is put in charge of a fundraiser and its full $50(!) budget. Rather than blink herself to wealth, Samantha holds onto her integrity and works to raise more money.

Via her powers Samantha could have just about anything she wants — but what she wants is Darrin and her children. She says in one episode, "Now listen to me, Darrin, you may have given up but I haven't. I enjoy taking care of my husband and my children in the everyday mortal way. I like things the way they are. If I didn't, I wouldn't be here."

Samantha's new aversion to using magic, and Darrin's desire that she desist, is an expression of their wish for a normal life. This pursuit of "normalcy" might very well have struck a chord in the 1960s, a time when political and social changes were pervasive.

Granted, this choice does seem odd. If one has magic powers, why not use them for everyone's betterment? *Bewitched* addressed this issue in a 1965 episode, "A Is for Aardvark," where Darrin finds himself confined to bed and Samantha gives him some temporary powers. Darrin goes wild with his new abilities. Nevertheless, he soon realizes its drawback: When you don't have to work for things, they don't mean as much.[12] This understanding of the true things that matter is further supported by series creator William Asher, who said, "The show portrays a mixed marriage that overcomes by love the enormous obstacles in its path. Samantha, in her new role as housewife, represents the true value in life. Material gains mean nothing to her."[13]

According to Herbie J. Pilato's *Bewitched Forever* book, even Montgomery at first couldn't comprehend her character's refusal to utilize her powers until the character was presented to her in comparison to film hero Shane, the great gunfighter who one day lays down his weapons. As Pilato puts it, "There was a certain dignity to Samantha's decision to hold back on her power just as there was for Shane to control his fast draw."[14]

While *Bewitched* has similarities to *I Love Lucy*, in at least one regard the program differs. Lucy's sitcom life was a series of frustrating — if funny — attempts to break out of her traditional role. By contrast, Samantha finds fulfillment in hearth and home. Therefore, if feminism is about women's choices — even if those choices are "traditional" — then *Bewitched* supports the tenet. Writer Ron Smith concurs: "Though she may not have always seemed so, Samantha was an independent woman; it was her decision to surrender her sorcery."[15]

Though Samantha may have been in many ways "traditional," she was never subservient. In "How Not to Lose Your Head for Henry VIII, Part 1," she compares Darrin to Bluebeard (whom Samantha has met): "[He] was more of a gentleman than you've been tonight." In another she vocalizes a complaint of many housewives when she says to Darrin, "Tell Larry if I have to make one more dinner for a client, I want to go on the payroll."

Just as Samantha was far from the oppressed housewife, Darrin was far from a monster. Despite the torture that his mother-in-law often inflicted on him, Darrin never walked away from his responsibilities. In one episode Darrin concedes to Samantha, "When we were married, you made a big sacrifice for me." As pointed out by Asher, the Stephens marriage is based on mutual understanding and equality. Darrin loves Samantha for who she is, not what she can do for him; Samantha loves Darrin regardless of his being mortal or not.

—⟡—

If, for the sake of argument, Sam was oppressed, what then of Sam's mother Endora?

Endora was played with relish by Agnes Moorhead, who, as one author put it, "hissed every line, cran[ed] her neck like a demented pelican, [and] thrust her painted nails into Kabuki-like positions"[16] as part of her performance.

Endora was a troublemaker — quite literally, the mother-in-law from hell. She never referred to Darrin by his real name, preferring alternatives like Delwood, Dobbin, and Durwood. In one episode, Darrin intones that Endora learned cruelty from the Marquis de Sade. Endora corrects him: "It's not true. He was just a classmate."

"Durwood" (dead wood?) and the rest of mankind was just no match for Endora. If Samantha is the poster child for restrained womanhood, then Endora is the symbol of what one risks suppressing female power. Endora represents witchcraft's revenge, payback to persecuting mortals. And payback is — literally — a mother.

—⁓—

There are various readings to *Bewitched*. In some ways, the series is a lesson in Freudianism. Endora, and her devil-may-care ways, represents the instant gratification of the id; Darrin the cautious ego; and Samantha, the superego, the mediator.

Similarly, *Bewitched* can also be viewed as a metaphor for the 1960s with Samantha as pseudo-hippie. Just as the era's hippie culture stressed a return to a more hands-on approach to life, so too does Sam with her desire to do cooking, cleaning and scrubbing without any magical shortcuts. In this reading, Endora, with her addiction to superficiality, represents the bourgeois generation while also tipping her broom to the international "jet set." There is even evidence that she and Samantha's father Maurice have a marriage of convenience since, though they remain married, they seem to live separate lives.[17] Just as many parents of the era couldn't understand the commune living and other choices of their children, Endora cannot comprehend Sam's desire not to "live life to the fullest," i.e., interact with witches and warlocks (the "in" crowd) or fly around the world (like the aforementioned pleasure-seeking jet set). The relationship between mother and daughter is a clash of generations and, unfortunately for him, Darrin is just a pawn in between.

Continuing metaphors, *Bewitched* is in sync with another aspect of 1960s America: the Cold War and threat of nuclear devastation. If Samantha possesses certain capabilities and chooses not to exercise them, then she is an allegory for unmitigated power. With her choice not to use her magic, Samantha conveys an important message: We will restrain our power; we will not "twitch" just because we can; we will not disrupt the laws of nature. We will not split the atom.

In its own way, *Bewitched* even addressed other issues then plaguing the country like religious tolerance and race relations. As Samantha states in one episode, "I belong to the greatest minority of them all — I'm a witch." In another, Endora calls her son-in-law a "bigot" for lumping all witches together as cauldron-stirrers. In another, Samantha informs daughter Tabitha about different religions, saying, "Everyone is allowed to believe what they want to, *if* they want to believe." In a later episode, when zapped back to the Salem witch trials, Samantha takes up for the accused: "The people you persecuted were guiltless!"[18]

With her insightful comments and contemplated actions, along with being this series' mediator and frequent savior, Samantha is its ethical center. Not only does she refuse to use her powers selfishly, but Samantha is also her show's necessary counterbalance against indulgence (i.e., Endora's life) and greed (as represented by Darrin's boss Larry Tate and the advertising industry which employs him and Darrin). Samantha is also the linchpin which holds this family together and bridges its separate worlds — the mortal, the immortal, the present, the past.

In the end, Samantha is a strong, individualistic woman willing to make her own life choices and possessing the convictions to live by them.

Out of the Bottle

Six months after ABC's success with *Bewitched*, NBC, with the help of producer Sidney Sheldon, launched *I Dream of Jeannie* (1965–1970). In it, a female genie is set free from her bottle by a young astronaut after he crashlands on an island. Grateful to be liberated, the genie, named Jeannie (played by Barbara Eden), follows ancient moral code and devotes her life to her rescuer. She pledges forevermore, "Thou may ask anything of thy slave, master."[19]

Again, as with *Bewitched*, on the surface *I Dream of Jeannie* looks like the ultimate male fantasy. After all, what man wouldn't want a pretty, scantily clad woman living in his house and calling him "master"? In fact, at the time of the program's premiere, *TV Guide* compared *I Dream of Jeannie*, with its "master" and "slave" references, to the Marquis de Sade![20]

Such a limited interpretation fits only the program's premise. As with *Bewitched*, the power dynamic of the show is communicated in *Jeannie*'s animated opening. In it, though Jeannie is ultimately returned to her bottle, her knowing eyes later appear through the glass and we realize that this is not a woman (or genie) to trifle with.

Sheldon seemed to agree, saying that the show was, ultimately, about a "man and his supposedly servile woman" and adding later, "I write about women who are more capable than men at what they are doing."[21] This view is shared by series writer Edgar Penton: "Although [Jeannie] insists on calling Tony 'master' and proclaims that her only desire is to grant his every wish and obey his every whim, more often than not, she's the one who controls *him*." And co-star Larry Hagman said, "The question is, who was the 'slave' and who was the 'master'?"[22]

These statements from producer, writer and star are more than conjecture. Throughout the series, Jeannie regularly displays independence. In the pilot, once astronaut Tony Nelson (Hagman) has sprung Jeannie from her bottle, she explains that she had been imprisoned there for hundreds of years for refusing to marry the evil Blue Djinn.

Barbara Eden's magical presence as Jeannie upturned the stagnant lives of all the men around her and even NASA on *I Dream of Jeannie* (1965–1970).

With this disclosure we quickly learn just how determined a genie can be: willing to endure imprisonment rather than be forced into marriage.

Later in that same episode, after Tony has decided that he has no room in his life for a genie, he tricks Jeannie back into her bottle and attempts to leave her. But Jeannie later escapes and clandestinely returns with him, materializing in his Florida home. "Thou has deceived me!" she yells, later calling him an "ungrateful master!"

Throughout the series, Jeannie shows herself to be both independent in thought and sly in intelligence. In "A Secretary Is Not a Toy," Jeannie decides her master needs a promotion and the way for him to get one is for her to become secretary to Tony's superior, General Peterson. Tony forbids (famous last words!) Jeannie from doing anything to influence his career. To keep Jeannie in "her place," Tony orders her to watch three movies that are consecutively airing on TV. But Jeannie isn't to be restrained. With a blink, Jeannie put the movies on fast-forward. She then blinks herself into General Peterson's office. Technically, Jeannie has done what Tony has asked of her, but ultimately also did what she wanted.

Not only was Jeannie's so-called master no match for her, neither was any other mortal. In "The Second Greatest Con Artist in the World," Jeannie outsmarts an unscrupulous millionaire.

—◦◦◦—

Tony never asked for a genie any more than Darrin asked to marry a witch. Once Jeannie becomes a part of his life, Tony asks her to do three things: (1) keep her identity a secret (how exactly would he explain her?); (2) not use her magic (which, like Darrin's request, illustrates Tony's desire to live normally); and (3) not grant him any wishes (ditto). These are reasonable — even noble — requests; they seem as much for Jeannie's protection as anything. Jeannie could easily be exploited. After all, what would happen if some foreign government found her? Even NASA, Major Nelson's employer, might have tried to make use of Jeannie had they known. Why bother to send rockets to the moon when Jeannie can blink you there? For her own safety, it was necessary for Jeannie (and Tony) to keep her abilities under wraps, just as Samantha hid her powers from others on *Bewitched* and just as Superman and the Incredible Hulk kept their identities secret. Therefore, rather than Tony as Jeannie's oppressor, it makes greater sense to view him as a protector.

However, despite his stance, sometimes Tony (like Darrin before him) is not above using Jeannie when other options fail. In one episode, Tony and fellow officer Roger Healy are to live in the desert to test their endurance. With no food, 100-plus degree heat during the day and below freezing at night, they soon have no qualms about turning to Jeannie.

Similarly, in the episode "The Greatest Entertainer in the World" with guest star Sammy Davis, Jr., Tony has to get Sammy to perform for the general's upcoming party. Tony goes through all the proper channels but nothing works, so it's Jeannie to the rescue. With a blink, she makes Sammy appear in the living room.

In "Jeannie and the Kidnap Caper," Tony orders Jeannie to not grant him any more wishes. All goes well until Tony finds himself kidnapped and Jeannie has to rescue him. Jeannie would save Tony's life again in the episode "Who Needs a Green-Eyed Jeannie?"

—◦◦◦—

There are few characters who have been played with as much joy as Barbara Eden brought to Jeannie. In most episodes, rather than serving their masters, genies just want to have fun. The most resonating image from the series is Jeannie laughing unto herself as her master Tony flails away helplessly. Consider the episode where Tony has to explain a suddenly appearing babbling brook in his kitchen. All the while, a miniaturized Jeannie is laughing from her vantage point. Eden has said:

> Jeannie wasn't a wimp or a robot. She really had a mind of her own. People in the women's movement would sometimes say, "How can you call him master?" My own personal little bit of philosophy is that I don't think what we say is as important as what we do. She was saying "Yes, master," but she was always doing her own thing.[23]

As evidence of Jeannie "doing her own thing," consider the episode where Jeannie wants to learn to drive but Tony forbids (famous last words!) her from taking lessons. Jeannie doesn't listen. In this episode's conclusion, Jeannie is seen smiling behind the wheel as she tears down the road with Tony running behind.

As with *Bewitched, Green Acres* and other series, here the male figure has found himself within a surreal setting[24] and, because of it, it is the female who is less frantic than he. *Jeannie*'s director Gene Nelson said, "[Larry] Hagman had this marvelous energy and kind of nervousness about his character that really registered on film and Barbara played right into that with Jeannie as the calm one."[25]

There is a childlikeness to Jeannie's character, but she is not "infantilized." Jeannie's naiveté makes sense. Unlike Samantha, who though a witch was every bit a modern woman, Jeannie has lived most of her life bottled up. Emerging suddenly in 1960s America, Jeannie is ignorant of the world. In a way she is more akin to *The Beverly Hillbillies*, dumbfounded by the sight of the "cee-ment pond," than she is to Samantha. Because Jeannie has been sheltered most of her life, she cannot be viewed as a metaphor for the women of the 1960s any more than Jed Clampett can be viewed as representative of men.

There's another important distinction between *Jeannie* and *Bewitched*. Unlike Darrin and Samantha, Jeannie and Tony are *not* married. Jeannie and Tony don't marry until the penultimate season by which time Jeannie has also largely stopped referring to Tony as master.[26] Therefore, since for most of the show Jeannie and Tony were little more than roommates, it's inaccurate to view *Jeannie* as a parable for married life.

Jeannie was one of the first television shows to feature a man and a woman living together without benefit of marriage. (Additionally, technically, this was also TV's first older woman-younger man romance as well.) Luckily, the fact that Jeannie was a genie, a magical creature, seemed to nullify any "living in sin" accusations. The following season, the same logic would be applied to *The Ghost and Mrs. Muir*.

Jeannie is, in essence, a romantic comedy, boy-meets-girl. From the second episode, a romance between the two leads is hinted at with Tony falling as hard for Jeannie as she does for him. In fact, in episode two, Tony tells Jeannie, "You're the greatest thing that's ever happened to me," a detail that is seldom mentioned in recaps. And he's right. For when Tony freed Jeannie from that bottle, he also freed himself from his own dull, militaristic existence. Jeannie is, literally and figuratively, a free spirit whose free-wheeling way does not adhere to the strict rigidity of military life.[27]

The choice of Tony Nelson's career was a careful one for Sidney Sheldon. In creating the series he asked himself, "What kind of man would be most embarrassed by having a genie?"[28] This opposites-attract, clash-of-worlds is what *Jeannie*'s true message is and it's a premise that would largely be copied — minus the magic — in *Dharma & Greg*, where a New Age wife infiltrates a stuffy old-money family.

I Dream of Jeannie, built around an old-fashioned man and a free-wheeling woman, also seems to be a metaphor for the generation gap. Jeannie was like one of TV's first hippies. Certainly she had an appetite for adventure. Even her harem costume seems to suggest a hippie's weeds.

A much discussed element of the series is Jeannie's bottle. True, for years Jeannie was imprisoned in it but was it really a prison for her? She returns to it to sleep. And panic always arose whenever the bottle was lost or was in danger of being destroyed. Could Jeannie's bottle be, as Virginia Woolf might have called it, a room of her own?

Man and Machine

Other series of the *Bewitched* ilk have popped up over the years. Consider *My Living Doll* (1964–1965). This one-seasoner starred Julie Newmar as Rhoda the Robot, a "woman" made entirely of wires and gears.

After Rhoda's creation by government scientists, she is placed in the care of army psychologist Dr. Robert McDonald. (Government involvement? An army shrink? *Doll* debuted one season before *I Dream of Jeannie*.) It is the doctor's job to transform this android from total machine into "perfect woman." (In order to calm the neighbors in regard to this unmarried "woman" co-habitating with an unmarried man, it was explained that Rhoda is a mental patient being treated by Dr. McDonald!) McDonald was played by Bob Cummings, who was working the same playboy shtick he did in *Love That Bob*.

On the surface, this series too was male fantasy: a voluptuous Julie Newmar robot who could be programmed to do anything her male "owner" wanted her to do! With such factors, no wonder *My Living Doll* is often cited as one of the most sexist series in history. But, again, this is from people who have never watched an episode. As Smith has pointed out, although "the sophisticated humor possible in satirizing man's passion for the perfect (and perfectly controllable) woman turned to sitcom formula mush," he noted:

> [Newmar's] sense of fantasy fun and her unique combination of intelligence and imagination showed through.... She was funny as the misunderstanding Robot AF709 that took commands literally, suffered mechanical failures that left her acting drunk or dizzy, yet remained unperturbed by the chaos around her.[29]

In the series, all of Dr. McDonald's attempts to mold Rhoda go awry. In one episode, "My Robot, My Warden," Dr. McDonald is under a deadline to finish a proposal for his book "How Not to Be Dominated by Females." But, as one might have guessed, the title of this work will prove ironic. In order to finish, Dr. McDonald gives Rhoda the command to prevent him from leaving the house for the next 24 hours. Rhoda is happy to oblige but shortly thereafter Dr. McDonald decides that he needs to leave. Still, Rhoda has her orders and McDonald's attempts to get out prove futile. As often happened with Jeannie and Tony, here again a man's attempt to boss around a woman proves disastrous ... for him.

This theme is revisited in "Rhoda's Forgery" when McDonald asks Rhoda to copy a Picasso. Rhoda does, expertly, even down to the artist's signature. She does it so well that soon an art dealer has mistaken it for the real thing. In the end, Dr. McDonald has painted himself into a corner.

But, despite the "problems" Rhoda caused in his life, McDonald was not above utilizing her when it was convenient. In one episode, he takes advantage of Rhoda's calculating abilities to win at dice.

Newmar has said of her character, "Rhoda is the ultimate consciousness, the ultimate reality, the ultimate freedom. She is the quintessence of humanness. As I play her, the robot is coming closer to the ideal in humanity, and the humans around it are becoming more and more like robots."[30]

This theme (intersecting mankind with machine-kind), as outlined by Newmar, has been addressed in other series, notably via the android Data from *Star Trek: The Next Generation*. With these characters, their literalism may cause confusion at first but ultimately prove illuminating to those around them. Ultimately, they remind humans of their humanity.

Ironically, the general premise of *Doll*, this "sexist" show, was replicated two decades later in the 1980s comedy *Small Wonder* (1985–1989). However, since that show revolved around a robotic little girl and not Julie Newmar, it was free of accusations of sexism. Similarly, mechanics aside, McDonald's quest to create the "perfect woman" is only marginally different from other Pygmalion scenarios, i.e., *My Fair Lady*, a film and play usually free from complaints of patriarchal oppression.

Conclusion

Despite variations that exist from series to series, in the end, these three women-focused programs do have at least one thing in common. In all of them, their power (be it magical, mechanical, logical or symbolic) disrupts the status quo of male spheres. Therefore, if, as some persist in believing, series like *Bewitched*, et al. are about men attempting to squash female power, then they are also about these same men failing in their attempts.

"She Works Hard for the Money"
TV's Women at Work

The reward of labour is life. Is that not enough?—William Morris, "News from Nowhere"

As long as there's been TV, there have been fictional representations of working women on it. Yet you wouldn't know it from most articles on the subject. For example, in recapping a 1971–1981 study on women on television by the National Commission on Working Women, its author states that "finally," in this period, "female TV characters have entered the work force."[1] A decade later, in 1991, *Working Woman* magazine perpetuated this misconception: In an article, the editors stated, "Not long ago there were simply too few realistic TV career women to warrant such an article [as this]."[2]

In October 1995, the magazine revisited the subject when they put Cybill Shepherd on their cover to celebrate (again) that women on TV "finally" had "real jobs." They also said that *Mary Tyler Moore* was "TV's first truly modern working woman" because she was the "first female sitcom lead not using the workplace as a hunting ground or a stopgap on the way to marriage."[3]

But from Ann Sothern on *Private Secretary* to *Our Miss Brooks*, these women were seen working (and working far too hard) to ever hunt for a husband. Mary Richards was not the first to keep business separate from pleasure.

Granted, women on TV in the 1950s and 1960s were more likely to be wives and mothers than lawyers or doctors but, as noted previously, labor stats of the era reflect this as accurate.[4] Over the years, as more women entered the workforce, television followed suit. The reason we have more female doctors, lawyers, and business executives on TV today is because we have more in real life.

Sometimes even when authors acknowledge TV's early working women, they still give them short shrift. Unable to ignore *Our Miss Brooks* and *Private Secretary*, they just downgrade them for having "traditional" occupations like teacher or secretary. But certain jobs became "traditionally" female because, traditionally, females have held them. Even today, according to the National Center for Education, 82 percent of public school teachers are female.[5] According to the Department of Labor, 92 percent of all RNs are female.[6] If these are the numbers today, what were they like in 1950?

Even if statistics didn't back them up, there's still no reason to diminish the women who held them. Just because something is traditionally "women's work" doesn't mean it isn't important; being a nurse is an important job, as is being a teacher

In her 1991 book *Backlash*, Susan Faludi doesn't devalue the jobs of working women on TV, she just degrades the women. She states, "Early television actually offered quite a number of single-woman shows, although they featured hapless schoolmarms, maids and typists in such fare as *Private Secretary*, *Ella Miss*,[7] *My Friend Irma*, *Our Miss Brooks*, and *Meet Millie*."[8]

As in *Working Woman*, Faludi offers sweeping statements about various working women. Unfortunately, they're not borne out in the shows. Many words describe Susie of *Private Secretary* and *Our Miss Brooks* but "hapless" isn't one of them.

The incomparable Eve Arden played Connie Brooks on *Our Miss Brooks* (1952–1956). The character was known for her wit and professional acumen.

The Teachers

The comedy *Our Miss Brooks* (1952–1956) told of high school English teacher Connie Brooks of Madison High. Starring Eve Arden, the show began on radio in 1948 and later transitioned to TV. Coming with Miss Brooks to TV were back-up characters Osgood Conklin (played by Gale Gordon), the prickly principal; dim-bulb biology teacher (and Miss Brooks' crush) Mr. Boynton (played by Robert Rockwell); and nerdy student Walter Denton (Richard Crenna).

If Miss Brooks was a "hapless" caricature, then why was Arden made an honorary member of the NEA and honored by the organization?[9] Why did she repeatedly get asked to join school boards and address teachers' meetings? And why did one fan, a teacher, mail her a "diploma" reading, "Thank you for recording the fact that we are not all poker-faced leftovers."[10]

A 1994 paper for the Australian Association for Research in Education by Erica Williams, "Seductress or Schoolmarm: On the Improbability of the Great Female Teacher," also takes a different view of Brooks:

> There is a voice that insists on speaking, … the alto voice of *Our Miss Brooks*, the witty female pedagogue…. Miss Brooks I do recall as a "towering figure," able to rise above the absurdity of a range of pedagogical and administrative events in order to stand and deliver parody in ways that marked her as transcending the mundane.[11]

Despite evidence of her being extremely capable, due to a secondary plot of Miss Brooks' unrequited love for Boynton, she is inevitably described as "husband hunter."[12] But, instead of "husband hunter," Miss Brooks could actually be considered just a strong early image of female sexuality. Mr. Boynton, though knowledgeable on his subject, wasn't very bright. Yet he was handsome. Connie didn't seem to want Mr. Boynton for his intellect and she didn't need him financially. Hence Connie's crush was mainly physical in nature, making her a precursor of sorts to the ladies of *Sex and the City*.

If Miss Brooks is thought of this way, then what we have here is a woman "of a certain age" (Arden was 40 when the series began), desirable and desiring of men and not shy about it. In one episode, after preparing dinner for Mr. Boynton, Miss Brooks spies the TV and wonders, "Maybe if we watch wrestling, he'll get some ideas."

Despite her crush, Miss Brooks' job and self-respect were never undermined. Miss Brooks (and Arden) were just too dignified to be desperate. In that regard, she is far removed from the "contestants" on such contemporary shows as *The Bachelor*. (You've come a long way, baby?)

Despite her occasional longings, Miss Brooks could never hold her tongue long enough to act on her impulses. As Michael McWilliams states, "[Brooks] could never resist sacrificing a bed partner for the Last Word."[13]

Always ignored in recaps of *Miss Brooks* is the series' final incarnation: In 1956, Connie took a new job at an elementary school. There, gym teacher Mr. Talbot (played by Gene Barry) openly attempted to woo an uninterested Miss Brooks. So was she really that desperate?

Despite all this evidence, why are Connie Brooks (and Susie of *Private Secretary* et al.) often described as "husband hunters"? Because it's easy. By labeling her a husband hunter, it quickly disposes of her. Her professionalism, intelligence, and humor can all be expunged. The "husband hunter" moniker is to working women on TV what wardrobe is to TV's wives and moms — a way to quickly dismiss them.

Furthermore, the "husband hunter" label begs an interesting question: Why is it if Diane and Sam flirt on *Cheers* that's romantic comedy but with Miss Brooks it's "desperation"?

One answer is that TV, at that time, couldn't be so up front with sexuality. If Miss Brooks wanted Mr. Boynton, it would have to be for matrimony. "Hooking up" didn't exist in 1950s TV.

If husband-hunting women (like Sally Rogers on *Dick Van Dyke*) did exist then on TV, it's because they've been a popular TV stock character along the lines of the sarcastic maid or butler. But it's an archetype that has a male equivalent, namely in the persona of the would-be Lothario, like the two "wild and crazy guys" from *Saturday Night Live* or Kirk from *Dear John*, who all too often found themselves played as punchlines.

Regardless, there's more to Miss Brooks than just, maybe, marriage. Miss Brooks was portrayed as both liked and respected by her pupils and peers. In one episode they stage an intervention when they think she is working too hard.

Miss Brooks was also the smartest person in this series. In one episode, when an anonymous threatening letter arrives, everyone thinks they are the intended victim … except for Connie. While Conklin and Mr. Boynton make "bullet-proof" vests, Connie laughs (mostly) behind their backs. Author Sam Frank called Miss Brooks "keenly intelligent,"[14] while another writer wrote:

> Arden played [Brooks] with a brassy, wisecracking self-assurance that made her more than a match for her three running battles: her power struggle with her pompous principal (an anti-authority streak), her endless effort to drum knowledge into the head of a dim-witted student

named Walter, and her battle to snare the shy biology teacher who never seemed to pick up her amorous hints.[15]

Eve Arden won an Emmy in 1953 for the series. She built a career on playing wise-cracking women in films like *Mildred Pierce*. When she came to TV she brought her wit with her. Her Connie has the fastest, sharpest comebacks in TV history. Arden's gift was that she could deliver these killer lines but still come across as likable. And though she was only 5' 7", Arden always dominated those around her. She'd wipe the floor with Ally McBeal.

What *Our Miss Brook*s beget would be carried on elsewhere on the small screen.

Though a supporting character, a truly dignified teacher was Miss Landers, "the neatest teacher in the whole school," according to Beaver on *Leave It to Beaver* (1957–1963).[16] Miss Landers (played by Sue Randall) is compassionate and forward-thinking. In one episode, she delivers a speech on how boys and girls should have respect for each other. In another, when Kenneth, a new boy, confesses it's him and not Beaver who has been stealing, Kenneth explains to Miss Landers that it's because he has no friends. But Miss Landers says she's his friend.

Other teachers abounded in the '50s and '60s. On *Mr. Peepers* there was English teacher Mrs. Gurney (played by Marion Lorne) and music teacher Rayola Dean (played by Norma Crane). On *Dobie Gillis*, actress Jean Byron played Dr. Burkehart, a teacher of math and Egyptology(!). On *Andy Griffith* (1960–1968), teacher Helen Crump (Aneta Corsaut) "served [the community] in admirable ways."[17]

Education on TV took a serio-comic turn with *Room 222* (1969–1974). Set at racially diverse Walt Whitman High, *Room 222* followed the work of some devoted teachers and administrators including guidance counselor Liz McIntyre (played by Denise Nichols). Though fellow teacher Pete (played by Lloyd Haines) and Liz were involved, their relation-ship was kept outside school. Their mature relationship marked a new high in terms of adults behaving like adults on TV.

After *Room 222*'s first season, the show dropped its intrusive laugh track and began to focus on subjects like drugs and delinquency. The fact that Haines and Nichols were black also helped integrate racial issues.

As a counselor, Liz McIntyre had her hands full. She often took her job home with her and struggled to see that all students were treated fairly. In one episode, she butted heads with her principal to see that a boy with behavior problems was helped. In another episode, Liz takes on the strident principal of another school. He says, "The schools have their function, the jails have theirs."

To which Liz replies, "I guess the question is … which are we?"

After being a book, musical, and movie, it seemed natural that *The King and I* would come to TV. It did as *Anna and the King* (1972). The TV version starred Yul Brynner with Samantha Eggar as schoolteacher Anna. Anna, a young widow with a son (another early single mom), came to Siam in the 1860s to teach the king's many children by his many wives.

The "stubborn, strong-willed"[18] Anna was never afraid to put her foot down even if it was in a high-button shoe. In one episode, she learns of a newborn baby who is for sale. Horrified, she buys the infant herself though it angers the king. Anna's rebellion sets her apart even among her fellow TV teachers. It's one thing to stand up to a principal, it's another to defy a king!

Brenda Vaccaro starred in *Sara* (1976), a series about a schoolteacher in the Old West. Though Sara had come to Independence, Colorado, in the 1870s to educate "young'ns," she ended up schoolin' the town. Described as "strong-willed"[19] and "feisty,"[20] Sara had progressive views that did not endear her to the all-male school board.

During its run, *Sara* tackled a variety of topics. In the premiere, Sara allows a half-breed to attend her schoolhouse. She accuses the citizenry of using the boy as a scapegoat for their anger over the Indians.[21]

In more modern times, two wonderful female teaching images could be found on *Fame* (1982–1987), a series based on the 1980 film about the real-life High School of the Performing Arts in New York (and a kind of precursor to *Glee*). Debbie Allen is the best remembered cast member. As dance teacher Lydia Grant, she often barked out orders but her bark was worse than her bite. Underneath, she was dedicated. One author described Grant as a "strong-willed, no-nonsense but sensitive, caring character."[22]

Lydia's toughness and passion was evident in various episodes. In one she dumps a boyfriend when he's critical of her students. In another, she confronts a student over her rapid weight loss.

Lydia's best friend was English teacher Elizabeth Sherwood (played by Carol Mayo Jenkins). Surrounded by students ready to break into song at any moment, Sherwood at first seemed out of place, but she held her own. In one episode, she declared, "What I teach is important!" Like Lydia, Ms. Sherwood often took her job and concern beyond the classroom, for example the time she followed a student home only to be confronted with the abject poverty he lived in.

Besides *Fame*, television has offered other school-based shows, and female educators haven't been absent. Bridget Fitzgerald (Meredith Baxter) was a schoolteacher on *Bridget Loves Bernie* (1972–1973); Emily Hartley (Suzanne Pleshette) was a teacher on *The Bob Newhart Show* (1972–1978); and Lynn Redgrave starred in *Teachers Only* (1986–1987).

The Secretaries

Susie McNamara of the comedy *Private Secretary* (1953–1957) is hardly "hapless" or "husband-hunting" either.

Certainly the actress who played her, Ann Sothern, was no retiring figure. According to legend, Sothern, while under contract to MGM, once had her appendix unnecessarily removed in order to get out of a film she didn't want to make. Another time, she sent a letter to Grace Kelly chastising the future princess for her romance with married actor Ray Milland. Said Sothern about the missive, "She received it. I sent it certified mail."[23]

Luckily Sothern had the talent to back up her pluck. Lucille Ball said of her, "[She's] the best comedienne in this business, bar none."[24]

As portrayed by Sothern, Susie was a total professional. Susie has been described by one source as "pretty, efficient, and worldly wise"[25] and as "ultra-efficient" by another.[26] Rick Mitz wrote, "[Susie] was independent and self-assured and had dignity and — even when she brought [her boss] Mr. Sands in his coffee—you knew that if he didn't treat her well, she just might dump the pot over his head 'by accident.'"[27]

Susie also had an interest in the opposite sex (one critic praised the series for Sothern's "good-hearted take-charge sex appeal"[28]). But she wasn't interested in her boss, talent agent Mr. Sands (played by Don Porter). Besides, as *TV Sirens* puts it, much like Miss Brooks, "[Susie] could never reconcile her romanticism with her repartee."[29]

Besides, most *Secretary* episodes revolve not around dating but various "schemes and scams that Susie undertook to rescue her boss from trouble." Susie was always "relaxed and poised and smooth, even in the most outrageous situations."[30] In many ways, Susie was a precursor to characters in *Nine to Five* and *Ugly Betty*, often saving her boss from himself. Case in point: In one

On *Private Secretary* (1953–1957), Ann Sothern's character Susie McNamara held a supposedly subordinate job position, but she regularly usurped her male boss's (Don Porter) authority.

episode, Mr. Sands is attempting to recruit a Garbo-esque actress but his attempts fail. When Susie tries, she succeeds. Other episodes also illustrate this same scenario:

- Susie poses as a maid to convince a wealthy couple not to pull their backing from an upcoming show.
- Susie convinces an overly protective mother to let her daughter be a kid and not be in show business.
- Susie shows an actor that all his publicity stunts are hurting his career.

Detect a pattern?

Like *Our Miss Brooks*, Sothern's *Private Secretary* trumps allegations leveled against women on TV at that time. Like Arden, when Sothern came to TV, she was "of a certain age"; she was 44 when the series began. It's also worth noting that in *Private Secretary*, there is no intrusive mother, nosy father, big brother or roommate under foot. Susie was a woman on her own long before Mary moved to Minneapolis.

What Sothern started would be followed. In his first TV effort, Bob Cummings played a *truly* hapless real estate agent, Robert S. Beanblossom, on the sitcom *My Hero* (1952–1953).

The title was ironic. Beanblossom was a bumbler, constantly having to be rescued by his secretary Julie Marshall, played by Julie Bishop. (He was the alleged "hero" of the title, she was the "my," giving her top billing.)

One episode has both Beanblossom and his equally inept boss, flailing about when Julie's on vacation. Unable to operate equipment, etc., both men realize they can't survive without Julie. The boss calls Julie "the best secretary a man ever had."

My Hero stuck around for one season. Cummings returned quickly in *The Bob Cummings Show* (a.k.a. *Love That Bob*) (1955–1959) where he played Bob Collins, a professional photographer whose office-studio was stocked with voluptuous fashion models. Also there was his secretary Charmaine "Shultzy" Schultz, played by Ann B. Davis, today best remembered as Alice on *The Brady Bunch*. Everything Davis was as Alice, she was as Shultzy — dependable, common-sensible, and full of vinegar when necessary. *The Great TV Sitcom Book* finds various reasons to celebrate Shultzy:

> She was the one we truly cared about. She had unending energy and lust for — well, lust. With her hair tied up in a little kerchief and her body hidden in baggy clothes, she was the down-to-earth counterpart to all the girls who sashayed into the office. She was substantial ... someone you could talk to, laugh with, have a good time with.[31]

—◄◊◊◊►—

As iconic as any secretary was Della Street, Perry Mason's indispensable right arm on *Perry Mason* (1957–1966).

Mason had been in movies and on radio before TV. On TV, Raymond Burr had the lead while Barbara Hale co-starred as "cool and efficient" Della.[32] Though Mason was a lawyer, he and his team (which also included PI Paul Drake) often functioned less like legal eagles than as detectives. In most episodes, Mason's legal expertise usually only mattered at the end when his questioning caused a witness to confess.

According to Newcomb, there's a dynamic to the Mason trio with Mason the legal mind while

> Paul Drake, the private investigator, represents the more physical aspects of the case. He will probe private lives, follow up leads, trace missing persons. Della Street, the ever-present secretary, represents the mental activity that will be involved, and is always armed with a stenographic pad in which she records essential details.[33]

Repeatedly, Della proved herself a skilled observer and pseudo-policewoman. In one episode, Della posed as a man's wife to get by authorities. In another, she breaks into a hotel room and uncovers documents that Perry needs for trial. Critic David Cuthbert said of Street: "[I]n terms of impact, she was a major element of the show.... I never thought of her as a secretary, or anything as menial as that — I thought of her as Perry Mason's partner."[34]

—◄◊◊◊►—

With apologies to Susie and Della, TV's most overworked secretary has to be Jane Hathaway (played by Nancy Kulp), assistant to stuffy banker Mr. Drysdale on *The Beverly*

Hillbillies (1962–1971). How overworked was she? In one episode, "Miss Jane" can't accept an invitation because as Mr. Drysdale explains:

MR. DRYSDALE: I would love for her to go but it would cost me $300 to replace her.
MISS HATHAWAY: Three hundred dollars?
MR. DRYSDALE: Is it my fault you do the work of four women?
MISS HATHAWAY: It certainly is.

Among other things, Miss Hathaway's the most under-employed character in TV history. Educated, knowledgeable about art and literature, even an expert on birds, she is an intellectual among those who can't appreciate it. (In some ways she's like Diane Chambers years later, slumming on *Cheers*.) But Miss Jane never played dumb. She doesn't think twice about throwing out obscure facts or poetry even though she knows it will fall on dumb ears.

As David Marc has noted, Hathaway is the "moral paragon" of the series, reminding Mr. Drysdale of his greed and Mrs. Drysdale of her snobbery. As Kulp put it, "I think she felt she had to protect [Mr. Drysdale] from himself, and she had to protect the Clampetts from him."[35]

Marc also points out, "The Clampetts often do not understand what she is talking about when she breaks into Elizabethan soliloquies…, but they do understand Miss Jane as a 'nice' person and are happy to treat her as one of their own."[36]

Yet, despite the abuse she often endures, there remains an underlying respect from everyone towards her; she's always called "Miss."[37]

In recent years, Hathaway has become a lesbian icon based, stereotypically, on her mannish appearance. But this is not evident in shows. If anything, Jane is one of TV's most lusty heterosexuals. She makes no secret of her amorous feelings for Jethro, even occasionally pouncing on him. Kulp said of her character's randiness, "She knew how absurd it all was; but she thought, 'What the hell.'"[38] And as McWilliams has pointed out, "[Miss Jane] never let her looks stand in the way of what she wanted."[39] There is something empowered about Miss Jane's wanton desires. Like Miss Brooks, Miss Jane is not interested in Jethro for intellectualism; she once described him as "a magnificent skyscraper with an uncomplicated penthouse." Rather, she's interested in her own gratification.

Actually, Miss Hathaway is about the only sexual persona in this asexual series. Jed's a content widower, and money is Mr. Drysdale's only aphrodisiac. Only "prim" Miss Jane has integrated her intellectual and sexual selves.

—◈◈◈—

More seriously, one of the most acclaimed series of the 1960s was *East Side/West Side* (1963–1964), a gritty drama about social worker Neil Brock (George C. Scott).

Many aspects of the series are noteworthy. First, with its unsentimentalized treatment of child abuse, racism, and poverty, it presented a realistic look at an America far removed from sitcoms. Secondly, Brock answered to a female boss, Frieda Hechlinger (played by Elizabeth Wilson).

Finally, co-starring with Scott was Cicely Tyson. Tyson played Brock's secretary, June Foster, with a "strong, resourceful, sharp-edged professionalism."[40] June's role extended far beyond pencil-sharpening. Said one author, "[She] fully participates in the affairs of [the] social services agency."[41] She is also shown to be unafraid to correct or criticize Brock, usually with Brock eventually admitting he's wrong.

With her role on *East Side/West Side*, Tyson became the first African American actress to have a recurring part in a primetime non-comedy.[42] She also began an acclaimed acting career highlighted by her work in *The Autobiography of Miss Jane Pittman* and *Roots*.

In the 1970s, TV secretaries of the era were a brilliant lot. And none more so than actress Marcia Wallace on *The Bob Newhart Show* (1972–1978). Wallace's character, Carol Kester (later Bondurant), worked as secretary for Newhart's character, psychologist Dr. Bob Hartley, and for dentist (and self-styled Romeo) Dr. Jerry Robinson. Wallace has said:

> I get very upset when people say, "Oh, you played that dumb secretary." Not only was Carol not a dumb secretary, but she was a pretty independent gal.... She dated and it didn't ever quite work out, but she wasn't a loser by any means and she had a life that wasn't dependent on having a man.... She became the hub of the office. She kept things going.[43]

As the "hub" of the office, Carol had to contend with both doctors' delusional pronouncements and odd patients. Luckily she could handle it. Carol had great comebacks. Consider:

PATIENT: Is Dr. Hartley free?
CAROL: No, but he's reasonable.

JERRY: I should have gone to law school.
CAROL: That's what most of your patients say.

As one author concluded, Carol seemed "always to have the upper hand in the social transactions around the office."[44] Perhaps this was because Carol was so good at her job; in one episode, she is named "Secretary of the Year" by the *Chicago Sun-Times*. In another, she is honored in a contest held by the other building secretaries.

Wallace created such an impression that years later she appeared as Carol on *Murphy Brown*, playing the one secretary Murphy didn't fire.

TV secretaries came full circle with Jennifer Marlow (played by Loni Anderson) on *WKRP in Cincinnati* (1978–1982). Essentially the continuation of Sothern's Susie, Jennifer was blond, beautiful and significantly wiser than her boss. It wasn't Jennifer who dropped live turkeys from an airplane.

Jennifer's been described as "hyper-competent."[45] McWilliams said of her, "[She was] smarter than her boss, sharper than her colleagues [and] successful in deflecting the advances of office creeps," adding that in her performance, Anderson "was a monument to impregnability and self-respect."[46]

Her impregnability and self-respect were evident in the witty ways she rebuffed the come-ons of co-worker Herb Tarlek. Jennifer also exhibited concern and empathy. When Les Nessman won a broadcasting award, Jennifer shocked everyone when she agreed to be Les' date for the dinner. She helped Herb repair a rift in his marriage. And she went to visit Herb when she learned that his "vacation" was actually a hospital stay.

Despite her beauty, Jennifer was not resented by her co-workers; she was liked by all. And like TV's great superheroines (examined later), she seemed to "own" her beauty and sexuality and, with it, her power. No man was a match for her in terms of the proficiency with which she did her job or the grace in which she conducted her life.

Another of TV's great secretarial success stories was on *Silver Spoons* (1982–1987). Erin Gray was in this sitcom about a child-like toy company exec, Edward (played by Joel Higgins), who one day learned he has a straight-laced son (played by Ricky Schroeder).

Though the character, Kate Summers, was usually referred to as a secretary, that term is incomplete. Even in the beginning, her character seemed to be more advisor than assistant. Often she was the only thing between her boss and financial disaster.

In fact, eventually in the show, Kate was named CEO. And while such extreme upward mobility is rare, in sitcoms anything is possible. Nevertheless, since Kate was played so intelligently, her ascension seemed not only plausible but appropriate.

This being TV (especially '80s TV *a la Who's the Boss?* and *Scarecrow and Mrs. King*), boss Edward and Kate had to have an undercurrent of romance between them. The two eventually started dating. They married in the 1985 season.

Several years after the series, Gray noted some viewers' unique reaction to her character:

I looked at [Kate] as a heroine.... This is a woman who went from secretary to CEO. I liked that transition. It took me five years to get there. The producers wrote that and worked with me and helped develop that. The sad commentary on that is, most of the women who came up to me saw an aspect of my character that I did not see. A lot of them would come to me and say, "So, you married the boss, huh? Good girl! We like that!" My reaction was, yes, I married the boss, but never once did it cross my mind that that's how I got to be president.... I was so disappointed that women had these thoughts. I hadn't allowed it. It came as a surprise to me.[47]

Gray's fascinating first-person experience in regard to how people — women — reacted complicates this issue of TV featuring accomplished women. What's the point if they are negated by the audience they are intended for? Does this help explain why other images of strong women, reaching back to *Our Miss Brooks*, never seem to get a fair shake?

—❧—

Throughout TV history, other female secretaries have distinguished themselves. Cara Williams was a secretary on *The Cara Williams Show* (1964), a program produced by her own production company. In it, she worked for Fenwick Diversified and made herself indispensable by devising a filing system no one else could figure out.[48]

Former film star Eleanor Parker played an executive secretary to a seldom-seen movie producer on *Bracken's World* (1969–1970). There was a TV version of *Nine to Five* (1982–1983; 1986–1988). And in an early episode of *LA Law* (1986–1994), actress Susan Rutan became a heroine to real-life secretaries when her character Roz confronted her boss and insisted on a raise. "I'm worth what I'm worth," she told him.

The Maids

Actress Esther Rolle, who played maid Florida on *Maude*, once said, "There is nothing wrong with being a maid, or a nurturer, as long as you are not stupid. These types of roles are the roles I'm interested in, those of the voiceless."[49]

The long history of sitcoms built around "the help" is a commentary on the American class struggle. It is about the revenge, or at least the triumph, of the working class against the bourgeois. While the families on *Hazel* et al. are wealthy enough to employ full-time domestics, these same people are usually helpless when it comes to raising their children and conducting their businesses. In the end, they are dependent upon the "lower-class," the supposedly less-educated Hazels to do it for them.

TV's first prominent maid was the star of *Beulah* (1950–1953). This African American maid, working for a white family, was originally heard on radio's *Fibber McGee and Molly*. After first being played by a white man(!), the radio role was later assumed by Oscar-winner Hattie McDaniel.

When the show came to TV, McDaniel did not make the transition.[50] TV's first Beulah was Ethel Waters, who would be Emmy-nominated for her work, the first African American actress ever so honored. Waters left after two years, replaced by Louise Beavers.

Like *Amos 'n' Andy, Beulah* today is a lightning rod for controversy. Beulah was certainly cast in a traditional Mammy mode: she was a robust, childless, black, working for white employers.

At the time of the original airing of *Beulah*, it was a double-edge sword for African Americans. Though the program may have often portrayed blacks in stereotypical strokes, it was no doubt positive for many black Americans to see representations of themselves in the media.

Years later when other images of African Americans existed, the NAACP campaigned to have reruns of *Beulah* removed from local stations. They were largely successful.[51]

But, in regard to *Beulah*, everything is not so black and white. Though physically Beulah may have been stereotypically conceived (Waters was allegedly ordered to gain weight for the role),[52] and the program opened with Beulah saying she's "always in the kitchen but never knows what's cookin'!," Beulah herself was not dumb. In fact, Beulah is usually the problem-solver. As Jannette Dates points out, "Beulah was central to the plot in that she guided the family to a safe conclusion, as she alone restored balance and normalcy to the household."[53]

Other authors concur. One described Beulah's employers as "fully reliant on Beulah to come to their aid, run their household, and take part in raising their son."[54] This is evident in many episodes, such as the installment where Beulah begins to worry that her bosses, Mr. and Mrs. Henderson, are growing apart. To solve this, Beulah does some careful "meddling," eventually resulting in the couple renewing their vows.

Later episodes follow this theme. In one, when the son of one of Beulah's friends starts hanging out with delinquents, Beulah's sets him straight.

Surprisingly, Beulah's altruistic nature has been criticized. Dates qualifies her earlier statement by saying, "Viewers could not conceive of Beulah wanting to be anything but what she was or of her fighting for her children to have a life more self-fulfilling than her own."[55]

But is this true? Was Beulah's life too entrenched with her employers? If so, that's a claim that can also be leveled at the title character in *Mr. Belvedere* and Mr. French of *Family Affair*. Along these same lines, series about white domestics (like Hazel) are not questioned if their leads are involved with their employing family. Are we therefore applying one standard to black women that we aren't applying to white ones?

Other details should also be pointed out. First, Beulah was shown to have a life away from her job. She had friends (such as Oriole, played by Butterfly McQueen) and she was not asexual; she had an often-seen boyfriend named Bill, owner of a fix-it shop.

Other episodes also enhance Beulah: In one, she and Mrs. Henderson participate in a local play. In another, Beulah is involved in a bidding war as someone tries to entice her from the Hendersons.

Even episodes where Beulah might, arguably, be portrayed "negatively" should first be viewed as sitcom rather than racial commentary. In one installment, Beulah mistakes a misplaced baby carriage as evidence that the Hendersons are expecting. But they aren't. Did Beulah jumps to conclusions? Yes. But such wrongful assumptions are common to comedy, from Lucy to *Three's Company*, not just ones with black female leads.

No such double standard was imposed upon Amelia "Sarge" Sergeant, the maid on *The Dennis O'Keefe Show* (1959).

O'Keefe, a former film actor, starred as newspaperman Hal, a widower. He, his son Randy and Sarge shared a penthouse apartment in New York City. Hope Emerson was Sarge. Alex McNeil described Sarge as "formidable" (and as Emerson stood 6' 2", Sarge was towering).[56]

In the home, Sarge cooked, cleaned and was "mom" for Randy. Hence, she was treated as a member of the family; she joined the family at mealtimes and called her boss "Hal."

Additionally, like many other TV "live-ins," Sarge was always around to take Hal down a notch when necessary. Though Hal was not a bumbler, he did occasionally need upbraiding. This was evident in an episode where Hal takes up with a socialite who wants him to behave more as a member of his "class" should, which to her mind involves him changing how he raises his son and treats "the help." Soon, the "new" Hal is driving everyone nuts. So Randy and Sarge plan to show Hal the level of his pretentiousness. Later, at Hal's big society party, the boy and maid adopt their own obnoxious airs. It isn't long before Hal sees the error of his ways. The socialite is soon dismissed and household harmony is restored.

If Sarge often seemed to be in charge on *Dennis O'Keefe*, she was nothing compared to the title character on *Hazel* (1961–1966). Watch any episode of Shirley Booth's series and you'll discover there's no question about who is running this household. Though the maid, Hazel ruled the roost with an attitude that was the bossiest, most opinionated and irrepressible in TV history. As TimsTV.com aptly describes the situation:

Oscar- and Tony-award winning actress Shirley Booth played irrepressible "domestic engineer" Hazel Burke on *Hazel* (1961–1966).

George Baxter [an attorney] was always in control of everything at the office, but almost nothing at home. When he returned home from the office he entered the world of Hazel. She ran the Baxter household more efficiently than George ran his office. She was always right, knew exactly what needed doing, and preempted his authority with alarming, though, justified regularity.[57]

As another author wrote, "[Hazel] is characterized as 'meddling' and as causing 'misadventure' in her attempts to run the household but ultimately it is her job to keep order—both literal and ideological—in the house."[58]

If Sarge beget Hazel, then Hazel laid the groundwork for Maude and Roseanne. In fact, in various episodes, Hazel refers to herself as a "domestic engineer," a linguistic precursor to Roseanne's "Domestic Goddess."

Hazel, along with superlative cooking and child-care skills, is also a good baseball and pool player, golfer and bowler who repeatedly trounces the men in her league. She was also strong in spirit. In one episode, Hazel, over the objections of her boss Mr. B (as she calls him), invites a parolee to stay in "her" home because she *knows* she can rehabilitate him. In another, Hazel and a friend are taken hostage by gangsters. In the end, the mob is no match for Hazel. Ordered to make breakfast, she slips tranquilizers into their eggs. When they nod off, the cops rush in.

Hazel is also portrayed as a vital and active woman. She gets gussied up (often in her prized mink stole) and goes out on dates with various gentleman.

Hazel was played by Shirley Booth, a stage legend and Oscar winner. One critic said, "Miss Booth playing Hazel is roughly tantamount to John Barrymore playing Henry Aldrich, but probably no one could do it better."[59] Booth's performance is an effervescent explosion. She is a dynamo of energy.

Over the years, Hazel has been labeled a busybody (a term almost exclusively applied to women). But what does "busybody" imply? Someone who refuses to sit on the sidelines. Hazel's so-called meddling is a quasi-feminist statement (she refuses to be silenced) and an assertion on behalf of the working class; she will not be devalued no matter what her "status."

—◦◦◦—

Another (primarily) maid character was played by Imogene Coca on *Grindl* (1963–1964).

Coca was already a TV legend thanks to *Your Show of Shows*. In *Grindl*, the actress' second sitcom,[60] she played a maid-nanny–Jill-of-All-Trades hired weekly by different employers. The premise was perfect for Coca's ability to comedically reinvent herself (not unlike the mythical creature with whom her character shared a name).

Grindl wasn't as brazen as Hazel. (Who was?) But she was no wimp. In the opening credits we see Grindl bang her umbrella on a car when it nearly runs her over in the cross-walk. In one episode, in typical Cold War TV fashion, Grindl gets embroiled with some Russian spies. On her job, she and the seven-year-old she's taking care of get kidnapped by enemy agents anxious for some rocket fuel the boy's father has invented.

Smart in her predicament, Grindl doesn't panic or endanger her charge. If anything, she's resourceful, tricking her Russian captors into letting her and the boy wait out the eve-ning in the boy's bedroom while the goons wait downstairs for the parents. Upstairs, Grindl ties sheets into a rope so they can lower themselves from the window.

After some slapstick, the spies get eliminated by an explosion that levels the house — but not Grindl or the boy. Afterwards, Grindl is hailed as a hero and honored by the U.S. government.

—◦◦◦—

The same year as *Grindl*, a different maid, more sentimental than slapstick, also arrived.

Inspired by the 1947 film, TV's *The Farmer's Daughter* (1963–1966) told of Katy Hol-strum (played by Inger Stevens), a Minnesota farm girl with a Norwegian accent who goes to work as a governess for widowed Congressman Glen Morley (played by William Windom).

As anyone familiar with TV knows, the governess-boss relationship was just backdrop for a serio-comic romance destined to end in marriage. This sort of set-up reoccurs often, as in *The Nanny* where the accents were different but the outcome the same.

From early in *The Farmer's Daughter*, love was in the air, even if neither of the two principals recognize it. After two seasons, the two tied the knot.

Even before the marriage, however, Katy and the Congressman's relationship, even as "employer" and "employee," was depicted as one of equals. Each morning Katy sits at the breakfast table next to her boss and his mother (the latter played by the regal Cathleen Nesbitt).

Even on her way to the altar, Katy was not depicted as "husband-hunting." In one episode she ends a date (with guest star Peter Graves) early when she finds she's more knowledgeable about political issues than he.

Another telling episode is "Behind the Man." In it, the Congressman gives an interview where he reveals too much about his dependence on Katy for legislative suggestions. The press picks up on this and Katy's fame bruises the Congressman's ego. Morley is even too wounded to listen to Katy's good ideas regarding a new working mother's bill ... until Katy devises a way for him to hear her out.

Inger Stevens, the lead of *The Farmer's Daughter*, brought poise to her role as the farm girl-cum-governess-cum-political wife. McWilliams has dubbed Stevens the most "serenely beautiful woman to ever grace a sitcom"[61] and her exceeding serenity places her within the company of Elizabeth Montgomery and Ann Sothern. Panic did not become them. And why should it? Especially when they are more savvy than the men around them.

—⟨∾∾⟩—

Another refined nanny arrived five years later. Inspired no doubt by *Mary Poppins*, Juliet Mills was a most unusual nanny on *Nanny and the Professor* (1970–1971). Though this nanny couldn't fly, that didn't mean she wasn't like Poppins. Like Julie Andrews' character (or years later ABC's real-life Supernanny), television's Nanny Figalilly had a crisp English accent and an old-fashioned air. Certainly her blue cape and rain hat bespoke of a prior time. And like Poppins, this nanny possessed some mysterious skills.

First, quite inexplicably, Nanny Phoebe arrived on this family's doorstep unannounced — and in the nick of time. Mr. Everett, a widower father of three, had just had his fifth nanny quit over frustration with his brood.

Immediately upon her arrival, this new nanny manages to charm everyone. And mysterious things start to happen:

- It seems Nanny always knows who's at the door or on the phone long before anyone answers them. (A little bell — that only the audience can hear — alerts us that something magical has just occurred.)
- Thanks to his father's old telescope and Nanny's special touch, one of the little boys makes an amazing discovery.
- When daughter Prudence and the professor both want something (a role in the school play for her, a new job hire for him), Nanny wishes upon a star and utilizes "pixie powers" to make everything come out okay.

Then things get odder: In one episode, Nanny's radio starts playing programs from the 1930s. In another, her passport is discovered and it lists her age as 107!

Nanny was always cagey regarding its mysticism, leaving it up to the characters (and the viewers) to try to figure it all out.

But regardless of whatever abilities Nanny might have had, she was still a pretty neat lady, always doing the right thing. In one episode, she works to protect a wilderness area. In another, she helps an eccentric recluse re-enter the world.

—⟨∾∾⟩—

Quite different from Nanny Figalilly, yet of the Hazel archetype, was Alice, the maid for TV's *The Brady Bunch* (1969–1974).

Adored by Gen X, Alice (played by Ann B. Davis) is a vital member of this blended family. After all, how many families take their maid on vacations like the Bradys always did? The Bunch wouldn't be the Bunch without her.

Among other traits, Alice often served as the only civil link between the girls and the boys whenever the house divided by gender, which was often. For example, in the episode about trading stamps, it is Alice who holds the family's many books until an agreement is reached. Later, it's Alice who comes up with the idea of a gender-neutral building of a house of cards to settle the problem.

Alice is also a great problem-solver. In one episode, Alice is the linchpin in solving the case of Carol's missing earrings (after Cindy had borrowed them without asking). And Alice got Greg off the hook when he was discovered with cigarettes.

As TVAcres.com puts it, "Alice is there to lend a hand, console a troubled child or serve coffee or a midnight snack to her employers when they can't sleep or arrive home from some social function."[62] Interestingly, though childless herself, Alice seems to understand child psyches. In retrospect it seems no accident that she is the center square in the series' opening grid of faces.

Throughout the series, Alice remains happy and content, secure in the knowledge that she's good at her job. In one episode, she says, "I can take care of this house standing on my head." Alice is also a peerless (and busy) cook. Once, when Mrs. Brady asked what they'd do without her, Alice replies, "Probably eat out."

But Alice has other talents too. In one episode, we learn she's a skilled bowler (like aproned sister Hazel). In another, she wins a jingle-writing contest. And Alice isn't asexual. Though over forty, she has an ongoing relationship with Sam the butcher. Yet, solid as they are, neither seems anxious for marriage.

Between Sam, Mr. and Mrs. Brady and her Bunch, Alice has crafted for herself a pseudo-family. Like the Bradys themselves, her "family" is one joined by love, not biology. Her blending into this already blended family seems to prefigure Mary Richards' later "What is a family?" speech to her workplace "family" in the final episode of *Mary Tyler Moore* in 1977.

—◦◦◦—

Another type of blended family, and a far more serious treatment of the "domestic," arrived in the U.S. via PBS in the early 1970s.

Upstairs, Downstairs (1971–1975) told the stories of two "families" who resided in London at the turn of the 20th century. Though the lives of the two "families" constantly intersected, *Upstairs, Downstairs* was a series about different worlds — the upper class and the lower class.

The series was the idea of British actresses Jean Marsh (who played maid Rose) and Eileen Atkins. Both women had had a parent, as they say in England, "in service." Marsh said, "People never seemed to write intelligent parts for servants in plays, so Eileen and I thought that it would be a nice idea…."[63]

When *Upstairs, Downstairs* arrived in America via *Masterpiece Theatre*, it became one of the most successful series in public TV history. Its success was in keeping with 1970s' audience's preferences for working class shows (*All in the Family* et al.) and historic dramas (*The Waltons* et al.).

In *Upstairs, Downstairs*, the two families were the "upstairs" Bellamy family and the "downstairs" servants. The Bellamys were wealthy and connected by blood and money and anchored by patriarch Richard. The "downstairs" "family" consisted of a multi-generational group of servants who served the Bellamys and were headed by butler Hudson. In contrast to those above-stairs, the below-stairs family is linked only by common employment — and their lower station. And yet they did have cohesiveness; in one installment they all sit down to Christmas dinner.

Like U.S. programs about servants, *Upstairs, Downstairs* was a story of classes, only this time with the line between "us" and "them" more deeply drawn. The lovable overbearing nature of Hazel would not have been tolerated. Which is not to say that early blows in class war didn't occur. In the premiere, new maid Sarah threw the gauntlet on her first day by knocking on the front door, not the servants' entrance!

Throughout the series, the Bellamys are frequently portrayed as miserable — drowning in their personal problems and wary of social-climbing outsiders. They are also helpless without their servants. This aspect of the series, this topsy-turvy-ness, where the lower class actually has the upper hand, is best illustrated via the character of Rose. She's portrayed as wise, and her young mistress Elizabeth thinks nothing of seeking advice from her. In one episode, Rose warns "Miss Lizzie" that her new gentleman caller will want his "pound of flesh." Later, Elizabeth concedes that Rose was right.

Episodes occasionally focused solely on the lives of those downstairs. In one installment, Rose is almost spirited away by a handsome sheep farmer from Australia, a country that he assures her is less class-conscience than England. Though Rose eventually rejects life "down under," her near-departure conveys to the Bellamys that there is more to the people below-stairs than they thought. Their servants have dignity and dreams all their own.

—◊◊◊—

Esther Rolle's legendary Florida Evans was originally introduced on *Maude* (1972–1978). As forceful as Hazel but with greater social awareness, Florida was one of the few *Maude* characters who could butt heads with Bea Arthur's lead. As McWilliams wrote of Rolle-Florida, "As [Maude] strained to prove her Democratic credentials, Rolle peered over the cake tin and smirked."[64]

As in *Hazel*, the dynamic of who was boss and who was employee was often inverted. In Florida's first episode, as if to prove her liberal modernism (or relieve her guilt), Maude goes out of her way to make her new black maid feel "at home." When Florida arrives, Maude panders to her with all sorts of out-of-touch good intentions. Maude tells Florida that unlike other maids, she will use the front door, not the back; she will eat meals with the family, not in the kitchen; and she will join the family for their afternoon cocktails. But Florida isn't interested. She explains she'll use the back door because it's closer to the garage; that she prefers to eat alone; and that she doesn't believe in drinking midday. Later, the two ladies exchange this dialogue:

FLORIDA: Now, the first week'll be on a trial basis.
MAUDE: Oh, Florida, don't be ridiculous — you're not on trial.
FLORIDA: I know —*you* are.

That sort of interaction — Florida as the voice of bottom-line realism — would remain throughout her time on the series. But before Rolle came to *Maude*, she repeatedly spoke of bringing authenticity to working-class characters. The actress said, "I refuse to believe that there's any role that can't be played with some dignity. I don't do roles that I believe are derogatory…. Florida was an upward striver, and she's still viable today."[65]

—⁓—

From the fertile ground of *All in the Family*—which had spawned *Maude*—came *The Jeffersons* (1975–1985), a series with its own maid character every bit as plain-spoken as Florida. *The Jeffersons* told of an upwardly mobile African American couple who moved out of working-class Queens and into a high-rise apartment in Manhattan.

The Jeffersons ran for a decade. And while the boastful George Jefferson and his wife Louise were in the title, the series also featured their sharp-tongued[66] maid Florence (played by Marla Gibbs, who had "the most beautifully timed wisecracks this side of Eve Arden"[67]).

Like Florida, Florence served as this series' voice of reality, there to puncture the ego of her employer, Mr. Jefferson. Joe Garner elaborates:

> Florence had no tolerance for her undersized, overbearing boss and would pass up no opportunity to go toe to toe with him. In fact, a good deal of the show's comedy emanated from them — the arrogant uppity boss who demanded deference from someone he'd like to feel superior to, and the employee who refused to let him forget from whence he came.[68]

Regularly, Florence got the last word.

Since Florence was such a consistent laugh-getter, it's easy to forget other details about her. In one episode we learn that Florence is the head of her labor union. In another, she demands that Mr. Jefferson offer her a pension. In another, we discover a different side to Florence when, one morning, Louise and George discover a man in their kitchen; it turns out he's a "friend" of Florence's who has spent the night.

Florence was portrayed as a smart, mature woman. And though she was black and a maid, her working for a black family sidestepped the criticism that haunted *Beulah* and others. (In other words, the type of criticism that reappeared with *Gimme a Break* in 1981.)

Nell Carter was a Tony Award winner before she came to TV as Nell Harper on *Gimme a Break* (1981–1987). In it, as Jannette Dates points out, "Carter's own strong personality was quite evident in the program, for Nell, the performer and the character, was always in control."[69]

Yet, in the series, since Carter was a live-in housekeeper for a white family (a widower father and his three daughters) and since Carter was African American and overweight, her sitcom was accused of racism. The controversy begs a question: Can an African American actress who *happens* to be overweight ever play a maid and not be a "Mammy"? Should all African American actresses (unless Ally McBeal–thin) turn down these roles? Such a request is not something asked of white actresses.

At times, *Gimme a Break* addressed its critics. Perhaps the most overt moment was in an episode in which Telma Hopkins debuted as Nell's childhood friend Addie, now an upwardly mobile lawyer. Addie had come to town to reunite with Nell. Addie arrives at the home of the Kaniskys (the family Nell works for) only to learn that Nell's at the Laundromat. As she waits for Nell's return, Addie talks about the achievements of modern black women: "[I'm] not that special. I'm only one of thousands of today's black women who are out there making it. It wasn't easy, but thank God, we finally put to rest that old stereotypical image of the black woman as nothing but an Aunt Jemima."

Cue Nell, who bursts through the front door, laundry basket in hand, red kerchief on head. "I'm home!" she yells.

As the two characters reconnect and then spar, they hash out many of the criticisms that had been lodged at the show itself. Was Nell a "sellout" for doing a job that many consider stereotypical but which she found meaningful?

Hopkins became a permanent member of the show's cast and the ying to Carter's yang in a Lucy and Ethel sense and also in defusing some of the alleged one-sidedness in terms of its depictions.

—◦◈◦—

Other TV maids who have mattered over the years have included Mary Wickes' Martha, working for a "retired" opera star (Ezio Pinza) on *Bonino* (1953); Louise Beavers and later Amanda Randolph working for Danny Thomas on *Make Room for Daddy* (1953–1964); Nancy Walker's Mildred, a "wisecracking, acid-tongued, sarcastic woman"[70] and housekeeper on *McMillan and Wife* (1971–1977); and Elizabeth Pena in *I Married Dora* (1987–1988). Collectively, they laid the groundwork for such latter "domestic divas" as Fran Drescher in *The Nanny* (1993–1999) and Conchata Ferrell's Berta on *Two and a Half Men* (2003–).

The Waitresses

Even in the nicest of establishments, being a waitress isn't glamourous. Waiting tables means all day on your feet, working for less than minimum wage and hoping that your tips make up the difference. From time to time, TV has shown us images of these blue-collar women.

It makes sense that TV's first important waitress would be on the Chicago-originated *Studs' Place* (1949–1952). The show's creator and star, Studs Terkel, is America's great oral historian and his most famous tome, *Working*, dealt with employment in America.

Terkel's early TV program was unusual: A gentle comedy-drama, it took place at a local watering hole, Studs' Place, and was largely unscripted, with the show's core cast of four improvising most dialogue.

The cast, along with Terkel (who played himself), consisted of Win Stracke as Wynn, the handyman; Chet Roble as Chet, the pianist; and Beverly Younger as the waitress, Grace. Years after the series ended, Terkel said of Younger and her role:

> [She] revolutionized the idea of a waitress. Until then, the waitress was stereotyped, gum-chewing, Brooklynese. Beverly had been an actress in stock companies, traveling week to week…. [D]uring her stock days she didn't eat in fancy hotels, she ate in diners. So there was the waitress. Someone, a mother, a woman, maybe married, maybe not. And she learned from them.[71]

TV's most famous waitress came in 1976. She would go on to dish out wit with daily specials for nine seasons — a run longer than those of *Mary Tyler Moore* and *Charlie's Angels*. And yet so many retrospectives end up ignoring *Alice* (1976–1985).

Based on the movie *Alice Doesn't Live Here Anymore*, *Alice* told of Alice Hyatt who, after her husband's death, hopes to start a new life in California as a singer. But while driving cross-country with her teenage son Tommy, their car conks out. Alice and son are forced to set up "temporary" residence in Phoenix and she gets a job as a waitress at Mel's Diner.

On TV, Alice was played by Linda Lavin. Mitz said of Lavin's performance, "[She] turned Alice into her own character — warm and witty and knowing.... She was somewhere between Mary Richards and Anne Romano; she was a reactor. She didn't do dumb things. She was sensible and calm."[72]

Though *Alice* always went for laughs — this was a sitcom — the series was realistic in its portrayal of work and home life.

Though a talented singer, Alice had few other "marketable skills," no doubt a frustration being felt by many "displaced homemakers" at the time. She needed to take whatever work was available, i.e., waitressing.

Mel's wasn't that great and Mel, the owner, though deep down kind-hearted, was notoriously cheap. Alice and her fellow waitresses lived for, and on, their tips. Alice's working conditions were not luxurious while her faded pink uniform was unflattering and her work load heavy. It took its toll; in the opening credits, we see Alice soaking her feet.

Amid criticisms that work on television is often glamorized, *Alice* took a hard look at America's minimum-wage workers. For example, Alice couldn't afford much. She didn't have a vast wardrobe nor a grand apartment; she slept on a fold-out sofa in the living room, while her son took the only bedroom.

But despite it all, Alice never got discouraged thanks to the women she worked with. Vera (played by Beth Howland) and Flo (played by Polly Holliday) were different from Alice (and each other), but were all in the same boat — having to deal with rude customers, with Mel, and trying to earn money to pay the rent. One author said of the series, "[*Alice*] guaranteed a place for groups of discontented but mutually supportive women in the sitcoms of the '80s."[73] Mitz said, "[T]he subliminal message of 'Alice' was that Sisterhood is Powerful."[74]

Frequently sisterhood was all these women had as they often stood up for themselves. In one episode, Mel hires a waiter and the women learn he's earning more than they are. Mel's reasoning for the disparity: He's a man. Forming a united front, the women walk. Of course, all is resolved by closing credits but by then Alice has made a point to her employer — and all of America.

Other issues related to work and women were also addressed. In one episode we learn that the waitresses have regularly been coming in to work for free on Sundays to clean up the store room. But that changes when Mel installs a time clock to track his waitresses' hours. Though offended by the penny-pinching, Alice, Vera and Flo obey the new rules and punch in each day. But that also means that they punch in on Sundays. When Mel later gets the reports, he fumes at having to pay overtime. But Alice, Vera and Flo stand their ground, demanding to be paid for *all* their work.

Even out of the diner, Alice was often hit with double standards. In one episode, Alice auditions for a local singing job. Though she nails her number, she doesn't get the position since management considers her "too old."

As can be discerned from these examples, for nine seasons Alice and her shifting cast[75] fought the good fight. As dismal as her day job sometimes seemed, Alice never gave up on her dream of being a singer. Later, though, she began attending night school.

The messages of *Alice* seemed to have a consciousness-raising effect on many, including the show's star. During the run of the show, Lavin emerged as an outspoken advocate for working women and for the passage of the ERA.[76]

TV's next waitresses appeared on a sitcom originally titled *It's a Living* (1980–1985). Set in a Windows on the World–type restaurant atop an LA skyscraper, the show originally starred Susan Sullivan. Sullivan left after a few episodes for *Falcon Crest* and just before ABC pulled the series for "retooling." When the show returned, it had a new title, *Making a Living*, and a new lead, ex-*Mary Hartman* star Louise Lasser.

In either incarnation, however, the breakout star was Ann Jillian, who played tough-talking sexpot Cassie. Cassie was like a sister to Jennifer of *WKRP*. Like Jennifer, Cassie was not a "dumb blonde." She had a lightning quick wit — especially when it came to putting down self-delusional piano player Sonny and icy hostess Nancy. Though the show's characters showed diversity, all had one thing in common: They needed to work. Dot was a struggling actress; Jan was a single mother who attended college during the day. Even Lois (Sullivan), a married mom with two kids, worked there to help support her family.

Despite some frothy elements, the series sometimes attempted to address larger issues. In one, Lois hesitates when her daughter invites her to her school for career day. Lois is worried she'll embarrass her daughter because she's "just a waitress" while other moms are doctors and lawyers. Ultimately, Lois realizes there's no shame in working an honest job for an honest wage.

In another episode, Jan (played by Barrie Youngfellow) finds herself going into debt. Attempting to keep her head above water, she takes on additional jobs and a day-long schedule of constant work. Soon her "foolproof" schedule falls apart, causing her to do three jobs at once — wait tables, make sales calls and sneak into the back to write out hand-calligraphied invitations. The multi-tasking doesn't sit well with boss Nancy. But what choice does Jan have? At the end of the episode, after the restaurant closes, her fellow waitresses pitch in to help Jan make her deadlines.

Another episode has hostess Nancy losing her job because she's "too old." Subsequent episodes have the waitresses taking a self-defense course and dealing with invasion of their privacy when Nancy is ordered to search their lockers.

When *It's a Living* debuted, critics who didn't ignore it lambasted it as ABC's latest T&A (the network was then airing *Three's Company*). Special contempt was shown for the ladies' allegedly low-cut uniforms.[77] Actually, though, the uniforms (which featured a skirt below the knee) showed less cleavage than Faye Emerson did in the 1950s. Here again, we have a case where, instead of focusing on what these women did or said, people preferred to focus on what they wore.

The Nurses

Long before *Nurse Jackie*, TV characters have been donning whites, strapping on stethoscopes and telling stories of life, death, medicine and miracles. Inasmuch as the nursing profession has always been and remains overwhelmingly female, it's not surprising that the majority of nurses on TV have been female. What is equally unsurprising is how stoically these women have been depicted.

Probably TV's first nurse of note was Nancy Remington (Patricia Benoit), the school nurse on the sitcom *Mr. Peepers* (1952–1955). *Mr. Peepers* told the story of a nerdy high school teacher (Wally Cox). The show was one of TV's earliest hits. But since Nancy was a supporting character — that is, until her marriage to Mr. Peepers — she didn't get much air time. When she did appear, she represented herself well. "A fine young woman, eminently worthy of marriage to the protagonist," according to the definitive work on the subject, *The Changing Image of the Nurse* by Philip A. Kalisch and Beatrice J. Kalisch.[78]

The first program to feature a nurse as a lead was *Janet Dean, Registered Nurse* (1954). It ran for one year and featured no other regular characters besides Janet. The series was conceived as a tribute to real-life nurses and, at the end of each episode, Dean would break the fourth wall to promote the profession.

Former film actress Ella Raines starred as ex-military nurse Janet Dean (Raines also produced the series with Joan Harrison), a private-duty nurse (which allowed her to take on different assignments weekly). Raines brought cool dignity to her character and, in the process, to the profession. The Kalisches sing this nurse's praises, noting she was portrayed as a "dynamic woman, a problem solver and an individual of initiative."[79]

Unlike some medical programs, *Janet* did not center on obscure medical conditions. Instead, it tended to stress interpersonal dramas. The program's weekly emphasis on patients' minds and spirits often caused Dean to do as much personal counseling as hands-on care. But in doing either, Dean proved herself a "savior and protector of the weak."[80] In one episode, Janet learns that a small boy's problems are his over-protective parents. Dean then takes it upon herself to remedy the situation.

Some episodes featured more action-oriented plots. In one, Janet bravely enters a stalled elevator, its car hanging precariously, to treat a patient inside. In another, Janet has to foil a bank robber out to kill an eyewitness — a man under Janet's care.

Among the qualities that Dean exhibited was a modern mentality. In one episode, she cares for a bigoted patient. The woman's views come out when she and Janet stare at an oil painting of one of the woman's ancestors:

> PATIENT: Miss Dean, that's the general.
> NURSE DEAN: General Stonehill?
> PATIENT: Nathaniel Stonehill, my great-great-great grandfather, seventh governor of this state, commander of the Third Continentals, twice wounded in action and three times cited for gallantry, once by General Washington himself who called him the hero of King's Point.
> NURSE DEAN: I don't wonder why you're proud of him, I would be too.
> PATIENT: They don't understand those things down in the city. Why should they? Foreign, hybrid stock.
> NURSE DEAN: What do you think most Americans are?
> PATIENT: More's the pity. We'd been better off if they'd stayed where they belonged and left the country to pure-bred Americans.
> NURSE DEAN: You mean the Indians?

With the existence of scenes like this from the 1950s, so many assumptions about how women were portrayed — and racism addressed — seem forever altered.

Another nurse of note arrived in 1955 when Frances Mercer played Ann Talbot on *Dr. Hudson's Secret Journal* (1955–1957). Kalisch and Kalisch say of this supporting character:

> [She] appeared to be the perfect nurse and ideal woman. Although she was occasionally referred to as the superintendent of nurses, in fact she was Dr. Hudson's personal assistant. Her virtues were legion: patient, discreet, attractive, competent, loyal, and devoted to Dr. Hudson. Yet she was no mere rubber stamp, and often she offered opinions contrary to Dr. Hudson's and corrected some of his temperamental excesses.[81]

In one episode, we see Hudson request that Nurse Talbot stay in the room during a doc-tor-patient consultation. We also see that Nurse Talbot is not above criticizing the doctor; she once corrected his use of "who" with "whom."

Though Kalisch and Kalisch do lament that we never see Talbot out of uniform or learn much about her home life,[82] that was customary for TV at the time. We knew little about Perry Mason or Joe Friday. It wouldn't be until later, in shows like *Hill Street Blues*, that characters' personal life — and demons — spilled over into the professional.

⎯⎯✦⎯⎯

Even in the comedies of the era, nurses were presented professionally. On *Hennesey* (1959–1962), Jackie Cooper played Lt. Charles J. "Chick" Hennesey, a young medical officer stationed in San Diego. Abby Dalton played his nurse, Martha Hale. As the Kalisches point out, Nurse Hale "never let an opportunity pass to prove her feminine prowess at outwitting [the guys]."[83]

Nor did Martha ever fail to point out sexism. In one episode, when a surgeon decides to quit practicing to move to Paris, there is suspicion among the men that his "sudden" decision is the influence of his fiancée. Luckily, Martha's there to say, "As soon as there's a woman involved, you have to make her the heavy." Later, we learn that Martha's right. It is solely the decision of the surgeon to resign. Meanwhile, we learn that his fiancée, though supportive, is troubled by his retiring.

Dalton's role on *Hennesey* would beget a career of playing straightforward women. She'd continue in this vein as the wife of the title character on *Barney Miller* (in the pilot of that series) and then as Julia Cumson on *Falcon Crest*.

⎯⎯✦⎯⎯

Even with Janet Dean, etc., for nurses on TV, past was prologue for what the Kalisches call the "single best image of the professional nurse in television history."[84] This program, the hour-long drama *The Nurses* (1962–1965), focused on the lives of two women at fictional Alden Hospital: nursing vet Liz Thorpe (played by Shirl Conway) and her young charge Gail Lucas (played by Zina Bethune). Twenty years before *Cagney & Lacey*, *The Nurses* was the first television program to co-star two women in leading roles.

The Nurses was exemplary in its treatment of the profession. According to the Kalisches, "[N]urses and nursing emerged in a positive but not exaggerated light. Most of the nurse characters demonstrated balanced, well-rounded personalities.... The nurses were problem solvers. Rather than waiting for a physician to arrive on the scene and deliver an order, nurses identified problems and found solutions."[85]

Nurse Thorpe was the consummate professional, adept in her field and with her pri-orities straight. For her, patient care came first, even if that meant disagreeing with a (male) doctor. In one episode, when a female narcoleptic is being treated and the doctors can't determine if her illness is psychosomatic or something else, Nurse Thorpe lectures a physi-cian, "[We] took her on because she was an interesting case. The hospital has no right to lose interest now without helping her a little bit."

As played by Conway, Thorpe had a knowledgeable calm about her as well as weariness, understandable for someone who's been on her feet for eight hours. Conway made her char-acter heroic and realistic.

Nurse Thorpe was also portrayed as an advisor to Nurse Lucas. As in other TV medical dramas like *Dr. Kildare*, *The Nurses* was built around a mentor-student dynamic. Though Nurse Lucas was new to the field, she was never afraid to stand up for herself. In one episode, when an injured infant arrives at the hospital, Gail suspects abuse but the treating physician refuses to acknowledge that well-off parents could harm their child. Lucas keeps pushing until the doctor tells her to be quiet. Gail responds, "Don't try it! Don't try and say 'Nurse' and expect me to fall two paces to the rear and say, 'Yes, doctor'!"[86]

In another episode, Gail is dating an intern. Though they are smitten with each other, Gail's manner is troublesome to him. At one point, frustrated with him, she asks, "What do you expect from me, doctor? Just moonlight rides and giggles?" She goes on to state she's "not playing the husband game."[87]

In the tradition of the golden age of TV, *The Nurses* was forward and fearless in addressing an assortment of social and political issues, including the death penalty, abortion (ten years before Roe v. Wade), euthanasia, domestic violence, and substance abuse.[88] In one episode, Nurse Lucas is attacked and nearly raped. Hospital authorities refuse to give credence to her story, going so far as to suggest "she asked for it."[89]

Though well-done and well-reviewed, *The Nurses* faced problems for being what it was. Built as it was around two women, the program proved a tough sell to male viewers who were then TV's most desired audience. Ratings remained tepid, so in 1965 the show was overhauled. Two male doctors were added and the name of the show changed to *The Doctors and the Nurses*. Why the guys were added seems obvious: to create an equal ratio of men to women in the cast and attract more male viewers.

The changes did not go uncriticized by *TV Guide* (who had twice put the series on its cover). They wrote, "Out of sheer diplomacy, I think it should be called *The Nurses and the Doctors*. The producers have made a lot of money out of the nursing profession, and it would have been more politic to give the nurses top billing."[90]

But even after the changes, the women were not shunted aside. In the first episode of season three, Nurse Lucas implores a physician to report a case of child abuse even if it does risk his career. In another, "The Witnesses," a deranged police officer kills two men in a bar and seizes Liz as a hostage.

The Doctors and the Nurses would last just one year.

In the drama *The Nurses* (1962–1965), Zina Bethune and Shirl Conway played RNs Gail Lucas and Liz Thorpe, respectively. Their series presented a realistic portrayal of the medical profession and the women in it.

Julia Baker, the lead character of the comedy *Julia* (1968–1971), was also a nurse. Yet this detail usually takes second priority to another factor: Julia was black.

The debut of *Julia* marked the first time an African American woman was seen regularly on TV in a non-stereotypical role (i.e., not a maid). In fact, it was the first time an African American of either gender was seen in a solo leading role.

In many histories, *Julia* is often written off as a series that, despite a black lead, held no political viewpoint, a program that could just as easily have starred a white actress. Even the authors of *The Complete Directory to Prime Time Network TV Shows* recall the series as "more notable for its casting than its content."[91]

But, again, memory does not serve. Many episodes of the series address race in an upfront manner:

- In one episode, Julia's son Corey meets a young girl (played by Jodie Foster) while playing. The little girl invites Corey to her birthday party. Corey accepts. When Julia drops Corey off at the girl's home and is greeted by the girl's mother, it becomes clear that the mother didn't know Corey was black. When Julia returns later to pick him up, the mother "compliments" Julia on her son's manners and his ability to "fit in with other children." It's an awkward exchange. Julia later comments to her friend Marie that the woman at the party "was sincere. A little too sincere, if you know what I mean."
- Julia gets set up on a blind date and when her date arrives he bumps into one of Julia's neighbors. Later, he complains about the "color scheme" of Julia's building: "too white." This leads to an conversation with Julia eventually accusing him of reverse bigotry. She states, "I'm prejudiced ... against prejudice."
- Julia's son and Marie's son want to earn extra money. Marie suggests they do shoeshines. The children do a brisk business until Julia finds out and confronts a confused Marie. Julia explains that she will not have her son shining shoes; it's a throwback to a time when many black men could find no work *but* shining shoes for white men. But the two ladies talk and soon realize that jobs don't have prejudices, only people have prejudices.

Despite these incidents, Julia was still criticized — even for her single mom status (her husband had died in Vietnam) which supposedly supported preconceptions about "absent" black fathers. But star Diahann Carroll pointed out that Doris Day and Hope Lange (on *The Ghost and Mrs. Muir*) were widowed mothers on their shows and no one was challenging them.[92]

The program was also attacked for its "unrealistic" portrayal of black America. Before *Julia*'s debut, critic Robert Lewis Shayon wrote that the show was "a far, far cry from the bitter realities of Negro life in the urban ghetto, the pit of America's explosion potential."[93] And *Time* said, "[Julia] would not recognize a ghetto if she stumbled into it, and she is, in every respect save color, a figure in a white milieu."[94]

Even Julia's home and wardrobe were taken to task. According to some, her apartment was too large, her off-duty wardrobe too fancy. (Though as a full-time nurse and a war widow entitled to a military pension, Julia's salary certainly placed her in the middle class.)

The program was never able to appease its many critics. As Carroll would relate later, though *Julia* was "not conceived as a documentary," the burden took its toll on producer Hal Kanter and on her. Carroll saw her weight drop to 99 pounds as she weathered the storm.[95] Finally, at the end of season three, she chose not to return.

While *Julia* is mostly remembered for desegregating primetime, the program is also interesting in terms of gender.[96] First, Julia was unabashedly on her own. She never had a regular man nor any overzealous mother. Though her boss Dr. Chegley and fellow nurse Hannah could be viewed as quasi-parents, they were not intrusive. And when they did cross a line, Julia put them in their place as in one episode where Chegley has gone behind Julia's back to get her a deal on a car. When Julia finds out, she informs him that she doesn't need help.

Secondly, Julia's need to work full time *and* raise her son (in contrast to, say, Lucy Carmichael's ability to stay home) echoed an increasing number of families — mainly headed by women — who were also facing these same concerns. There are even episodes concerning Julia's attempt to secure an affordable, responsible sitter for her son, echoing the daycare dilemma often faced by working families.

In the end, there are a myriad of messages to *Julia*, both race- and gender-related. And though, in regard to either, the show may not have been any more overtly feminist than it was a voice for civil rights, it was certainly far more than it is usually remembered as.

—✧✧✧—

Even today *Marcus Welby, MD* (1969–1976) seems to be TV's definitive medical series. Debuting in 1969, *Welby* was a huge hit, becoming ABC's biggest hit up to that time and their first number one show ever.

Robert Young played Dr. Welby and brought to the series the same fatherly warmth he had in *Father Knows Best*. The father-doctor connection was one the series encouraged. Rather than working out of a clinical hospital, Welby worked from home. (In fact, the home exterior was the one used on *Leave It to Beaver*, now only more verdant.)

In the show, Dr. Welby was partnered with a young protégé, a recent medical grad (played by James Brolin) who functioned as a sort of pseudo-son. Elena Verdugo played Consuelo Lopez, Dr. Welby's "mature and efficient" nurse.[97] Kalisch and Kalisch describe the character as "friendly, enormously valued by her employers, skilled and interested in their patients … with a moderately active social life, … always open to new friendships and experiences."[98]

Verdugo, formerly of *Meet Millie*, worked hard to see to it that Consuelo was not a stereotype or, as the Hispanic actress put it, a "mamacita."[99] Said producer David Victor, "I assured her that she was going to [play] a very intelligent, well-versed character who was not going to 'Yes, master' the doctor and was able to tell him to go to hell if she had to."[100]

Verdugo got her way. She eventually created such an impression that soon she was as much a star of the series as Young and heartthrob Brolin. Consuelo sometimes took center stage. In one episode, her character undergoes a hysterectomy. In another, she deals with the death of her mother. We also learn during the series that Consuelo originally dreamed of being a doctor but, since her family couldn't afford it, she became a nurse instead.

Verdugo's visibility on the show brought with it results. Over the years, according to Verdugo, many women told her they pursued a nursing career because of her. During its airing, Verdugo was also recognized by the American Society of Medical Assistants.[101]

—✧✧✧—

Though not a medical drama *per se*, one of the great nurse images of the '70s came via the cop drama *The Rookies* (1972–1976) and its character of Nurse Jill Danko (played by Kate Jackson), wife of rookie officer Mike Danko.

Originally the series was to focus on three young male police officers, but Jackson exuded so much vitality she soon became the show's breakout star, regularly receiving more fan mail than her co-stars. Producer Aaron Spelling soon started granting more airtime to his newly minted name. As Jackson has said, "I would have more to do when the scripts called for me to be kidnapped, which happened often."[102]

True, for drama, Jill often found herself held hostage but, when she did, she never dissolved into a weepy mess. Rather, she always remained collected, often taking part in her rescue. Consider:

- Some gangsters seize an operating room during surgery. Danko is there. While the male surgeon and others retreat, Jill emerges as a leader. Later, she engineers a plan to smuggle one of the Rookies into the OR by disguising him as an intern.
- When a strung-out drug addict storms the hospital demanding methadone and holds Jill at gunpoint, her quick thinking defuses the situation.

But it didn't take Jill being kidnapped to illustrate how smart she was. In innumerable episodes she is a pivotal part of cases; she is the fourth Rookie. Repeatedly, Jill is consulted on any cases with medical overtones. Often she is called upon to uncover medical evidence in order to catch a criminal. And she's always there to nurse any of the Rookies when they get injured.

This is not to say Jill was "soft." In one episode, Jill believes that a police captain is subjecting officers to unnecessary danger. After treating an officer, the captain comes in asking if the officer will be okay. "I'd have said 'yes,' until you came in," Jill replies.

With all this, why isn't Jill better remembered? Perhaps Jackson's follow-up success on *Charlie's Angels* has caused Danko to be dwarfed. Perhaps because the show was *The Rookies*, and not *The Rookies + 1*, it's easy to forget what an important part of it Jill was.

—⁂—

Then there was *M*A*S*H* (1972–1983).

In its early years *M*A*S*H* didn't always do well by its women characters. Except for Major Margaret Houlihan, none were ever featured prominently beyond being a cute Army bunny there for Hawkeye to hit on.

Even Houlihan was originally depicted as very unlikable: short-tempered, loud, and so by-the-book that it undermined any compassion. Then, to add insult to injury, she was saddled with the nickname "Hot Lips" (carried over from the movie *M*A*S*H*), a moniker that was, we assume, ironic.

Nevertheless, no one ever questioned Houlihan's abilities. Critic Marvin Kitman praised the "professionalism" that actress Loretta Swit brought to her character.[103] And of all the series' primary characters, it is Houlihan who takes the war most seriously, never turning the OR into a theater of dark-humored schtick. Though she was tough on the women under her command, deep down she knew what really mattered. She said of her nurses, "They're terribly unruly and undisciplined and I thank God for each and every one of them when those casualties roll in."

*M*A*S*H* was on for over a decade. The show is perhaps the best example of a series whose characters evolved. With time, Radar grew into a man and Klinger dropped the dresses. But the most significant change was in Houlihan, who became much more multi-dimensional after she dumped Frank Burns and married and divorced a philandering fellow officer.

Swit had an understanding of her character that allowed her to inhabit Houlihan's many sides. She said, "I find her terribly *human*. That's really the most endearing quality Margaret has."[104] One author summarizes the development of the character while placing it within a historical context:

> Through inner development brought about by her marriage, subsequent divorce, and the painful process of reconciling her strong passions with an understanding of the authentic human communication of love, she matures as the series unfolds through the years. The series writers increasingly shift our attention to Margaret's function as a paraprofessional, highly skilled nurse and generally effective administrator as the drive in the United States for the passage of the Equal Rights Amendment intensifies. Thus, the two times are intertwined — 1970s values are successfully implanted in the social relations of the 1950s.[105]

In the early 1980s, Michael Learned, formerly of *The Waltons*, returned to TV as Mary Benjamin, RN, on *Nurse* (1981–1983).

Based upon the book by Peggy Anderson, the series told of middle-aged Mary Benjamin, who returned to her nursing career after the death of her doctor husband. She was described in a press release as "not only a nurse but a mature, attractive woman alone in the big city after a long and happy marriage."[106]

Despite Mary's years out of nursing, when she returned, her reputation preceded her. She was remembered and treated as an exceptional RN. In the first episode, she's made head nurse for one of the floors, overseeing all care and supervising both veteran RNs and young aides who respect her experience.

Along with her duties, Mary was often called upon to run interference with doctors. This was especially true with Dr. Adam Rose, a mercurial sort played by Robert Reed. (No more Mr. Brady!) Throughout the series, Rose and Mary frequently butted heads but there was always respect between them. Refreshingly, there was never any hint of romance between the two.

The Kalisches say of *Nurse*, "[T]he image of the profession was overwhelmingly positive without being romanticized or distorted."[107] *Nurse* steered clear of soap opera and never delved that deeply into personal lives. In fact, it only peripherally examined Mary's non-hospital hours. Instead, episodes focused on real medical issues like reproductive choice, dying with dignity, and anorexia. In all of them, Benjamin played a vital part in their on-air resolution.

Much of the program's believability was thanks to Learned, who brought the same sort of stoic intelligence to this role as she had to Mrs. Walton. In the process, she gave TV another great image.

From the same team that had ushered in *Hill Street Blues*, TV's most acclaimed police show, came the esteemed hospital drama *St. Elsewhere* (1982–1988).

Set at the fictional St. Eligius (nicknamed "St. Elsewhere") in Boston, the series brought to the airwaves a collective of strong female characters, both doctors and nurses. Chief among them was Nurse Helen Rosenthal, perhaps TV's most direct descendant of *The Nurses'* Liz Thorpe.

Christina Pickles played the role and McWilliams is a fan, describing the character (and Pickles' performance) as "supremely intelligent": "Though far from impervious to the chaos of St. Eligius, she isn't overwhelmed either — she's a professional.... A working mother who can assert her identity without losing her femininity (she's smarter than her male colleagues)."[108]

One of the show's few characters to remain for its full duration (and only woman), Nurse Rosenthal, in six seasons, ably dealt with: Leading her fellow nurses on a strike and fighting her own breast cancer. Though the program would often embrace eccentricities, Nurse Rosenthal remained real. Unlike many of her co-workers who often engaged in work-related romances (a prelude to the sex-crazy ways of *Grey's Anatomy*), Rosenthal always put professionalism and patients first.

———✶✶✶———

Beginning in the late '80s, the comedy *Empty Nest* (1988–1995) featured Nurse LaVerne Todd. Though played for laughs, she nevertheless emerged as a no-nonsense, capable, and highly professional RN.

Played with Southern fury by Park Overall, LaVerne managed "her" medical office with a hand that was soft with patients and tough on her boss. She regularly ordered around her superior, Dr. Weston (played by Richard Mulligan), a man who seemed generally intimidated by her.

Said one author about Laverne, "[She was] a nurse with attitude, an Ozark-accented, outspoken, but highly efficient professional who sometimes treated Dr. Weston like his youthful patients."[109]

LaVerne showed just how seriously she took her work in one episode, a hysterical takeoff on *An Officer and a Gentleman*. In it, LaVerne (in full Lou Gossett mode) must oversee the final training of Nurse Cobb, a newly graduated male nurse played by Phil Hartman. Their first meeting begins civilly enough but then LaVerne lets him know she means business:

> LaVerne: Well, it's gonna be a real pleasure workin' with you... *Now fall in, you slimy worm*! I can't believe what they done sent me — a boy nurse. You think I'm gonna be easy on you 'cause you ain't got darts on your blouse. You think that, don't you, boy?!
> Cobb: No, I — I don't think you understand —
> LaVerne: "You"?! The ewe is a female sheep. Is that what you think I am, boy?

Due to LaVerne's tough-love embodiment of the profession, during the series, Overall was often honored by various nursing organizations around the country and bestowed with certificates and awards.[110]

Other notable nurses included Julie London on *Emergency!* (1972–1977); Mary Wickes on *Doc* (1975–1976); Mary McCarthy and Madge Sinclair on *Trapper John, MD* (1979–1986); Conchata Ferrell (before *Two and a Half Men*) as the aptly named Nurse Thor on a sitcom called *E/R* (1984–1985); and Mary Ellen Walton (Judy Norton-Taylor) in the last seasons of *The Waltons* (1972–1981).

The Doctors

Though, as in real life, female physicians on TV may be less prevalent than female nurses, that doesn't mean that they do not, and have not, existed.

Almost unbelievably, TV's first notable female doctor appeared in 1952 and 1953: The New York–produced *City Hospital* starred stage actress Ann Burr as Dr. Kate Morrow. Then, in the early 1960s, *Ben Casey* (1961–1966) featured a female doctor, anesthesiologist Dr. Maggie Graham, played by Bettye Ackerman.

Originally, Dr. Graham was to act as a low-key romantic partner for Dr. Casey (Vince Edwards). But despite this prescribed relationship, Dr. Graham was not relegated to just a shadow character. In fact, she was often seen as the calm, wise voice of this series, almost as much a mentor to Casey as Dr. Zorba, his fatherly supervisor. In an episode where Casey is butting heads with an intern, Dr. Graham straightens him out:

> GRAHAM: Why don't you get off his back?
> CASEY: Get off his back?! What has he been doing, crying his heart out to you?
> GRAHAM: Nothing of the kind. You're supposed to be his friend. Why don't you act like one?
> CASEY: We're supposed to act like doctors. This is a hospital, not the Southside Boys' Club.
> GRAHAM: So, you're a chief resident. You've got responsibilities. Does that mean you can't treat your staff members like human beings?

Another female TV physician was June Lockhart as Dr. Janet Craig on CBS' *Petticoat Junction* (1963–1970). Lockhart, whose *Lost in Space* ended the year before, joined *Petticoat Junction* in 1968 after the death of Bea Benaderet.

Though *Petticoat* was not known for its social statements, it could not introduce a female MD into this small-town microcosm without touching on sexism. Hence, when Craig first arrived in Hooterville, its residents — especially the older menfolk — didn't take to the "lady doctor." But, in time, she managed to win them over with warmth, professionalism ... and her cooking. In fact, soon Dr. Craig was fully accepted as a beloved community member. So much so that, in subsequent installments, when Dr. Craig considers leaving (the first time to be with a new suitor, the second to work with a well-known neurologist), the citizens pull out all the stops to get her to stay.

For the town, it's good she didn't leave. They needed her. In one episode she's able to cure Uncle Joe, though he's the town's last hold-out in accepting her. In another, she brings modern medicine to a hillbilly family who are resistant to doctors.

Ralph Levy, director for the series, has praised Lockhart and the sensibility she brought to her role: "[She possesses] the one-sensible person quality.... [An] image of beautiful stability — a warm, mature but still beautiful woman surrounded by nuts."[111]

TV's first series built solely around a female physician was *Julie Farr, MD* (1978–1979). Dr. Farr first appeared in TV movies (*Having Babies* and *Having Babies II*) before getting her own series. In the movies, Julie specialized in pediatrics; in the series, she became head of a hospital's internal medicine unit.

As with *Nurse*, *Farr* often addressed personal, medical and ethical issues. The series even courted controversy as in an episode where a rumor spreads that Julie and another female doctor are lovers. When Julie hears the gossip, her concern is not for herself but how this unfactual information might affect the other doctor. In this episode, sisterhood really was powerful; even on the brink of becoming victims of gossip mongers, a female professional is looking out for another.

Actress Susan Sullivan, who had bounced around on screen (in *Rich Man, Poor Man* and *The Incredible Hulk*), took on the series' title role having first appeared in one of the movies. As Sullivan would show later on *Falcon Crest*, she's an intelligent, sophisticated actress and she imbued her character with those same qualities, making Farr an effective healer.

—◦◦◦—

Other female physicians have also appeared over the years. On the western *The Road West* (1966–1967), Kathryn Hays was featured as a kind of *de facto* doctor: Her character, Elizabeth Reynolds, was a doctor's daughter and had absorbed much medical knowledge. Throughout the series' run, acting as the Dr. Quinn of her day, Elizabeth handled many an emergency. On CBS' *Medical Center* (1969–1976), Corinne Camacho played Dr. Jeanne Bartlett in its early seasons. On *The Interns* (1970–1971), Sandra Smith played intern Lydia Thorpe, a name strikingly similar to that of the head nurse of *The Nurses*, Liz Thorpe. Shelley Fabares played a grad of Harvard Medical on *The Brian Keith Show* (1972–1974). And on *Doctor's Hospital* (1975–1976), Zohra Lampert played neurosurgeon Norah Purcell, a character who has been described as "dedicated, compassionate, and able to maneuver skillfully past anti-female barriers."[112]

Maud Adams starred as the "heroically caring, rational and dependable" Dr. Judith Bergstrom on the critically lauded *Chicago Story* in 1982[113]; Shelley Hack was one of a trio of dedicated doctors on *Cutter to Houston* (1983); and female physicians were featured on the "post-feminist"[114] *Heartbeat* (1988–1989).

The Reporters

You've heard the one about the pen being mightier than the sword?

Since the dawn of the printing press, numerous real-life women have proven that point, deflating the myth of the press as just a boys' club. Early real-life pioneers include Nellie Bly, radio's Dorothy Thompson and TV's Pauline Frederick.

Fictional TV, too, has also often shown us some women reporters. TV's earliest woman reporter was on *Big Town* (1950–1956). *Big Town* told of Steve Wilson, crusading editor-in-chief of the *Illustrated Press* newspaper. First played by Patrick McVey and subsequently Mark Stevens, Wilson took on organized crime and government corruption.

For five seasons, Wilson's star reporter was Lorelei Kilbourne. Various actresses played Kilbourne including Mary K. Wells, Julie Stevens, Jane Nigh, Beverly Tyler and Trudy Wroe. As played by any, Lorelei was shown getting stories and sometimes getting mad, even calling out her boss. In one episode, she orders him to "get off your soapbox!" when she thinks he's using the paper as a pulpit. Later, she complains of his assigning of stories: "You bounce me around like a yo-yo!"

What Lorelei began would be carried on by others. For the live series *Byline* (1951), Betty Furness played the lead character "The Reporter," a newspaperwoman whose "beat" was tracking down international criminals. The series (also known as *News Gal*) lasted only a short time but is an interesting footnote for women on TV and in Furness' amazing career.[115]

Foreign Intrigue (a.k.a. *Dateline: Europe*) (1951–1955), shot in Europe, went through several casts during its lifespan while always maintaining the same premise: one or two globe-trotting reporters involved in international incidents. In the show's early years, Jerome Thor starred as reporter Robert Cannon. Co-starring with him was Sydna Scott as reporter Helen Davis. Though both worked for Consolidated News, that didn't prevent them from trying to one-up the other when it came to getting stories as in one episode where they are both taken hostage. Cannon falls into the trap first, followed by Davis. She tells him, "That's what you get for trying to beat me to a story."

As a reporter, Davis usually did as much sleuthing as writing. Throughout her adventures, dealing with everything from counterfeiters to war criminals, she was determined and fearless. She's sent down dark alleys and into seedy store fronts. She's a gritty gal who, even when at the wrong end of a gun, maintains her wits.

More likely to cover government corruption and international crime than flower shows and garden parties, Sydna Scott played Helen Davis on *Foreign Intrigue* (1951–1955).

Another early reporter who can't be ignored is Lois Lane of *The Daily Planet*.

On *The Adventures of Superman* (1952–1957), Lois was played by two actresses. And like the dueling Darrins on *Bewitched*, fans have long debated who's better, Phyllis Coates or Noel Neill.

Coates was the first, appearing in the show's premiere season. According to the author of a book on TV's *Superman*: "[Coates'] Lois Lane vilifies Clark Kent and matches him step for step...."[116] According to Coates herself, "I was *never* aware of not being liberated. I worked hard.... I had to, maybe to prove women could take the load just as much as men."[117]

Noel Neill (who had played Lois in two *Superman* serials) took over the role in season two. Though her Lois was less hard-edged, that didn't mean she was a doormat. As Glut and Harmon state, "Unlike the comic book Lois, whose main reasons for living were to expose Superman's secret identity and to marry him, the television Lois was more concerned with her job as a crack reporter."[118]

Whether played by Coates or Neill, Lois is always proving her mettle. She doesn't think twice about fighting with her editor, Perry White, when her opinion differs. In one episode he forbids her from going to a location because he's concerned about her safety, but Lois defies him and heads out the door. In another, about to testify before a crime commission, Lois starts getting death threats. White and Clark Kent implore her not to appear but she refuses. Grossman says, "Although she is aware of the danger ... [Lois] presses forward. The star reporter feels her appearance is more important than any threat on her life."[119]

And that's just for starters. In "The Superman Silver Mine," Lois confronts an impostor and shocks him when she pulls off the man's stuck-on mustache! Lane is competitive too. In the episode "The Unlucky Cat," she says to photographer Jimmy Olsen, "If Clark is going out by himself, you can bet he's after a good story. Why should we let him get it? I'll finish early and this afternoon we'll go out and snoop around."

Like so many of her TV contemporaries, Lois was not a "husband hunter," nor were there any fireworks between her and Kent. If anything, Lane showed a sarcastic streak when assessing Kent's masculinity, especially compared to Superman. She once said to Clark, "Don't tell me there's some man in you after all."[120]

Nor was Lois depicted as gaga over the Man of Steel. As Glut and Harmon state, "Lois and Superman hardly ever had any romantic entanglements.... He had little time for her romance and she seemed more concerned with getting scoops for the *Planet* than anything else."[121]

In numerous episodes, Lane often found herself captured by crooks or in some peril — Superman had to have *someone* to save — but even then, Lane never became Penelope Purebred. She always remained calm and collected and never waited to be saved. Instead, she plans ways to save herself. In one episode, she got trapped in a mine shaft. Rather than wait, Lois attempts to finds ways to dig out. Meanwhile, the man stuck with her is a panicked mess.

This reversal of gender stereotypes is evident throughout the series. Consistently it is not Lois but Jimmy Olsen, cub reporter–photographer, who is always causing trouble, and either Lois or Superman have to bail him out.

In contrast to *Mary Tyler Moore*'s Mary Richards — a later woman of the newsroom — who always (quite famously) referred to her boss as "Mr. Grant," Lois didn't address her boss any differently than any of her male co-workers. Throughout the series, Lois refers to her boss, editor Perry White, as "sir" or "Mr. White" but mostly as "chief,"[122] the same way Clark Kent did. If gender equality didn't exist in Mary's Minneapolis, it did in Metropolis.

—◦◦◦—

The inversion of traditional gender roles is one that was further explored in the sitcom *Dear Phoebe* (1954–1955). Dapper Peter Lawford starred as Bill Hastings, who worked at the *LA Daily Blade* writing the lovelorn column under the name of Phoebe Goodheart (hence, "Dear Phoebe").

If having a man write the lonely hearts column was unusual, so was another columnist: "Mickey" Riley, the paper's chief sports writer. Mickey was a woman. She was played by Marcia Henderson.

Perhaps even more radical was that while Hastings remained anonymous, hidden behind his byline, everyone in town knew Mickey was a lady ... and didn't mind. We see in episodes that she's regularly recognized by readers and sought out for her opinions. In writing about the primarily male world of sports, however, Mickey did not sacrifice her femininity — or humor. In one scene, a waiter inquires about a boxing match. "Who do you like?" he asks.

"The referee. But he's married," Mickey replies.

Borrowing a page from the movie *The Front Page*, *Phoebe*'s characters often talked in fast, overlapping sentences, the same sort of style later used on *Moonlighting*. And, like *Moonlighting*, *Phoebe*'s duo often traded jabs with Mickey always holding her own. Mickey was never above putting Bill in his place or even her boss as in a Christmas episode where she called the latter "Scrooge."

—⁕—

Another important woman of the press was on *Wire Service* (1956–1957), a series with three different, rotating stars. Actors George Brent and Dane Clark were two, actress Mercedes McCambridge was the third.

By the time of *Wire*, McCambridge had already won an Oscar for 1949's *All the King's Men* and had already been named by Orson Welles as the world's "greatest living radio actress." She went on to give one of the great vocal performances by voicing the demon in *The Exorcist*. Between these career highs, there would be her role as Trans Globe News Service reporter Katherine "Kitty" Wells.

In one of McCambridge's episodes, she stumbles upon a story and, alone, doggedly pursues it. As the episode begins, Wells is at the airport when the shooting of a famous jockey takes place. Wells cancels her flight and calls her editor, John (she calls him by his first name; take *that*, Mary Richards!) to let him know she's going to follow up on her only lead: a runaway eyewitness.

After some questioning of airport personnel, Kitty learns the witness' name. Using the reporter's "secret weapon"—the phone book—she's then off to the man's house. There, Katherine proves herself a tenacious reporter. She divulges to the missus that when she saw her husband at the airport he was with another woman! Is Wells' disclosure her digging for extra sizzle?

For most of the episode Katherine is actually more interested in getting a story than the killer. But her doggedness helps flush out the witness and the gunman. Then, suddenly, it's up to her to find the witness before the killer does!

Kate is depicted as being good and respected in her job. Her editor doesn't question her when she phones; he doesn't send a male reporter to shadow her.

McCambridge brought seriousness to the character. Wells is determined. And there is nothing that supports "husband hunter" accusations. In fact, when her co-worker, Martha, attempts to set her up with a guy, Kitty refuses, putting deadlines before dating.

All in all, *Wire Service* is an exceptionally well done series and, McCambridge is one of TV's most fascinating, and sadly forgotten, working women.

—⁕—

Another actress who moved to TV from movies was Shirley MacLaine. She came to episodic television for the first—and last—time playing Shirley Logan, a globe-trotting reporter for *World Illustrated* magazine in *Shirley's World* (1971–1972).

Logan, like the actress who played her, was portrayed as spunky and political. Logan is also happily single, accomplished in her career and respected by her peers. All in all, the character comes across as the complete "new woman" that revised definition of womanhood born from the second wave of feminism and who, in TV, can count Mary Richards as midwife.

That said, some of Logan's independence did not come without a fight.[123] MacLaine had to challenge the show's older male producer over the issue of making Logan a "free woman," i.e., sexually active but not tied down. In the end, though Logan may not have been as "free" as MacLaine had hoped (the actress seemed to entertain the idea of a man in every port), the character is depicted as being fully on her own. Even Logan's male editor was neither lover nor pseudo-father figure. (We hardly saw him at all, he was usually just on the phone.)

While the series would never take on the overt feminism MacLaine had hoped for, it was progressive. In one episode, Shirley stuns a doorman when she walks into her hotel one morning and he realizes she's just coming in from the night before! In another episode, set in London,[124] Shirley storms a gentlemen's club to end its "men only" policy. Later, in Japan, Shirley tries to prevent a forced marriage.

When not striking out for women, Shirley is embracing other causes. In one episode, she assists an aged colonel take on an oil company. In another, she promotes a broke street artist.

In other episodes, Shirley was less political but still involved. She didn't think twice about injecting herself into a story, if necessary. One episode has Shirley in Hong Kong stumbling onto a blackmail plot. During this half-hour, Shirley fought off two goons, operated a crane, and turned the tables on a blackmailer.

—◆◇◆—

Continuing with the rebirth of many of *Mary Tyler Moore*'s ensemble after they left WJM (Gavin MacLeod on *The Love Boat*, etc.), Ed Asner also soon returned to TV. But unlike his co-stars, Asner played his previous MTM character on *Lou Grant* (1977–1982).

This time around, though, Asner played it straight. His Grant was now the editor of an LA daily newspaper and, as such, had to deal with a cadre of reporters. One of them was hard-working Billie Newman, played by Linda Kelsey.

Billie didn't arrive until the series' fourth episode. Newman starts out unhappily stuck in the newspaper's "Today" section which runs fluffy feature stories. It's the section that Lou still calls the "women's section" and its offices "the henhouse."

Things take an upturn for Billie in her first episode when, while in New Mexico to interview a playwright, the playwright turns up dead. Was it foul play?

In the newsroom, Grant doesn't believe that a "lady reporter" can cover such a story and sends out city staffer Joe Rossi. Rossi is a rumpled "Woodward wannabe" who has his own ideas about "a woman's place" in the newsroom, and elsewhere. After meeting Billie, Rossi doesn't bother to hide his disregard for her. He barely speaks to her and when he does, it isn't pleasant:

ROSSI: What's your name again?
BILLIE: Billie Newman.
ROSSI: I can't picture a reporter named Billie.
BILLIE: How about a president named Jimmy?

Eventually Billie's hunch that the death was suicide proves correct and her skills impress Lou. So much so that he hires her.

Though now co-workers, the tension between Billie and Rossi would never abate and their sparring was no flirtation; these two didn't like each other. In one episode, she and

Rossi are again at loggerheads as each attempts to one-up the other on a story. In the end, Billie outsmarts him and scores the coveted front page.

Throughout the series, Billie proved herself a hard-working, ethical reporter. At least twice she went "undercover" to seek out a story. Once she was provided with police protection after a story of hers resulted in threats. She was also unafraid to take a stand. Once she challenged Lou when his editing changed the slant of her article. Once she chastised her fellow reporters when she thought their reporting about a candidate was giving an inaccurate view.

Her professionalism endeared her to many real-life women reporters. Kelsey has said, "I had a lot of women journalists say [to me], 'Keep it up, you're doing this for us. You keep on your editor and you keep asking for the good jobs and don't you let Rossi get to you.'"[125] Kelsey even fielded offers from journalism schools to speak to their graduating classes.[126]

In retrospect, Billie Newman was like Mary Richards 2.0. Like Mary, she was very human, but less insecure. Billie broke through the glass ceiling, up from "Style" to the newsroom. She even referred to Mr. Grant as "Lou."

—◦∿∿◦—

Other women of the press who helped pave the way for *Murphy Brown*: Celeste Holm worked for *The New York Express* on *Honestly, Celeste* (1954). Before *Gilligan's Island*, Jim Backus was a newspaperman in the comedy *The Jim Backus Show* (1960) which co-starred Nita Talbot as Dora, a reporter. Barbara Rush was the Washington correspondent for the *New York Bulletin* in *Saints and Sinners* (1962–1963). Bernadette Peters was a liberal-minded news photographer married to an older conservative on *All's Fair* (1976).

The American Girls (1978) starred Debra Clinger and Priscilla Barnes as producers for a *60 Minutes*–like TV show called *The American Report*. They traveled the country in an RV ferreting out stories.

Stockard Channing was a TV consumer advocate on *The Stockard Channing Show* (1979); Susan Anton was a daredevil reporter *a la* Brenda Starr in "Stop Susan Williams!" (1979), a segment of NBC's *Cliff Hangers* program; Joanna Gleason was the producer of a local radio program on *Hello, Larry* (1979–1980); and Helen Shaver was a TV news anchorwoman on the drama *Jessica Novak* (1981). (Shaver had a similar role on the series *WIOU* almost a decade later.)

Earlier, Mariette Hartley was a TV news anchor on the short-lived sitcom *Goodnight, Beantown* (1983–1984), prefiguring her own hosting of CBS' *The Morning Program* in the late 1980s. Lucie Arnaz was the host of a call-in radio show on *The Lucie Arnaz Show* (1985). Twice in the '80s, Suzanne Pleshette played reporters, first in the sitcom *Suzanne Pleshette is Maggie Briggs* (1984) and then in the comedy-drama *Bridges to Cross* (1986).

A few years later, Jamie Lee Curtis and Ann Magnuson both worked for a trendy Chicago lifestyle mag on *Anything But Love* (1989–1992).

The Lawyers

Decades before *Harry's Law*, TV had already welcomed its first female attorney. June Havoc played lady lawyer Willa "Willy" Dodger on the Desilu-produced sitcom

Willy (1954–1955). (And all women on were TV housewives!) When the series began, Willy was practicing in her hometown, a New Hampshire hamlet where she lived with her father, sister and her sister's son. Mid-season, the series changed its locale to New York where Willy worked as counsel for a vaudeville organization.

From the premiere episode, Willy's knowledge of the law is evident. She's always quoting legalese and referencing obscure laws. We also learn that, though new in town, she is already being considered for town supervisor.

We also learn, via conversations with her sister, that Willy had chosen law over marriage. It seems that before heading to college, Willy fielded several offers of matrimony ... and turned them down.

Despite her skills, Willy usually took on cases far from federal import. In the opener, she defends a dog which has allegedly crossed over into a pasture and caused a cow to stop giving milk. Willy treats the case like she's in front of the Supreme Court. Preparing for trial, she doesn't hold back. When the male plaintiff stops by her office, Willy won't be intimidated. She starts by removing the man's hat since he failed to when he walked in.

In the end, Willy wins the case, having researched the pasture and then researched arcane property law. The episode's denouement is a front page headline: "Willy Dodger Refuses to be Cowed!"

One of *Willy*'s later episodes has the shadow of sexual harassment. Guest star Hal March asks Willy to be his associate on a big case but he's more interested in dating her than working with her. It's a ploy Willy doesn't appreciate.

Later, in various episodes, Willy uses her expertise for a variety of social justices: She helps build a home for an orphaned seal; helps an elderly woman prove her competence; and aids the family of her building's janitor.

—⧼⧽—

About a decade after *Willy*, Jean Arthur became the latest star from Hollywood's "golden age" to bring her talents to primetime and she also became its second lady lawyer. On *The Jean Arthur Show* (1966), she played Patricia Marshall, a sophisticated, well-known attorney in private practice.

In contrast to Willy, who often worked pro bono, Patricia was a gun for hire, and she didn't always represent the most upstanding clientele. In fact, a supporting character was a cartoonish mobster. Patricia was always bailing him out of some fix.

Arthur, 49 when she starred, radiated a tony elegance. In the series she was, as one character put it, "class, real class." But beneath that style was a tough barrister. Patricia thought nothing of chastising police officers, judges, or the prosecution. She once called one principal a "fathead." And in a scene in the morgue, it's her mobster companion, not her, who faints.

Luckily, Arthur's well-bred demeanor overrode harsher aspects of her character and she retained her likability. It also helped that the characters she sometimes represented were so exaggerated.

No matter who her client was, Patricia had compassion for them, illustrating that this was a multi-faceted woman: glamourous, outspoken, idealistic, and unapologetic.

—⧼⧽—

Another early female TV esquire, and its most fervent feminist this side of Maude, was seen in the TV adaptation of *Adam's Rib* (1973).

As one might recall, the 1949 film told the story of two attorneys married to each other but representing opposite sides in a case that hinged on gender issues. The small-screen version, starring Ken Howard and Blythe Danner as Adam and Amanda Bonner, never quite achieved the bristling energy of the film version but it tried.

During the series' run, about every episode took on matters of sexist double standards. In one, Amanda takes a restaurant owner to court after he refuses to serve women wearing pants; in another, Amanda takes on the case of a young girl who wants to play on an all-boys baseball team.

While Adam wasn't as active as his wife was on these issues (he was an old-fashioned kind of guy), he was supportive of her. In fact, near the end of the series, he was encouraging her to run for City Council.

—•◦•—

In the 1970s came TV's first hour-long drama about a female attorney. Along with *Amy Prentiss* and *Dear Detective* (discussed later), the legal drama *Kate McShane* (1975) was part of a wave of "independent woman" dramas that popped up during the decade. (It's interesting that, today, '70s TV is usually remembered only in terms of *Mary Tyler Moore*.)

Multiple factors contributed to the rise of female-centered dramas including the arrival of the modern women's movement and changes in demographics. From men and women choosing to delay marriage to the rise of single parent (often single mother) households, women now had greater say in the programming they watched.

Unfortunately, even with these shifts, these dramas didn't last long, each the victim of low ratings.

But the fact that these series existed at all is notable in itself, shifting the blame—if there is blame—away from supposedly misogynistic (and, assumedly, male) network executives to the public, men and women, who for whatever reason didn't choose to watch these watershed programs.

When *Kate McShane* began, its star, 46-year-old Anne Meara, was primarily known as half of the comedy team Stiller and Meara. As Kate, Meara was "gutsy"[127] and "independent, aggressive and soft-hearted, tough and argumentative but within reasonable human bounds."[128] But rather than being embraced by viewers as a resounding positive portrayal, *Kate* was the first casualty of the 1975 season.

Despite the legal gray areas she encountered, Kate was a crusader, always on the side of good. And in keeping with her serious work, Kate conveyed a serious persona. She was no fashion plate; Kate cared about cases, not clothes.

—•◦•—

Women lawyers had better luck the next decade, thanks to Steven Bochco and his *Hill Street Blues* (1981–1987) and *LA Law* (1986–1994) series.

On *Blues*, Veronica Hamel played Joyce Davenport, the "capable, contentious lawyer from the Public Defender's Office,"[129] who, according to one author, was "presented as an intelligent, professional woman."[130]

LA Law showcased various female attorneys including Grace Van Owen (played by

Susan Dey), Ann Kelsey (played by Jill Eikenberry) and Rosiland Shays (played by Diana Muldaur). The Shays character especially galvanized opinion and evolved the image of the female attorney, so uncompromising and unsympathetic was she. Diana Muldaur, who played the role, has said, "I really wanted her to represent the new executive woman: someone who was totally accepted, as a peer, by the men she worked with, but who wasn't part of any old boys' club."[131]

Muldaur has often spoken about people's reactions to her character. Upon the actress' exit, even one of the show's writers attempted to absolve himself. He told her she "played it differently than we wrote it."[132] The character was so strong that ultimately she could only be cast out by having her fall down an elevator shaft, like some sort of sacrifice to appease angry (male?) gods.

Lighter fare has seen its share of women on or before the bench. Gretchen Corbett was Beth Davenport, the love interest of Jim Rockford, on *The Rockford Files* (1974–1978). Said one critic, "Beth Davenport ... is a very strong character, and her relationship with James Garner seems loving and healthy."[133]

Diana Muldaur (again) played a judge on *The Tony Randall Show* (1976–1978). Post–*Girl from UNCLE* but before *Hart to Hart*, Stefanie Powers was attorney Toni "Feather" Danton on *The Feather and Father Gang* (1977). On it, Powers worked with her dad, a reformed con man, to "cheat the cheaters."[134]

In ABC's acclaimed sitcom *The Associates* (1979), a group of young attorneys apprenticed at a Wall Street firm. It featured Alley Mills (later of *The Wonder Years*) as Leslie Dunn, a recent Columbia grad from a working class family, as well as Shelley Smith as Sara James, a New York blue blood with a razor-sharp wit. Smith's beautiful but far-from-dumb character was, like Jennifer on *WKRP*, another strike against the "dumb blond" stereotype.

Connie Sellecca was a down-to-earth attorney whose boyfriend Ralph was often seen flying around on *The Greatest American Hero* (1981–1983). *It Takes Two* (1982–1983) starred Patty Duke as a mom with a law degree. Supporting her were Richard Crenna, as her doctor-husband, and future stars Helen Hunt and Anthony Edwards as her almost-adult children.

Over the years the sitcom *Night Court* (1984–1992) featured a rotating cast of female prosecutors played by Paula Kelly, Ellen Foley, and Markie Post. Playing opposite Mr. T in *T and T* (1987) was Ali Amini as attorney Amanda "Amy" Taler. While he worked as a detective, she worked to put the bad guys behind bars.

Finally, Florence Stanley was like a tougher Judge Judy on *My Two Dads* (1987–1990). Her best moment occurred in an episode where teenager Nicole (Staci Keenan) got dumped. The judge relates her own story of once being stood up. When Nicole asks whatever happened to the guy, the judge says, "Life's funny. Years later he appeared before me on an insider trading charge.... Fifteen years. No parole."

The Cops

Television's first recurring policewoman arrived 17 years before *Police Woman* and 25 before *Cagney & Lacey*: In the syndicated *Decoy* (1957), Beverly Garland starred as New York Police Officer Casey Jones.

Decoy owes much of its structure to *Dragnet*. Like it, *Decoy* was conceived as a tribute to America's police (specifically police women) and episodes were allegedly taken from real-life cases.

Dragnet's lead provided voiceover for each episode; so did Casey Jones. She even occasionally broke the "fourth wall" and addressed the audience directly, giving the character a uniquely authoritative voice.

As with *Dragnet* too, the personal life of the character was a non-issue. We knew "just the facts" about Joe Friday and such was the case with Casey. Throughout *Decoy's* 39 episodes there were few hints about Casey's background. In fact, Garland only recalled one scene that was set in Casey's apartment and that was just a simple telephone scene with no other actors.[135]

Casey brought a far greater compassion (what would have been called a "woman's touch") to her policing than Friday did. "Good" and "evil" was not always easily discerned on *Decoy*. Officer Jones often

Twenty-five years before the debut of *Cagney & Lacey*, Beverly Garland played policewoman Casey Jones on *Decoy* (1957). From left to right, George Mitchell, Garland and Frank Overton.

wrestled with moral issues and sometimes felt sympathy for the guilty. In the pilot, Jones arrests a woman, a near-victim of rape who killed her attacker. At the end, she walked the woman out with her arms around her. When did Friday do that?

During its run, the series took on many other so-called "women's issues" including unplanned pregnancy and feminist sisterhood. Regarding the latter, in one episode, five-year veteran Jones related the story of her first assignment to a new policewoman. It's an image of a supportive female partnership long before Cagney and Lacey.

The show also addressed other tough subjects. There was a sensitive portrayal of a brain-damaged adult; in "Scapegoat," Casey must stop a distraught mother from killing her mentally retarded baby.

Though called *Decoy*, Jones seldom acted in a decoy capacity. Rather, she was always the center of the action and 90 percent of the time worked alone.

Decoy took its realism and responsibility to real-life policewomen seriously. (The show even employed a former New York policewoman to act as advisor.) This commitment was evident at the conclusion of the pilot where Casey addressed the camera. Her speech set the tone for the series:

Remember [policewoman] Jean, the girl I talked to? She has a degree from the University of Southern California. She's a fully qualified chemist. Edna was a nurse. Marion was a social worker. I studied, believe it or not, to be a ballet dancer. Down the line you name it and we've done it. Today, tomorrow, next week, we'll pose as hostesses, society girls, models, anything and everything the department asks us to be. There are 249 of us in the department. We carry two things in common wherever we go: a shield—called a "potsie"—and a .32 revolver. We're New York's finest. We're policewomen.

Though "Decoy" was produced for only one season, it was heavily syndicated afterward as *Policewoman Decoy*. The show had an impact even though it's little remembered today. Beverly Garland once said, "[T]hroughout my life, I've had ten or twenty women come up to me and tell me that they saw me on *Decoy* and because of it they became a policewoman."[136]

———✥———

Remarkably different from *Decoy* was TV's second policewoman and the first to appear regularly on network TV.

The Mod Squad (1968–1973) told of three once-troubled, now redeemed youths ("One white, one black, one blonde," according to ads) who are tapped by the LAPD to form a youth-oriented crime-fighting unit.

Remarkably, *The Mod Squad* was inspired by a real-life initiative. Before entering television, show creator Bud Ruskin was a member of LA's Sheriff's Department and once served on a team of boyish-faced flatfoots.

Ironically, the series, cutting edge in 1968, was conceived much earlier. For years, the script gathered dust before Aaron Spelling recognized its cross-sectional appeal. For Spelling, *Mod Squad* encapsulated his ability to anticipate audience desires, fuse genres, and take advantage of "fringe" culture. With *Mod Squad*, Spelling was as successful as ever. For over-35-ers, it was an old-fashioned cops-and-robbers show. For "kids," it showcased fellow young people who were radical and rebellious.

In keeping with their "rebel" persona, the Squad had a code of conduct: They wouldn't "fink" on friends or their generation; they also wouldn't carry guns, a nod (one supposes) to the era's peace movement.

Julie (Peggy Lipton) was the female on the team. Daughter of a San Francisco prostitute, Julie had been picked up for vagrancy and, like her two male colleagues Linc and Pete, was given the choice of jail or "going straight." She chose straight.

Julie was considered a full member of the team; there were no concessions for the group's lone "girl." She's always in on all the action; she's listened to and respected. In the pilot, Julie realizes that a clue, "the D-room," means the dark room at an area nightclub.

Julie was also often undercover. During the series, she posed as a hippie, a high school student, and a starlet. In one episode, she even took a bullet.

Though the show's dated today due to its "groovy"-laden dialogue, it still has its merits: because of Julie and because this threesome helped usher in a new era for TV police, away from stick-straight Joe Friday days and into the realm of cool cops. In their break with tradition, *The Mod Squad* paved the way for *Miami Vice* and other TV bad-asses.

———✥———

The Mod Squad gave a leg-up for female flatfoots, but it was the season after that shield-wielding women really came into their own.

The first of that year's "lady cops" premiered over ABC one week before *Police Woman* began on NBC. *Get Christie Love!* (1974–1975) was an attempt to bring "blaxploitation" to TV. In movies, Pam Grier had already played action-oriented women, so why shouldn't something like that work on TV?

ABC hired its own beautiful black actress, Teresa Graves (formerly of *Laugh-In*), to bring a Grier-like character to primetime. In taking the role, Graves became the first and — to date — only African American woman to star in her own hour-long network dramatic series.

More than 20 years later, *Christie* is recalled as camp due to its title and the show's overly affected "jive" talk; one episode has a thug, who has blown Christie's cover, uttering, "Our lady fox is a pig!" Meanwhile, Christie's infamous catchphrase "You're under arrest, Sugar" has long been the subject of contempt. But Love's lingo doesn't seem any more ridiculous than Kojak's "Who loves ya, baby?" or Baretta's tough-guy talk.

Officer Love should be remembered for her wit that regularly silenced would-be Romeos. Consider:

MAN: Howdy. My friends call me "Cowboy."
CHRISTIE: You have friends?

In looking at episodes today, it's impressive to see all that Christie was. The book *Shaded Lives* praises Christie as "tough, smart and sexy" and as showing "young women ... the possibility for a convergence of strength, respect and femininity."[137]

Graves described her character: "Christie's bright, young and kicky. She knows her business but she's a lady. She's fun.... She does everything professionally. [But] she's not a super woman. She's tough, but she's still a woman."[138]

When the program began, ABC promoted it with sex and action; their famous tag line was "Beauty, brains and a badge!"[139] While some might recoil at such titillation (and alliteration), it should be noted that the network would soon push the sex appeal of *Starsky and Hutch*. If one is "exploitation," then aren't they both?

Christie didn't deserve its criticism. Love wasn't depicted as dumb, weak, or promiscuous. And she was often seen entering dangerous, unpredictable situations alone, able to take care of herself.

In the pilot, Love finds herself cornered by a thug in a high-rise hotel room. The fight sequence that ensues is no-holds-barred. In the end, it's him, not her, who goes flying off the balcony. A later episode sees Christie flip a drug dealer over her shoulder.

Get Christie Love! was not high-brow television. But as in blaxploitation films, the series did address a few weightier issues. In one episode, Love goes up against a prejudiced police captain. In another, she takes on the stereotype-busting undercover assignment of aviatrix.

Appreciation was finally voiced at the time of Graves' death in 2003: *Entertainment Weekly* eulogized her Love as "teasingly tough, alarmingly inventive."[140]

—◦◦◦—

Despite the presence of *Christie Love* (and the earlier *Decoy*), TV's most famous lady of the law, before *Cagney & Lacey*, was Pepper Anderson on *Police Woman* (1974–1978) starring Angie Dickinson.

Dickinson has given impressive performances in everything from *Rio Bravo* to *Dressed to Kill* and in Europe is considered a successor to Marilyn Monroe. Author Michael McWilliams says of her:

> She's better than just about any project — movies or TV — she's ever been connected with ... she can do more with a raised eyebrow and melancholy grin than most of her leading men can do with a lifetime of histrionics.... She plays [Pepper Anderson] as if she were doing *Hedda Gabler* at the Circle in the Square.[141]

Dickinson was 43 when she debuted the role on the anthology *Police Story*. Executive producer David Gerber said later, "There was a fantastic audience reaction to [her episode]. We convinced Angie that a series would not get dull because, as a vice squad officer, she does a different 'cover' character every week. She's not playing a fantasy super-chick."[142]

Retrospectives of *Police Woman* have not always been appreciative. One latter-day critic called the series "irrelevant."[143] (Would a police drama featuring a man ever be so labeled?) Criticism of the series usually starts with the character's nickname "Pepper." One author says "Pepper" is a name for a cat, not a cop.[144] But it was Dickinson's idea; she said, "Somehow I can't imagine a woman police officer named Lisa."[145]

Other criticisms usually address Pepper's undercover jobs. Pepper did occasionally go undercover as a go-go dancer or prostitute, but real policewomen are more often called upon to pose as "ladies of the evening" than CEOs. Besides, Pepper's other undercover roles included jewel fence and teacher.

Though the 1970s were not the "dark ages," looking back at *Police Woman*, it is striking to see how progressive the show was. First, there's a gritty feel to the series. This wasn't a soft-focus treatment. The series addressed various tough issues: drug abuse, rape, racism (in one episode, Pepper has to protect a militant activist), mental illness, and runaways.

Secondly, like Casey Jones, Pepper viewed herself as just a cop, not a "female cop." She was accepted as part of the team by her fellow officers; there were no concessions to the "lady" in their midst.

Furthermore, there was never any romance between Anderson and her superior Bill Crowley (played by Earl Holliman). Those who say there was are projecting romanticism.

And, contrary to what is often reported, Anderson did not exist only as a decoy. On the contrary, in one episode, Pepper is part of a sting operation, eventually bringing down one perp all on her own. After he's caught, he vows revenge. Pepper later asks Joe why it's always her, the female, who gets threatened. Later in this same episode, Pepper finds herself experiencing a strange series of events including a break-in. Pepper's reaction to these events is one of great honesty, a more truthful response than any male TV officer would have been allowed.

In the climax of this episode, outside a rustic cabin, Pepper is cornered by her stalker, the father of a man Pepper put in prison. What's interesting in this scene is that once Pepper learns (at gunpoint) the man's identity, she remains unapologetic about sending the man's son to jail even if it further angers him. Back at the station, Pepper's co-workers have now discovered the man's identity and his plans to ambush her. After alerting the park police, they rush to the mountains. A ranger arrives but is shot in the shoulder. Pepper grabs a tree branch and knocks away the gun. Though the men are en route, by the time they arrive, Pepper has saved herself.

Pepper also brought humanity to her job. *TV Guide* said, "Few women have ever seemed so tough and so tender."[146] Her concern was about more than just getting the bad guys as seen in this exchange:

PEPPER: Any word?
BILL: Yep, she's with her brother. Joe and Pete are tailing them.
PEPPER: That poor kid, it really makes me sick.
BILL: Pep, will you stop worrying? It's going to be okay!
PEPPER: She's a 12-year-old kid, how can I help but worry about her?
BILL: Pepper, we're onto it. It's going to be okay, okay?!
PEPPER: Remind me to keep telling myself that.

Ultimately, whether wielding a tree branch or worrying about a young victim, Sgt. Pepper Anderson was an inspiring character. When the series premiered in 1976, *Time* described Pepper as "brave" and "self-reliant."[147]

—⟨∿∿⟩—

Nineteen seventy-four was a boon year for women in law enforcement ... at least on TV. Along with Christie and Pepper, TV also saw *Amy Prentiss* (1974–1975) starring Jessica Walter.

Created by Francine Carroll, *Amy Prentiss* told of a high-ranking San Francisco police-woman who, after the death of the chief, is named his replacement. Prentiss' ascension to the top brought with it resentment. In the pilot, Amy has a male subordinate tell her, "If you had the instincts of a cop...." Later, she is disinvited to a luncheon of officers' wives. Amy laments about both groups, "I wish they'd trust me more." The public is no better. One sleaze asks a group of officers, "You actually take orders from the broad?"

As if that's not enough, in this same installment, on the crime front, Amy has to cope with internal corruption and take down a mad bomber. Before the end, Amy is even forced to arrest a long-time family friend.

Prentiss was also a single mom (her husband had died in a plane crash) with a teenage daughter (played by Helen Hunt).

Spun-off from *Ironside*, *Amy Prentiss* could have been one of the great breakthrough series of its day. But only four episodes aired before it got yanked. Nevertheless, in her short airtime, Walter must have made an impact: She won the Emmy that year for Best Actress.

—⟨∿∿⟩—

The wave of female police officers continued with *Dear Detective* (1979). Based on a 1977 French film, the series starred Brenda Vaccaro as Kate Hudson, an LAPD detective and a divorcee with a preteen daughter. Mother and daughter enjoyed a harmonious relationship and shared a home with Kate's mother.

Taking place at the station and at home, *Dear Detective* is tough to categorize as it's an awkward mix of police drama and humor. The series seemed to want to copy *The Rockford Files* which tempered crimefighting with irreverence. But *Dear Detective* could never quite achieve a balance. The show's humor seemed strained and the program's switch to straight-out police procedural then seemed jarring. Perhaps the fact that Hudson was a cop, not a PI, made the difference.

This said, *Dear Detective* is not a complete failure. Vaccaro does wonders in her role; her character is marvelously human, maybe a little flawed, but far from insecure, and tough when necessary. At the same time, she's not hard or impersonal, criticisms that would later be hurled at Helen Mirren's *Prime Suspect*.

What is also refreshing is how respected Hudson is by men. She is fully supported by her male superior and is admired by her all-male team. Later, Cagney and Lacey would wish they had it so good.

Kate's personal life was also much of the series. Kate had a good relationship with her daughter — very *Gilmore Girls*. While the generations might occasionally clash, there were no knock-down mother-daughter arguments. And though Kate didn't *need* a man, she did have one, just as McCloud had a significant other. Hudson's love interest was Richard Wayland, a professor of Greek philosophy. He didn't care for the dangers of Kate's career, but he did care for her. As refreshing as Kate's work relationships were, so too was this personal one: evolving, age-appropriate and realistically played.

At work or home, Kate was always portrayed as together. She was not undergoing a mid-life crisis. She didn't obsess over her weight. With tweaking, *Dear Detective* could have become excellent. Unfortunately, it aired for only two months.

While the so-called "new woman" was a hit in sitcoms (i.e., *Mary Tyler Moore*), they didn't endure in hour-long dramas.

—◦◦◦—

Hunter (1984–1991), though running concurrently with *Cagney & Lacey*, never got credit for bringing to the screen its own excellent female officer.

The series was a Stephen J. Cannell Production. He was known for *The A-Team*, so critics tended to practice a severe double standard. Had *Hunter* sprung from Steven Bochco, it might not have been so ignored.

In *Hunter*, Stepfanie Kramer played Sgt. Dee Dee McCall. From its debut, McCall was seen as the full partner of detective Rick Hunter (played by Fred Dryer), which begs the question, why wasn't the show titled *Hunter & McCall*? (Or *McCall & Hunter*?) Many viewers always wondered if Hunter and McCall would eventually team up romantically. That question was eventually posed to Kramer. She responded:

> Absolutely not. It may be a fantasy in the minds of viewers, but it's not the basis for the series. The relationship we have on the screen is the core of the show. It's what distinguishes it from other cop shows.... The basis for the relationship is strong respect and friendship.[148]

Kramer's take is supported throughout the series. In fact, romance between Hunter and McCall would seem like a step down. As Hunter once told his partner, "Think about wedding vows. They're a distant second to the unspoken bond between partnered police officers. I mean, you and I are supposed to die for one another, right?"

Kramer should also be acknowledged for the brave off-camera stance she took midway through the show's run. At the beginning of the show's fifth season, an episode called for McCall to be raped. It was a scene that Kramer refused to perform.[149] McCall had already endured a sexual assault in a previous season. It was part of a multi-episode story and was treated sensitively. To Kramer, having the character victimized again was, in her words, "exploitative and unnecessary [and would] perpetuate the image of violently violating women."[150]

Kramer issued an ultimatum, "[The] rape scene is out ... or I'm out." It was a brave, unusual stance. Brave in that it was an actress putting her job on the line and unusual in that normally such protests are over money, not principal. Ultimately, Kramer was victorious. The actress returned to the series and the script re-written.

Kramer's stand should have made her one of the great feminist heroines of the era. But it didn't. Historically her protest has all but been ignored as 1980s primetime has just been labeled "backlash."

—◦◦◦—

Another show that defies "backlash" is the British-produced *Dempsey and Makepeace* (1985). In this syndicated action-packed series, American Michael Brandon played rogue American cop James Dempsey, recently banished to Britain after exposing police corruption. Across the Atlantic, the New York City cop is assigned to British police undercover unit SI-10 and gets paired with a partner who is British and female.

Harriet "Harry" Makepeace (actually Lady Harriet Alexandra Charlotte Makepeace) was played by cool blond Glynnis Barber. Makepeace was described by one author as "a sharp-witted woman,"[151] and by another as "a martial-arts–savvy electronics wizard [and] ace policewoman."[152]

As one can imagine, this duo was a culture clash. Their oil-and-water relationship mirrored many Anglo-American relations, with the Yankee living down to "ugly American."

Dempsey didn't like his "girl" partner. He also disliked British crime-solving methods, finding them slow and anti-productive. He further antagonized his new colleagues by refusing to give up his gun.

Similarly, Makepeace had contempt for her new partner, finding him crass and violence-prone. The show's pilot is filled with Makepeace's tough pronouncements to him: "Don't you 'babe' me!" and "I don't take orders from you!" Later, she excuses his bad behavior by explaining to others, "He's American." Even the show's ad copy played up the diametrically opposed duo: "Bad Boy meets Cultured Pearl." The characters' names are symbolic, his conjuring up the American prizefighter, hers ("make" + "peace") reflecting her more understated manner.

Despite the premise of a single man paired with a single woman, little romance was hinted at (at least on screen[153]), probably so that the show could emphasize its cops-and-robbers action. Instead of longing glances, it was insults that filled this series' episodes. In fact, Dempsey and Makepeace seemed to have a less intense bond than Starsky had with Hutch in the '70s.

Nevertheless, in true cop fashion, when bullets were flying, the two were there for each other. And as *Syndicated TV* points out, it was not unusual to see "the female cop rescue the male cop"[154] as in the pilot where a fight breaks out in a hotel kitchen. Dempsey is about to get cleavered when Harry disables the assailant.

Makepeace was heroic, but also a lady. Like fellow kick-ass lass Emma Peel, she could do more with a karate kick than her male cohorts could do with a hundred punches. One supposes, when you're an aristocrat you learn how to keep your hands clean even when dealing with the worst grime.

—◦◦◦—

One of the more controversial female officers in TV history arrived via *Lady Blue* (1985–1986).

Jamie Rose starred as policewoman Katy Mahoney, often referred to in the press as "Dirty Harriet" due to her sometimes brutal — but effective — methods. (Rose admitted that she watched Clint Eastwood movies as research for her role.) As the *New York Times* noted when the series debuted, "Katy is actually rather petite and fragile looking. But her no-nonsense manner and a .357 Magnum quickly convinces criminals that she means business."[155]

When the series began, Mahoney had just been reassigned to the "Matron Squad" due to her tendency towards excessive force. But that switch didn't alter Katy; she continued to shoot first and ask questions later. And to defy authority. In the premiere, she's removed from a case by her superior but ignores him and continues to investigate.

As soon as *Lady Blue* debuted, it became a pariah. Two months in, the National Coalition on Television Violence cited the series as TV's most violent program.[156] TV critics were no kinder and soon ABC pulled it.

But, in retrospect, *Lady Blue* exists as an interesting experiment, an attempt to recast the hardcore cop genre with a female lead. It was notable, if not successful. Maybe the producers did go overboard with their female commando. Perhaps the show was a victim of sexism: Was such rebellion, contempt for authority, and brutal tactics considered too "unfeminine"? We had seen rebel male cops (Baretta, etc.) before, but is it different with a woman? Perhaps *Lady Blue* was ahead of its time. In 1991, when Thelma and Louise went on their shooting spree, they were heralded as newfangled feminist icons. And, unlike Thelma and Louise, at least Dirty Harriet was on the *right* side of the law.

—◦◦◦—

Other female TV cops: Barbara Anderson, an aide on *Ironside* (1967–1975); helicopter pilots and heroes Joanna Cassidy and Pamela Hensley on *240-Robert* (1979–1980); and Anne Marie Martin as the partner of the super hardcore *Sledge Hammer!* (1986–1988). Meanwhile, the graphic Aussie-import *Prisoner: Cell Block H* (1980) took place in a women's prison; it featured female correctional officers, often outnumbered by women inmates.

The Detectives

As early as 1951, TV featured women working as PIs to solve crimes.

That year, film star Anna May Wong starred in *The Gallery of Madame Liu-Tsong* (1951). Wong (age 44) played Liu-Tsong, owner of a worldwide chain of art galleries. Madame's business gave her the opportunity to travel and to solve mysteries involving everything from stolen treasure to murder. As the solo star of her own series, Wong claims various firsts: that of being TV's first female detective and of being the first Asian-American to helm their own program.

Unfortunately, *Madame Lui-Tsong* lasted only a few months. Equally unfortunate, according to a Wong biographer, neither films nor scripts have survived to the present.[157] Hence, we cannot say how Madame Lui-Tsong was portrayed or just how empowering she might have been. But inasmuch as Wong was the series' only star, it's pretty safe to assume she carried the majority of it and that it was her crime-solving abilities that took every episode to its resolution.

—◦◦◦—

It was not long before other female sleuths sprang up. The crime-solving Mr. and Mrs. North — the *Hart to Hart* of their day — began life in *The New Yorker*. From there, they were a Broadway play, then a film and radio series. Then they came to TV from 1952 to 1954.

Jerry North was a wealthy publisher of mystery stories. He and his wife, Pamela, often stumbled onto murders which they then solved. In most episodes, it's actually the Mrs., not the Mr., who finds the clues, as in an installment where she recognizes the photo of a suspect in the house of the victim.

In one episode, Mr. and Mrs. North (played by Richard Denning and Barbara Britton) are on a case when Mrs. North overhears a conversation about a man named "Hunch." Mrs. North deduces — correctly — that that man must be a bookie. Who else would have such a nickname? The episode ends with the gun-wielding killer cornering Mrs. North in her garage. But Pamela doesn't panic. Soon, with some carefully thrown groceries, she disables the crook.

In another, the couple is being held hostage. All seems lost until a dishrag, well-wielded by Mrs. North, causes the bad guy to drop his gun.

In yet another, Mrs. N. is locked in an upstairs bedroom while her husband is downstairs at the wrong end of a pistol. But Mrs. North doesn't wait to be saved; she uses a metal shoe horn and a shoe to dislodge the hinges of the door. Once freed, she makes her way to the basement to flip the breakers, plunging the house into darkness and giving Mr. North the chance to take down his assailant.

The same year the Norths debuted, so too did the Bakers of *Biff Baker, USA* (1952–1953). Alan Hale (later of *Gilligan's Island*) and Randy Stuart starred as Biff and his wife Louise, globe-trotting importers whose travels always got them involved in international intrigue.[158] Louise was never a damsel in distress. She shows a lot of fearlessness. In

One of the most popular he-she detective series on TV in the 1950s was *Mr. and Mrs. North* (1952–1954) starring Barbara Britton and Richard Denning.

one episode, when Biff goes behind the Iron Curtain, he does so without telling his wife. But after Louise finds out, she follows him.

In another, when she is being used as a human shield by a gun-toting unsavory, the heel of her shoe disables the gunman.

There's an even better example of Louise's mettle in an episode when Biff and a group of men are being held at gunpoint. Louise manages to sneak up behind the gunwoman. "Louise!" Biff yells out.

"That's the oldest trick in the book," the gunwoman replies. But, this time, it's real. Louise grabs the woman, grabs the gun and frees not only her husband but all the men.

———✥✥✥———

Similar in format to *Biff Baker* was *The Thin Man* (1957–1959), a series based on some well-regarded novels. The glamourous married detectives Nick and Nora Charles were played by William Powell and Myrna Loy in some classy big screen mysteries. A decade after the Charleses' last film, the characters were resurrected for TV. Peter Lawford and Phyllis Kirk played Mr. and Mrs. Charles while the couple's famous dog, Asta, was played... by Asta.

Though filling the shoes of Powell and Loy was just about impossible, Lawford and Kirk nevertheless did cut two dashing figures, elegant and at-ease. As in the movies, each mystery was often just backdrop for banter. Though Lawford and Kirk's dialogue didn't zing with as much zip as their big-screen predecessors, their sophisticated conversations were well-done interplays between two shrewd minds. The Charleses' exchanges were often punctuated with sexy references. In one episode, Nora has been used to smuggle a rare gem. Nick eventually confronts the villains, lambasting them for taking advantage of "sweet, innocent Mrs. Charles." Nora exclaims, "Innocent?!"

Up until that time, the Charleses were probably TV's most kissy-faced couple. Almost every scene ends with a smooch. And though, in keeping with the times, they had separate beds, episodes inevitably ended with either Nick or Nora breeching that divide.

Romance aside, though, when the Charleses got to solving a murder, they worked as a team. Though fist-throwing was mainly the duty of Nick, Nora was always right there in the action. As one author notes about TV's Mrs. Charles, "[She] was not mere sidekick but her detective husband's true moral and intellectual equal."[159]

———✥✥✥———

A variation on the husband-and-wife detective team was *Glynis* (1963–1965). Like *Murder, She Wrote*'s Jessica, Glynis Granville was a mystery novelist (author of *Murder Takes the Bus*). Also like Fletcher, she always found herself stumbling onto real-life crimes. In Glynis' case, though, it wasn't so odd as she was married to an attorney.

Glynis was conceived as a showcase for the unique qualities of actress Glynis Johns. It was a valiant attempt to be both sitcom and mystery but wasn't completely successful. Nevertheless, whether played for laughs or intrigue, Glynis was always depicted as smart and resourceful. In nearly every episode, we are witness to her excellent detective skills.

In various episodes we also see that Glynis can take care of herself, as in the episode where a would-be murderer attempts to hunt her down in the mountains. Though at one point he has his gun aimed at her, Glynis creates a distraction and runs off, eventually hiding in an abandoned well. Once the coast is clear, she pulls herself out. If *Glynis* resembles *Murder, She Wrote*, you should see *The Snoop Sisters* (1973–1974). Eleven years before *Murder, The Snoop Sisters* brought to TV the legendary Helen Hayes and Mildred Natwick, who played two elderly but spirited golden girls named Ernesta and Gwen Snoop. In their series, the ladies regularly became embroiled in mysteries and merrily went about solving them.

These two were far from dotty. Repeatedly they demonstrated how brave they were, confronting suspects or breaking and entering to uncover clues. They continually confound killers and cops alike with their quick thinking. Once they passed themselves off as temps to gain entry to an office.

Even when they are not solving a crime, the ladies are depicted as active. In one episode we see them jogging. Later, we see them bowling. They even take part in some of the action-adventure elements of the show. Author Richard Meyers celebrates the program's Gray Panther–ness by noting, "Helen Hayes leaping into a karate stance has to be seen to be believed."[160]

Hayes was 73 and Natwick 65 when they began the program, thus bringing to television two more inspirational images of women over 40.

Notably as well, no one could accuse them of "jiggle."

—⁓—

Perhaps no program has been more vilified than *Charlie's Angels* (1976–1981). From its debut, it was a hit with viewers and a target for everyone else.

Despite the premise of the series — three women working together, unaided and successfully, in a traditionally male field — critics have never stopped carping. One author states that the show "reinforces the patriarchy" since the three central women are employed by a man (Charlie).[161] Meanwhile, another calls it "misogynist"— but doesn't explain why.[162] That same author compares the relationship of the show's three female leads to their unseen boss as "a version of the pimp and his girls: Charlie dispatches his street-wise girls to use their sexual wiles on the world while he reaps the profits."[163]

This latter statement — the Angels categorized as whores — is especially harsh. Comparing these law-enforcing women to prostitutes is more anti-woman than anything that ever transpired in the series.

Among details that disprove this pseudo-feminist propaganda is that not only were the women of *Charlie's Angels* not prostitutes, they weren't even promiscuous. In the show's six years, none of its leads were ever seen in bed with a man.

Secondly, if working for a man on TV makes you "a prostitute," then most of TV's females would also have to be similarly labeled: Mary Richards worked for Lou Grant; Murphy Brown worked for producer Miles; and even Cagney and Lacey answered to a male superior.

In various critiques of the show, much is also made about Charlie's anonymity. We — and the Angels — never see his face, just hear his voice. But is this misogyny? If it is, then what do we make of the setup on *Magnum, PI*? Magnum never met his boss, mysterious millionaire Robin Masters. According to *Charlie's Angels'* "show bible," Charlie's anonymous in order to protect his employees from kidnapping.[164]

This focusing on Charlie is silly anyway in that his role was minimal. He functioned more as narrator than participant. He sets up each week's plot, then disappears.[165]

If anything, far from "pimp-like," Charlie is more the great emancipator. In the program's opening, which fills in the Angels' back story, we learn that all the Angels[166] were alums of the police academy who, after graduation, found themselves assigned to gender-stereotyped jobs like meter maid. It's Charlie who recognizes their abilities and "promotes" them to more important work. (The premise of women being under-appreciated before being elevated has since been replicated in shows like *Alias*.)

As cruel as some have been to Charlie, they've been even harsher on Bosley, the associates' one resident male whose job entailed everything from bookkeeping to working undercover. Author Susan J. Douglas is especially dismissive, calling Bosley a "eunuch" in charge of the "harem."[167] Obviously, Douglas missed episodes where Bosley engaged in romances with guest stars Pat Crowley and Janis Paige. This anti–Bosley rhetoric begs the question: Would this author have been happier if Bosley was less "eunuch-like," perhaps constantly hitting on his co-workers?

Throughout the series, all of the Angels proved themselves skilled detectives who didn't get their jobs on their looks. Sabrina (Kate Jackson) was adept at finding clues and was brilliant undercover. She was described in the show's bible as "educated, refined, and elegant"; she was also fluent in five languages and knew karate.[168] It's been written that Sabrina was the main detective and the other two "decoys."[169] But Webster's defines "decoy" as "someone used to lure or lead another into a trap."[170] And the actions of the other Angels disprove this.

Kelly (Jaclyn Smith) was the toughest. Having grown up an orphan, Kelly knew how to take care of herself. In one episode, she responds to sexual harassment from a truck driver by dropping him to his knees.[171]

Jill (Farrah Fawcett) is as a former champion swimmer. Later she would become a race car driver, taking third at LeMans.

Kris Monroe (Jill's little sister, played by Cheryl Ladd beginning in season two) was no slouch either. In one episode she wrestled an alligator — and won.

In the fourth season, after Jackson left, Shelley Hack joined as Tiffany Wells. A top grad of the Boston Police Academy, Wells was Ivy League–educated and proved her smarts in various episodes, including one where the Angels were on a supposedly deserted island. But a roaming peacock makes Tiffany believe the Angels aren't alone; "[Peacocks] are not indigenous to this latitude, or even this hemisphere."

Despite the cast changes, the program stayed the same. As the *LA Times* pointed out, the women always prove themselves "independent, intelligent, resourceful, and brave."[172] Like many of their female forbearers, these women didn't wait around for a man to help them; these were women of action.

The trio of Angels were not depicted as competitive with each other either. In the tradition of male TV partnerships, like on *Dragnet* and *Adam-12*, they were a team. And they weren't superficial. Conversations always pertained to work, not boyfriends.

As mentioned earlier, the Angels were moral, even old-fashioned. In none of their episodes did the Angels bed a man, a stat which isn't matched by *Magnum* or *Matt Houston*. In fact, once when such a scene was written in (for episode #5), Jaclyn Smith objected and appealed to have it excised.[173] It was.

Even attempts to interject double entendres were opposed. Producer Barney Rosenzweig, who later produced *Cagney & Lacey*, implored Spelling, etc., to be strictly PG. He recalls, "[I told Spelling], it's not just boys — girls are watching, women are watching. I've read the mail! I've got three daughters that love the show! These women are role models, and you are insulting over half your audience with these lame sexist jokes!"[174]

Rosenzweig's rant was not caprice. For all the talk that the show's success was based on "jiggle," *Angels* had a huge female viewership. A poll conducted during season one showed that *Angels* had been seen by 62 percent of male viewers and *68 percent of female viewers*.[175] TV critic Ben Brown originally lambasted the show but changed his mind after a conversation with a friend's young daughter. She said she loved the show's heroines for being in control, driving fast and outwitting men.[176]

Still, despite evidence, many continue to slam *Charlie's Angels*. Issue (again) has been taken with the Angels' undercover assignments as nurses and cheerleaders. But the Angels also went undercover as truck drivers, football players, and stuntwomen.

Repeatedly *Angels* has a yardstick applied to it that's never applied to anyone else. When male stars run and jump, it's "action-adventure"; when women do it, it's "jiggle." The most famous (infamous?) episode of *Charlie's Angels* is "Angels in Chains": The trio goes undercover as inmates at a women's prison, eventually being assigned to a chain gang. Though they eventually escape, the Angels are linked in wrist irons for a time. This episode, supposedly ripe with S&M symbolism, has come back to haunt the three stars. Yet what happens here is identical to the film *The Defiant Ones*. Therefore, if "Chains" is exploitative, then is *Defiant Ones*? In Charlie's Angels *Casebook*, the authors defend the "Chains" episode: "[It] portrays the Angels as intelligent, capable professionals, and having all three work undercover together allows for more of the easy group repartee...."[177]

Even the "jiggle" factor has been overstated. It's not like this was TV's first time showing sexy women. Faye Emerson, Dagmar and others came before them. In the movies, America had already seen Jane Russell and Marilyn Monroe. Furthermore, on the show, Kate Jackson was never in a bathing suit and Fawcett never in a two-piece. Compare these details with series like *Tarzan*, with the bare-chested Ron Ely, or *Magnum, PI* with the oft-shirtless Tom Selleck. Is this male jiggle? And what of *Sea Hunt*? Lloyd Bridges often bared his chest, as did all the actors on *Flipper*. Compared to these men, the women of *Charlie's Angels* seem downright Victorian.

Similarly, we must also recognize that "beefcake" has fueled many hit series. Why did women watch *CHiPs*? And what of Tom Wopat and John Schneider of *The Dukes of Hazzard*; Ty Hardin of *Bronco*; Barry Williams of *The Brady Bunch*; Kirk Cameron of *Growing Pains*, etc. Furthermore, it's no accident that the opening credits of *Trapper John, MD*, *Dave's World*, *Starsky & Hutch*, and even *Cagney & Lacey* (which featured Martin Kove) contained shots of their male co-stars bare-chested.

The "jiggle" label that has been forced onto *Angels*—much like a scarlet letter—is not surprising. Since men's body parts don't "jiggle" (at least the parts that can be on television), it's a term that can only apply to women, creating a double standard.

What has befallen *Angels* is what befalls many women: No matter their achievements, they just get evaluated on their looks. From its debut, *Angels* was addressed in terms of its stars' appearance. This doesn't happen with male leads. When *Vega$* debuted, it was written of in terms of entertainment value, not wardrobe.

Similarly, a show like *Starsky & Hutch* (1975–1975) about two male detectives who sometimes went undercover in traditionally male occupations (stuntmen, wrestlers) didn't set off any alarms. CBS' *Simon & Simon* (1981–1988) was about two male PIs who once found themselves "undercover" in a nudist colony. What was their comeuppance?

An interesting near coda for *Angels* occurred in the series' penultimate season with the episode "Toni's Boys." It starred Barbara Stanwyck as Antonia McQueen, who also owned a detective agency. She staffed her agency with three young, attractive *male* investigators.

This episode was meant to spawn a spin-off but the secondary series never happened. If it had, would *Toni's Boys* have been described as "whores"?

Today, decades after *Charlie's Angels'* debut, the supposed "jiggle" of the show seems pretty tame compared to Madonna and *Maxim* magazine. And what lingers isn't pin-up poses, but the Angels' great athletics. These women run, leap, even skateboard. Whether it was an influence is debatable but these characters' able-bodied personas certainly seem to dovetail well with the fitness culture of the 1970s.

What also endures is their professionalism and sisterhood. Ironically, it's a level of seriousness that was not replicated in the movie remake from 2000, a supposedly more "enlightened" time. The new Angels (Cameron Diaz et al.) didn't have the same maturity as the originals. To these latter-day Angels, fighting crime seemed like a fluke.

Years after TV's *Angels* departed, programmer Fred Silverman stated that the series was "at the forefront of women's lib."[178] And Rosenzweig said, "There would never have been a *Cagney & Lacey* without the foundation laid by *Charlie's Angels*."[179]

Even Ayn Rand once stated she was a fan, saying, "The [series] is about three attractive girls doing impossible things."[180] In a paper by Chris Matthew Sciabarra, he analyzes Rand's affinity for *Charlie's Angels* and compared the show's story structure to Rand's famous works. He notes Rand's reoccurring "images of three" and observes how this motif was reflected in *Angels*. Furthermore, he implies that these TV "angels" conjure up pseudo-religious comparisons, "a secular counterpart to the Christian Holy Trinity." According to Sciabarra, "[T]here can be little doubt that the three heroines of the story exemplify the true, the good and the beautiful, as they vanquish the false, the bad, and the ugly."[181]

———◦◦◦———

The creation of producers Arlene Sidaris and Joyce Brotman, *The Hardy Boys/Nancy Drew Mysteries* (1977–1978) rotated *Drew* episodes with *Hardy* episodes every other week.

Nancy Drew began in fiction in 1927 and, in the '30s, she was featured in four feature films.

As she'd been in books, Nancy on TV didn't worry about her hair or what to wear — not when there were mysteries to be solved! For example, in "The Mystery of the Solid Gold Kicker," when Nancy's friend George claims to have seen the body of a dead woman through a window, and the police won't believe her, Nancy's hunt for clues is on.

George says that the woman seemed to have been hit with a crystal vase. But when Nancy searches for glass fragments, nothing turns up. She then asks the house's owner, "Can I see your vacuum cleaner?" When that search turns up nothing, Nancy presses on, eventually Dumpster-diving to find glass shards.

Throughout the episode, Nancy's detecting skills outshine the cops and, eventually, flush out the criminal. From the warm engine of a parked car, she determines that a witness was lying about being home all night; from the attempted theft of a supposedly useless item, Nancy realizes what someone was trying to cover up.

Along with smart, Nancy is also brave. In this same episode, in a crime lab, Nancy is confronted by a ski-masked man. The unarmed Nancy doesn't panic; instead, realizing that having people around is not what this guy wants, Nancy throws a chair out the window. The noise brings others running. Later, when Nancy is fleeing from a pursuer, she removes her hat and throws it down a corridor, fooling her follower about her direction. In the end, Nancy solves the mystery and even saves the big football game!

Throughout all the mysteries she solved, Nancy also showed a variety of skills, including being a pilot (a carryover from the books).

Pamela Sue Martin originally played Nancy and was able to project keen intelligence without smugness. But as brilliant as she was, Nancy wasn't popular. Her 50 percent of the series couldn't equal Shaun Cassidy's *Hardy Boys* half. Sadly, soon into her own series, *Nancy* became an also-ran.

In an effort to retain the show's original concept, the Boys and Nancy were merged into one series. Martin (wisely) objected to the trio concept and departed. Actress Janet Louise Johnson became Nancy but appeared only twice before *Nancy* disappeared altogether and the program became all–*Boys*.

As capable as she was, in the end, Nancy couldn't compete against Cassidy's cuteness. It's ironic that one of the best-ever female TV teens was ultimately undone by the audience she was best suited for: teenage girls.

———

Another renowned detective with a legacy as long as Nancy's is Agatha Christie's skilled amateur Miss Jane Marple. For many fans, it's PBS' Joan Hickson (in a 1984–1992 series) who is the definitive Miss M.

Though she debuted the same year as *Murder, She Wrote*, Miss Marple wasn't quite as spry as Jessica Fletcher. But that didn't mean she wasn't sharp-minded. As Alan McKee writes in an essay on the series: "Her frail physical appearance contrasts with her intensely blue eyes, and the way she dominated the scenes in which she appears."[182] But while some underestimate her, local authorities never do. Whether she is at home or on holiday, it is not uncommon for police to seek her out.

Unlike Jessica, Miss Marple is not one to shadow law enforcement. She is also less likely to take part in action-oriented resolutions; she's English, after all. Miss M.'s crime-solving is all mental, deduced over cups of tea. When she is proved right, and later thanked, she offers up only a smile and a simple "Not at all...."

———

Near the other end of the spectrum was PI Claire McCarron (played by Margaret Colin) on *Leg Work* (1987). In one recap, this character is dismissed as "a nubile private eye who spent much of her time posing and complaining about the dating scene...."[183] That's untrue.

Leg Work was like *Mary Tyler Moore* with a crime twist. Along with finding a new roommate and shopping for one, the single McCarron also took on various PI assignments large and small. *Leg Work* was a sort of female *Magnum*— a detective story mixed with odd-ball bits of humor. Producer Frank Abatemarco said that he wanted to "bring a true sense of reality to the world of the private investigator."[184] To that end, as often as we saw Claire grilling suspects, we also saw her doing dull paperwork or attempting to collect from dead-beat clients.

Despite occasional car troubles and problems related to being a woman in a "man's job," McCarron, per Thrillingdetective.com, always "handled her cases with wit and intelligence."[185] And she always got the crook. In one episode, McCarron's knowledge of sign language unraveled the mystery. In her lead, Colin brought a likability and a quirky humor to her role.

Unfortunately, *Leg Work* was slotted on Saturday nights against stiff competition. Only ten episodes aired before it was yanked. Hence *Leg Work* became a programming footnote and another example of a missed opportunity.

Other notable female detectives, "official" or not, on the air over the years included: *Mannix*'s (1967–1975) associate Peggy Fair played by Gail Fisher; Lee Meriwether on *Barnaby Jones* (1973–1980); Kate Mulgrew in the title role of *Mrs. Columbo* (1979) (later retitled *Kate Loves a Mystery*); and Loni Anderson and Lynda Carter on the short-lived *Partners in Crime* (1984) (who also saw their show evaluated more on the looks than content).

The Spies

TV's greatest sitcom as satire was the spy send-up *Get Smart* (1965–1970). One writer said, "[It's] the equivalent of Dada as applied to the world of espionage."[186]

The series starred Don Adams as secret agent Maxwell Smart, who was actually anything but. Smart was no 007; even his secret agent code number — 86, bartenders' shorthand for someone who's had enough — signified his ineptitude.

By utter contrast, Max's female partner (and love interest) Agent 99 had a code number just one digit short of perfection.[187] Agent 99, played by Barbara Feldon, is yet another example of a woman on TV smart and good at her job. Feldon's 99 was no bimbo. She was smarter than Max. In fact, she was easily the series' smartest person. The recurring good guys from the organization CONTROL were as inept as the evil lot from their enemy organization KAOS.

TV Sirens says of Feldon, "[She] subverted masculine hierarchies with a sly feminine force."[188] Another author called her "cool-headed."[189] Donna McCrohan, in her book *The Life & Times of Maxwell Smart*, says, "[She had] an arch innocence, a sensible worldliness, beauty, poise, the ability to radiate intelligence without having to say a word."[190]

Regularly, 99 saves both Max and the day. Consider:

- In one episode, Max and another spook find themselves alone with a killer on a deserted isle. Luckily, 99 arrives in time to rescue them.
- In another, 99's quick thinking saves her and Max when they find themselves trapped in a submarine with a torpedo heading for it.

As McCrohan puts it, "Without [99's] presence of mind, Max is doomed."[191]

Among other things we know about 99: She speaks several foreign languages, is a martial artist, and possesses a grand vocabulary. She was also too forgiving. One of the series' ongoing gags had 99 always coming up with a solution only to have it later ripped off by Max. Consider this exchange:

99: We can use Mr. Bunny to get out of here.
MAX: Ninety-nine, I'd like to handle this myself.... Mr. Bunny, you can help us get out of here.

Repeatedly, when faced with Max's arrogance, 99 never did more than roll her eyes. As Ron Smith notes, "It was achingly funny — or just plain aching — to see 99 waste her affection on an oblivious Max."[192] With time, viewers probably just once wanted 99 to smack Max upside the head. But, as explained by the show's writers, it was redundant to give 99 snappy comebacks; she didn't have to try to make Max look like a fool, he did that himself.[193]

The two eventually became romantic, then married. The interplay between 86 and 99 owes less to Nick and Nora Charles than it does to Don Quixote and Sancho Panza with 99 as Panza, the put-upon second banana, smarter and savvier than the lead but whose role is one of compassion as she works to keep her partner alive.

—◦◦◦—

Syndicated over various U.S. stations, the Brit-produced *The Protectors* (1972–1973) told the story of a trio of international investigators.[194] The Man from U.N.C.L.E. Robert Vaughn played Harry Rule, the London-based head of the team. Tony Anholt, later of *Space: 1999*, co-starred as Paul Buchet, who made his home in France amid computers. Finally, Nyree Dawn Porter had the role of Lady Caroline Oglivie (a.k.a. the Contessa di Contini) who lived luxuriously in Rome when she wasn't out kicking butt.

Like Emma of *The Avengers*, the contessa was an integral part of this team and, once again, no concessions were made for the "girl" in their group. She was never in distress; if anything, her judo and fencing often saved her partners' lives. In one episode, when the trio jumps into a dune buggy, the contessa grabs the wheel; the guys ride shotgun.

Throughout the series, the contessa regularly garnered more airtime than Buchet, mainly because there was so much she could do: distract the enemy, infiltrate grand salons, go undercover (who would suspect her?), and shoot like a sniper. For sure, the contessa did more than her share in disabling her show's evildoers.

Evildoers also didn't stand a chance against the women of *Codename: Foxfire* (1985). Joanna Cassidy played Elizabeth Towne, a former CIA operative handpicked by the brother of the president to head up a special counter-intelligence team. Joining Towne were Maggie Bryan (played by Sheryl Lee Ralph), a cat burglar going straight, and Danny O'Toole (Robin Johnson), a New Yorker with killer driving skills.

Brooks and Marsh say of them, "[T]hey were hard-nosed and tough, or elegant and sophisticated, as the assignment demanded."[195] During their months on the air, the trio proved themselves effective in working together whether they were dismantling a nuclear warhead or protecting a foreign dignitary. Had they endured, *Foxfire* could have picked up where *The Avengers'* Emma left off.

Her Own Boss

If women on TV often toiled in jobs where they answered to someone else, they just as often were seen as both bosses and business owners. As early as 1952, former film star Lynn Bari starred in *Boss Lady* as Gwen F. Allen, the owner of a construction company. It aired on NBC for 12 episodes.

A more enduring female business owner arrived via *The Roy Rogers Show* (1951–1957). Dale Evans co-starred as the owner of the Eureka Café; her business often had to take second place to her riding out with Roy to track down outlaws.[196] Said husband Roy about his real-life wife's on-air persona, "When Dale came along she got into fights and everything. She gave the leading lady a better part and the people liked it!"[197] As Savage puts it, Dale was "capable and fearless."[198] Dale was always *in* the action, not standing off to the side.

In one episode, she and Pat Brady, the duo's sidekick, are holed up in a cabin with outlaws outside. Roy rides in to try to rescue them. When he arrives, Pat draws his guns and gets ready to shoot. Luckily, Dale stops him: "No, Pat, they'll kill Roy!" Dale sends their dog Bullet out the window to create a distraction. Still, Pat gets overeager and ends up shot in the shoulder.

Eventually the outlaws are put on the run. Dale exits the cabin, telling a member of Roy's posse, "Take care of Pat. He's injured." She then jumps on her horse and rides off to join up with Roy.

Dale could always stand up for herself. In one episode, when one guy gets fresh, Dale retorts, "Don't call me 'Babe'!" If further proof of Dale's feminist leanings are needed, consider this after-dinner exchange between Dale and an older woman that she, Roy and Pat are visiting:

DALE: Ma, you and I better attend to these dishes.
MA: Oh, they can wait. You go attend to your horse.
DALE: Roy and Pat will do it for me.
MA: Roy and Pat nothing! You can't handle men by letting them know you have to depend on them. They'll get the upper hand if you do.
DALE: You have a point.

Then, in the final frames, Roy and Dale often, literally, ride off into the sunset, with Dale, not dallying behind, but alongside.

—◦◦◦—

On TV, Dale Evans wasn't the only restaurant owner, or tough gal, in the Old West. Miss Kitty of *Gunsmoke* (1955–1975) owned the Dodge City saloon and was portrayed, with brains and backbone, by Amanda Blake.

On radio's version of *Gunsmoke*, Miss Kitty was clearly a madam; on TV, there's little evidence that Miss Kitty was practicing the world's oldest profession. Why then does the madam myth persist? Is it sexism? Can viewers not conceive of a successful woman who doesn't trade on sex? In his book on TV westerns, J. Fred MacDonald says, "Kitty Russell ... epitomized the tension between social respectability and the demands of a single woman making a living on the frontier."[199]

Though always treated as a lady (always addressed as "Miss Kitty"), she's also "one of the guys," an equal to Matt Dillon and the other Dodge men. Regularly she is sought out for counsel. During discussions, Kitty's a participant. Her opinions matter and show her to be of greater intellect than many around her — even Doc, who is less worldly than she.

Throughout *Gunsmoke*'s 20-year run, Kitty proved herself to be formidable. She owned a successful business and managed a large staff. She had backbone too. Said one author, "[When] tough customers did in her saloon what tough customers usually do ... Kitty had the resolute strength to lay down the law."[200]

Kitty was gutsy. She thought nothing of standing up to a man, or a group of them. In the episode "Wheland's Men," where Kitty has to play poker to save Dillon's life, she's as cool as they come. "You got brass, lady," one of the outlaws tells her after she wins.

In the episode "The Lost," Kitty's stagecoach is toppled and, rather than wait there to be saved, she takes it upon herself to go look for help. On her journey, Kitty comes upon a "wild child," an abandoned girl who lives feral in the woods. Unknown to Kitty, an unscrupulous family (led by guest star Mercedes McCambridge) is hunting the girl to exhibit her like an animal. When the family catches Kitty with the girl, they take both hostage. It's now up to Kitty to save them both — and she does. Prying herself loose from her restraints, Kitty then frees the girl, then grabs a gun when one of the woman's sons attempts to stop her.

Among other traits, Kitty also had a maternal streak. And was the least judgmental person in town. She often takes in boarders, giving sanctuary to untrusted minorities and people who, like her, are outside social norms. In her humanity, Miss Kitty removes a stereotype that has been thrust upon her, from both history and TV critics.

—⟡⟡⟡—

Of course, it wasn't just in the Old West that women owned businesses.

Anne Jeffreys, formerly of *Topper*, starred in the comedy *Love That Jill* (1958) as Jill Johnson, the high-powered owner of a New York modeling agency. Co-starring with Jeffreys was her real-life husband (and former *Topper* co-star) Robert Sterling. He played Jack Gibson (Jack and Jill, get it?), the owner of Gibson Girls, Manhattan's other top modeling agency.

Jack and Jill were supposed to be business rivals and were also to have a romantic interest in each another. Like *Moonlighting* (a show also with a fashion slant), their bickering was supposed to be perceived as elaborate, though chaste, foreplay. But, that said, business often took precedence over love. These "friendly" rivals would jettison witticisms whenever a new face was up for grabs. In this business of beauty, things could get ugly.

In one episode, Jill misleads Jack into thinking she's headed to Paris instead of a dude ranch to sign a new discovery. However, a loose-lipped model spills the beans, so when Jill arrives at the ranch, she finds Jack already there!

As the battle begins, there appears to be more than just money at stake. Jack loses his cool when he sees handsome guest star Chuck Connors take an interest in Jill. Throughout the episode, it's Jack who is the lovesick one.

As an executive on *Love That Jill*, Jeffreys was the *chicest*, most stylish vision on 1950s TV. Dressed in tailored suits with swept-up hair and gesturing with her horn-rimmed glasses, she could teach Alexis Carrington about power dressing. Jill Johnson seems to continue the line of tough executive women that began with Joan Crawford in the 1940s and then got carried on through *Dynasty*.

Make no mistake, though, Jill wasn't just style. As depicted in the series, she's a power player, holding court behind her desk and ordering around male assistants. This is a woman whose business has been built on good deal-making, not tears or playing dumb.

—⟡⟡⟡—

Though not as glam as Ms. Johnson, Kate Bradley, owner of the Shady Rest Hotel on *Petticoat Junction* (1963–1970), knew what she was doing too.

A sole proprietor, Kate was both a competitive businesswoman and a community pillar. To keep her hotel afloat, she regularly butted heads with "arch rival" Selma Plout and with railroad efficiency "expert" Homer Bedloe.

But it wasn't just money that motivated Mrs. Bradley. She was also a dedicated activist, always at the forefront to save the Cannon Ball, the ancient steam engine that is the social and economic lifeline of Hooterville.

Kate Bradley is feisty. In various episodes she contests a ticket for jaywalking; plays peacemaker to two feuding train conductors; and gives parenting tips to a man who's neglecting his son.

As played by Bea Benaderet, Kate was a centered business owner and even-keeled mother. Said McWilliams, "Whether dealing with … the cantankerous sarcasm of Granny, or the spirited antics of Billie Jo, Bobbie Jo, and Betty Jo, Benaderet provided a calm center to centrigual lunacy."[201]

Much of that lunacy on *Junction* was the product of Kate's Uncle Joe, a shiftless sort with many wild schemes. In one episode, Joe tricks two women, Henrietta and Gertrude, into thinking that the Shady Rest is a spa and that Kate is a perfectly preserved 75-year-old! In the end, the two women figure out Joe's ploy and, upon checking out, tell him and Kate that despite it all they have learned one thing:

> HENRIETTA: [We know] what keeps you young and attractive.
> GERTRUDE: Your secret, Mrs. Bradley, is hard work.
> HENRIETTA: We have never seen anyone tackle work like you do.
> GERTRUDE: You're incredible. You're not 75, like this old rascal would have us believe, but you're still an incredible woman.

Junction was a staple of CBS' rural line-up for years, alongside *Green Acres* and *The Beverly Hillbillies*. At the height of its popularity, 1963, *Petticoat* ranked fourth and attracted 30.3 percent of the viewing audience.[202] Ironic then that Kate Bradley, one of TV's most preeminent business women (and, for that matter, mother figures), often gets omitted from discussions of gender on TV.

In the 1930s and '40s, Barbara Stanwyck had been one of the movies' most prominent actresses. Like many of her contemporaries, she later moved to TV, beginning in 1960 via her anthology *The Barbara Stanwyck Show*.

But even with that success, Stanwyck would still make her biggest splash with *The Big Valley* (1965–1969) where she played Victoria, the matriarch of the Barkley clan. Stanwyck had excelled in Westerns in film and was at home with the genre on TV too. But before taking the role, she made it clear what she wouldn't be:

> I'm a tough old broad from Brooklyn, don't try to make me something I'm not. If you want someone to tiptoe down the Barkley staircase in a crinoline and politely ask where the cattle went, get another girl.[203]

One of cinema's toughest, most resilient leading ladies, Barbara Stanwyck brought that same sort of grit to her role as rancher and land owner Victoria Barkley on *The Big Valley* (1965–1969).

In nearly every episode of *Big Valley* there is a display of Mrs. Barkley's grit. In one, which centers on a land dispute between the Barkleys and some squatters, one squatter arrives at her home with a gun. This inspires Victoria's son, Nick, to reach for his firearm. But Victoria's not having it. "Oh, put down that ridiculous gun!" she orders as she grabs the squatter's rifle.

In another episode, when a California earthquake buries Victoria and others under an old church, Victoria takes charge. Buried along with her is a young Charles Bronson playing Tate, a fellow worshiper—but not a law-abiding one. Nevertheless, he and Victoria are everyone's best bet for survival ... until Victoria sees Tate gulping liquor. (He had a stash hidden on him.) She solves that problem by shattering the bottle.

In another episode, she easily handles a rifle, fighting off a group of outlaws single-handedly. In another, she impersonates a criminal to get herself thrown in jail; she wants to learn about the prison's deplorable conditions.

Torey L. King wrote in a study of the actress's career, "As Victoria Barkley, Stanwyck regularly confronts life-threatening situations and hostile adversaries. And like some mythic figure, Victoria triumphs over all, out-shooting and outsmarting her (usually male) opponents."[204]

⎯⎯⎯~∿∿∿~⎯⎯⎯

Based on the *Washington Post*'s Katherine Graham, *Lou Grant*'s (1977–1982) Mrs. Pynchon ran her newspaper, the *Los Angeles Tribune*, with the same sort of iron hand/velvet glove that Graham has been celebrated for. Starring in the role was Nancy Marchand (later Octavia, matriarch of *The Sopranos*).

As Mrs. Pynchon, the actress was Emmy-winning, able to project regality without tripping into haughtiness. McWilliams summarized her by stating, "Bitchy, regal, tough-minded, Marchand refused to be one of the boys only because it would be a step down."[205]

Mrs. Pynchon was well-bred and "of a certain age," a woman who wore education and sophistication with aplomb. Marchand said of her, "She was a titan. She could do anything."[206]

As "boss," Mrs. Pynchon often had to make tough decisions and fight the good fight, be it with Lou or others. In one episode, when stolen medical files are passed on to one of her reporters and the reporter refuses to divulge his source, a tempest erupts. Mrs. Pynchon takes a stand with the courts. Mrs. Pynchon questions her editors, "So, we newspaper people are only above *some* laws?" When Lou compares the situation to the Pentagon Papers, Mrs. Pynchon responds, "But that was a matter of national importance. I don't think this case is comparable."

Other times, she had to take other unpopular stances. In one installment, the wife of one of her senior editors has taken a paid position with a candidate. Pynchon believes this constitutes a conflict of interest and says that the woman will have to resign from her job or he will be fired from his.

⎯⎯⎯~∿∿∿~⎯⎯⎯

Over the years, other working women, large and in charge, have also been seen. On primetime's first hit soap *Peyton Place* (1964–1969), Constance Mackenzie (played by Dorothy Malone) owned a bookstore; Wrangler Jane was a shopkeeper (and good shot) on

F Troop (1965–1967); Nancy Walker owned a talent agency on *The Nancy Walker Show* (1976); actresses Bess Armstrong and Lynnie Greene, on *On Our Own* (1977–1978), worked at an ad agency and answered to Toni McBain, played by Gretchen Wyler; and Shelley Fabares played an ad exec on *One Day at a Time* (1975–1984). Fabares "wiped everybody off the set with her wicked impersonation of an aging prom queen let loose in the business world."[207] Restaurants were owned by the title characters on *Angie* (1979–1980) and *Flo* (1980–1981) and by Mrs. Garrett on *Facts of Life* (1979–1988).

During the 1980s, TV counted numerous female execs and business owners. Sheree North headed a DC think tank on *I'm a Big Girl Now* (1980–1981); actress Holland Taylor played one of her trademark power women on the Tom Hanks–Peter Scolari sitcom *Bosom Buddies* (1980–1982); Shirley Hemphill (formerly of *What's Happening!*) took on the "stuffed shirts" of corporate America in *One in a Million* (1980); Beatrice Arthur, between *Maude* and *The Golden Girls*, ran her own hotel on *Amanda's* (1983); and Yvette Mimieux managed a department store on *Berrenger's* (1985).

The 1980s were also the heyday of the primetime soap, a genre that brought to TV some extraordinarily powerful working women. Far from "backlash," this was arguably the best era ever for women on television thanks to the soaps. Certainly for actresses over 40, the primetime serial finally brought a platform big and regal enough to contain these women's hard-edged glamour and "tough dame" personas.

The divas were led by Joan Collins whose career-defining Alexis turned *Dynasty* (1981–1989) into a megahit. McWilliams called Collins the "Queen Bee of prime-time soaps."[208] Collins' crisp English diction and ultra-thin cigarette inspired a generation of drag queens. Collins said of her character, "If she wanted to make a decision, she made it and faced the consequences...."[209]

Diahann Carroll joined *Dynasty* in 1984 playing, in her own words, the "first black bitch on television."[210] Stephanie Beacham played devious Sable Colby on both *Dynasty* and *The Colbys* (1985–1987). One author said of her, "[She was the] only bitch strong enough to give Joan Collins second thoughts."[211] Co-starring with Beacham was Barbara Stanwyck as the respected Colby matriarch, running her business ... and becoming involved with a younger man.

On *Dallas* (1978–1991), Barbara Bel Geddes, Alexis Smith and Donna Reed all at one time had roles. Oscar winner Jane Wyman returned to TV at the age of 70 to play Angela Channing on *Falcon Crest* (1981–1990) and gave the "most acid portrait of divahood ever to reach primetime."[212]

Others who came to *Falcon Crest* included Gina Lollobrigida, age 57, and Lana Turner, 64. Turner previously had practically invented this sort of role on the early primetime soap *The Survivors* (1969–1970).

Bette Davis, age 76, starred as the owner of the namesake hotel in the pilot for *Hotel* (1983–1988). She was followed by Anne Baxter, 61, who continued on the program until her death in 1985. Ava Gardner was on *Knots Landing* (1979–1993) in 1985. That series also featured Donna Mills, Michele Lee, and Joan Van Ark.

Erudite social critic Camille Paglia said of some of these queen bees:

> When the history of feminism is rewritten accurately, Joan Collins' performance as Alexis Carrington on *Dynasty* and [Donna Mills'] as Abby Cunningham on *Knots Landing* will be seen as pivotal roles in popular culture that had a revolutionary impact on women's behavior and self-image.[213]

The Nuns

Of course, women did not have to sport shoulder pads or run empires to be imposing on TV. For many Catholics there's nothing more formidable than a nun. Over the decades, TV has brought forth its share of sisterly images. And no one can accuse them of "jiggle."

TV's most famous nun was Sister Bertrille, played by Sally Field on *The Flying Nun* (1967–1970). A series with one of the oddest premises ever, *The Flying Nun* followed a nun whose light weight and ornate habit, combined with the tropical winds of Puerto Rico, where her convent was, allowed her to fly.

In *Where the Girls Are*, Susan Douglas is hard on Sister Bertrille. Douglas states that despite the Sister's ability to fly, she is undermined by her chaste state.[214] But certainly female role models don't have to be sexual in order to be "relatable"? Sister Bertrille's convent life, rather than being repressive, could just as easily be interpreted as female-centeric: She is living in and among other women in a self-managed, near-separatist community.

Next Douglas derides the Sister's coronet by calling it "a paper airplane on steroids."[215] Yet Sister Bertrille's attire is historically accurate.[216]

Finally the author takes issue with Bertrille's early crash landings.[217] But these stumbles — played for slapstick — are only in the show's early episodes. With time, our Sister gets control of her "wings" and enjoys only the most graceful descents.

Sister Bertrille's ability to fly should not be undervalued. Her ability is impossible according to the (man-made?) laws of physics. For the Wright Brothers it took years of experiments to get airborne; Sister Bertrille only needed a headwind.

In many episodes, Sister Bertrille's flying saves the day and sometimes saves lives. In one episode she assists a fisherman by serving as an "eye in the sky" and leading him to fish-infested waters. In another, she saves a drowning woman.

As the series continued, Bertrille's flying ability became more incidental to the series. After the first season, it was no longer necessary for her to be aloft to work her magic. In one (nearly flight-free) episode she taught an illiterate man to read. In another she broke through the emotional wall around an orphaned boy.

For a program often tagged silly, *Nun* actually broached a variety of weighty topics. In one episode, the archdiocese hears of this supposedly flying nun. He dispatches a psychologist to the convent to cure the "mass hysteria" (a loaded, female-oriented term). In the end, though, it's the shrink who thinks he's crazy when he sees Sister Bertrille take to the sky. Once again, traditional male science and theology is no match for female power.

Besides being about female ability, *Nun* is also pro-environmental. Bertrille is in harmony with Mother Nature. Rather than being a tale of "man against nature," it is instead about a woman at one with the elements.

During its life, *The Flying Nun* also explored (believe it or not) male-female partnerships, ones that were free of sexual content. Sister Bertrille often journeyed into town to see Carlos, a good-hearted but swinging playboy who owned a local disco. Carlos' contacts were sometimes needed by the nuns. Carlos and Sister Bertrille had a brother-sister dynamic. And though Carlos often stated he'd had enough of Sister Bertrille's "hare-brained schemes" (much like another Latin male once voiced to another empowered woman, Lucy Ricardo), he ultimately ends up doing what the Sister wants. The reason for Carlos' frequent turnaround is one as old as the world (and "The Word"): In the end, while the nuns might need Carlos' assistance with earthly things like money, Carlos needs them for redemption.

The "Carlos Factor" also demonstrates one of the most refreshing aspects of this series: It's pro-religion. In a departure from how religion, especially Catholicism, is usually portrayed, none of these nuns ever questioned their vows. Contrast this with *The Thorn Birds* where a man of the cloth gives in to temptation.

Nothing in the show was ever sacrilegious. And, hence, episodes could not be based around lies or dating scenarios. Therefore, its comedy usually arose out of the strained relationship between Sister Bertrille and her Mother Superior.

Mother (played by Madeleine Sherwood) didn't care for her novice's frequent flying. Yet, in the same way that *Bewitched*'s Darrin ended up often needing Samantha's magic, Mother sometimes called on the Flying Nun to take to the sky.

In her role as Mother Superior, this mother, literally and figuratively, represented not only her own old-fashioned ideas but also a strand of pre-reformation Catholicism. Therefore, *The Flying Nun* is about the generation gap with the Mother Superior standing in for all mothers who were at the time also concerned about the way their daughters were choosing to lead their lives. Sister Bertrille was flying away from the nest and challenging traditions and expectations.

—◦◦◦—

Though Sister Bertrille was a tough act to follow, TV has given us other notable nuns. *In the Beginning* (1978), produced by Norman Lear, starred Priscilla Lopez as Sister Agnes, who ran an inner-city community center. Her radical ideas often (in shades of *All in the Family*) were often opposed by her superior, Father Cleary (played by McLean Stevenson).

In *Sister Kate* (1989–1990), Kate, played by Stephanie Beacham, was a no-nonsense nun with deep faith and major attitude. She headed Redemption House, a Catholic residence for orphans. Inside, seven kids ran wild, having already driven off three priests. Then Sister Kate arrived. Kate was modern and post–Vatican II. Among other unorthodox factors, she had also kicked the habit, preferring instead secular dress.

Kate's disposition was hammered home in the pilot when one of her girls sneaks out to a golf course to meet a boy. Just after the would-be lovers arrive at their trysting place, a shed, thunder is heard and lightning cracks the ground. Sister Kate walks in wielding a nine-iron. "What are you doing here?" the boy asks.

"I've come to up my handicap," replies the Sister. (In reruns, this line was changed to "I've come to hit some balls.")

While not quite Kate, another gutsy nun could be found on *Father Dowling Mysteries* (1989–1991) in the personage of Sister Steve. *Dowling* was about a crime-solving priest (Tom Bosley). His assistant, a streetwise sister, was played by third-generation TV star Tracy Nelson, daughter of Ricky and granddaughter of Ozzie and Harriet.

In solving the weekly mystery, Sister Steve had to depend not only on God's grace but on her own smarts and bravery. After all, nuns don't carry guns. In the show, it seemed like all of the "heavy lifting" fell to the Sister — including going undercover as a card dealer, a noblewoman and (gasp!) a lady of the evening. (Shades of Mary Magdalene?) By the end of every episode, Steve broke the case, not her vows.

All in a Day's Work

Though certain occupations lend themselves to TV — police officer, lawyer, etc. — in the 60-plus years of television programming, a diverse number of other careers have also been depicted and have often been enacted by women.

Begun immediately after *Private Secretary*, *The Ann Sothern Show* (1958–1961) re-envisioned Sothern as Katy O'Connor, the assistant manager of an upscale hotel, the Bartley.

This time around, Sothern's character had the inner office and her own secretary. But she had no designs on her boss or any other male. Katy is having too much fun. As the show's theme says, "All the guys fall for Katy...." In various episodes, Katy (or "Miss O'Connor" as she's always addressed) tracked down some jewel thieves and championed the cause of Native Americans.

After *My Little Margie*, Gale Storm returned to TV in *The Gale Storm Show: Oh, Susanna!* (1956–1960). Storm was Susanna Pomeroy, the social director for a *Love Boat*–like liner. She often butted heads with the ship's captain and once told a suitor, "No man brushes off Susanna Pomeroy and gets away with it!"

In *The Adventures of Tugboat Annie* (1958), Minerva Urecal, 62, was the owner and the skipper of the *Narcissus*.

On the comedy *Broadside* (1964–1965), a group of WAVES was stationed in the South Pacific and their commanding officer (Kathy Nolan) once informed her superior, "We joined the WAVES to help fight the war, not to sit in some back area...!"

Other military women have included Eileen Brennan, as Army Captain Doreen Lewis on TV's *Private Benjamin* (1981–1983), and Beverly Archer as Gunnery Sergeant Alva "Gunny" Bricker on *Major Dad* (1989–1993).

Women scientists could be found on the *X-Files*–like *Top Secret, USA* (1954–1955) starring Gena Rowlands; on *The Time Tunnel* (1966–1967) featuring Lee Meriwether; and on *Salvage 1* (1979), where Trish Stewart played an explosives expert helping junk man Andy Griffith get to the Moon. Diana Muldaur was an anthropologist on TV's *Born Free* (1974) and Oscar-winner Celeste Holm was a blunt press secretary on *Nancy* (1970).

Actresses playing actresses could be found on *So This Is Hollywood* (1955); *Two Girls Named Smith*; *Mona McCluskey* starring Juliet Prowse (1965–1966); *That Girl* (1966–1971) starring Marlo Thomas; *The Betty White Show* (1977) and *Love, Sidney* (1981–1983) with Swoosie Kurtz.

Marilu Henner was a cabbie, art gallery worker and single mother on *Taxi* (1978–1983) and Lynn Redgrave was a hospital administrator on *House Calls* (1979–1982).

Writers — of considerable success — could be seen on *The Dick Van Dyke Show* (1961–1966) in the personage of Rose Marie; on *McCloud* (1970–1977) which featured Diana Muldaur as the lead's girlfriend, and via Loretta Young in *The New Loretta Young Show* (1962–1963); Pat Crowley on *Please Don't Eat the Daisies* (1965–1967); Hope Lange on *The Ghost and Mrs. Muir* (1968–1970); Bess Armstrong on *All Is Forgiven* (1986); and Ellen Burstyn on *The Ellen Burstyn Show* (1986–1987).

Meanwhile, Elinor Donahue was Ellie the town pharmacist on *The Andy Griffith Show* (1960–1961); Whitney Blake (Hazel's "boss") was an interior designer on *Hazel* (1961–1965); and there was a female carpenter — named Ralph no less — on *Green Acres* (1965–1971). Ulla Stromstedt was an oceanographer on *Flipper* (1965–1966); Yvette Mimieux was a criminologist on *Most Deadly Game* (1971–1971); and Joanna Cassidy was a TV producer on *Buffalo Bill* (1983–1984).

In 1985, even the U.S. president was a woman — on *Hail to the Chief* (1985) starring Patty Duke.

Conclusion

This long list of TV working women roundly disproves the resilient myth that no woman worked on TV before Mary Richards went to Minneapolis.

But even then, all these women, whether they worked in traditional or non-traditional careers, represent more than just their job titles. What is resonating about working women on TV is how seldom — if ever — we saw women portrayed as bad at their jobs. Miss Brooks was a good teacher; Susie McNamara, a skilled secretary; Sgt. Casey Jones, a good cop; and Hazel, a domestic engineer without peer.

That being the case, then what was the message that these images ultimately sent? What did they convey to little girls who were watching them and to real-life women either thinking about careers, or working in them already? And what do they still communicate to generations after?

— 6 —

"Sisters Are Doin' It for Themselves"
Single in the City

A woman needs a man like a fish needs a bicycle.—famous feminist slogan

Sitcoms about young women living in big cities and Making It On Their Own have never left us. Though they might have peaked in the 1970s with *Mary Tyler Moore* and her clones, such later fare as *Suddenly Susan, Caroline in the City, Ally McBeal,* and even *Sex in the City* have shown the endurance of this feminized subset.

To fully appreciate the Single Woman program, note the lack of shows built around single men carving out their careers. Usually when programs are about men, the mister is married (*He & She* with Richard Benjamin, *Everybody Loves Raymond*) or he is in some way a parent (think *Bachelor Father* through *Full House*). (NBC's short-lived *The Single Guy* is an exception.)

Usually, when people think of Single-in-the-City–type sitcoms, they think of *Mary Tyler Moore.* When she debuted, Mary Richards, smart but a little insecure, and on her own for the first time, struck a major chord with women as she mirrored them, other college-educated young women who also wanted to experience life before settling down to marriage and motherhood — if they "settled" at all.

Though the Independent Woman genre reached its high during *Mary Tyler Moore*'s seven-year run, Mary wasn't TV's first woman to be on her own or, for that matter, to turn the world on with a smile.

Technically, programs like Ann Sothern's *Private Secretary* and Eve Arden's *Our Miss Brooks* fall into the Independent Woman category since both were about unmarried professionals living on their own. But Ann and Eve are separated from Mary if only because these ladies were both over 40 when they began their TV endeavors. Hence, their more mature personas and degree of work experience disconnect them from many of the single women who arrived later.

Gale Storm's second sitcom, *The Gale Storm Show,* could also be considered a precursor to *Mary.* But *Storm*'s concentration on her character's work life, as opposed to focusing (more or less) equally on work and home, makes her show more "workcom."

Nevertheless, even excluding these programs, before *Mary* in 1970, and *That Girl* in 1966, there had already been a few ladies who helped pave the way for Mary's move to Minneapolis.

Stars in Their Eyes

TV's earliest single ladies tended to move away from home in pairs and to have dreams of show biz.

The high number of early programs that featured not one but two single women can be explained in a couple of ways. First, for whatever reason, few early TV characters ever lived alone: *Mr. Peepers* lived with his mother and even swinging bachelor Bob Cummings shared a house with his sister. In the case of early single career gals, their co-habitating acknowledged the post-war housing shortage and real-life economics: How could any young, fresh-from-college woman afford to live alone in New York City?

Secondly, partnered pairs (male or female) helped conjure up images of great comedy teams: Laurel and Hardy, Abbott and Costello and, of course, Lucy and Ethel.

Meanwhile, the high percentage of young women pursuing entertainment careers can also be explained. First, having a show biz bent allowed opportunities for unusual situations—from outrageous antics to funny costumes. Secondly, it allowed these programs to incorporate musical elements. This genre mixing would be a formula for later shows like *The Partridge Family* and *Glee*.

Both a duo and a show business slant was in TV's very first notable "single gals" series, *The Girls*. This live series debuted in 1951 and told the story of friends Cornelia and Emily, who recently graduated from Bryn Mawr (!). They had just come to New York to make their dreams come true—Cornelia as an actress, Emily as a writer. The two leads seemed to embrace both flapper-dom (the show was set in the 1920s) and progressive roles for women during their short run.

Not long after *The Girls*, TV saw the debut of *Two Girls Named Smith* (1951). According to a 1951 *Radio-TV Mirror*, *Smith* followed the "[u]ps and downs of big city living for two small town girls...."[1] Cousins from Omaha, they had left home for the big city. Babs was intent on being a singer while Fran hoped to be a fashion designer. While waiting for their breaks, Babs worked as a stenographer, Fran for East Side Fashions.

Two girls named Peggy played the two girls named Smith. Twenty-year-old Peggy Ann Garner, who had starred in *A Tree Grows in Brooklyn*, played Babs Smith, the aspiring songstress. (Garner was later replaced by Marcia Henderson.) Peggy French co-starred as Peggy Smith, the dress designer.

Two Girls aired from January to October 1951. Before it left the air, Babs got her big break by winning a role on Broadway. She said upon getting the job, "I never dreamed anything so wonderful could happen to a little girl from Omaha!"[2]

Four years after *Smith*, *So This Is Hollywood* (1955) told of two would-be performers out to make their mark in the movies. Former child actress Mitzi Green was featured as Queenie. Queenie herself was a former child actress now grown up and working as a stunt woman (a career that was slapstick-convenient). Co-starring was Virginia Gibson as Kim Tracy, a would-be starlet who mostly worked as an extra.

Though in the series both Queenie and Kim had resident boyfriends, it was fame, not marriage, they desired. Queenie and Kim's commitment to their careers was such that they once hung out on the docks because of a rumor that a director was looking there for an actress for his next picture. In another episode, Queenie decided to pose as a foreign film star to infiltrate a Hollywood party. In another, the duo staged an impromptu performance in their apartment to impress an agent.

If these situations sound very *Laverne & Shirley*, the comparison is fair. Like those later ladies, Queenie and Kim possessed both an adventuresome spirit and a desire to make their dreams come true. And while during *So This Is Hollywood*'s run stardom eluded them, they never quit.

Other single show biz aspirants could be found on *Those Whiting Girls* (1955–1957).

Successful singer Margaret Whiting played a slightly fictionalized version of herself on *Those Whiting Girls* (1955–1957), one of several series of the era that followed unmarried women pursuing show business careers. Jerry Paris is on the right.

Debuting as a summer replacement series for *I Love Lucy*, *Girls* was produced by Desilu Productions specifically for the talents of songstress Margaret Whiting, who starred as herself. In fact, the series was a family affair with Whiting's sister, Barbara, also playing herself.

In the show, the sisters lived in a Los Angeles home with their mother (played by Mabel Albertson) while pursuing their careers: Margaret as a singer, Barbara an actress.

While the women did date, neither seemed set on marriage. Besides, men tended to get in the way. This is the case in one episode where a frustrated Barbara threatens to move out. To get her to stay, Margaret's physician beau Joe suggests some "reverse psychology." But, as can be expected, the plan backfires and Barbara packs up and leaves.

Once she moves out, Barbara discovers that her struggling actress wages won't get her much of an apartment. She ends up leasing a converted garage with a broken back door and a weird neighbor. When mother and sister visit, it makes them realize that they should never have listened to Joe. Later, when Joe shows up, Margaret doesn't care to hear any more from him; she tells him, "The only thing I want to hear from you is the front door closing."

While the character of Barbara was written to be slightly impulsive, all three of these ladies packed a mighty wit. In the same episode, Dr. Joe attempts to explain the female mind to Margaret and her mother until Mom points out the obvious:

JOE: I'm just saying a girl is different from a man.
MOM: Is that what you learned at medical school?

Not only is this series notable for another portrayal of two single women, it's also interesting in that the Whitings played themselves. This self-reflexive technique (as seen on *Seinfeld* and *Ozzie and Harriet*) added a sense of realism to the series. Those Whiting girls weren't just playing normal women pursuing careers, they *really were* these women pursuing careers.

Similar in many ways to *Whiting* was *My Sister Eileen* (1960–1961). Based on a play, *Eileen* told of two sisters, would-be writer Ruth and her younger sister, would-be actress Eileen. By pinching pennies in their hometown, the sisters were able to move to New York City — chaperone- and den mother–free — to chase their dreams ... even if it meant residing in a dingy basement apartment (foreshadowing *Laverne & Shirley*'s later Milwaukee digs).

Elaine Stritch played Ruth and, though only 34 at the time, already possessed her gravel voice and special way with a quip. In one episode, she scores with the following exchange when a new beau of Eileen's comes to the door:

MAN: I hope I have the right apartment.
RUTH: You have. We're the one who got the wrong one.

Ruth's blunt manner also kept a roof over their heads. She wasn't above withholding the rent from the landlord or telling him off until he agreed to make some repairs. As can be surmised, Ruth was the more worldly of the two sisters and the less romantic. She was suspicious of men who were interested in her little sister; in one episode, she tells Eileen, "Listen, all men are like most men."

While Eileen went on auditions, Ruth spent her evenings writing stories. During the day, she worked as a reader for a theatrical agency. Her boss valued her opinion. In one episode, her suggestion that the female character in a play be made older was adopted by the playwright. Unfortunately, in this installment, unbeknownst to Ruth, changing the age of the character causes her sister to lose the part. Well, that's show biz....

Taking into account *Two Girls Named Smith* and *My Sister Eileen*, the debut of *That Girl* (1966–1971) seems to very much fall within the continuum of this already-established genre. Here again, a young woman has moved to the Big City to pursue a career.

If *That Girl*'s Ann Marie wasn't a breakthrough in terms of women on TV, the show still has the distinction of being one of the most debated programs in history with opinions still divided between those who see her as a feminist landmark and those who believe she was undermined by the presence of her steady boyfriend, among other factors.

Though the show's original title was *Miss Independence*,[3] the character's chosen profession of acting led one author to opine, "The erratic nature of her employment undermined everyday routines of working life, position[ing] her independence as highly precarious...."[4]

Yet Ann Marie did fully *pursue* her career. She'd studied theatrics in college and continued to hone her craft in New York City. We also learn that, if necessary, she had a fall back; she previously worked as a teacher.

Adding to Ann's independence is the fact that throughout the series we see that her parents are not 100 percent behind their daughter's career. But that doesn't deter our heroine. Like Lucy, who was always getting her show biz dreams clipped, Ann Marie was always also having to stand up to opposition.

Even after Ann took up with boyfriend Donald and marriage seemed like a foregone conclusion, she continued to plug away at her career. When the series ended after five seasons, Ann was no closer to fame and not much closer to marriage either. She was engaged, but the series ended before the wedding. The latter was a conscious choice on behalf of Marlo Thomas: "If her story ended with a marriage [female viewers] might think that that was the only way to have a happy ending."[5]

But Ann Marie's career isn't the only aspect of the series often taken to task. She lived on her own without a father figure or pseudo-chaperone in sight, but one historian still questions her autonomy, especially in contrast to Mary Richards. He says:

> [In the opening credits] Mary is shown driving along a highway, away from the sprawling suburbs. The leaving-home motif suggests the rushing-railroad title shots of *That Girl*, the most prominent working-girl comedy of the years immediately preceding, but in traveling by train, *That Girl*'s Ann Marie signaled that she was still dependent, broke, little-girlish. Mary, alone behind the wheel of her car, provides a more mature and self-contained image....[6]

This is interesting, but is it accurate? While symbolically the train tracks of *That Girl* could be viewed as a link, an umbilical cord back to Mommy and Daddy, we must take into account the faster speed and greater distance that Ann travels by rail compared to Mary in an auto. (We should also consider the impracticality of Ann keeping a car in New York as opposed to Midwesterner Mary.)

Other aspects of the two shows' opening credits are also interesting. While Mary in hers quite famously threw her hat up in the air in a freedom gesture, that hat nevertheless would eventually have to fall. In contrast, in Ann Marie's montage, she flies a kite and keeps it aloft. Does Ann's freedom have strings attached ... or are her dreams simply taking flight?

Furthermore, in both programs' openings, both Mary and Ann are seen walking around their town, breaking out of the generally considered female domain of the home and symbolically taking back the streets. But Mary is in leafy Minneapolis while Ann Marie has the courage to take on the mean streets of the Big Apple.

Of course *That Girl* gets its greatest complaints due to the fact that Ann had a boyfriend, Donald Holliger (played by Ted Bessell). Was he a stand-in for Daddy? A would-be concession to the patriarchy?

That Girl co-creator Sam Denoff saw him as neither, just a device. He said, "We learned from geniuses, like Sheldon Leonard and Carl Reiner, that if a main character has responsibility to someone they're funnier. Because if you just go off by yourself and do what you want there are no consequences. Lucy wasn't as funny when Desi wasn't there. Nor was Ralph Kramden or any of those comedy stars."[7]

If in some episodes Ann seemed to "answer to" Donald, there are just as many when he's dependent upon her. In one, reporter Donald is only able to obtain an interview with an opera star because the man's become smitten with Ann. In "The Mating Game," Donald's story on a TV dating show hinges on Ann acting as a contestant. In the latter, while Donald ends up getting his story, he also becomes jealous when Ann goes off on her date. In another episode, he becomes jealous of Ann's old boyfriend; in another, he's driven crazy by a fashion photographer's interest in That Girl.

From Ann helping Donald with his career to him being frequently worried she'll leave him, it all begs the question: Just who is dependent on who?

Besides being able to strike out on her own, Ann was also noble and socially aware. In various episodes she fought for what was then called "women's lib," protested for the environment and against stereotyped portrayals of Hispanics. She even turned down one acting part because she refused to do nudity.

That Girl wasn't the first "single girl" sitcom but the series nevertheless was transitional because it came along when it did—at the very dawn of the modern feminist movement. And it was more popular and longer-lasting than some of its predecessors, giving a growing number of young women a better chance to emulate her.

Working Girls

Not all of TV's "single gals" were would-be stars. One of *MTM*'s most direct ancestors is *Meet Millie* (1952–1956).

Like other early shows, *Millie* began on radio before coming to TV. The TV version starred Elena Verdugo as young, single Millie Bronson, a secretary who shared a New York brownstone with her mother. Again, such shared living quarters should not be interpreted as dependency but as a nod to realism or, perhaps, a concession to (presumed) morality.

Long before Mary Richards moved to Minneapolis, Elena Verdugo played single working woman Millie Bronson on *Meet Millie* (1952–1956).

Few episodes of *Millie* have survived to the present day. What does remain is eye-opening. First, we often see Millie sporting pants! This is nine years before Mary Tyler Moore donned Capris on *Dick Van Dyke*. We also often see Millie break the fourth wall of her series and give a wink to the audience—a sign of sly omniscience. Then there's Verdugo herself. When she began in *Millie* she became the first Hispanic actress to helm her own network series.

Florence Halop played Millie's mother. And though Verdugo and Halop were only three years apart in age, Verdugo's youthful zest and Halop's studied performance as an older woman, complimented each other perfectly. (Halop would later have a career renaissance playing the role of Florence on *Night Court*.) Halop's portrayal of Mother Bronson, a character neither dotty nor a burden, makes her a sort of early Golden Girl.

Many recaps of the series state that its premise was that Millie's mom was always looking to marry

Millie off. But, for most of the series' run, Millie had a steady boyfriend — Johnny Boone, Jr., the son of Millie's boss. Hence, Millie was not really on the market. But even with Johnny's presence, Millie should not be assumed to be a woman after marriage. Of the episodes of *Millie* that have survived, the most frequent theme is not about weddings but about the battle of the sexes.

In one episode, Millie and Johnny are not speaking as they have just had a tiff over where to take a joint vacation. Johnny wants to go fishing; Millie wants to go to a nearby lodge. The next morning at the office, Johnny gets some advice from his dad who lectures him on how to "handle a woman." It seems that the elder Boone has had a disagreement with his own wife just the night before because she wants to spend a week in the country and he wants to go golfing. Mr. Boone is planning to get his wife to reconsider by applying reverse psychology — the old "soft soap," he calls it. He's already purchased some flowers (he points out a bouquet on the desk) to butter her up and he has planned a fancy dinner for her for later that night. Then, as Mr. Boone explains, when she's feeling most content ("purring and off her guard"), he will hit her with his plans for the golf trip. She'll feel guilty for her "selfishness" and change her mind. Mr. Boone says, "Women are so gullible that they'll swallow baloney all day long if you slice it right. When P.T. Barnum said there's a sucker born every minute, he was referring to women."

At that moment, Millie, still mad, walks in. She sees Johnny and says not a word. Johnny, on the advice of his dad, launches into the "soft soap," telling Millie of the sleepless night he had and that he wants to apologize. He says:

JOHNNY: (*about to go in for the kill*): If you really want me to go to the mountains with you and your mother, I'll forget my fishing and go.
MILLIE: Really, Johnny? Oh, gee, you're being so sweet about it and now knowing how you really feel, I'll tell you what, Mom and I would love for you to go with us.
JOHNNY: *What?!* You were suppose to say I could go fishing!
MILLIE: Huh?
JOHNNY: Sure, Dad said if I soft-soaped you —
MILLIE: Oh, he did?! So that's why you were so sweet! And I suppose these flowers were part of the soft-soaping act too. (*Millie picks up the flowers.*) Well, you can soft soap the janitor with them! (*She tosses the flowers out the door.*)
MR. BOONE: B-b-but, Miss Bronson, those were my flowers. I bought them for my wife.

The thrown flowers land all over Mr. Boone's wife who happened to have been in the hallway at that time. Wet and covered in blooms, Mrs. Boone enters. After Millie's explanation, Mr. Boone attempts spin control:

MRS. BOONE: John, what is the meaning of this?
MR. BOONE: I got them for you.
MRS. BOONE: For me? ... Well, it's no use, you're not going golfing.

From what we see, Millie was not depicted as dependent on "her man." And she didn't think twice about standing up to him or his father.

Verdugo remembers her character as being the "central figure, the peacekeeper" of the show,[8] mediating between those around her just as Mary Richards would later run interference between Murray and Sue Ann. Hence, Millie, like so many other TV females before and after, seemed to be another calm center in the middle of a comedic storm.

Just as later audiences have never had a chance to "meet Millie," they've also been denied knowing Jeannie MacLennan of *Hey, Jeannie* (1956–1957).

Hey, Jeannie was created as a showcase for actress-singer Jeannie Carson. The English-born Carson starred as a Scot who had just arrived in America. The show built its episodes around Jeannie's wide-eyed wonderment of the USA.

While Jeannie was an innocent abroad, such naiveté didn't mean that she was dumb. In fact, in the series' premiere, on a bus tour of Washington, DC, Jeannie shows she knows more about U.S. history than the tour guide does. In that same episode, a drive by the Capitol makes Jeannie decide she wants to stay in America because being in America means she can become anything — even a U.S. Congresswoman!

What follows is a telling fantasy sequence: Jeannie envisions herself as Representative Jeannie. As a member of Congress, she is a woman of power with a huge desk and a male secretary who sits on *her* lap. Later in the dream, Jeannie's military man boyfriend arrives to sweep the lady of the House off her feet! He proposes marriage, but Jeannie won't forgo her career. "You can't ask me to give up my constituents!"

Later episodes have Jeannie continuing with her immersion into America. In one, she goes to Boston to commemorate Paul Revere's ride. In another, she applies for citizenship. She even gets to take part in the legal process in one episode when she's an eyewitness to an auto accident.

Throughout her adventures, Jeannie remained idealistic. She once helped a group of "girl rangers" build a new playground and was briefly both a police officer and a member of the WACs.

In the series' second incarnation during its single season, *Jeannie* got overhauled and she became a flight attendant. Even airborne though, Jeannie remained Jeannie. In one episode, she helped some farmers survive a drought.

In retrospect, it makes sense that Doris Day would eventually have her own single-gal-in-the-city sitcom. She practically pioneered that persona via her big screen comedies. As McWilliams put it:

> A lot of people owe Doris Day. Every time Shelley Long deflects Ted Danson's advances on *Cheers*, or Bess Armstrong has a hard day at the office on *All Is Forgiven*, or Judith Light is tempted by Tony Danza on *Who's the Boss?* ... a tribute is being paid to the Queen of Modern Romantic Comedy.[9]

When Day first came to TV in *The Doris Day Show* (1968–1973), she played a former singer (handy so that the star could sometimes sing) who, after being widowed, moved to her father's farm with her two young sons. Charming and innocuous, the first format of *Doris Day* lasted for one season. By season two, changes were made. Day wrote in her autobiography:

> By the end of my first year in television I came to realize that if the program was to continue successfully, it was up to me to take over....
>
> I hired new producers and new scriptwriters and worked out a new locale and concept for the show.... I worked with writers, set designers, costume designers, makeup and music — there wasn't an aspect of the show that I didn't get into.[10]

When *Doris* returned in the fall of 1969, Day's character, Doris Martin, was now a city dweller and working mother. During the summer she had gotten a job in San Francisco as a receptionist for *Today's World* magazine. Gramps and the farm were gone though her two boys still appeared.

Thanks to Day's greater involvement, and exuding more sophistication, the series began to hit its stride. Interestingly, in the series' second season opener, in some not-so-subtle symbolism (and similar to *Mary Tyler Moore*'s later drive to Minneapolis), Doris is seen driving herself over the Golden Gate. Still later in the opening, Doris is seen traipsing through the streets of San Francisco, again following in the tradition of *That Girl*.

In the second incarnation, *Doris* took on weightier issues. In the first episode, when Doris applies for her job, she is faced with possibly having to hide that she's a mother since her employer questions the commitment of women with children. Finally, refusing to feel ashamed, Doris discloses she's a widowed mother of two — and gets the job.

Later episodes also dealt with modern life, especially women's lives. In "The Health King," a handsome fitness fanatic, about to be featured in the magazine, takes a fancy to Doris. And she to him. When the two go on a "working date," Doris' boss Mr. Nicholson (played by McLean Stevenson) worries about "little Doris" out alone with such a high-energy gentleman. The boss grows more panicked when the date runs late and Doris still hasn't returned. But what the boss doesn't know is that Doris and her date have just been soaked by a rainstorm and returned to the man's apartment to dry their clothes. It's an innocent situation (like one right out of one of Day's films) but Mr. Nicholson thinks the worst and starts calling the man's apartment, much to Doris' consternation. She does not take kindly to the idea of a chaperone or to her boss' assumption she can't take care of herself.

Another episode from season two has the loaded title "The Feminist." In it, Doris' male boss has failed to secure the rights to a famous "women's libber's" new book, so he decides to send Doris in his place to see if she can accomplish it. Leaving no stereotype unturned, when Doris goes to the writer's hotel, she has completely de-feminized herself. She arrives attired in a man's suit and a fedora, and sporting a riding crop (!). Soon both women are smoking cigars. The famous feminist is depicted as masculine as well as angry and anti-male. Doris, playing her "role," is a hit with the writer and gets the woman's work for *Today's World*.

One would think that would be the end until later that night Doris runs into the writer again. This time the woman is being wined and dined by the suave male editor of a rival publication. But now the feminist is shown to be feminine, a little coy and completely smitten with her date. Faster than you can say "cliché," Doris' magazine has lost its exclusive.

This particular episode is interesting. Of course, it obviously buys into a rash of stereotypes about feminists — that they are angry women whose problem is that they can't get a guy. But, beyond that, this episode also dares to address something else: that the relationship between the genders is far more complex and complicated, fraught with issues of wariness, desire, need and mistrust, than such concepts as equal pay for equal work can encompass.

That *Doris Day* would do an episode like this is not surprising. During this time, as the women's rights movement emerged, numerous sitcoms did a "women's lib" episode. Some of them: *Batman*, *Green Acres*, and *The Beverly Hillbillies*. Almost all of them end with all the principals returning to their traditional roles, mirroring many of the old "gender role reversal" episodes that various sitcoms had done years before.

The cynical view of feminism is not surprising. Television is usually mocking of the new and radical, and likes to support the status quo. Hence, feminism on TV often found itself belittled or dismissed. But television tends to do that with all social movements. For hippie and beatnik cultures, TV ignored their artistic and political messages and, instead, zeroed in on their more stereotypic aspects. When the Robert Bly–led "men's movement" of the 1990s happened, various TV shows, including *Murphy Brown*, savagely satirized it.

As can be assessed, Doris Martin is repeatedly shown to be a skilled, trusted secretary. She's often sent out to get big stories. In one episode, she's so sought-after that she gets recruited away by a reclusive millionaire. All goes well until the millionaire's erratic schedule interferes with Doris's time with her kids. She now has to weigh her options — the same sort of choices that all working mothers sooner or later have to face.

In other episodes Doris campaigned against air pollution and fought the YMCA to join her son on a "Father-Son" weekend.

In the fall of 1971, *The Doris Day Show* underwent yet another transformation. Suddenly, Doris Martin was now a single, childless full-time career woman. Even the dog had disappeared. In her final incarnation, she got a promotion. No longer a receptionist, Doris was now an accomplished reporter. In keeping with her new "urban girl" persona, Doris had not only an exciting job but also boyfriends (like guest star Peter Lawford). Only for want of Mr. Grant was Doris not now Mary Richards.

While during her last incarnation, Doris had her share of dates, most episodes focused on her professionally. Doris usually got involved in the stories she was covering. She often stuck up for the little guy, as in the time she painted herself into a corner aiding a lovable artist. Another episode found Doris faking her way into a hospital to get the scoop on a safecracker. In one episode, she even briefly assumed the role of *Today's World's* editor-in-chief.

This incarnation was the last for *Doris Day*. The show ended in 1973. It's notable that of the show's versions, the longest-lasting was the one with Doris on her own.

—◦◦◦—

Though as we've seen, series about single young women are nearly as old as TV itself, *Mary Tyler Moore* (1970–1977) nevertheless did become a watershed program, as influential in its way as *All in the Family*.

The success of *Mary* would soon usher in other female-centered sitcoms all following the comedic travails of young women pursing various big-city careers; a good half dozen of them would debut between 1971 and 1975. So why did "Mary" and her imitators strike such a chord?

Simple: demographics.

By the 1970s, times had changed. While the average age for a woman to marry had only risen by one year, from 20 to 21,[11] the number of women who were married decreased sharply. In 1950, 82 percent of American women were married; by 1970, this number was 61 percent.[12] (Today, 51 percent of American women are without a spouse.) Hence, since there were so many more single women out in the world, they no doubt felt a greater need to "see" themselves on TV.

Other factors also helped. That *Mary* debuted in 1970, the same year that a protest at the Miss America pageant in Atlantic City ignited the modern feminist movement, would also have to be a cause.

After *MTM* arrived, one of the first sitcoms to follow her path was *Funny Face* (1971) starring Sandy Duncan. Duncan played Sandy Stockton, a single woman who had moved to California to attend UCLA and become a teacher. In a nod to some of her forebears,

Sandy worked for Prescott Advertising Agency as an actress in TV commercials. (This detail was written in so that Duncan could occasionally show off her musical chops.)

Debuting in 1971 as part of CBS' powerhouse Saturday night line-up (which included *MTM* and *All in the Family*), *Funny Face* was an immediate hit whose old-fashioned plots proved a counterbalance to the tough issues and loud decibels of its *All in the Family* lead-in.

As for storylines, *Funny Face* made *That Girl* look like *Inherit the Wind*. Typical scenarios had Sandy experiencing dating mishaps or trouble with a TV repairman. Unfortunately, just as the series was taking off, Duncan took ill. Eventually diagnosed with a tumor, she later required surgery and her recovery necessitated the end of *Funny Face* after 13 episodes.[13]

Duncan bounced back and CBS gave her another shot. The renamed, reconfigured *The Sandy Duncan Show* debuted in the fall of 1972. Sandy was still Sandy Stockton but now worked for the Quinn and Cohen Advertising Agency. Though most of Sandy's misadventures stayed pretty featherweight, sometimes she got some depth. She once nabbed a purse snatcher and on another occasion had to choose between doing an ad for a shoddy soap or doing the right thing. Unfortunately, when she returned to primetime, her series got switched to Sunday nights and, once there, Sandy's ratings-challenged series lasted just three months.

Diana Rigg, formerly of *The Avengers*, returned to TV in her own sitcom, *Diana* (1973–1974). While the series could easily have fallen into a safe pattern of cute situations (and sometimes did), with Rigg at the helm it sometimes took some risks.

First, far from being the "All-American girl," Rigg's character, Diana Smythe, was a British divorcee, having left her ex overseas to pursue a career as a fashion coordinator for a New York department store.

Before the series debuted, Rigg boasted about the "new woman" she was bringing to TV, "She's very sophisticated, in her thirties, with lots of boyfriends. And she's not untouched by human hands."[14]

Formerly Emma Peel on *The Avengers*, Diana Rigg, as Diana Smythe on *Diana* (1973–1974), was just one of the many notable actresses packaged into "independent women" sitcoms in the 1970s.

Certainly Ms. Smythe faced many situations which spoke of a worldly sophistication. A running gag was that Diana had taken over the New York apartment of her brother who was out of the country. Unfortunately, he had forgotten to mention that he had loaned extra keys to many of his (male) friends. Hence, it was not unusual for Diana to arrive home (or wake up) and find a strange man in her apartment, many of them towel-wrapped from the shower. Of course, this situation is innocent, but the image of a single woman waking up to find a half-naked man in her home, and that woman not being worried about her "reputation," was progressive.

Other radical themes were also addressed. In one episode Diana begins dating a man who is not only much older but also the father of one of her friends! In another, Diana's platonic male friend Howard becomes her platonic roommate. (Early *Three's Company*?)

Throughout all her adventures, Diana Smyth is direct and confident. She never dissolves into girlish giggles. In one episode, Diana and her boss enjoy a pleasant and platonic dinner while the boss' wife is out of town. Unfortunately, the next day, her boss is racked with guilt over being seen out with a woman who's not his wife. Though Diana attempts to allay his fears (inverting the boss-employee dynamic) with common sense, it falls on deaf— and drunken — ears. Oh, well, she tried, and never once did she break into the panic the boss did.

—◦◦◦—

Ironically, for as much attention as Mary Richards gets, Mary's best friend *Rhoda* often gets overlooked.

On *Rhoda* (1974–1978), Rhoda Morgenstern was a vividly drawn character and perhaps TV's best second banana since Ethel Mertz. Self-deprecating but shrewd, eager for romance but unwilling to hold her tongue, everything about Rhoda, from her head scarves to her sarcasm, seemed stunningly individual. On *MTM*, she provided a dose of stinging vinegar that contrasted with Mary's sunny disposition. It's no surprise that Rhoda would get her own spin-off. For her own series, New Yorker Rhoda left Minneapolis and returned to the Big Apple.

When it debuted, *Rhoda* was a hit thanks to star Valerie Harper's comedic talents and some first-rate support from Nancy Walker as Rhoda's mom and Julie Kavner as Brenda, Rhoda's younger sister. Frequently the series bested *Mary* in the ratings.

While the name was the same, the character had changed. She was once chubby and messy, but when Rhoda got to New York, it seemed like she had been reinvented. Rhoda was together, perhaps too together. On her own, Rhoda didn't seem as funny as when she was living under Mary (something that often happens with spun-off characters). The aspects of Rhoda that America first came to love were now largely seen in Brenda, who had weight problems as well as man and mother issues.

Rhoda (1974–1978) was a spinoff of *Mary Tyler Moore* with Valerie Harper as the evolving and relatable heroine Rhoda Morgenstern.

If Rhoda the character went through various changes, so did her series. During its run, Rhoda was single, then married, then divorced; she would work for a department store and later for a costume company; and she'd have a number of on-again, off-again boyfriends. Even her mother disappeared for a time when Nancy Walker briefly starred in her own two series.

Rhoda's October 1974 marriage, to wrecking company owner Joe Gerard, was a turning point for the character and the series. And the hour-long special wedding episode was a cultural event, complete with fans throwing viewing parties.[15]

But as significant as her marriage was, it paled in comparison to her divorce in 1977. In dumping her spouse, Rhoda was TV's first notable female character to go through an on-air marriage dissolution. Her onscreen actions sent a message: Even on TV, you didn't have to stay in an unhappy union.

Rhoda was a metaphor for the 1970s, the so-called "Me" decade, where self-improvement was an obsession. After all, wasn't Rhoda the ugly duckling who became a swan, the little sparrow who spread her wings?

—◆◇◆—

Following in the footsteps of Rigg, in 1975 Lee Grant became the latest acclaimed performer to come to TV where she also played a single woman in the city.

But in *Fay*, Grant's character, Fay Stewart, was not a recent college grad. Instead, she's a 43-year-old grandmother. Fay was also a recent divorcee, having finally walked out on her unfaithful husband after 25 years.

On her own for the first time in a quarter of a century, Fay moved from the suburbs to the city, got an apartment and a job as a secretary to two radical lawyers. Her uptight daughter and stuffy son-in-law didn't approve of Mom's new life while her ex-husband wanted her back, an option Fay wouldn't consider.

Within this framework, *Fay*, like some other series of the era (e.g., *Adam's Rib*), dared to address some timely "women's issues." In one episode, Fay journeys with her bosses to Washington to work on a case about equal rights. In another, Fay's daughter's desire to return to college is in conflict with her husband's wishes. In another, Fay's friend Lillian uses Fay as inspiration in order to exit her own bad marriage.

Fay was pretty progressive and highly reflective of its time. Fay was very much like the women Betty Friedan documented in *The Feminine Mystique*: women of a "certain age" who had already tried marriage and motherhood only to discover they wanted more.

Unfortunately, *Fay* had one of the shortest runs of all this era's "single" sitcoms. Weird time slots and clashing creative visions for the show doomed it. Among those who lament its demise is author McWilliams, who wonders what the talented and outspoken Grant could have brought to the role had she continued:

> As Fay, Grant could have pulled together the strands of her career: social persecution (Fay was seen as an oddball for leaving her husband); feminine survival (she insisted on independence); and grown-up sensuality (she had no intention of remaining faithful to her ex). I don't mean to slight Grant's other accomplishments or to suggest that *Fay* was a masterpiece. But the two together might have produced a Queen.[16]

—◆◇◆—

Karen Valentine was the breakout star of the high school–set *Room 222* (1969–1974). When school let out, Valentine quickly returned in her own sitcom.

In *Karen* (1975), she starred as Karen Angelo (how these characters almost always have the same name as the actresses playing them!). Angelo lived in DC and worked for Open America, a citizen's lobby group.

Along with being young, pretty and perky, Angelo was also idealistic. (Shades of Ally McBeal?) Her organization's job was to expose government corruption. And though some of Karen's attempts to do so crossed over into farce, there remained good intentions and a positive message in her program. In one episode she investigates a shady defense contractor; in another she speaks out against illegal surveillance. Once, she even chose work over marriage when her boyfriend, a Congressman, proposed.

—*∕∕∕*—

Karen lasted a season as did the similar *On Our Own* (1977–1978). These short lifespans were typical for these shows. Despite the high numbers of them in the '70s, few caught on with the public. Out of all of *Mary*'s imitators, only *Doris Day* and *Rhoda* made it more than one year. The best that can be said of this nod to the new female demographic is that they were around longer than attempts to package single women in dramas (*Dear Detective*, *Amy Prentiss* et al.).

Even if the independent woman series reached its high-point during the 1970s, spurned on by the rise of the modern feminist movement and the charms of Mary Tyler Moore, the genre has never completely left us. As mentioned, this type of show has staying power. Since *Mary* and her imitators, there's been *Sara* starring a pre–*Thelma and Louise* Geena Davis, *Suddenly Susan* and *Caroline in the City* as well as *Ally McBeal*, *Kristin* with Kristin Chenoweth, *Less Than Perfect*, *Eve* and *2 Broke Girls*, among others. Tina Fey's *30 Rock* seems like a full-on *MTM* homage with Fey in the Mary role, Alec Baldwin as her Lou Grant, Tracy Morgan as the show's Ted Baxter, and Jane Krakowski as its Sue Ann. Both series are even based in the world of TV.

What accounts for this genre's endurance, in fact their plethorization since the '70s? Well, how better to showcase the talents of young and fetching comedic actresses? And what network wouldn't want to launch the next *Mary Tyler Moore*, a program that was popular and acclaimed? But is there more?

In many ways, the women of *Those Whiting Girls* and *My Sister Eileen* were far tougher and tart-tongued than most of their 1970s (and after) sisters. As a group, the former are closer to sitcom queens Arden and Sothern than they are to Karen or Sandy. This latter generation of single women on TV were less sure of themselves than their predecessors. This begs the question: Was the vulnerability of a Mary or an Ally a sign of "backlash"?

As more real-life women delayed marriage and moved into the work force, they, like Mary et al. probably knew that while they could make it on their own, they also might not have had all the answers. Hence, they needed heroines, like Mary, who weren't superwomen but just women, perfectly human and wonderfully relatable.

— 7 —

"Femme Fatale"
Television's Secret Agents and Super Heroines

Power is neither male nor female.—Katherine Graham

They are the exotics of the TV landscape. They are the progeny of the silent era's *Perils of Pauline* and the comic pages' *Brenda Starr*. They are the crime fighters, super women, and female spies of the small screen. They have lived in jungles, in cities and in outer space. They have unusual powers or unparalleled skills, or both. They run the gamut from Batgirl to Buffy, from Sheena to Xena. And their presence on television shows how diverse, strong and liberated women on TV have always been.

They are often ignored in histories; when these women *are* mentioned, they are usually dismissed for being too cartoon-y, too far-fetched, to have any relevance. But to discard a Bionic Woman or a Wonder Woman would require us to similarly disregard their male counterparts (Superman, etc.) and all types of speculative fiction including the works of H.G. Wells, etc.

Regardless of their costumes and sometimes cutesy names (Honey, Cinnamon), the heroines discussed here are portrayed as resilient and courageous. And, as media scholar Kate Kane has pointed out, "They don't do housework."[1]

And while many of these women are sexy, their female-ness is a non-issue. For them, saving the world takes precedence over male attention. They use their bodies only in terms of athleticism.

Even when some heroines use their sexuality (like Cinnamon in *Mission: Impossible*), they—at the risk of gender studies speak—seem to "own" their sexuality in a way that previous sex symbols didn't. Compare Emma Peel from *The Avengers* with the persona of Marilyn Monroe. On- and off-screen, Monroe exuded a naiveté bordering on ignorance. Consider her pose over the subway grate in *The Seven Year Itch*. Monroe is oblivious to the peep show she's supplying. By contrast, Emma has complete awareness and command of her allure.

It is also worth noting that despite the often sexualized images of many TV heroines, many were created or influenced by women behind the scenes. A husband-wife team under the name G.G. Fickling created Honey West.[2] *The Girl from UNCLE*'s first treatment was penned by Martha Wilkerson.[3] *Avengers* publicist Marie Donaldson coined the name of its heroine: she derived it from the character's need to have "male" or "m-appeal." Hence, Emma Peel.[4]

Often derided are these women's form-fitting bodysuits. Call them leotards or cat suits, these characters almost always wore them. While this type of attire is body-conscious, these uniforms now appear as precursors to modern athletic wear. Skiers, swimmers, and others

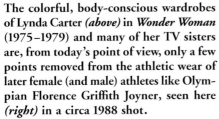

The colorful, body-conscious wardrobes of Lynda Carter *(above)* in *Wonder Woman* (1975–1979) and many of her TV sisters are, from today's point of view, only a few points removed from the athletic wear of later female (and male) athletes like Olympian Florence Griffith Joyner, seen here *(right)* in a circa 1988 shot.

(male and female) now don skin-tight lycra for competitions. In 2000, runner Cathy Freeman competed in the Olympics in a form-fitting running suit — and won gold. In 1985, tennis star Anne White played Wimbledon in a similar outfit. With their long-sleeved, long-legged shinny tightness, they looked like something from Batgirl's closet.

Even Wonder Woman's costume can now be seen as prophetic. The running "shorts" of female track stars have gotten shorter and tighter; they are now nearly identical to Wonder Woman's star-spangled trunks. Certainly the apparel favored by Wonder Woman was no more unusual, or less functional, than the exotic attire of Florence Griffith Joyner.

The wardrobe favored by superheroines also follows social-fashion history. The garments of the turn-of-the-century (hoop skirts, whale-bone corsets) limited movement. As female dress styles simplified, liberation ensued.[5]

Sheroes

TV's first superheroine was the solo star of TV's *Annie Oakley* (1952–1956). This half-hour western was aired in first-run syndication. Unlike the real Annie, the TV Annie seldom toured in shows and, when she did, it was only to raise money for charity. Instead, on the series, Annie functioned as her town's *de facto* deputy, making her not only TV's first female action star but also its first female law officer.

Annie was portrayed as the fastest sharpshooter in the West; when it came to guns, no man could compete. In one episode, when a local boy challenges Annie to a quick draw contest, she takes up the dare and beats him with ease. Annie manages to shoot the boy's gun right out of his hand after first banking her shot off a bell.

Gail Davis, a former rodeo rider, starred as Annie and, impressively, performed her own stunts. One of the series' best takes place when Annie, her younger brother Tag and two other men are riding in a stagecoach. Two black-clad outlaws ride up and demand valuables. When the driver attempts to fight them off, he gets shot in the shoulder. As the bandits ride away, one of them fires a shot to spook the horses into a run. Annie and the others are now stuck in this runaway coach, but Annie doesn't panic. Leaving the "menfolk" inside, Annie crawls out the window and onto the roof. From there, she jumps onto the backs of the horses and seizes the reins. Ever fearless, Annie then turns the men back towards town just before she unharnesses one horse and rides off in pursuit of the gunmen.

As evidenced here, TV's Annie Oakley, despite her pigtails, was not "cutesy." Press kits described her as "hard-ridin'" and "quick-shootin'" and the show's opening showed her in action sequences — like riding by at full gallop, able to shoot a hole through the center of a playing card. *Cowgirls* author Candace Savage listed the skills of Oakley: "[She was] cook, caregiver, a daring trick rider, a roper, a teamster and a tracking expert. There was nothing she couldn't do well."[6]

In addition, Annie never pined for some guy or worried about her hair or clothes; she never rode side-saddle. In one telling exchange from an episode, two outlaws talk:

> OUTLAW #1: Who's afraid of a girl?
> OUTLAW #2: I am when it's Annie Oakley.

Like *The Lone Ranger, Annie Oakley* was aimed primarily at children, making it part of the "kiddie western" genre (as opposed to "adult" westerns like *Gunsmoke*). With its young viewers in mind, the series was as non-violent as possible. Annie never shot to kill. Her aim was so perfect she could shoot pistols out of people's hands. Once Annie shot the disguise off of an outlaw. Annie even did her part for gun safety, in one episode telling Tag, "Guns are to protect people, not hurt them."

Don't let the pigtails fool you, as *Annie Oakley* (1952–1956) was TV's first female action hero and a sharpshooter equal to any man. Gail Davis played the title role.

Annie was fearless and moral.

She was a sharp-eyed detective and regularly saved the lives of men. Men listened to her too, even Lofty, her town's chief deputy. Lofty always followed her orders not because he had to but because Annie was right. Author Savage went on to say,

> For some of us "little ladies" ... Annie and Dale [Evans] were more than a simple diversion. These cowgirls were our idols and they beckoned a world to us.... If our playmates thought we should run the cafe, we refused to play by their rules. True to the cowgirl spirits, we wanted into the game as equals.[7]

Though there was always a romantic undercurrent between Annie and Lofty (played by Brad Johnson), the series steered clear of "mushy" stuff. Hence, Annie was no "husband-hunter."

Interestingly, though Annie was never a wife, she was a pseudo-mother. Presumably Annie and her brother Tag were orphans; their parents were never seen and seldom, if ever, mentioned. Annie — who was supposed to be in her late teens or early twenties — did all the "motherly" things for her little brother: saw him off to school, made him wash behind his ears, etc. Hence, though not biologically, Annie's full custody of Tag seemed to make her a *de facto* mother. And if Annie is a mother, then this also makes her another kind of TV pioneer — one of its first single "moms" (and a working one to boot!).

At the end of *Annie's* run, Gail Davis toured with Gene Autry's rodeo show, often recreating some of the series' tricks. After that, she retired. Davis later proved a popular guest at Western conventions. The actress came to take her notoriety in stride. She said, "As far as I'm concerned, I'll be Annie Oakley for the rest of my born days."[8]

She passed away in 1997. *Ms.* magazine's December '97 issue paid tribute to various notable women who had recently died. Along with Mother Teresa and Princess Diana, also mentioned was TV's Annie Oakley, Gail Davis.[9]

—◦◦◦—

Not long after *Annie Oakley* appeared, she was followed (again in syndication) by *Sheena, Queen of the Jungle* (1955). Based on the comic strip, *Sheena* told the story of a female Tarzan, a protector of the jungle and its inhabitants. Twenty-six episodes of the series were made and aired, a full decade before Ron Ely's *Tarzan*.

Shot in Mexico (subbing for Africa), *Sheena* starred former Vargas girl Irish McCalla, who Hal Erickson in *Syndicated Television* describes as an "intelligent, creative woman who brought the two-dimensional heroine to life."[10]

McCalla was the perfect Sheena: Five feet nine and platinum blond, she was the full embodiment of the iconic hero. Even today the shot of McCalla in the show's opening, contrasted against the darkening "African" sky, is a commanding image. One author begins there and then takes TV's Sheena to another near-mythical level:

> Seen within the context of the greater symbolic and mythic tableau of which Sheena is a part, this character takes on added dimension. She is, I believe, a personification of an element of what Graves called "the grammar of poetic myth," a strong, heroic and feminine figure from which goddesses are made.[11]

Sheena, an able fighter and athlete, is *more* than that. As the white goddess, she is a link between the Dark Continent and the outside world, between past and present, while embodying the best qualities of both. Her goddess-like qualities underscored by her basic goodness. Like other TV superheroines, Sheena's actions come from a place of good. For

Sheena, being heroic is her duty. Her motives are ecological and humanitarian. Her mission is to protect. Once this is achieved, Sheena asks for nothing in return. In fact, in one episode, a tribe offers her gold ... which the adventuress refuses.

As in the comics, TV's Sheena spoke in pidgin English (understandable considering her lack of formal education) and wore leopard skin. Though much has been written about Sheena's "provocative" dress, her costume exposed no more than the bathing suits of the era; for comparison, see the swimwear of film star Esther Williams.

Despite assumptions, *Sheena* wasn't about sex. Her sexuality didn't matter in the midst of this drama. Sheena and her cohort Trader Bob (played by Christian Drake) are portrayed only as co-crusaders; no romance. Decades before women in America — that urban jungle — would be sharing work spaces with men, Sheena, Queen of the (real) Jungle, was seen working with a man in an equal setting. McCalla herself noted of her character, "She was, in my mind, strong, honest, kind and could accept help from the white hunter, Bob, as any friend would without giving up her own independence."[12]

Besides, as with *Annie*, Sheena had little time for love. In every episode Sheena is the catalyst for action. As Richard Lamparski noted, "[T]he scripts had Sheena very much in command. In a complete reversal of roles, it was Sheena who always came to [actor] Drake's rescue."[13] Throughout the series, Sheena demonstrated physical feats. In one episode, after Sheena takes off into the jungle, Bob laments, "The way she travels, she'll be half a day ahead of me."

Beyond her physicality, Sheena also proved herself a perceptive detective. Traipsing through the jungle in one episode, Sheena saves Bob from a trap by spotting an oddly hanging vine. In another, Sheena saves Bob after a tribesman with a knife sneaks up behind him. After she wrestles the boy to the ground, Sheena attempts to communicate with him in Swahili and other tribal languages. Since the boy refuses to talk, Bob attempts to figure out who he is. Sheena ultimately identifies the boy's tribe by the clay on his feet.

The significance of *Annie Oakley* and *Sheena* on television should not be undervalued. Not only did they present to young female viewers heroic role models, they also weakened a theory about children and television. It's long been thought that while girls would watch shows about boys, boys wouldn't watch shows about girls. The success of *Sheena*, etc., deflates this myth and speaks well for the "equal opportunity" that boys were willing to apply to programming. It also speaks well of the (mostly) male programmers of the 1950s who helped bring these images to air long before anyone heard of a "women's movement."

This attitude exhibits a level of maturity that many contemporary (mostly male) writers don't show when recalling programs like *Sheena*. Rather than giving these shows a fair shake, they usually just focus on Irish McCalla's figure and why *some* men and boys might have watched. But to remember *Sheena* only in terms of its star's appearance is done at the expense of acknowledging this character's abilities, a reluctance to take women seriously — a type of wholesale sexism that women have long battled.

—◈◈◈—

TV heroines entered a more modern era with *Honey West* (1965–1966). Based on a series of pulps by G.G. Fickling, Honey made her first TV appearance in a 1965 episode of *Burke's Law*. Played by Anne Francis, Honey cracked a case right under the nose of lead Amos Burke.[14]

That wouldn't be the last case Honey cracked. She was soon spun-off into her own half-hour series, making her network TV's first action-adventure heroine. For the series, Francis continued in the role. Co-starring were John Ericson, as Honey's PI partner Sam Bolt, and Irene Hervey, who played Honey's Aunt Meg.

In the series, Sam Bolt possesses many of the characteristics one might normally ascribe to the "girl": He's the one who's always admonishing Honey not to take so many risks (which she does anyway). One author has said that Honey West made [Man from UNCLE] Napoleon Solo "look like *Mr. Peepers*."[15] Honey is also often compared to 007 in that both maintained an arsenal of clever gadgets. For Honey, her lace garter belt doubled as a gas mask and her earrings were bombs. These two-in-one weapons seem symbolic: These female adornments transformed into life-taking tools illustrate, that like the woman wearing them, they are not as benign as they might appear.

As TV historian Julie D'Acci has pointed out, while the detective shows of the era featuring men usually played up action elements in their openings, *Honey*'s credits juxtaposed action with sex.[16] In the opening, there are glamourous portraits of a slinkily attired Honey. These shots are then followed by photos of Honey in a judo pose or holding a man in a headlock. Following those is an extreme closeup of Francis' puckered lips, her pre–Cindy Crawford mole plainly visible. After that, more action shots. While some might interpret this sequence as projecting mixed messages, it can also be viewed as placing *Honey West* further within Bond territory, since 007's prowess with women was every bit as potent as his spy skills.

Still, even for a character this sexy, sex was far from the program's *raison d'etre*. It wasn't something Francis emphasized. She once said, "I just played her tongue-in-cheek and had fun with her. I could never do the real heavy sex stuff 'cause I got the giggles."[17]

If, at first, Francis' form in a tight black leotard was meant to appeal to male viewers, with time the audience seemed to shift to women. One of the show's original sponsors was Consolidated Cigars but when they departed, ads for more female-oriented products (Sunbeam, Diet Delight) came in.[18]

Furthermore, just as the series was about to premiere, Gilbert toys manufactured a Honey West doll. Though girls could later purchase an evening dress for it, the doll arrived in the character's trademark black leotard, suggesting that she was about action, not attraction. One source states that during its year of production, the Honey doll outsold Barbie![19]

Network TV's first true action-adventure heroine was Anne Francis in *Honey West* (1965–1966). Honey was a super sleuth and black belt.

Maybe that's not so surprising. Despite her many personas, Barbie could never be everything Honey was: unattached, self-employed, tough and unafraid to speak her mind (in one episode, she tells Sam to "get off his male ego!"). And no Barbie could be described as Julie D'Acci described Honey: "resourceful, willful, and adept at action-adventure. [Viewers saw] Honey talking her way out of scrapes, speeding off to solve cases ... [and] disposing of villains with kicks, chops and flying leaps."[20]

How cool was Honey? She drove a convertible and had a pet ocelot. (Said Francis about her animal co-star, "I had to have my tetanus shots every six weeks."[21]) And Honey always displayed a savoir-faire. Consider this dialogue when Honey nabbed a jewel thief:

> THIEF: Honey West? Well, well, well, a girl private eye. Don't you know a woman's place is in the home?
> HONEY: This is no time for a proposal. Just hand over the loot.

In a late interview, Anne Francis said, "You wouldn't believe the letters I get from Baby Boomer career women. Many tell me it was Honey who made them realize that marriage and motherhood weren't the only options. It's staggering to think that this little show could have that kind of an impact."[22]

—⚬⚬⚬—

Even with *Honey West* having been a modest hit,[23] and the fact that TV had already seen *Sheena* and *Annie Oakley*, there had never been anything quite like Emma Peel of *The Avengers* (1965–1967) when she arrived in '65.

Played with cool sophistication, athletic grace and mischievous slyness by Diana Rigg, thirty-some years after her debut, Mrs. Peel remains an icon. In 2002, she was picked by *TV Guide* as the sexiest star in TV history.[24] And Lucy Lawless has said she based much of Xena on Rigg.[25] Even the world of high-fashion has repeatedly resurrected Emma's style, and strength, with such designers as Versace filling their catwalks with Mrs. Peel's sleek style.

So why does Emma still resonate? Perhaps because Mrs. Peel was contemporary and, therefore, more relatable. Annie Oakley was a historic figure; Sheena was out of time as she was set in inner Africa. Mrs. Peel was *now*.

The Avengers began airing in England in 1961. Originally, it starred Patrick Macnee and Ian Hendry as crime fighters. That format lasted a few episodes before Hendry left and Macnee, as dapper John Steed, was paired with Cathy Gale, played by Honor Blackman. Though the program proved popular in the UK, Blackman elected to leave after the first season to become a "Bond Girl" in the 007 film *Goldfinger*.[26]

Enter Diana, now Dame Diana Rigg. Many actresses had already auditioned to replace Blackman when 28-year-old Rigg was brought in. Macnee remembers:

> [Diana] had this total, complete technical comedic style.... She had a very sharp and lively imagination and understanding of what a woman, a woman like her, would say in any given situation — however outrageous or mad....[27]

Presented with a blank slate to create this new Avenger, producer Brian Clemens constructed a character that melded perfectly with Rigg's style.

The character of Mrs. Emma Peel has been described as "an English Rose with the ability to toss a man over her shoulder as if he were a sack of feathers."[28] Highly educated, she would quote Faust and, at one time, at an alarmingly young age, single-handedly ran her father's business empire. Over the series' course, Peel would also be shown to be a sculptress and musician and to have knowledge of all the major sciences.

What remains a mystery is how this well-bred woman acquired her butt-kicking abilities. The program's opening doesn't give any clue. She is simply described as a "talented amateur" and as a young widow whose husband, a test pilot, has been lost at sea and presumed dead. In their first episode, Peel and Steed are already working together; we have no back story on how they teamed up.

According to Macnee, Mrs. Peel was envisioned as being "a shade softer" in character than Gale. The "warmly witty" relationship between Peel and Steed was modeled on the Thin Man movies of the 1930s[29] that featured amateur married sleuths Nick and Nora Charles and who enjoyed a friendly verbal jousting and rapid-fire repartee. Like Mr. and Mrs. Charles, the Avengers' interchanges also contained a lot of innuendo which American censors let slide.

But Mrs. Peel (like Charlie's Angels later) never acted upon her sexuality. She was not "loose"; she was very much a lady. After all, though her husband was missing, Mrs. Peel still considered herself married. The only flirting she did was with danger.

Despite Emma's chastity, she was still of the moment. According to Macnee, the characters' personas were carefully crafted: "To counterbalance John Steed's preference for living in the past, Mrs. Peel would be strikingly futuristic."[30] In the show, Steed would embody the traditional British Empire; Mrs. Peel, its new mod era. And yet there would be no generation gap. One author said *The Avengers* exemplified "the meeting in the middle of old and new ... over a glass of champagne."[31]

This contrast was evident in the pair's choice of clothing. Ultra-Edwardian Steed was always attired in a suit, bowler hat and umbrella. By contrast, Mrs. Peel's wardrobe consisted only of the latest creations from Carnaby Street and her trademark "emmapeelers" — jumpsuits made of stretch jersey. Peel's streamlined wardrobe was practical and suitable for her.

Yet that didn't mean the series didn't use the Peel character to play on stereotypes. As one *Avengers* aficionado put it, "The men are doing things women should be doing, the women are doing things men should be doing and there doesn't seem to be division between these gender characteristics."[32] Example: One episode concludes with Steed and Peel riding a motorcycle with a sidecar — Emma is at the controls while Steed is the passenger.

Even with her individualism Mrs. Peel was not emasculating. As has been pointed out, "Diana was independent without being strident. She could even be John Steed's superior without wrecking his ego."[33] Rigg said about her alter-ego, "Emma is totally equal to Steed. The fighting is the most obvious quality."[34] Producer Clemens said that he wanted to make Steed "fight like a woman" or at least a gentlemen. Hence, Steed seldom used a gun, preferring to wield his umbrella instead.[35] Meanwhile, Mrs. Peel fights with graceful, athletic judo chops.

"Cool" is the word when it comes to Emma. Perhaps that's why this character lingers. Yes, Annie Oakley was great but she was a country girl; and as wonderful as Honey West was, there was always something working-class about her. By contrast, Mrs. Peel exuded an aristocratic air even as she rolled in the dirt. Perhaps the best assessment of her comes in an episode where kidnapper Z.Z. Von Schnerck says, "I needed you, Mrs. Peel, a woman of beauty, of action, a woman who could become desperate and yet remains strong, a woman who could become confused and yet remain intelligent, who could fight back and yet remain feminine. You, and only you, Emma Peel, have all these qualifications."[36]

For a series that was always just this side of camp, *The Avengers* nevertheless possessed an underlying message about female empowerment. One fan wrote, "[T]he women always prevail, sometimes with assistance from Steed, in ways that show how resourceful and rational they are. He provides a top-and-tail presence to mark equilibrium, but his partner is often the agent of change."[37]

Diana Rigg's departure from the series in 1968 did not spell the end of *The Avengers*: Britain's ITV resurrected Steed for 26 internationally syndicated episodes of *The New Avengers* (1976).

Macnee returned. Joining him were Gareth Hunt as Mike Gambit, an avenger who would do some of the more masculine "heavy lifting," and a pre–*Ab Fab* Joanna Lumley as Purdey.

Though any female Avenger after Rigg will probably always be in her shadow, Lumley's Purdey (whose name was borrowed from a shotgun) left her own impression. Said one fan, "[Purdey] was an amalgamation of the best elements of her predecessors. Her character had the sophistication of Cathy Gale; the allure, athleticism, humor and venom of Emma Peel.... Basically, Purdey was an incredible creation and one which Joanna settled into from episode one."[38] Said another about the character, "[She's] the Sweetheart of Her Majesty's Secret Service, a liberated and sexually active (presumably, since this is still British TV in the '70s) woman in a bouncy Dorothy Hamill 'do who fends off the advances of virtually every one of her fellow agents with bon-vivant good humor."[39]

—*∿∿∿*—

Though not as fistfight-inclined as Emma, another super woman of the 1960s was also a fierce femme fatale. Fashion model by day, secret agent by night, Cinnamon Carter was a member of the Impossible Missions Force on *Mission: Impossible* (1966–1973).

Barbara Bain brought the sleek Carter to life. She said of her role, "[I]t was at the time the most wonderful series role for a woman on television."[40]

As the only female member of the IMF force, Carter's presence could be tokenism if not for the fact that she was such a vital part of the team.

That said, the Carter character, though fascinating, is at times dichotomous. In many episodes Cinnamon functions mainly as a "decoy," a sexy distraction so that the team's male members can proceed unobserved. This begs the question: Does Cinnamon's function to distract men make her, even within this context, a stereotype? Or does it make her a powerful soldier in the war on terrorism — and in the battle of the sexes?

Carter's role seems to suggest that women's most potent powers lie in their allure, a theory also being promoted at the time in the book *Sex and the Single Girl*. Bain said, "Cinnamon clearly used her femininity to keep the bad guys diverted, but that's probably as valid today as it was then and always will be."[41]

Though much of Cinnamon's power was sexual, it was still *power*. Her look-but-don't-touch allure possessed a Medusian effect. Like the character of Stupefyin' Jones in *Li'l Abner* (played on stage and screen by Julie Newmar), a simple glance or "hello" from Cinnamon could render men helpless. Hers was not physical power as much as it was one of mystic charisma mixed with biology. It's an ability that would also be seen in *Star Trek*'s "Mudd's Women" episode where three gorgeous women render the male crew awestruck.

The use of sexual prowess in espionage is not without foundation. Consider Mata Hari. Then, during World War II, U.S. spy Betty Pack (code name: Cynthia) became the mistress of a French diplomat in order to gain access to the French Embassy. At the end of the war, when Pack was asked about the morality of what she did, she replied, "Wars are not won by moral means."[42]

While Cinnamon never went that far, she knew her forte. In *Impossible*'s pilot, as the other members are given their assignments, the team leader leaves Cinnamon for last, finally turning to her and saying, "And you, Cinnamon, your job...." Cinnamon interrupts, "My job's only doing what comes naturally."

This said, however, Cinnamon's skills extended beyond beauty. In numerous episodes, the fate of that week's mission is in her hands. Moreover, since she often went undercover, she is often in far greater danger than any of her male cohorts since she is usually in much greater proximity to that week's evil despot. *The* Mission: Impossible *Dossier* states that, by the fifth episode of the show, "Odds on Evil," "Cinnamon graduates from minor distraction to major player."[43]

In some episodes, like "The Exchange," there is no emphasis at all on Cinnamon's femininity. Instead, she is depicted as a resilient spy, brave and unwavering even when tortured. In the episode "The Short Tail Spy," as White notes, Cinnamon foils an assassination attempt and, later, when fellow Agent Briggs (actor Steven Hill) is taken hostage, Cinnamon "saves the day."[44]

Among other abilities she possessed, Cinnamon was a master of disguise. Some of her *trompe l'oeil* impersonations included many non-traditional career women including: photographer, doctor, archaeologist, outlaw gunrunner and head of a state's prison system.

In early episodes, there was an ongoing flirtation between agents Carter and Roland Hand (played by Martin Landau); after those, any subtext was dropped and their relationship became strictly business. Ironic then that more recent TV series move in the opposite direction with male and female characters only marking time before falling into each other's arms (or beds); consider *CSI* and *Bones*.

—⊶⌇⊷—

If the success of *The Avengers* and *Mission: Impossible* made it seem like the world was awash in secret agents in the 1960s, in terms of TV, it was. Thanks to the Cold War and the big-screen success of James Bond, TV shows like *I Spy*, *Mission: Impossible* and even *The Wild Wild West* were also successful and were all about out-of-control governments and secret missions.

One of the era's most notable spy shows was *The Man from UNCLE* (1964–1968). *Man* concerned agents Napoleon Solo (Robert Vaughn) and Illya Kuryakin (David McCallum) of UNCLE, the United Network Command for Law Enforcement. Each week they did battle with THRUSH, the Technical Hierarchy for the Removal of Undesirables and the Subjugation of Humanity.

Man was a hit and spawned a spinoff, *The Girl from UNCLE* (1966–1967). When it came time to launch TV's first hour-long adventure show designed for a woman, the first treatment was written by a woman. Originally titled *The Lady from UNCLE*, that draft was done by Martha Wilkerson, a writer and wife of an NBC executive. Eventually, the program morphed into *The Girl from UNCLE* with a lead character named April Dancer.[45] While the demotion from *Lady* to *Girl* might be regrettable, was it malicious? Note that Batman's Robin was the *Boy* Wonder and Green Hornet's aid, Kato, was often referred to as a "boy." Was the term a matter of age, not gender?

After an unsuccessful, unaired pilot with another actress, the series that finally went forward starred 23-year-old Stefanie Powers.

Allegedly, Dancer was originally conceived as a "decoy" character — perhaps a sister to Cinnamon Carter. How "feminine" this superheroine was going to be was a topic of discussion. Series producer Norman Felton had his opinion, stating, "A girl who's looking for someone to hit doesn't appeal to me."[46] Hence, the original April was not expected to partake in much action. But David Victor, supervising producer, would later disclose, "Since [Stefanie] came in so strong and so powerful ... she became sort of an equal of the other agents, rather than being a neophyte."[47] And, indeed, in *Girl from UNCLE*, the character would be a forceful presence who could hold her own in any situation, including the occasional brawl.

Like Honey West, when April hit the air and got a male partner. Since *Man* had gained an unexpected female following thanks to David McCallum, producers decided that something similar would be good here too. Hence, cute, blond English actor–pop singer Noel Harrison (son of Rex) became agent Mark Slate.

Powers and Harrison proved a groovy pairing. Along with Powers' model looks and physicality (she was at the time a three-mile-a-day runner and an active swimmer), she also brought to the role an air of mod sophistication. April never lost her cool. In the climax of "The Mata Hari Affair," April engages in a fight with a male, managing at one point to kick a knife out of his hand. Unfortunately, he's then able to grab a metal pipe and is about to bring it down upon her; partner Slate fires his gun and manages to wound the man. April's cool response: "Pretty nifty with that shooter, luv."

Contrary to that climax, most *Girl* episodes feature Dancer as able to save herself ... and the free world. As *Spy TV* notes, "Dancer was portrayed as being as capable as her partner."[48] In the episode "The Mother Muffin Affair," which featured Boris Karloff in drag (!), April is paired with cross-over character Napoleon Solo; the two are an effective, equal team. There's no condescension in Solo's approach to April; she's just another agent.

Consider as well "The Dog Gone Affair" where April found herself suspended above a vat of piranha, slowly being lowered. She doesn't wait to be rescued. Instead, she whips out her walkie-talkie and by extending its antenna, she's able to flip the switch for the pool's cover. Thanks to her quick thinking, she won't be eaten alive.

Based upon examples like that, April Dancer truly is one of TV's great superheroines — a worthy precursor to TV's later female spies in shows like *Alias* — even if, at times, *Girl from UNCLE* remains a hit-or-miss affair. Some episodes are entertaining as action ... or camp. But other installments are just too silly for their own good; the episode "The Little John Doe Affair" has to be one of the most boring, anticlimactic hours in the history of primetime. The fluctuating quality of the series was no doubt due to its high turnover of writers. For the series' 29 episodes, 18 different scribes supplied scripts.[49]

Through it all, April Dancer always remained the centerpiece of the show and Powers always brought the same sort of glamour to it that she would later bring to *Hart to Hart*. And thanks to that, in terms of superheroines, none can claim to be more "cool" than her.

—◊◊◊—

If *Girl from UNCLE* attempted to walk the line between action and camp and didn't always succeed, that was not a problem for another '60s series. But as over-the-top as *Batman* (1966–1968) was, its one female superheroine always made herself heroic.

A ratings phenomenon at its outset, ABC's colorful but formulaic *Batman* was sinking fast by season two. In an attempt to revive the program and attract two new demographics — men over 40 and pre-pubescent girls — producers decided to introduce Batgirl, a female crime fighter, to turn the Dynamic Duo into the Terrific Trio.[50]

Much has been made over the years about the choice of the name Bat*girl* over the more mature Bat*woman*.[51] But it was actually not the producers of the TV show, but the people behind the comic book who christened the character. Because the character of Catwoman was already established, the comic book writers feared confusion. Hence, the female crime fighter became Batgirl.[52]

Other reasons may have existed as well. As we saw with *Girl from UNCLE*, Batgirl's biological age may have been a factor. Batgirl's name, like that of Robin the Boy Wonder, may have indicated her overall status among these heroes. Even after Batgirl's introduction, Batman was still the elder statesman with Robin and Batgirl functioning, to some extent, as apprentices.

As many Bat-fans know, before Batgirl began, the producers first filmed a never-aired ten-minute test film which debuted Yvonne Craig in the Batgirl role. Remembers Craig, "When we did the pilot, Batgirl was supposed to be not only as good as the guys but *better*. She ended up though being this cute little bland character, when she could have been more in the style of Katharine Hepburn."[53]

Craig is being a little harsh. In aired episodes, Batgirl was shown to be feisty and sly. In fact, Batgirl is one of the most emancipated female characters in pre–1970s TV (and that's saying something!). On every level, Batgirl-Barbara Gordon is liberated: She's a college graduate, has a full-time job, and not once on the series is she husband-hungry.

Furthermore, consider how self-defined Batgirl was. As the daughter of the police commissioner, Barbara knows all about the city's super-villains who still run amok despite the efforts of Batman. So, Barbara reinvents herself as a crimefighter. No one knew (except for butler Alfred who, of course, knew everything) who she really was — not even her father.

Despite Batgirl being portrayed as an apprentice of sorts to Batman, she was not dependent on him. After all it's Batgirl who: shut off the giant magnet in "Ring Around the Riddler," freeing Batman, and later freed herself from a web of whiskers after switching on a set of lawn sprinklers (she had been tied up by Lord Ffogg and Lady Peasoup). She also displays excellent detective skills. In her second episode, Batgirl figures out that the Riddler's clue of a "ring" means a boxing ring, not jewelry.

She's brave too. Batgirl never hesitates before confronting crooks. She always stood her ground or, when necessary, stormed a villain's hideout as bravely as Joan of Arc led her brigade.

Her fighting was cool, too. The series' producer Howie Horwitz was adamant that Batgirl fight only in a "feminine" matter. According to Craig, "He didn't want [Batgirl] to do anything his daughter wouldn't do."[54] This aspect of the character was not one that the actress objected to. She said, "The thing that pleases me most about the character of Barbara Gordon is that while she's the active, agile type, she still retains her femininity."[55] For Batgirl, when it came to fighting, there would be no punches. Instead, she would rely on athletic kicks. Luckily, Craig (who did most of her own stunts) was a trained dancer. In the series, the kicks which once thrilled audiences now clobbered criminals.

Craig said about her performance, "I played Batgirl like she was having a great time."[56] And it shows. Throughout the series, Batgirl doesn't do anything without a smile. In one episode, Batgirl is holding her own against five henchmen before the Dynamic Duo come in:

ROBIN: Five men against one girl isn't fair!
BATGIRL: Oh, I don't mind, I'm rather enjoying it.

Though Batgirl's addition didn't reverse the show's ratings slide (it was cancelled at the end of season three), the program has since become a rerun staple. And, today, we know that Batgirl served at least half of her purpose. Though Craig had her doubts she'd attract more young females — "I'd figured that at that age, they'd be more interested in Robin" — she has come to discover otherwise. Said the actress, "So many women come up to me today and say, 'I saw you and I loved you. You gave me courage and an idea of what I could do.'"[57]

"Batgirl was ... a good role model. She was take-charge and quick to assess a situation and take action on it. And she wasn't violent — she was wily and quick-witted."[58]

Three years after the series, the crimefighters were reunited for a public service announcement publicizing the Federal Equal Pay Law. Though Adam West didn't take part and was doubled by Dick Gautier, Burt Ward (Robin) and Craig did appear. In the 30-second spot, Batman and Robin are tied up in a warehouse with a bomb ticking. In sweeps Batgirl. But before setting them free, she first sets them straight:

BATGIRL: I've worked for you for a long time and I'm still paid less than Robin.
ROBIN: Holy discontent!
BATGIRL: Same job, same employer means equal pay for men and women.
BATMAN: No time for jokes, Batgirl.
BATGIRL: It's not a joke, it's the Federal Equal Pay Law.

In this spot, as in the original series, Batgirl remains informed and formidable, and strikes yet another blow for women.[59]

❧❧❧

Similarly suited to Batgirl and a "superheroine" in the classic sense was *Wonder Woman* (1976–1979), whose most famous TV incarnation arrived in 1976.[60]

Though created in the 1940s by a man, everything about *Wonder Woman* is pro-woman. According to her origins story, she comes from a race of Amazons who broke free of male-dominated societies to live by themselves on Paradise Island. Their society is a strict matriarchy, devoid of men and male influence. Even the resilient metal — found only on Paradise Island — that would later make up Wonder Woman's bracelets was called feminum! (As noted in the comic, Wonder Woman's trademark bracelets were worn symbolically by all Amazons to remind them of the shackles they had broken free of.)

In 1976, Wonder Woman became TV's first true female superhero to helm her own weekly series.

It's flabbergasting that Wonder Woman could ever be considered anything but empowering. Yet one author has said, "This girl [*sic*] used her brains and her body. But as tough and powerful as she was, Wonder Woman never used her powers to advance her own interests."[61] What?! As if Wonder Woman's expressed mission of defeating Nazis and other evildoers was not worthy and of equal importance to her as to anyone else.

Other attempts to undermine the series also come across as empty. One critic upbraids Wonder Woman's cover identity, Diana Prince, by stating, "In both incarnations [of the series], Diana Prince put on glasses and worked as a secretary in low-cut dresses."[62]

Actually, no. During the show's first season, set during World War II, Prince was a yeoman and wore a uniform. In later seasons, set in the modern day, Prince was an operative for a DC-based government agency and resided in the nation's capital. Though now she did not sport a uniform, her on-screen wardrobe was demure. The character seemed to favor brightly colored blouses with professional-level necklines, buttoned-down (and buttoned-up) dress shirts and boat neck sweaters. The only flesh she usually bares is when she rolls up her sleeves to get to work. In one episode, Diana went undercover as a maid whose uniform is downright dowdy, even on star Lynda Carter.

Wonder Woman only ever had one co-star, Steve Trevor (played by Lyle Waggoner). Originally, Trevor was a World War II fighter pilot whose wartime crash on Paradise Island sets in motion the need for Wonder Woman to return to civilization and assist the Allied powers.

Synopses of the series calling Trevor Diana Prince–Wonder Woman's "love interest" are incorrect. In the show, the two never went on a date or kissed. Moreover, in seasons two and three, set in the present day, Waggoner obviously could not play the same character he had during the war years. So, instead, he played Steve Trevor, Jr. Steve, Jr., like Diana Prince, now worked for the IADC (the Inter-Agency Defense Command), a CIA-like agency. Since Diana Prince–Wonder Woman was the same person (and ageless) but Steve wasn't, there would have been something vaguely disturbing — and May-December! — in any love relationship between the two. Hence, no romance happened.

Furthermore, in the series, Trevor only had minimal screen time anyway. Like Charlie of *Charlie's Angels*, Steve was usually only seen at the beginning as that week's plot got set up and at the very end, after all had been resolved.

If Trevor got air time in between, it was usually only when he was taken hostage. Then it was up to Wonder Woman to save him. Whenever Wonder Woman emerged on the horizon — come to save the day! — Trevor was always relieved that help had arrived.

But while Steve and other citizens were always grateful to see her, the Nazis and latter-day crooks were not. There was nothing that Wonder Woman couldn't do. Though not a deity herself, she was more powerful than any of them. She possessed: the Wisdom of Athena, the Strength of Hercules (take that, Kevin Sorbo!), and the Speed of Mercury. Wonder Woman was not only a great runner and high-jumper but also an expert swimmer and javelin thrower. For many young female fans witnessing Wonder Woman's sheer physicality, it might very well have inspired them to follow her lead and take advantage of various Title IX opportunities. (Title IX was an educational amendment that gave girls equal access to high school sports. It went into effect in 1972.)

TV's *Wonder Woman* was cast to perfection with former Miss America Lynda Carter. One author has said of Carter's iconic performance, "[She was] poised and natural even while running around in an outlandish outfit."[63]

Starlog described TV's Wonder Woman as "aloof but light-hearted, witty but dedicated.... Cool but capable of caring." They said of her alter ego Diana Prince, "[S]he maintains a proud twinkle in her eyes that tells her audience (but never her adversaries) that there is more behind those dowdy glasses than the world will ever know."[64]

The authors of *Fantastic Television* state that in the series, "Ms. Carter has some gutsy women's movement speeches."[65] In one episode, Prince is paired with an old-fashioned male and the two exchange many barbs. "This is the best idea since women's suffrage," Diana tells him at one point.

In both incarnations of the series, Diana obtained her jobs not due to her looks but due to her skills, an admirable fact considering Diana's later career as a government agent.

This show and its star left a lasting impression. Carter has commented, "Wonder

Woman sparked something inside girls that told them they could be powerful."[66] But perhaps it was Paradise Island's queen, Diana's mother, who summed her up best when she sent her eldest offspring off and said, "Go in peace, my daughter. And remember, in a world of ordinary mortals, you are a Wonder Woman."

—◦◦◦—

Superwomen dominated 1970s TV. Concurrent with *Wonder Woman* was another small screen heroine, also the subject of debate. One author has labeled her the "Bionic Bimbo."[67] Bionic? Yes. But "bimbo"? Certainly not by definition — she wasn't dumb nor slutty.

Then in 1996, *Ms.* magazine dismissed *The Bionic Woman* (1976–1978) because the title character "smiled too much."[68] But the book *Sheroes* says that the Bionic Woman "seldom smiled."[69]

So who is this person? Will the real Bionic Woman please stand up?

Spun off from *The Six Million Dollar Man*, the Bionic Woman was Jaime Sommers (played by Lindsay Wagner) who was a tennis pro (supposedly one of the best) and the girlfriend of Steve Austin (the aforementioned Six Million Dollar Man) before she became bionic. When she nearly died in an accident, she was rebuilt by the government into the world's first mix of woman and machine. Once recovered, Sommers embarked on a new life. She had to. She has been changed, physically and emotionally, having experienced this odd "rebirth." She jettisoned boyfriend Austin (though they remained friends) and quite ethically retired from tennis. She also began to work for the government in undercover assignments.

Between missions, Sommers worked as a teacher. The show has been assailed for Sommers' non-bionic career. Said one critic, "[H]er cover was the femininely appropriate role of schoolteacher."[70] But making Jaime Sommers' "day job" a teacher adds an interesting aspect. For example, in one episode, the government wants to send Jaime undercover as a tutor for a foreign prince. But when Jamie hears of the plan, she puts down her bionic foot, refusing to mix her teaching with her other duties. She is further incensed that her cover could have negative ramifications for her charge. Only later, when she's convinced that her cover will serve to protect the boy, does Jaime agree to the assignment. Jaime's reluctance to trade on her role as a teacher plays up an important part of her character. Though it may just be a "cover" to some, to her, her work is important. And though she was nearly half machine, her devotion to it underscores her humanity. As one fan said, "The Bionic Woman was all woman, human and vulnerable — a fact which brought poignant sensitivity to her hard-hitting action-hero persona."[71] As *Starlog* put it:

> [She has] great determination to live the life she wants — not the life of a mechanical freak.... But once on assignment for Oscar Goldman, her narrow personal concerns are forgotten, and all her perceptiveness, her powers and her prowess are focused on the world-shaking problem at hand.[72]

Credit for creating this fully rounded character belongs to star Wagner. *Fantastic Television* states, "To Ms. Wagner's credit, her acting serves to enliven the series and make it truly fun to watch."[73] Lionel Siegel, a writer for the series, said, "The series benefited from Lindsay's warmth, charm, intelligence and sincerity."[74] Wagner also brought humor and common sense to the role, which enhanced the series and made the plots seem plausible, her character believable. For a character that was 40 percent mechanical, Jaime showed a lot of heart. In 1977, the TV industry recognized Wagner for her performance and awarded her an Emmy.[75]

Other condemnations of the series similarly come across as windmill-tilting. In her book *Where the Girls Are*, Susan J. Douglas takes the Bionic Woman to task for often going undercover in "traditional" female careers such as nun and beauty pageant contestant.[76] Unfortunately, Douglas doesn't mention the times she went undercover as a scientist, rodeo rider, and race car driver.

Author Susanna Paasonen, in assessing the pilot of the series, makes note of a run undertaken by Steve Austin and the newly rejuvenated Jaime. The fact that Austin, the Bionic Man, outruns Sommers causes Paasonen to write, "In spite of her technological prowess, Sommers remains a representative of 'the weaker sex.'"[77] But if Austin does outshine Jamie at this time, it could be because she is still learning to incorporate the bionics within her body. Later in the series, we learn that Jamie, now in harmony with her robotics, regularly runs a mile in 58 seconds — two seconds faster than Steve.[78] The technological advancements that had taken place in the years between Austin's rebuilding and Sommers' contributing to her increased speed.

The Bionic Woman is a lead character who is faster and stronger than any man she encounters. But, more importantly, beyond bionic abilities, Sommers, week after week, proves herself braver and more intelligent as well. Double agents, runaway robots, and (male) mad scientists are no match. While her speed, strength and supersonic hearing assist her in completing her missions, it is her intelligence that shines through and enables her to, in various episodes, dismantle a doomsday machine, rescue an ambassador, and avert a nuclear missile.

Often mixed in with her adventures is gender commentary. In "Kill Oscar," a renegade scientist (guest star John Houseman doing his best Dr. Evil) creates an army of female robots — "fembots." He praises his androids' abilities and the fact they are 100 percent "controllable." He tells one of his assistants, "Since when is thinking for herself an asset for a woman?"

Of course, as the episode plays out, the doctor's "fembots" are no match for Jaime Sommers. The Bionic Woman not only overpowers each but also sees to the destruction of the mad genius' headquarters. Ever compassionate, however, Jaime saves the scientist's life as his empire crashes down.

Once again, a parable has been laid out: Attempting to control women — by replacing them with robots or by trying to destroy one like Sommers — is a recipe for failure, one that the men of TV's *My Living Doll* and film's *The Stepford Wives* also discovered.

Rocket Girls

As if excelling in the past or in contemporary times weren't enough, TV heroines have also been seen in the far-off future via small screen science fiction.

Their presence in this genre is actually remarkable in that women and sci-fi has always been a sticky wicket. By and large, science fiction has been a genre skewing male. Hence, sci-fi has tended to be male-centered and male-focused and what women are featured, like the "Bond Girls," sometimes get little to do but look pretty. (Consider the women of TV's *Lost in Space*.) And yet, despite this trend, throughout TV history, various female characters have brought "girl power" to the galaxy.

TV sci-fi started in the 1950s in several cheaply produced but creative series aimed at kids. Long before the *Enterprise*, TV was filled with programs like *Flash Gordon*, *Rocky Jones*, and *Space Patrol*. And all these programs featured at least one female cast member. For example, there was once a time when "space cadet" was not an insult. That was during the heyday of *Tom Corbett, Space Cadet* (1950–1955).

Set in 2035, *Tom Corbett* told of cadets training at Space Academy. One of their instructors was scientist Dr. Joan Dale (played first by Patricia Ferris, then Margaret Garland). Dr. Dale has been described as "educated, intelligent, independent and capable."[79] Besides being a tough instructor (her tests nearly flunked out some), Dale was also one of the universe's most profound thinkers. In one episode she is described by a villain as one of the "greatest minds in the galaxy." Among her inventions was "hyper-drive" (to *Tom Corbett* what "warp speed" was to *Star Trek*).

Meanwhile, over on *Space Patrol* (1951–1952), actress Nina Bara was Tonga, an evil outer space queen. She was also the show's breakout character. In fact, she was so popular with little girls that, according to Bara, the network starting getting mail from parents saying either Tonga had to change or they'd forbid their children from watching. It seems too many daughters were picking up bad habits from this sci-fi siren![80]

But Bara's popularity with viewers excluded her from being excised. So, instead, the producers hit upon an only-in-sci-fi solution: In one episode, Tonga is apprehended by Space Patrol and they subject her to a "brainwashing" which rids her of evil. Unfortunately, during the procedure, Tonga's evil cousin, Baccaratti, mars the process. Thereafter, while Tonga was almost always good, she did, sometimes, relapse. Bara said of her role, "I enjoyed playing Tonga greatly, because she was such a changing character, one minute she was the soul of propriety and the next she was off to double-cross everybody. However, the end result was always good as she fought the influence of Baccaratti or saved the [good guys] in spite of herself."[81]

Tonga's alteration is fraught with symbolism. In her conversion from "bad" to "good," is Tonga being stripped of her individuality? Turned into a Stepford astronaut? Or was the process more the evil cast out?

It seems fair to say that when she was bad she was very bad, but when she was good, she was great. When evil, Tonga was as a formidable enemy. But when good, she was depicted as a valuable team member, eventually assuming the role of Assistant Security Chief, a precursor to Yar on *Star Trek: The Next Generation*.

Tonga's position meant she often faced danger and, like Yar, she always rose to the challenge. In one episode, Tonga has the duty of carrying secret information to Venus. Abducted by the evil Baron Von Kreitz en route, she finds herself imprisoned aboard her own ship. Later, Tonga risks radiation to turn her rocket into a flare and signal her fellow Space Patrol members.

In another episode, Tonga goes to a radiation plant on Saturn's third moon to investigate mismanagement. There, she dismisses the plant's head for incompetence which causes him to vow revenge. But, in the end, he's no match for Tonga's wit or strength.

Sharing the ship with Tonga was Carol (played by Virginia Hewitt) who was also a brilliant scientist. Just as Tonga had once invented the Radurium Glove for the treatment of burns, Carol invented the Agra Ray, a device which speeds up the growth process to revitalize desolate planets. (A similar device, named Genesis, would later be featured in *Star Trek*.)

Like Tonga, Carol is shown to be brave and conscious of her duty — and rebellious. In one story, Carol pursues a criminal from Mercury to Mars despite orders not to.

Another early space saga only came to the small screen after a successful theatrical career. As in movie serials, TV's *Flash Gordon* (1953) centered on three characters: Flash (played by Steve Holland), his associate Dale Arden (played by Irene Champlin), and the eccentric Dr. Zarkov (played by Joe Nash).

Though Flash was the lead and handled most of the action, Dale was depicted as an integral part of this trio. In one episode, she doesn't think twice about jumping on the back of a henchman to take him down.

In their book on early sci-fi, authors Lucanio and Coville state, "Dale was far from [a] passive and helpless creature.... Dale not only packed a ray gun and could hold her own in a fight, but more importantly she possessed an emotional strength...."[82] Proof of both of these qualities can be found in "The Lure of Light." In it, Dale is kidnapped by an evil queen. The renegade ruler wants to find out about a new device which allows rockets to travel faster than light. But even when faced with death, Dale refuses to answer. Dale's bravery results in — believe it or not — her death! The ruler kills Dale because Dale can't be broken. Thankfully, in this episode, Flash is later able to journey back in time to prevent Dale's demise.

As if all that weren't enough, Dale was also portrayed as a futuristic feminist. In one episode, when the team travels back to the "ancient past" of 1950s America, Dale asks Zarkov for details:

DALE: The women, Dr. Zarkov, what were they like?
DR. ZARKOV: Well, instead of filling their heads full of knowledge about astrophysics, atomic research, electronic phenomenon like a certain young lady we know —
DALE: Yes, well what did they do? Sit home and knit?
DR. ZARKOV: Well, I wouldn't say that was all they did but they certainly knew their way around a kitchen better than they did a laboratory.

At the end of this exchange, the look of disgust on Dale's face is timeless.

Meanwhile, over on *Rocky Jones, Space Ranger* (1954), the cast included female character Veena (played by Sally Mansfield). She often did the "women's work" on the ship — from acting as teacher of boy cadet Bobby to sewing uniforms — but she also was called upon to act as a translator and to act as navigator.

Perhaps just as importantly, Veena was depicted as a strong, fully involved member of this crew and was portrayed as far more intelligent than some fellow officers, especially Winky, a sort of outer space Gilligan.

TV's early space shows, despite their low-tech sets and low-rent effects, presented a clear vision to any little girl watching — that in the future, there was space for them.

For most, TV science fiction reached its zenith with *Star Trek* (1966–1969). As most Trekkers know, from the program's conception attempts were made to make the cast multicultural and sexually integrated to project creator Gene Roddenberry's vision of a peaceable future.

As fans also know, in the series' unaired pilot,[83] the second in command was a woman. Actress Majel Barrett had the role, a character named Number One (a moniker later resurrected for *The Next Generation*).

It's been reported that NBC, after seeing the pilot, asked for various changes to be made, including, among others, that a woman not be so high-ranking. In *Inside* Star Trek:

The Real Story, a book by Herbert F. Solow, executive in charge of production for the series, and Robert H. Justman, the show's co-producer, the authors claim differently. They state that NBC did not object to a female officer per se, and in fact once sent a memo stating, "We support the concept of a woman in a strong, leading role." But the network did express doubts about Barrett (a relative unknown) being able to carry the part.[84] Barrett, however, was already romantically involved with series creator Roddenberry (the two would eventually marry). We can speculate that once Barrett was nixed, Roddenberry simply killed the character rather than see it played by someone else.

Despite the loss of Number One, there remained various strong women, even among its guest cast. Consider these: The T'Pau (played by Celia Lovsky) was a Vulcan matriarch in "Amok Time"; Joanne Linville was a Romulan commander in "The Enterprise Incident"; Diana Muldaur was a skilled (and mysterious) ambassador in "Is There in Truth No Beauty?"; Kathryn Hays was as an alien who risked her life to save McCoy's in "The Empath"; France Nuyen starred as Elaan, a spoiled would-be alien bride in "Elaan of Troyius"; Joan Collins was a pacifist and eventual human sacrifice in "The City on the Edge of Forever"; and Jane Wyatt guest starred as Mr. Spock's human mother in "Journey to Babel." (Wyatt would later recreate her role in a *Star Trek* film.)

In terms of recurring female characters, *Star Trek* also delivered. Though the less said about Yeoman Rand (played by Grace Lee Whitney) the better, there was Christine Chapel, the ship's head nurse, a lieutenant with a doctorate in bio-research. While her role might have been consolation, Majel Barrett made the most of it. Though, technically, Chapel was fulfilling a traditional female role, she wasn't subservient to medical officer McCoy. In one episode, McCoy has diagnosed himself with a fatal illness. He forbids Nurse Chapel from informing Captain Kirk. She rebels, stating, "I am a nurse first and a member of the *Enterprise* second."

Then there was the show's most high-profile female character, Lt. Nyota Uhura, played by Nichelle Nichols. Though one online Trekker dismisses Uhura, the ship's communication's officer, as a "telephone operator,"[85] such logic is faulty. If that's true, then, chief engineer Scotty was just a grease monkey.

Even objections to the female characters' uniforms — which featured short skirts and knee-high black boots — don't withstand scrutiny. As Nichols has said, "Contrary to what many may think today, no one really saw [the uniform] as demeaning back then. In fact, the miniskirt was a symbol of sexual liberation. More to the point, though, in the twenty-third century, you are respected for your abilities regardless of what you do and do not wear."[86] (Along with the functionality of the uniform, note that the male uniforms consisted of tight, black, clingy capri pants.)

Uhura, whose name was derived from the Swahili "uhuru" meaning "freedom," was the *Enterprise*'s fourth highest-ranking officer. The character was conceived as a linguistics scholar, fluent in a variety of languages, and a top graduate of Starfleet. She is further described in the show's "bible": "Her life philosophy ... reflects the warm, non-aggressive 'man–nature-oneness' culture of the 23rd century Bantu nation which became Earth's best example of blending advanced technology with a naturalistic agrarian philosophy."[87]

Occasionally Uhura got to show both brawn and brains. In the episode "Mirror, Mirror," she overpowers an alien holding her at gunpoint. Says author Alan Asherman in his book *The* Star Trek *Compendium*, "[In this episode, Uhura is] more forceful, adaptable and gorgeous than usual."[88] Later, in the episode "I, Mudd," Uhura is instrumental in the plan to prevent a takeover. In "Space Seed," she boldly defies Kahn (Ricardo Montalban) and claims loyalty to Star Fleet. In "Balance of Terror," Uhura takes over navigation of the *Enterprise*.

Despite these instances, Lt. Uhura, in most of the series' episodes, only got to do utter a few lines of dialogue, with "Hailing frequencies open, Captain" most common. Nervousness about Southern affiliates, among other excuses, was often cited as the reason why Uhuru was often seen but not heard. Nichols grew so frustrated by the size of her role that after season one she considered leaving the series. But she would eventually change her mind, at the request of one special viewer. As the actress relates in her autobiography, during the show's original run, at an NAACP fundraiser, she was introduced to a "big fan of *Star Trek*." That "fan" turned out to be Dr. Martin Luther King, Jr. When Nichols said she planned to leave the series, he implored her not to: "You *cannot* and you *must* not.... You have the first non-stereotypical role on television, male or female. You have broken ground... ."[89] Taking Dr. King's words to heart, Nichols renewed her contract and stayed for the series' duration.

King wasn't the only fan of Uhura. During the show's run, Nichols' fan mail equaled that of William Shatner and Leonard Nimoy.[90] Since the ending of the series, Uhura has gone on to receive even wider praise. As one author put it:

> In its own time, there's no question that [the role] was revolutionary.... A black woman on the bridge with an officer's rank able to order men about!... And Uhura was always an excellent officer. She never had hysterics on duty, never freaked out or made some error.[91]

The character of Uhura has even been labeled a role model by Mai Jamieson, America's first African American woman astronaut.[92]

—◦◦◦—

Almost 20 years after the end of the original, *Star Trek* was relaunched as a new series. In *Star Trek: The Next Generation* (1987–1994), greater care was taken to see that the future being enacted was open to everyone. Even the show's opening manifesto was altered from "where no *man*" to "where no *one* has gone before."

When the series premiered, there were three full-time high-ranking female characters. Dr. Beverly Crusher (played by Gates McFadden) was head of medicine. Deana Troi (played by Marina Sirtis), an "empath," had the ability to sense other people's emotions; she served as the ship's counselor. Troi occupied a seat right next to that of Commander Picard.

But perhaps the most radical of the show's females was Tasha Yar (played by Denise Crosby), head of security. By her position's nature, Yar was trouncing stereotypes. As one author described her, "[She was] tough, constantly suggesting force and almost obsessively protective of her superior officers."[93]

Crosby left the series after season one. Rumor has it the actress didn't like her lack of screen time. And, true, there just weren't that many fights on this new, less violent *Star Trek*.[94] Had the Yar character stayed on, she might have emerged as one of media's great feminist heroines, another Xena.

After Crosby's exit, the role was not recast nor another character added to even out the male-female ratio. Was this sexism or just a way of weeding out an already overpopulated series? In Yar's absence, ship security fell to a more traditional choice, resident Klingon Worf, a male.

With Yar out, the show found itself the recipient of some belated feminist criticism.

The show's two remaining women continued to be portrayed as they had always been—integral to the team of the *Enterprise*, both professionally and personally (they continued to take part in the staff's weekly poker games); but ultimately the physical and emotional needs (i.e., maternal needs) of the crew were the responsibility of women. Various assessments often censure *Trek* for this alleged bias.[95] Though, to be fair, historically, neither doctor nor psychologist are considered "traditional" female occupations.

In any event, let's be accurate: The final care-giving roles that the females filled had less to do with patriarchal oppression than it did with Crosby deciding to jump ship.

The charges of sexism were abated a bit in season two when McFadden also left and was replaced by Diana Muldaur as the ship's doctor. "Abated" because Muldaur's persona and performance were more "tough love" than tender mercies.

From her guest spots on the original *Star Trek* up through her work on *LA Law*, Muldaur has always played straight-talking women. Her year as Dr. Kate Pulaski proved no different. Pulaski was the only character (male or female) willing to regularly butt heads with the captain. Pulaski's manner irritated Picard as she regularly usurped his omni-command. In her willingness to defy authority, and with her oft-exhibited contempt for technology, Dr. Pulaski was similar to the *Enterprise*'s original MD, "Bones" McCoy. But in keeping with the revolving door nature of the series' females, Muldaur left after one year and was replaced by a returning McFadden.

In any form, and even within their "traditional" professions, the women of *The Next Generation* always held their own. Said one writer:

> In the 20th century, prominent professional women are heralded for succeeding in "a man's world"; that is not a factor in the success of women in *The Next Generation*. Women in [the program] have virtually every possible opportunity among which they can choose from, so it is not the case that the two women chose these professionals in the absence of other choices....[96]

Five seasons after the original *Star Trek*'s end, TV's next space adventure launched. Inspired no doubt by the success of *Trek* in reruns, there were high hopes for *Space: 1999* (1974–1976) among science fiction fans hungry for a successor to Kirk and company.

The program had an impressive pedigree. It was produced by Gerry Anderson (whose previous credits were *UFO* and *The Protectors*) and it starred then-married actors Martin Landau and Barbara Bain, both previously of *Mission: Impossible*. Barry Morse, previously of *The Fugitive*, filled out the cast.

Furthermore, the series was to spare no expense when it came to special effects. Especially well done was the climactic moment of the premiere which set everything in motion.

When *Space* began, it is supposedly 1999 (then the faroff future) and a devoted team of scientists is staffing the experimental space colony, Moonbase Alpha, on Earth's moon. In the premiere, an explosion, caused by nuclear waste on the moon's dark side, dislodges the moon from Earth's orbit, hurling it into space.

While the sets and special effects were impressive, it was hard to cotton to the leads as each was depicted as rather cold and detached. Even the interaction between Alpha's Commander Walter Koenig (Landau) and medical doctor Helena Russell (Bain), which was supposed to have romantic undertones, seemed a stalemate.

The guarded, formal relationship between these characters bears a similarity to the working relationship between Scully and Mulder on *The X-Files* years later. The comparisons between *Space: 1999*'s Dr. Russell and Dana Scully, also a doctor, is an interesting one, begging the question: Does a woman of science on TV always have to be so decidedly cool? To judge by the more recent *Bones*, apparently yes.

But, then again, these women held vitally important jobs, Dr. Russell's all the more serious after Alpha's break from Earth. If her manner reflected a no-nonsense personality, can anyone blame her?

While many now look on the interpersonal relationships in the series as a fatal flaw, the behavior of the characters might have been a conscious choice. Perhaps the detached quality that Alpha residents exhibited echoed the "detachment" of Alpha from Earth. Could the populace of Alpha have been suffering from mass depression? The breaking with the Earth, the shrinking of the sun, the possibility of never seeing family again could affect one's disposition.

Soon after its premiere, viewership for *1999* began to diminish and most critics chose to write it off as a failure. But, when looked at today, most episodes of *1999* hold up quite well, a bridge of sorts between the action-oriented original *Star Trek* and the more cerebral *Star Trek: The Next Generation*.

And Dr. Russell emerges as a feminist character. In the episode "Alpha Child," she is a staunch defender of a little boy though his presence might endanger others. In another episode, she would rather see an ancient satellite destroyed than risk any life due to its unstable power source.

Dr. Russell was in charge of medical care on Alpha and, though it's not in Alpha's flowchart, she often seemed to be second in command as well. In a season one episode, she and an away team take one of their transport ships (called "Eagles") to a newly discovered planet. She's clearly in charge and her mostly male crew members have no problem taking orders from her.

Starlog said of Russell, "[She's] solid, stolid, inventive and reliable.... [S]he distinguishes herself as a medical scientist of both the physical and the psychological." They further praised her "courage in terrifying situations."[97] One fan argued that Helena could never be lumped into any "screaming female" category because

she stood up to "Brian the Brain," she jumped aboard a glider to save [Koenig] in "Immunity Syndrome," she commanded the base in "AB Chrysalis," she nearly shot [fellow officer] Maya in "Dorcons," [and] she even contemplated mutiny in "Seed of Destruction."[98]

Continuing TV's long history of featuring women in sci-fi sagas, Barbara Bain (left) and Catherine Schell played Dr. Helena Russell and Maya, respectively, on *Space: 1999* (1975–1977) with Martin Landau (seated).

From the beginning, Russell was never afraid to stand up to Koenig. In the debut, outraged over some unnecessary derring-do, she informs him, "We need answers, not heroes."

Despite *Space: 1999*'s problematic first season, the series was renewed. In year two, new producers upped the action and defrosted the characters. (Also, Barry Morse left the show due to a contract dispute.) Most importantly, though, the producers brought in a new character, a female alien named Maya (translation: "gift from god") played by Catherine Schell.

Maya, discovered on an outlying planet, was the daughter of a renegade scientist going mad. In her debut, thanks to the Alphians, Maya learns of her father's life-destroying experiments and revolts against him (literally revolts against the patriarchy). Eventually Maya flees her home and joins the residents of Alpha where, shades of Spock, she assumes the role of Chief Science Officer.

Maya also has another ability: She's capable of transforming herself into any form — from bird to exotic alien. (This same idea would later give birth to NBC's *Manimal* in 1983.) This skill (assumedly some way of reconfiguring cells of the body) makes Maya an incarnation of the White Goddess: "I was in many shapes...."[99]

Maya's transformative abilities regularly saved missions and officers. In one episode, when a fellow Alphian (a male) is knocked unconscious by an intruder, Maya transforms into a black-clad ninja. Soon she is able to defeat the assailant. In another, Maya's metamorphosis into a bird allows her to fly off to locate stranded colleagues. In another, she's able to assume the form of a hideous space monster in order to infiltrate a group of them.

Besides her ability to morph, Maya also possessed a mighty brain. She regularly astonishes colleagues with her talent for calculating in her head. As with her physical skills, her brain comes in handy. In one episode, it is Maya who realizes that the reason a being is impervious to lasers is because it's not alive at all but a machine.

Maya's physical abilities coupled with her smarts made her the most powerful person on Moonbase. Meanwhile, her exceeding bravery makes her as formidable as Helena. In one episode, she and Dr. Russell defy orders by leaving Alpha in a stolen Eagle. They are off to rescue crew members and come across like an outer space Thelma and Louise.

Maya is one of the least sexualized of all the characters in this chapter. The form-fitting catsuits usually favored by TV heroines, like Seven of Nine on *Star Trek: Voyager*, are not part of Maya's wardrobe. When we first meet her, she is attired in long sleeves and skirt. After joining Alpha, she adopts their attire, which, though skirted, remains unprovocative and asexual.

Nevertheless, despite her wardrobe and avant-garde makeup, which included profound eyebrows and what one critic called "sideburns,"[100] Schell as Maya was a striking presence. She also gave a superb performance; she is unforgettable in the episode "The Dorcans," where her character faces capture by an enemy of her people. Had *1999* lasted, Maya might have become this series' breakout character. But viewers didn't return to the "new" *1999* and after 23 additional episodes, the series came to an end.

—◦◦◦—

Another female outer space image arrived a few years later via Colonel Wilma Deering in *Buck Rogers in the 25th Century* (1979–1981).[101] *Buck Rogers* lasted two seasons thanks to its broadly drawn characters (some just this side of camp), its colorful sets and aversion to larger social issues (unlike, say, *Star Trek*). Some of its success might also have arisen from the show's hearkening back to its Saturday movie serial days.

Erin Gray played Deering with serious conviction. After all, as Gray has explained, "She had a serious job."[102] Gray said of her role, "I developed my character according to the script that was given to me. She was a colonel, she was head of the fighters, she trained men to fight.... [T]he way it was presented was that I was right there with the lead scientists and it was my job to protect planet Earth."[103]

Throughout the first season, Deering did just that. Though Buck was the star, Wilma was seen acting autonomously and was an important part of every episode. She repeatedly proved herself a skilled pilot, like when she guided a volatile "space berg" through space. She was even a forceful hand-to-hand combatant. Wilma would also occasionally go undercover (as in the episode "Olympiad") and, from time to time, save Buck's life.

As important as anything pertaining to the character was her professional manner. In her relationship with Buck, there was a mutual respect, a recognition of each other's abilities and no romance.

But that was in season one; the character underwent alterations in season two. A new male producer was installed and the series' lone female producer exited. Gray's character, always in the action before, got sidelined in season two.[104] Also, her once practical, unisexual uniform was replaced with a white tennis skirt, making her character look like a space-age flight attendant. Gray stated:

> In the first season, she led the men, she had very definite ideas about how a raid should be performed. Suddenly, the next year, she's always on planet Earth and her role becomes very nurturing.... That bothered me, and what bothered me even more was that I allowed myself as a woman not to speak up. Why? Because we had a new producer the second year.... I knew that my character had a chance of disappearing. So, I didn't speak up. I stayed passive. But I kept my job.[105]

Gray's candor brings up a reality of this whole TV images business. That is, that it's a *business* with money riding on every ratings point. Performers often don't, or can't, risk having a say in how their characters behave. Actresses like Gray might want their characters a certain way but, in the end, they are hired hands.

Nevertheless, Gray's Deering earned her a place in the pantheon of sci-fi heroines both in the derring-do that she did and in the image she created. Gray said,

> It came as a surprise to me to discover how a character I'd portrayed affected so many women. I'm honored when women come up to me and say, "You were the reason I became a police officer, or joined the Air Force."[106]

The Villainesses

For every heroine or hero to become a heroine or hero, they have to have an adversary.

And though Tonga would turn "good" in *Space Patrol*, back on Earth such mind-altering technologies didn't exist. Hence, early action-adventures often featured all-out female villains. After all, as real life sometimes taught us, evil is not gender-specific.

So, in early TV, mixed in with the Klingons and others, there were a few ladies who were on the wrong side of the law. Yet, despite their criminal status, these characters' break with societal norms and refusal to obey rules of male society seem to make them, in this context, not so much villains as anti-heroines.

Certainly that was the case with *Terry and the Pirates* (1952). *Terry* begun as a comic strip in 1934, then was a radio program, and then a serial. In any incarnation, Terry Lee was an American Army colonel and pilot who had relocated to the Orient to track down a long-lost gold mine. Terry never found gold but did have some far-flung adventures along the way.

On TV, actor John Baer played Terry; he was of the blond and square-jawed variety. In other words, kind of bland. Luckily, he was surrounded by some colorful characters, like his nemesis, The Dragon Lady!

The term "dragon lady" was coined in *Terry and the Pirates*. Today, Webster acknowledges its origins and defines it as "a glamourous and often mysterious woman."[107]

On TV, the Dragon Lady was played by Gloria Saunders. And if Saunders' name doesn't sound very Asian, it's not surprising. The South Carolina–born actress was as Asian as apple pie. Nevertheless, she looked exotic enough by Hollywood standards at the time to eke out a career playing any number of "others"—gypsies, Indians, Arabs.

Regardless of heritage, Saunders cut an amazing figure in her role. Supermodel slim, often *poured* into form-fitting sheaths, Saunders' jet-black hair and extravagantly made-up eyes made her a menacing mix of beauty and power. Furthermore, the Dragon Lady is depicted as dangerously smart, smart enough to strike fear into Terry and other males. Her calm, contained persona radiated a cleverness, a resourcefulness, that communicated this was not a woman to trifle with.

A contemporary of *Terry* could be found on *The Affairs of China Smith* (1952; 1955). Dan Duryea played the title character, a rogue adventurer. The show's chief scoundrel, the "scheming"[108] "Empress," was played by actress Myrna Dell.

Another "bad girl" of the era was on *The Adventures of Fu Manchu* (1956). Even today, *Fu Manchu* remains fascinating as it is one of the few series in history built around a villain. Every week, the evil Dr. Fu Manchu (Glen Gordon) would unleash another plot to take over the world. His plans included smuggling dangerous germs and replacing world leaders with lookalikes. He always got foiled but that didn't stop him from plotting.

In carrying out his plans, the doctor was aided by his daughter Karamanch, played by Laurette Luez. In episodes, Fu Manchu got most of the dialogue, thus leaving little for Karamanch to say. Nevertheless, she was a foreboding presence as she stood by her father, ready to aid him in his schemes. Sometimes she did play an integral part: Often she was used to seduce or hoodwink innocents, a sort of evil Cinnamon Carter. Karamanch was charismatic, a femme fatale, certainly a precursor to Catwoman on *Batman*.

Speaking of which...

Batman (1966–1968) had its share of female villains like Ma Parker (played by Shelley Winters), the Black Widow (played by Tallulah Bankhead) and the Siren (played by Joan Collins). They were every bit as diabolical as the Joker and the Riddler. In fact, since all the show's female villains were portrayed as nasty as the show's male villains, that must count as some sort of gender equity.

Gotham's most famous female Bat-criminal (and the one who made the most appearances) was Catwoman, played by Julie Newmar and Eartha Kitt.

Newmar, whose previous TV appearances included a female devil on *The Twilight Zone*, *was* Catwoman and gave one the great performances in TV history. Funny yet sexy, campy but menacing; there are no wasted words or gestures in her characterization. As one critic noted, "Most villains on *Batman* had an over-the-top quality to them, Newmar, however, played Catwoman with a self-assured and empowered feel—a common thread throughout her career."[109]

The actress herself has said about her character, "It was a great role. Catwoman was so spontaneous and creative and maddening and sexy and insouciant."[110]

Catwoman was cool ... and bad. Like her more law-abiding super sisters, Catwoman doesn't worry about her weight or her hair and she doesn't do dishes.

Some of Catwoman's power was, of course, sexual. And yet her sexuality did not define her. She did not trade on her looks. After all, it wasn't love she was after — it was world domination!

Catwoman was also smart. She always concocted her own ingenious plans. She's in charge too, commanding a team of henchmen to do her bidding. She once told one of her lackeys, "Yours is not to reason why. Yours is to do as I tell you to. Or you'll keep tasting my cat-o-nine-tails."[111]

Her effect on the Caped Crusader went far beyond matters of law and order. As Ronald L. Smith wrote, "Catwoman was [Batman's] complete equal, and her ... every smirk and purr unnerved him."[112] Cat-woman's sensuous voice and costume even had an effect on the young Boy Wonder. In one episode, Robin tells Batman, "Y'know, Batman, I couldn't help but notice Catwoman's finely shaped legs."[113] Certainly the Penguin didn't have that sort of impact on the Dynamic Duo.

In her break with social norms, Catwoman, like Thelma and Louise, was breaking off from male society. And while viewers may not originally have hit upon Catwoman's feminist separatist mentality, many women nevertheless did see in her something they wanted to express themselves. As Nina Bara experienced earlier, Newmar often got fan mail from young girls, many with photos attached. The actress said, "I would get pictures from young girls in their homemade Catwoman costumes, telling me how they liked to dress up in them and act wicked."[114]

As noted earlier, Newmar was not the only TV Cat-woman. In the series' final

In a weird sort of equal opportunity, women on early TV were also seen in villainous roles, like "The Dragon Lady" (played by Gloria Saunders) on *Terry and the Pirates* (1952).

season, chanteuse Eartha Kitt took over the role making her, during *Batman*'s run, its only black super-villain.

In retrospect, it seemed most appropriate for Kitt to become Catwoman. Kitt had long been described as slinky, kittenish, and feline as a singer-actress-dancer. And she was wonderful in the role, bringing her *purr*-fect personality and razor-sharp diction fully to the proceedings.

Kitt was also different than Newmar. While Julie's performance emphasized comedic aspects, Kitt's Cat was more sinister. Kitt seemed to lay the groundwork for the less-campy, more macabre female villains of the later *Batman* feature films, like Michelle Pfeiffer in *Batman Returns*.

Unfortunately, the sexual undertones (played up between Batman and Catwoman when Newmar had the part) were dropped as the producers steered clear of interracial romance. This imposed distance did add a new dimension to the series. Many—though not all—of the female villains previously on *Batman* (notably Marsha, Queen of Diamonds, played by Carolyn Jones) had romantic designs on Batman. By contrast, Kitt's Catwoman wasn't interested in bedding or becoming betrothed to the Crusader.

Mention must be made of the appropriately named catsuit that Catwoman always wore. Though this costume certainly showed off the curves of both actresses, the attire did not seem to be gender-specific. The skin-tight body stocking was the uniform for some of Gotham's most famous and infamous; consider the green leotard that the Riddler wore, and Batman's blue tights.

Of course, compared to the Riddler, Catwoman's costume is much more weighted with symbolism. With her costume's hip-hugging tightness, it seemed to do Emma Peel one better. Its black color conjures up images of the dominatrix which then spirals into fetishism and bondage. When you then consider that Catwoman occasionally carried with her a whip, there's little denying what her attire hinted at. But is this bad or good? In Elisabeth Fies' article "Catwoman: The Creation of a Twentieth-Century Goddess," she labels TV's Catwoman both "femme fatale" and "nefarious temptress" and as the possessor of both a "dangerous femininity" and a "keen intellect."[115] All qualities that, in the end, add up to a very intimidating and powerful woman, one who was equal parts "bad girl" yet still "super-heroine."

—◦◦◦—

Finally, perhaps TV's greatest super villainess—and that's something!—arrived on the airwaves via *V* (1984–1985), the sci-fi miniseries about lizard-like alien invaders. After a successful limited run, *V* went on to become a series.

In *V*, a not-so-benevolent group of aliens—the "Visitors"—arrive on Earth claiming good intentions but secretly planning to exterminate all humans. Hiding their reptilian appearance behind human façades, the Visitors take over the media, herd human youths into mind-controlling organizations, and ship scientists off to camps. The parallels between the rise of the Visitors and the advent of the Nazis was not coincidental.

Actress Jane Badler gave the performance of her life as Diana, the Visitors' (literally) cold-blooded *de facto* leader. Diana has been described as "alluring and repulsive"; "a female Dr. Mengele"; and "arrogant [and] ambitious with a voracious appetite for food, sex and power."[116]

In regard to food, Visitors preferred to eat live meat; in one immortal scene, Diana swallowed a live rat. Her lust for sex was equally carnivorous. While most Visitors found humans repugnant, Diana showed no qualms about bedding down a few human males.

In 2004, *TV Guide* declared Diana one of sci-fi's greatest characters, saying she looked "suspiciously like a Texas cheerleader gone mad" and describing her as "omni-sexual" and "joyfully evil."[117]

Conclusion

The list of TV women includes everyone from Annie Oakley to the Dragon Lady, from Honey West to Catwoman, from Sheena to Xena: how can anyone maintain that women's roles on TV have ever lacked diversity? For all the many forms that these superheroines (and their dark sisters, the super-villainesses) came in, they did though always have a few traits in common: a sense of their own self-worth, their own strength and own personal power.

— 8 —

"Voices Carry"
A Conclusion

And all shall be well and all manner of thing shall be well. — Julian of Norwich

Despite ample evidence to the contrary — as this book has shown — there remain those who refuse to consider June Cleaver a feminist or anything but an oppressed image.

As television's programming history grows more populated, such quick summations of women on the small screen seem destined to continue. Too much space and effort is needed now to accurately convey the full spectrum of female TV characters; it's just easier to ignore or diminish them.

Often, now, when these dismissive statements are made, they seem less concerned with being accurate than they are in being incendiary, a way to foster some contained rage among (mainly, probably) women over how other women were supposedly once depicted with the ultimate point being ... what?

As mentioned in Chapter 1, the purpose of this book was never to say that all of TV's women have been positive and empowering. Admittedly, there are entire series where women have been either completely ignored or treated shabbily. Candidates for most chauvinistic series would have to include *Lost in Space* (1965–1968) where June Lockhart's character never did much but set the table on the *Jupiter II* spacecraft, usually with the assistance of her two equally under-represented daughters. When that series' Robot has more to do — and more personality — than any of the show's women, something is wrong, not just lost, in space. Meanwhile, on *The Dukes of Hazzard* (1979–1985), its only female character, Daisy, is mainly remembered for her cut-off shorts. That would be forgivable if just once she had played a vital role in any episode's plot. Here, too, something mechanical — the Dukes' car, the General Lee — got more airtime than Miss Daisy ever did. Even a series like *Happy Days* (1974–1984) has some 'splaining to do. Despite the classic Marion Ross mother figure, most of the women there existed only to fawn over the Fonz. The one time we saw a woman an equal to him — Roz Kelly's Pinky Tuscadaro — she was gone after only a few episodes.

Meanwhile, on *The A-Team* (1983–1987), the testosterone of that show was so heavy it drove off two women before the idea of having a female team member was abandoned altogether.

Other programs are less cut-and-dried. *Remington Steele* (1982–1987) is remembered today as a well-done detective farce in the mode of *The Thin Man* with Stephanie Zimbalist as a female PI with a dapper partner (played by Pierce Brosnan). Brosnan became that season's breakout star as many women swooned over his English accent and dashing looks. And though Zimbalist brought pluck to her role, she seemed to fade into the background as more and more time was devoted to Mr. Steele and his Bond-like abilities.

Additionally, the Linda Hamilton-Ron Perlman series *Beauty and the Beast* (1987–1990) is also problematic. It always seemed that Hamilton's character, attorney Catherine Chandler, would always fall into some mess that required rescue by the Beast. Still, *Beauty and the Beast* was a hit among female viewers who developed an affinity for the poetic, tortured soul of Vincent, the Beast.

Despite these issues, programs like *Remington* and *Beast* were popular with many female viewers even though they seemed to frequently lessen their female characters' roles. These series seem to be the small-screen equivalent of so many romance novels where Fabio-esque heroes swashbuckle into the lives of damsels in distress. This begs the question: Do suave Englishmen and poetry-quoting beasts trump our feminist ideals?

One could of course go on, turning over every possible rock in primetime, daytime, and children's programming (not to mention commercials, the life blood of the industry) to hunt out examples of TV's "sexism," though a better word than "sexist" would be "dated."

But in assessing the images of women on television, one must not only always consider the era in which these programs were produced but also, as mentioned in Chapter 1, "The Man Question." That is: Do these female images have a male equivalent somewhere in the TV lexicon? While Napoleon Solo, the Fonz and Magnum, PI, were cool, TV has given us some rather spotty male "role models." Add to all the Gomers and Gilligans: Archie Bunker, Herman Munster, and Al Bundy. Even some of our "heroes" often leave something to be desired. Could anyone ever be more dull than Joe Friday or a bigger bore than Batman?

—⁓—

The great Betty White, speaking on the role that television plays in directing real life, said, "What's wrong with it is what's wrong with us."[1]

She's right. If TV is too violent, perhaps that's because the world is too violent. If TV is, or has been, sexist, then so too is the society from which it emanates.

Luckily though, among whatever supposedly "sexist" images that might have been or which might still exist, the medium has always been expansive, giving us many more than its fair share of positive images of women — women who have ranged from Honey West to Janet Dean, from Casey Jones to Florida Evans, Jaime Sommers, Lucy Ricardo, Emma Peel, Tonga, Connie Brooks, Susie McNamara, Lois Lane, Julia Baker, Hazel, Batgirl, Della Street, Miss Hathaway, 99, Lily Ruskin, Victoria Barkley, Miss Kitty, Joan Nash, Wonder Woman, Nurse Jill Danko, Samantha Stephens, Cinnamon Carter, Margaret Anderson, Willy Dodger, Ann Romano, Donna Stone, Emily Hartley, Lt. Uhura, Molly Goldberg, Mrs. Muir, Annie Oakley, Sister Bertrille, Christie Love, Nancy Drew, Billie Newman, Helena Russell, April Dancer, Sabrina Duncan, and Maya and Margie and Sheena and Xena.

And there's not a "hapless housewife," "husband-hunter," or "decorative non-entity" in the bunch.

— Appendix —

The Myths of a Medium

If they have lied about Me, they have lied about everything.
— Alice Walker, "The Temple of My Familiar"

Anyone who has ever doubted that fictional women in early television usually get short shrift need only do a perusal of the popular (and "scholarly") literature on the subject. Once they do, they will soon see just how far afield most assessments are.

Below are just some of the examples I've come across in my research. They are excerpts from books, journals, newspaper articles and the web that each have a reductive, myopic, and incorrect view about the types of roles women played, and how they played them.

Of course, once these statements get published, they then get cited by other writers and slowly become "fact," even when they aren't.

"Over the years, network sitcoms have ridden alternating waves of feminism and backlash...."— from "Networking on TV: A Feminine Touch" by Felicia R. Lee, *New York Times*, November 29, 2003

"In the 1950s, Eve Arden as *Our Miss Brooks* and Lucille Ball as Mrs. Ricky Ricardo cavorted across the nation's television screens. Both were dizzy dames. Both alternatively tricked and kowtowed to the men in their respective series — teacher Brooks to School Principal Conklin, Lucy to her husband."— from *Hearth and Home: Images of Women in the Mass Media*, edited by Gaye Tuchman, Arlene Kaplan Daniels and James Benet, 1978

"In the earliest television sitcoms, women were portrayed — in shows like *Leave It to Beaver* or *The Donna Reed Show*— as home-centered mothers who occasionally went out to shop or socialize but whose 'sphere' was private rather than public."— from *The Girl on the Magazine Cover: The Origins of Visual Stereotypes in American Mass Media* by Carolyn Kitch, 2000

"Likewise, *Ironside* championed the strengths of the handicapped, but didn't exactly shriek 'girl power.' The only woman on the show was a black [sic] secretary [sic], who wheeled Raymond Burr around and sometimes said things like 'I've found the file' and 'Joe called.'"— from "Major film reprises womens' liberation" by Larry Good, *Aspen Daily News*, September 25, 2002

"But unlike the woman's pictures of the 1940s and '50s, in which women were the axis around which the story revolved, women on TV in this era were more often relegated to the sidelines."— from *Feminism and Pop Culture* by Andi Zeisler, 2008

"While [*Bewitched* and *I Dream of Jeannie*] deal directly with female power, their dilemma is not how to celebrate it, but how to curtail it."— from "Channeling: Please don't twitch" by Mary Dickie on www.eye.net, January 14, 1999

"[In the] first generation of successful female writers and producers[, those] working in the comedy genre include Diane English (*My Sister Sam, Foley Square, Murphy Brown*)...."— from *Watching America* by S. Robert Lichter, Linda S. Lichter, and Stanley Rothman, 1991

"*Mary Tyler Moore* liberated single-woman sitcoms from narratives dominated by husband hunting (e.g., *Our Miss Brooks, Private Secretary, The Lucy Show*), charming incompetent and/or troublemaking (e.g., *That Girl* and *I Dream of Jeannie*), or widowed motherhood."—from *Prime-Time Feminism* by Bonnie J. Dow, 1996

"The character of Lois Lane is one of the very few (if not the only) working women on television in the 1950s."—from www.web.mac.com/repotter/George_Reeves_Forever/Noel.html

"Edith Bunker is a nitwit with a heart of gold. Laverne and Shirley are dummies.... Maude is neurotic. Alice's ambition is to become a cocktail waitress."—from "Essays, New & Selected" by Morris Wolfe, *Saturday Night,* January/February, 1977

"The ramifications of this social propaganda were reflected in the television shows of the day: *Ozzie and Harriet, Leave It to Beaver, Make Room for Daddy, The Donna Reed Show, Father Knows Best,* etc. In these shows we saw the image of the happy housewife, who didn't seem to do anything but waltz around her beautiful home in her pretty dress...."—from "Review: *The Beauty Myth* by Naomi Wolf" by Laura Bryannan, www.homestar.org/bryanna/wolf.html

"Donna [Stone of *The Donna Reed Show*] was the stay at home mother of three in the 'perfect family' where the man had the final say in everything."—from "The Television Moms We Love" by Roz Zurko, associatedcontent.com, 2010

"*Our Miss Brooks* was one of the few 1950s comedies where the woman was not portrayed as an airhead or a fool."—from *Invisible Stars* by Donna Halper, 2001

"[T]he beautiful babe as superhero, however, certainly has its predecessors, and they didn't model empowerment so much as sexuality."—from "Goodbye, Murphy Brown, hello Buffy and Ally" by Gloria Goodale, *Christian Science Monitor*, February 5, 1999

"New sitcoms and shows such as *The Beverly Hillbillies, Green Acres,* and *All in the Family* laid feminist rhetoric in the mouths of incompetent characters. Women were under represented in television and played minor roles. They were portrayed as homemakers and subordinate individuals in order to counteract the Feminist Movement."—from "Impact of Television on Gender Roles" by Rayna Wiles, maskin.bxscience.edu, May, 2001

"But in the world of *Julia* the message was assimilation and the invisibility of race. Race was rarely mentioned."—from *Media Messages* by Linda Holtzman, 2001

"Not only do some programming executives personally want to expel the independent woman from the American set; their advertisers, who still view the housewife as the ideal shopper, demand it."—from *Backlash* by Susan Faludi, 1992

"Not that long ago, the rules for battling TV evil were pretty simple: Men did all the fighting and shooting, women all the screaming and nail-chipping."—from "Actresses Are Beginning to Get a Bigger Cut of the Action" by Craig Tomashoff, *Los Angeles Times*, November 20, 2000

"[S]ingle working women in *Private Secretary* and *Oh! Susanna* ... labored in stereotypical jobs and were often obsessed with [getting a husband]...."—from *Where the Girls Are* by Susan Douglas, 1994

"[*Mary Tyler Moore*] was one of the first TV shows to feature a single working woman as its title character...."—from "I Am Woman" by Rachel Giese, CBC.ca, March 8, 2005

"On the tube, the highest attainment a woman can honorably hope for is to be a frequency modulated geisha girl."—from "Women on TV" by Nicholas Von Hoffman, *Playgirl*, December, 1974

"In the 1970s, television's representation of women changed, allowing women to lead action-adventure series and to take on conventionally male tasks in those series."—from *Wallowing in Sex: The New Sexual Culture of the 1970s American Television* by Elana Levine, 2007

"Over the years, men have dominated the action genre on both the large and small screens...." — from "Two Steps Forward, One Step Back" by David Roger Coon, *Journal of Popular Film and Television*, Spring 2005

"There seem to be only three incarnations for middle-aged women in the media: (1) The Loser-neurotic-bitch; (2) the Grotesque — ax murderess, clown, mother-in-law; (3) the wife.... The Wife is perfectly coiffed, patient, smiling, always pouring coffee and DULL DULL DULL." — from "Why Can't Hollywood See That 35 Is Beautiful, Too?" by Caryl Rivers, *New York Times*, April 1, 1973

"Early [science fiction] series such as ... *Space Patrol* did not include any female characters." — from *Women & American Television: An Encyclopedia* by Denise Lowe, 1999

"Throughout the run, the Angels got in and out of jeopardy while relying on Charlie, their unseen detective [sic] boss, to bail them out.... In the male viewer's fantasy, he could be Charlie, ever supervising, ever needed...." — from *Watching Television* by Todd Gitlin, 1986

"Television women of the 1950s and 1960s didn't work much at all, although plenty of real women did." — from "Getting Real: TV slowly coming into focus on women in the workplace" by Ruth Richman, *Chicago Tribune*, May 18, 1997

On *Sex and the City*: "There hadn't been women at the center of a quest narrative before. No one had ever thought women were that interesting." — Naomi Wolf, quoted in *Entertainment Weekly*, 2008

"As dramatic programs with continuing casts and situations replaced the anthologies in the late fifties and early sixties, women became even more peripheral.... Only in situation comedies did women provide an active center. Women (and the working class) were ghettoized in the world of canned (and live) laughter." — from *Women Watching Television* by Andrea L. Press, 1991

"In the fifties and sixties women on television were portrayed as happy little housewives content to stay at home and clean while their husbands went out and earned the living." — from "The Three Waves of Feminism History," www.syl.com, 2007

"*Julia* never alluded explicitly to [the] civil and social unrest raging in America." — from *Shaded Lives* by Beretta E. Smith-Shomade, 2002

"In the beginning there was Lucy and for a decade or more the redheaded heroine of the fabulously successful sitcom *I Love Lucy* was television's image of the American Woman: a lovable, scatterbrained housewife, always trying to put one over on her husband and always found out in the end.

"Then there was Mary Richards...." — from "Flo, Sue Ellen, Alice: Taking a Closer Look at the Women We Watch on TV" by Gary Clark, *Family Circle*, May 19, 1981

"And so, that vast television audience out there will continue to view women on prime-time television as unliberated ding-a-lings, sex kittens, kooky housewives, lovable widows, crimefighters' secretaries and nosy nurses." — from "TV's Women are Dingbats" by Judy Klemersrud, *New York Times*, May 27, 1973

"But while Beulah was the title character of the show, her whole life revolved around the white family she served and her own family and independent life was invisible." — from *Media Messages* by Linda Holtzman, 2001

"On TV or in the movies, having children is a sure sign of mental health for female characters, especially those who stay at home.... Only recently in a post–[Andrea] Yates world can I think of any depictions of stay-at-home mothers that struggle with [the] loneliness or frustration that are the natural result of being locked up with kids all day." — posted by "Amanda" on Mousewords.blogspot.com, February 1, 2005

"Popular shows such as *Mary Tyler Moore* and *Laverne & Shirley* featured single women whose emotional nurturing came primarily from close friends rather than family. These characters enjoyed freedoms that had previously been taboo for women on television."—from *Sociology of Families* by David M. Newman and Liz Grauerholz, 2002

"An American woman on TV is portrayed as a stupid, unattractive, insecure little household drudge who spends her martyred, mindless, boring days dreaming of love—and plotting nasty revenge against her husband."—from "Television and the Feminine Mystique" by Betty Friedan, *TV Guide*, February 1, 1964

"America's working woman and her daily life had no place on TV's schedule; instead, the house-wife—busy or 'idle'—had taken over. On television, the working woman was the 'lost sex.'"—from *The Magic Window: American Television, 1939–1953* by James A. Von Schilling, 2003

"With the occasional use of sexy female secret agents—Cinnamon of *Mission: Impossible* and Stefanie Powers in the forgettable spin-off *The Girl from UNCLE*—they became among the first dramatic shows to use women as leads."—from *Glued to the Set* by Steven D. Stark, 1997

"The fact was clearly illustrated by the media of the time, television shows such as *Father Knows Best* and *Leave It to Beaver* idealized domesticity, placing women in a closed sphere where they only had to fulfill the roles of housewives and mothers."—from "Second-Wave Feminism," Wikipedia.com

"As the Bionic Woman, Lindsay Wagner could run faster and hit harder than any man—except for the Six Million Dollar Man, of course."—from *Radicals and Reactionaries: The Media Assimilation of the Counterculture*, 2001

"If women [on TV] have a profession, it's usually nursing, where they minister to men. If they are superior to men, it's because they have magical powers. If they are over 30 years old, they've got to be widows, almost always with children, so that they can't run around enjoying themselves like real people. And they're guaranteed to be helpless every fifteen minutes."—from "The Subversive Mary Tyler Moore" by John Leonard, *Life*, December 8, 1970

"*That Girl* seemed to say that women could pursue their own dreams and push social and cultural boundaries, as long as they stayed childlike and ultimately incapable of sustained autonomy. This seemingly contradictory depiction became a model for future female characters in nontraditional roles."—from *Women and American Television: An Encyclopedia* by Denise Lowe, 1999

"[T]he controlling value of patriarchal authority is evident in 1950s sitcoms like *Leave It to Beaver* or *Father Knows Best*, in which the correct resolution of a problem inevitably follows the wisdom of the father."—from *Living Room Lectures: The Fifties Family in Film and Television* by Nina Leibman, 1995

"The only woman ever to headline a musical show remains Dinah Shore."—from *The American Women's Almanac* by Louise Bernkow, 1997

"In the 1960s the shows *I Dream of Jeannie* and *Bewitched* insinuated that the only way that a woman could escape her duties was to use magic. Industry analysis Shari Anne Brill of Carat USA states, 'For years when men were behind the camera, women were really ditsy. Now you have female leads playing superheroes, or super business women.'"—"Social Aspects of Television," Wikipedia.com

"From the comic antics of Ann Sothern and Eve Arden there emerged the image of the working woman that reflected a widely held view of the time. Career women were single, working in jobs where the boss was a man, and single-mindedly focused on getting a man."—from *Murphy Brown: Anatomy of a Sitcom* by Robert S. Alley, 1990

"In *Charlie's Angels*, three women detectives master evildoers on weekly episodes—clad usually in bikinis, tight-fitting sweaters, or other revealing clothing."—from *Radicals and Reactionaries: The Media Assimilation of the Counterculture*, 2001

"How did our culture come to accept a woman who could snap back an answer as well as snap her gum? Good Girl Donna Reed has been replaced by Roseanne Barr Arnold, Mrs. Brady has been eclipsed by Mrs. Bundy." — from "In Celebration of the Bad Girl" by Gina Barreca, *New York Times*, September 1, 1991

"[Many TV series] have focused on the position of women within the late 1950s domestic sitcom concentrating on her passivity, marginality and oddly formal brand of femininity." — from "Domesticated Dads and Double-Shift Moms: Real Life and Ideal Life in the 1950s Domestic Sitcom" by Tasha G. Oren, University of Wisconsin–Milwaukee, 2003

"Ms. Moore's Mary Richards [was] a career woman in her 30s. She did not have to married, most unusual for 1970s primetime...." — from "Fast Forwarding Into TV's Past" by John J. O'Connor, *New York Times*, 1991

"Women were seldom shown employed but those who did enact occupational roles were confined to a narrow range of options ... housewife, receptionist and whore." — from *Ladies of the Evening: Women Characters of Prime-Time Television* by Diana M. Meehan, 1983

"The early sitcom also held Dad's other underlings in place. Mrs. Dad, for instance, was always trim, erect, loyal, like a well-bred whippet; but even she sometimes made trouble and had to be reminded how to roll over and play dead." — from "Dads Through the Decades: Thirty Years of TV Fathers" by Mark Crispin Miller, *Media & Values*, Fall, 1989

"Typically the representation of the female body was de-feminized and/or de-eroticized. The programs usually featured heroines who were either non-threatening matronly types ... or else zany women like Lucy Ricardo who frequently appeared clown-like, and even grotesque." — from *Private Screenings: Television and the Female Consumer*, edited by Lynn Spigel and Denise Mann, 1992

"Situation comedy comediennes such as Gracie Allen and Jane Ace [of *Easy Aces*] played Dumb Dora roles, while Lucille Ball, Joan Davis, and Gale Storm distorted their femininity with grotesque disguises." — from *Make Room for TV: Television and the Family Ideal in Postwar America* by Lynn Spigel, 1992

"By the time *Lucy* left the air, TV had already domesticated and desexualized its women, either by moving them happily back into homemaker roles on programs such as *The Donna Reed Show* and *Ozzie and Harriet*, or by removing from their arsenal the weapon of sharp humor." — from *Glued to the Set* by Steven D. Stark, 1997

"Even so, Mary Richards was out to build a life for herself. She would not be a man-hungry spinster like *Our Miss Brooks*.... Nor would her occupation be secretary, bank teller or maid — the big three of sitcom women." — from *Archie Bunker's America* by Josh Ozersky, 2003

Lucille Ball (right), pictured with frequent co-star Ann Sothern, played Lucy Carmichael on "The Lucy Show" (1962–1968).

"Lucy Ricardo was a far cry from the meek housewives appearing in shows like *Father Knows Best* and *Leave It to Beaver*."—from *Women in Comedy* by Linda Martin and Kerry Segrave, 1986

"From ABC's *Roseanne* to CBS' *Murphy Brown*, the network schedules are notable for the invigorating presence of strong women.... [T]he adoring subservient wife of *Father Knows Best* is a relic of the past."—from "TV Skewers Sexual Harassers But Stereotypes Still Flourish" by John J. O'Connor, *New York Times*, 1991

"Lovable Lucy was funny or silly but she wasn't ever sharp-tongued."—from *Family Circle*, 1981

"[On *I Love Lucy* and *Make Room for Daddy*,] the wife runs the house, rears the children, winnows out any possible source of irritation to her husband, and seeks to advance his career from what she alone sees as her place in the background."—Cecelia Agar, *New York Times*, 1958

"[I]t was *The Mary Tyler Moore Show* [*sic*] that first offered a more sophisticated, wittily realistic assessment of female friendship."—from "Better Than Sisters" by Mike Duffy, *Detroit Free Press*, March 9, 1995

"[F]or most women performers who made the switch [from film to TV], it was to act in a television series, the production of which was in the hands of men who fashioned shows that seldom broke new ground. Women's acting careers remained under the control of men."—from *Women Television Producers: Transformation of the Male Medium* by Robert S. Alley and Irby Brown, 2001

"[*I Love Lucy*] has proved to be timeless, despite the divorce of Lucy and Desi Arnez [*sic*] in the late fifties [*sic*]. Moreover, it depicts a woman; and television has traditionally been hostile to woman comedians...."—from *Why We Watch Them* by William Kuhns, 1970

"[I]f there was a heroine cop in a movie or TV show, she had to be the sexy lady who went undercover as a hooker and got rescued by a male."—from "Feminist exploitation as its very best: *Police Woman* the ultimate," *Chicago Sun-Times*, 2006

"[T]he traditional ways in which female characters have generally been represented in primetime television fiction: passive and powerless on the one hand, and sexual objects for men on the other."—from *Feminist Television Criticism: A Reader* by Charlotte Brunsdon, Julie D'Acci, and Lynn P. Spigel, 1997

"Tough, canny female cops have kept the beat for many years in American TV drama, though inevitably as deputies, sergeants or dolly detectives. They were always given a pat on the back for their *Charlie's Angels* antics, but never trusted with much authority."—from "Prime prospects," www.theage.com, 2005

"Classical television moms—like June Cleaver of *Leave It to Beaver*, at home all day in her wideskirted dress, endlessly cooking, cleaning house, and seeing to the children's every need—are no longer the only option portrayed...."—from "Women in Popular Culture" by Mary Magoulick in *The Encyclopedia of Women's Folklore and Folklife*, 2006

"While previously most women on prime-time television were positioned squarely within the nuclear family as homemakers and mothers, thereafter images of working women became first acceptable, with *That Girl* and *The Mary Tyler Moore Show* [*sic*], then common, and finally unremarkable."—from "Gender and Family in Television's Golden Age and Beyond" by Andrea Press in *ANNALS*, AAPSS, 2009

Regarding a pro-woman speech delivered by June Cleaver: "[I]t is certainly true that most viewers in the 1950s likely did not pick up on the nuances suggested here."—from *Women Television Producers: Transformation of the Male Medium*

Chapter Notes

Introduction

1. Ginia Bellafante, "Feminism: It's all about me!" *Time* June 29, 1998: 54+.

2. Susan Faludi, *Backlash: The Undeclared War Against American Women* (New York: Crown, 1991), pp. 161–167.

3. *Ibid.*, p. 143.

4. Christina Hoff Sommers, *Who Stole Feminism?* (New York: Touchstone, 1994).

5. Lisa Schwarzbaum, "We're Gonna Make It After All," *Working Woman* Oct. 1995: 32–36.

6. *Ibid.*, p. 35.

7. Jane O'Reilly, "At Last! Women Worth Watching," *TV Guide* May 27 1989: 18–21.

8. In case I missed an episode in which one of the wives or moms of the four classic family sitcoms of the 1950s (*The Adventures of Ozzie and Harriet, Leave It to Beaver, The Donna Reed Show* and *Father Knows Best*) fainted, it was necessary to consult the people who know these shows the best: the fans. Hence, on the website www.sitcomsonline.com, I posted inquires regarding fainting on the message boards for each of the four series. I received a surprising number of thoughtful and informed responses. None of them could cite an instance where one of the leading ladies fell dead away.

One respondent noted, "These women were a little stronger than that. Besides, what Earth-shattering problems did these women have & where they were fainting every five minutes? Rickys playing rock and roll? Princess doesnt have a date for the prom? Boom, there goes Margaret. I really cant picture that happening.

A fan of *The Donna Reed Show* noted that, though she believed Donna never fainted, daughter Mary did in the 1959 episode "April Fool."

Granted, this survey was less than scientific, so I welcome other replies. If anyone has evidence of Donna, June, Margaret or Harriet passing out, please let me know.

9. Susan J. Douglas, *Where the Girls Are: Growing Up Female with the Mass Media* (New York: Times Books, 1994).

10. Diana M. Meehan, *Ladies of the Evening: Women Characters of Prime-Time Television* (Metuchen, NJ: Scarecrow Press, 1983).

11. Other incorrect statements in regard to women on TV are discussed in this book's appendix.

12. Throughout this book, use of the term "early TV" refers not to television's experimental stages, which date back to the beginning of the 20th century, but to the late 1940s and early 1950s. It was only at this time that television's reach began to have social impact.

13. Tinky Weisblat, "The Adventures of Ozzie and Harriet," *Encyclopedia of Television*, edited by Horace Newcomb (Chicago: Fitzroy Dearborn, 1997), pp. 17–18.

14. Evidence of these hyper-condensed timelines can be found in the online articles "The Evolution of the American Housewife as Depicted by the Media" at peop le.virginia.edu/~sgv6f/Hius_316/fiftiesandsixties.html and "Ding ang Bato! The Rise of Super Hero(ines) and Violence on Local Television" at philjol.info/index.php/FEUCJ/rt/captureCite.503/473

15. David Marc, *Demographic Vistas* (Philadelphia: University of Pennsylvania Press, 1984), p. 102.

16. Camille Paglia, *Sexual Personae: Art and Decadence from Nefertiti to Emily Dickinson* (New York: Vintage Books, 1990), p. 47.

17. Donna McCrohan, *Prime Time, Our Time* (Rocklin, CA: Prima, 1990), p. 1.

18. Betty White, *Here We Go Again: My Life in Television* (New York: Scribner, 1995), pp. 274–277.

19. Tom Stempel, *Storytellers to the Nation: A History of American Television Writing* (Syracuse: Syracuse University Press, 1996), p. 247.

20. Watson, p. 184.

21. And, yes, there were many; see this book's first chapter.

Chapter 1

1. Bernard Timberg, *Television Talk: A History of the TV Talk Show* (Austin: University of Texas Press, 2002).

2. *Current Biography, 1955* (Dorothy Gordon), p. 239.

3. John P. Holms and Ernest Wood, *The TV Game Show Almanac* (Radnor, PA: Chilton Book, 1995); and Jefferson Graham, *Come on Down!!!: The TV Game Show Book* (New York: Abbeville Press, 1988).

4. *Current Biography, 1951* (Faye Emerson), p. 185.

5. Joan Flynn, "How Faye Emerson Got Into Television," *Los Angeles Examiner* April 1, 1951: 25.

6. Deb Myers, "Faye Emerson," *Cosmopolitan* Aug. 1950: 110.

7. Michael Soloman, "The 50 Greatest Game Shows of All Time," *TV Guide* Jan. 27, 2001: 25.

8. Graham, p. 24.

9. Ronald Smith, *Sweethearts of '60's TV* (New York: SPI Books, 1993), p. 127.

10. *American Masters: The Quiz Show Scandals* (PBS, 2002).

11. *Ibid.*

12. Ruth Duskin Feldman, *Whatever Happened to the Quiz Kids?* (Chicago: Chicago Review Press, 1992).

13. Examples of early anthology shows and the actresses who hosted them or appeared in them were culled from the following sources: Mark Lasswell, *TV Guide: Fifty Years of Television* (New York: Crown, 2002); Marc Robinson, *Brought to You in Living Color: 75 Years of Great Moments in Television & Radio from NBC* (New York:

Wiley, 2002); and Irving Settel, *A Pictorial History of Television* (New York: F. Ungar, 1983).

14. Philip A. Kalisch and Beatrice J. Kalisch, *Images of Nurses on Television* (New York: Springer, 1983), p. 6.

15. Lasswell, *TV Guide: Fifty Years of Television*; Robinson, *Brought to You in Living Color*; and Settel, *A Pictorial History of Television*.

16. Alvin H. Marill, *Movies Made for Television* (New York: Zoetrope, 1987).

17. Lasswell, *TV Guide: Fifty Years of Television*; Robinson, *Brought to You in Living Color*; and Settel, *A Pictorial History of Television*.

18. Tim Brooks, *The Complete Directory to Prime Time TV Stars* (New York: Ballantine, 1987), p. 685.

19. Michael McWilliams, *TV Sirens* (New York: Perigee), p. 186.

20. Lisa Schwarzbaum, "The Sketch Artist," *Entertainment Weekly* June 15 2001: 12.

21. *A Really Big Show: A Visual History of "The Ed Sullivan Show"* (New York: Viking, 1992).

22. Some of the great women of song are pictured on the air in Irving Settel's *A Pictorial History of Television* (New York: F. Ungar, 1983). Others can be found in Marc Robinson's *Brought to You in Living Color: 75 Years of Great Moments in Television & Radio from NBC* (New York: Wiley, 2002).

23. Joel Whitburn's *The Billboard Book of Top 40 Hits* (New York: Billboard, 1996) was invaluable in determining top female vocalists of the past fifty years and their songs. More to the purpose of this book, it was confirmed that all of the performers mentioned appeared regularly on television. Connie Francis performed her hit "Who's Sorry Now?" on such TV series as *American Bandstand* (for the first time in 1958) and on *The Patti Page Show*. Peggy Lee debuted "I'm a Woman" on *The Ed Sullivan Show* in December of 1962. As mentioned, the Supremes were regulars on *Ed Sullivan*. "Little" Peggy March was a favorite of Perry Como and often appeared on his series, at least once performing her hit "I Will Follow Him." Janis Joplin was featured on *The Dick Cavett Show* and on *Ed Sullivan* while the Shangri-Las once performed "Leader of the Pack" on *I've Got a Secret* in 1964. Marianne Faithfull performed "Broken English" on *Saturday Night Live* and Gloria Gaynor performed "I Will Survive" on *American Bandstand*, among other programs.

24. Linda Martin and Kerry Segrave, *Women in Comedy* (Secaucus, NJ: Citadel, 1986), p. 339.

25. *Ibid.*, p. 291.

26. "Hallmark Hall of Fame: The First 40 Years" (UCLA Film and Television Archive, 1991).

27. Vincent Terrace, *Television Specials: 3,201 Entertainment Spectaculars, 1939–1993* (Jefferson, NC: McFarland, 1995).

28. The best resources pertaining to women in broadcast journalism, and which were consulted for this work, are Edward Bliss, *Now the News: The Story of Broadcast Journalism* (New York: Columbia University Press, 1991); Judith Gelfman, *Women in Television News* (New York: Columbia University Press, 1976); and Marlene Sanders and Marcia Rock, *Waiting for Primetime* (Chicago: University of Chicago Press, 1988).

29. Michael Ritchie, *Please Stand By: A Prehistory of Television* (Woodstock, NY: Overlook Press, 1994), p. 98.

30. Cary O'Dell, *Women Pioneers in Television: Biographies of Fifteen Industry Leaders* (Jefferson, NC: McFarland, 1997), pp. 93–104.

31. "Primetime Pioneer," *People* Nov. 3 1997: 102.

32. Female sports stars, as seen on TV, are well documented in two books by Joe Garner: *And the Crowd Goes Wild* (Naperville, IL: Sourcebooks, 1999) and *And the Fans Roared* (Naperville, IL: Sourcebooks, 2000).

33. Lisa Miller, "Tribute: Joanie Weston," *TV Guide* June 7, 1997: 8.

34. Jane and Michael Stern, *The Encyclopedia of Bad Taste* (New York: HarperCollins, 1990), pp. 258–260.

35. Harry F. Waters and Janet Huck, "Networking Women" *Newsweek* March 13, 1989: 48–54.

36. Information on the life and career of Gertrude Berg was obtained from Gertrude Berg, *Molly & Me* (New York: McGraw-Hill, 1961) and Cary O'Dell, *Women Pioneers in Television: Biographies of Fifteen Industry Leaders* (Jefferson, NC: McFarland, 1997), pp. 41–52.

37. Betty White, *Here We Go Again: My Life in Television* (New York: Scribner, 1995), p. 276.

38. Sources consulted on the life and achievements of Lucille Ball included Kathleen Brady, *Lucille: The Life of Lucille Ball* (New York: Hyperion, 1994); Warren G. Harris, *Lucy & Desi* (New York: Simon & Schuster, 1991); Charles Higham, *Lucy: The Life of Lucille Ball* (New York: St. Martin's, 1986); and Joe Morella and Edward Z. Epstein, *Forever Lucy: The Life of Lucille Ball* (New York: Berkeley, 1990).

39. Edie Adams and Robert Windeler, *Sing a Pretty Song....* (New York: William Morrow, 1990), p. 332.

40. Joe Morella and Edward Z. Epstein, *Jane Wyman: A Biography* (New York: Delacorte Press, 1985), p. 263.

41. Al DiOrio, *Barbara Stanwyck: A Biography* (New York: Berkley Books, 1983), p. 176.

42. Judy Lewis, *Uncommon Knowledge* (New York: Pocket, 1994), p. 246.

43. Robin Morgan, *Saturdays Child: A Memoir* (New York: W.W. Norton, 2000), p. 85.

44. The long and diverse list of female talent working behind the scenes and in front of the camera that dominate these next few pages was compiled from a vast array of sources, not the least of which has been the final credits of various TV sitcoms and dramas. However, I would also like to acknowledge: Robert LaGuardia, *Soap World* (New York: Arbor House, 1983); Alex McNeil, *Total Television* (New York: Penguin, 1991), pp. 863–903; *Missing in Action: The Women Behind Television's Golden Age*. 2003. www.womenbehindtv.com; Cary O'Dell, "A Station of Their Own: The Story of the Women's Auxiliary Television Technical Staff (WATTS) in World War II Chicago," *Television Quarterly* Vol. XXX, No. 3 (Winter 2000): 58–67 and *Women Pioneers in Television: Biographies of Fifteen Industry Leaders* (Jefferson, NC: McFarland, 1997); Marion Purcelli, "The Gals Take Over," *Chicago Sun-Times* April 7–13, 1962: 24–25; www.Ralphedwards.net; Michael Ritchie, *Please Stand By: A Pre-History of Television* (Woodstock, NY: Overlook Press, 1994); Tom Stemple, *Storytellers to the Nation: A History of American Television Writing* (Syracuse: Syracuse University Press), 1996.

45. Ritchie, p. 11.

Chapter 2

1. Alex McNeil, *Total Television* (New York: Penguin, 1991), p. 478.

2. Stephanie Coontz, *The Way We Never Were* (New York: Basic Books, 2000), pp. 159–160.

3. These statistics were supplied by the U.S. Department of Labor. www.dol.com

4. Donna McCrohan, *Prime Time, Our Time* (Rocklin, CA: Prima, 1990), p. 60.

5. Betty Friedan, "Television and the Feminine Mys-

tique," *TV Guide: The First 25 Years* (New York: Simon & Schuster, 1978), p. 93.

6. Myriam Miedzien, *Boys Will Be Boys: Breaking the Link Between Masculinity and Violence* (New York: Doubleday, 1991), p. 4.

7. Coontz, p. 29.

8. David Marc, *Demographic Vistas* (Philadelphia: University of Pennsylvania Press, 1984), p. 1.

9. Irwyn Applebaum, *The World According to Beaver* (New York: Bantam, 1984), p. 318.

10. "More Liberated Than You Remember?" *TV Guide* Dec. 4 1993: 42.

11. McCrohan, p. 149.

12. Cary O'Dell, *Women Pioneers in Television* (Jefferson, NC: McFarland, 1997).

13. Hal Humphrey, "So What's New with Molly?" *Los Angeles Mirror* Sept. 9, 1961: 9.

14. Linda Martin and Kerry Segrave, *Women in Comedy* (Secaucus, NJ: Citadel, 1986), p. 162.

15. *Current Biography, 1960* (Gertrude Berg), p. 28.

16. David Marc, "Gertrude Berg," *Encyclopedia of Television*, edited by Horace Newcomb (Chicago: Fitzroy-Dearborn, 1997), p. 192.

17. Billy Ingram, *TV Party* (Chicago: Bonus Books, 2002), pp. 41–43.

18. Robert S. Alley, *Women Television Producers* (Rochester: University of Rochester Press, 2001), p. 12.

19. "Frannie's Turn," *TV Guide* Sept. 12, 1992: 9.

20. In 1960, Berg, age 62, returned to television in another creation, *Mrs. G. Goes to College*, where she played a woman beating the "empty nest" syndrome by enrolling at UCLA. It ran for a year.

21. John Javna, *The Best of TV Sitcoms* (New York: Harmony Books, 1988), p. 71.

22. Mary Desjardins, "Mama," *Encyclopedia of Television*, edited by Horace Newcomb (Chicago: Fitzroy-Dearbon, 1997), p. 986.

23. Gerard Jones, *Honey, I'm Home!: Sitcoms, Selling the American Dream* (New York: Grove Weidenfeld, 1992), p. 43.

24. Susan Sackett, *Prime-Time Hits: Television's Most Popular Network Programs* (New York: Billboard, 1993), p. 23.

25. Desjardins, p. 986.

26. Robin Morgan, *Saturday's Child: A Memoir* (New York: W.W. Norton, 2000), p. 100.

27. Joanne Meyerowitz, *Not June Cleaver* (Philadelphia: Temple University Press, 1994); and Deborah Werksman, *I Killed June Cleaver: Modern Moms Shatter the Myth of Perfect Parenting* (Bridgeport, CT: Hysteria Publications, 1999).

28. Martin and Segrave, p. 296.

29. Mark Crispin Miller, "Dads Through the Decades: Thirty Years of TV Fathers," *Media & Values* #48 (Fall 1989). www.medialit.org

30. Tom Hill, *TV Land to Go* (New York: Fireside, 2001), p. 152.

31. Michael McWilliams, *TV Sirens* (New York: Perigee, 1987), p. 135.

32. Tinky Weisblat, "The Adventures of Ozzie and Harriet," *Encyclopedia of Television*, edited by Horace Newcomb (Chicago: Fitzroy-Dearbon, 1997), p. 17.

33. Will Miller, *Why We Watch* (New York: Fireside, 1996), p. 118.

34. Michael B. Kassel, "Father Knows Best," *Encyclopedia of Television*, edited by Horace Newcomb (Chicago: Fitzroy-Dearbon, 1997), p. 596.

35. Ephraim Katz, *The Film Encyclopedia* (New York: Perigee, 1979), p. 1250.

36. McWilliams, p. 138.

37. *Ibid.*, p. 137.

38. As part of its exhibition "From 'My Little Margie' to 'Murphy Brown': Images of Women on Television," the Museum of Broadcast Communications (MBC) in Chicago presented the panel discussion "Leading Ladies: A Luncheon Salute to Television's Pioneering Women" on September 11, 1993. The panel consisted of actresses Gale Storm, Betty White and Jane Wyatt. Ms. Wyatt's comments were taken from this discussion.

39. Tim Brooks and Earle Marsh, *The Complete Directory to Prime Time Network TV Shows* (New York: Ballantine, 1988), p. 257.

40. Rick Mitz, *The Great TV Sitcom Book* (New York: Perigee, 1983), p. 108.

41. Tim Kiska, "Bundys Diagnosed as the Most Dysfunctional TV Family Ever," *Chicago Sun-Times* July 27, 1983, p. 29.

42. "More Liberated Than You Remember?" p. 42.

43. Billingsley wasn't treated second-class in the credits either; she got top billing. Hugh Beaumont came second; Tony Dow, third; and "Jerry Mathers as the Beaver" came in last.

44. Jones, p. 127.

45. McWilliams, p. 130.

46. Applebaum, p. 42.

47. *Ibid.*, p. 43.

48. Alley, p. 22.

49. Jay Futz, *In Search of Donna Reed* (Iowa City: University of Iowa, 1998), p. 2.

50. Lisa McLaughlin, "Paint by Numbers: Back to Donna Reed," *Time* March 10, 2003: 65.

51. Futz, p. 1.

52. *Ibid.*, p. 77.

53. "Tribute: The Television Generation Mourns Its Favorite Surrogate Mother, Tough But Tender Donna Reed," *People* August 3, 1992: 85.

54. Mitz, p. 150.

55. Futz, p.122.

56. *Ibid.*, p. 131.

57. *Ibid.*, p. 132.

58. *Ibid.*, p. 152.

59. *Ibid.*, p. 132.

60. *Ibid.*, p. 152.

61. *Ibid.*, p. 153.

62. *Ibid.*, p. 126.

63. *Ibid.*, p. 127.

64. *Ibid.*, p. 131.

65. *Ibid.*, p. 147.

66. Lynn Spiegel, *Make Room for TV* (Chicago: University of Chicago Press, 1992), p. 60.

67. *Ibid.*

68. Dick Dabney, "How Men Sold Out Their Manhood," *Washington Post* Dec. 6, 1981: C1+.

69. Joe Queenan, "Boobs on the Tube: How sitcom dads make all men look bad," *Men's Health* Sept. 2003: 130–131.

70. Michael Abernathy, "Male Bashing on TV," *PopMatters* Jan 9, 2003. www.PopMatters.com

71. Jennifer Reed, "Beleaguered Husbands and Demanding Wives: The New Domestic Sitcom," *Americanpopularculture* Oct. 2003. www.Americanpopularculture.com

72. Les Brown, *Les Brown's Encyclopedia of Television* (Detroit: Gale Research, 1992), p. 246.

73. Warren Bareiss, "The Life of Riley," *Encyclopedia of Television*, edited by Horace Newcomb (Chicago: Fitzroy-Dearbon, 1997), p. 958.

74. Brooks, p. 281.

75. Mitz, p. 39.

76. Donald F. Glut and Jim Harmon, *The Great Television Heroes* (Garden City, NY: Doubleday, 1975), p. 128.

77. Jones, p. 105.

78. Glut and Harmon, p. 135.

79. William A. Henry, *The Great One: The Life and Legend of Jackie Gleason* (New York: Doubleday, 1992), p. 231.

80. Kathleen Waits, "Battered Women and Their Children: Lessons from One Woman's Story," *Houston Law Review* 35, Rev. 29 (1998). www.omsys.com

81. Ron Powers, *The Beast, the Eunuch, and the Glass-Eyed Child: Television in the '80s and Beyond* (New York: Anchor/Doubleday, 1990), p. 250.

82. Audrey Meadows, *Love, Alice: My Life as a Honeymooner* (New York: Crown, 1994), p. 43.

83. McCrohan, p. 74.

84. J.D. Reed, "Diamond in the Rough," *People* Feb. 19, 1996: 42.

85. McWilliams, p. 166.

86. Reed, p. 42.

87. *Ibid.*, p. 180.

88. Ginny Weissman and Coyne Steven Sanders, *The Dick Van Dyke Show* (New York: St. Martin's, 1983), p. 45.

89. Jones, p. 146.

90. McWilliams, p. 200.

91. Ingram, pp. 38–40.

92. Marc, *Demographic Vistas*, p. 61.

93. Vincent Terrace, *Sitcom Factbook, 1948–1984* (Jefferson, NC: McFarland, 2002), p. 94.

94. McWilliams, p. 83.

95. Ronald L. Smith, *Sweethearts of '60's TV* (New York: SPI Books, 1993), p. 81.

96. Ellen B. Klugman, "Tribute: Hope Lange, 1933–2003," *TV Guide* Jan. 24, 2004: 14.

97. Joey Green, *The Partridge Family Album* (New York: HarperPerennial, 1994), p. 29.

98. *Ibid.*, p. 16.

99. *Ibid.*, p. 35.

100. *Ibid.*, p. xiii.

101. *Ibid.*, p. 47.

102. *Ibid.*, p. 20.

103. *Ibid.*, p. 22.

104. *Ibid.*, p. 21.

105. Ace Collins, *Lassie: A Dog's Life* (New York: Cader Books, 1993), p. 134.

106. Terry and Becky Dufoe, "June Lockhart: TV's Favorite Earth Heart Space Mother," *Filmfax* No. 80: 48.

107. Collins, p. 134.

108. In subsequent seasons, Day's series underwent a transformation, morphing into a *Mary Tyler Moore* clone. For discussion of that, see the chapter "Sisters Are Doin' It for Themselves."

109. Cynthia Gorney, "Good Night, Olivia: Michael Learned Comes Down From the Mountain," *Washington Post* Jan. 18, 1979: B1+.

110. *Ibid.*

111. Joanne Kaufman, "Learned Lessons," *TV Guide* Sept. 21–27, 2002: 52+.

112. Mary Ann Watson, *The Expanding Vista* (Durham, NC: Duke University Press), p. 53.

113. Hal Himmelstein, *Television Myth and the American Mind* (New York: Praeger, 1984), p. 146.

114. Marc, *Demographic Vistas*, p. 58.

115. *Ibid.*

116. Erik Barnow, *Tube of Plenty* (New York: Oxford University Press, 1990), p. 407.

117. Stephen Cox, *The Addams Chronicles* (New York: HarperPerennial, 1991), p. 38.

118. Brooks, p. 445.

119. Cox, p. 49.

120. Jones, p. 176.

121. Susan J. Douglas, *Where the Girls Are: Growing Up Female with the Mass Media* (New York: Random House, 1994), p. 137

122. Bart Andrews and Brad Dunning, *The Worst TV Shows Ever* (New York: E.P. Dutton, 1980), p. 110.

123. Nicholas Fonseca, "Guilty Pleasures: 'Mama,'" *Entertainment Weekly* July 23, 2004: 38.

124. McCrohan, p. 213.

125. Horace Newcomb, *TV: The Most Popular Art* (Garden City, NY: Anchor, 1974), p. 222.

126. Jones, p. 207.

127. Newcomb, p. 225.

128. McWilliams, p. 59.

129. Newcomb, p. 225.

130. New York state, where Maude was set, had already legalized abortion; *Roe v. Wade* would occur the following year, 1973.

131. Phillip Wander, "Was Anyone Afraid of Maude Finlay?" *Understanding Television*, edited by Richard Adler (New York: Praeger, 1981), p. 225.

132. Sackett, p. 240.

133. *Ibid.*

134. Though Ann reverted to her maiden name after her divorce, daughters Julie and Barbara kept their father's, Cooper.

135. Ella Taylor, *Prime-Time Families: Television Culture in Postwar America* (Berkeley: University of California Press, 1989), p. 87.

136. Susan J. Douglas, *Where the Girls Are: Growing Up Female with the Mass Media* (New York: Random House, 1994).

137. Susan Faludi, *Backlash: The Undeclared War Against American Women* (New York: Crown, 1991).

138. Bruce Guthrie, "Rolle Model," *People* Dec. 7, 1998: 144.

139. Mitz, p. 319.

140. Actually, even before her expanded role, Willona was notable. Originally, her character was supposed to be a mother of three who spent most of her time in the kitchen. But DuBois thought otherwise, saying, "No way! The days of the black mammies are over." Thus Willona emerged as a happily single and proudly sexual woman ("I like my coffee like I like my men: hot, black and strong"), a precursor to the independent black women of *Living Single* and *Girlfriends*.

141. Guthrie, p. 144.

142. Jones, p. 220.

143. Jannette Dates, *Split Image: African Americans in the Mass Media* (Washington, DC: Howard University Press, 1993), p. 272.

144. "Legacy: Isabel Sanford," *People* Dec. 27, 2004: 192.

145. Craig Tomashoff, "Tribute: Isabel Sanford, 1917–2004," *TV Guide* Aug. 1, 2004: 19.

146. As part of its exhibition "From 'My Little Margie' to 'Murphy Brown': Images of Women on Television," the Museum of Broadcast Communications (MBC) in Chicago, Illinois, presented the panel discussion "I Nurture, Therefore I Am: Images of Wives and Mothers on Television" on September 26, 1993. Taking part in that discussion were the actresses Barbara Billingsley, Susan Clark, Pat Crowley, and Shirley Jones as well as Dr. Mary Larson of Northern Illinois University. Ms. Clark's comments are taken from this discussion.

147. Tinky Weisblat, "Gracie Allen," *Encyclopedia of Television*, edited by Horace Newcomb (Chicago: Fitzroy-Dearbon, 1997), pp. 40–41.

148. Randolph would later enjoy more fame by being on *Make Room for Daddy*. Earlier, she had starred in what was perhaps TV's first series built around an African American lead, *The Laytons*. It aired from August to October of 1948 over Dumont.

149. Bart Andrews and Ahrgus Juiliard, *Holy Mackerel! The "Amos 'n' Andy" Story* (New York: E.P. Dutton, 1986), pp. 150–151.

150. *Ibid.*

151. Jonathon Green, *The Cassell Dictionary of Slang* (London: Cassell, 1998), p. 1029.

152. Melvin Patrick Ely, *The Adventures of "Amos 'n' Andy": A Social History of an American Phenomenon* (New York: Maxwell Macmillan, 1991), p. 197.

153. Pamela S. Deane, "Amos 'n' Andy," *Encyclopedia of Television*, edited by Horace Newcomb (Chicago: Fitzroy-Dearbon, 1997), p. 65.

154. Mary Ann Watson, *Defining Visions* (Fort Worth: Harcourt Brace, 1998), p. 29.

155. Andrews and Juiliard, p. 152.

156. Deane, p. 66.

157. Mitz, p. 103.

158. Sackett, p. 55.

159. Trudy Ring, "The Bob Newhart Show," *Encyclopedia of Television*, edited by Horace Newcomb (Chicago: Fitzroy-Dearborn, 1997), p. 193.

160. Joey Green, *Hi Bob! A Self-Help Guide to "The Bob Newhart Show"* (New York: St. Martin's Press, 1996), p. 43.

161. *Ibid.*, p. 49.

162. *Ibid.*, p. 6.

163. J. Fred MacDonald, *Blacks and White TV* (Chicago: Nelson-Hall, 1992), p. 188.

164. Gilbert M. Blasini, "Family," *Encyclopedia of Television*, edited by Horace Newcomb (Chicago: Fitzroy-Dearborn, 1997), pp. 586587.

165. *Ibid.*, p. 587.

166. Watson, *Defining Visions*, p. 73.

167. Tom Shales, "Comedy with Class," *Washington Post* March 19, 1984: C1+.

Chapter 3

1. *Current Biography, 1978* (Lucille Ball), p. 32.

2. Susan Stamberg, "Manipulation 101," *Electronic Media* October 1, 2001: 18.

3. Bart Andrews, *Lucy & Ricky & Fred & Ethel: The Story of "I Love Lucy"* (New York: Fawcett, 1976).

4. Horace Newcomb, *TV: The Most Popular Art* (Garden City, NY: Anchor/Doubleday, 1974), pp. 36–37.

5. Karen Hornick, "Overrated/Underrated: Sitcom," *American Heritage* Oct. 2003: 51.

6. Donna McCrohan, *Prime Time, Our Time* (Rocklin, CA: Prima, 1990), p. 50.

7. *American Masters: Finding Lucy* (PBS, 2005).

8. John Waters, "A career colored by Lucy," *Electronic Media* October 1 2001: 19.

9. "Meet Margaret Matlin." www.lucyfan.com/margaretmatlin.html

10. David Marc, *Comic Visions: Television Culture and American Culture* (Malden, MA: Blackwell, 1989), p. 46.

11. Lynn Spangler, *Television Women from Lucy to Friends: Fifty Years of Sitcoms and Feminism* (Westport, CT: Praeger, 2004).

12. Geoffrey Mark Fidelman, *The Lucy Book* (Los Angeles: Renaissance Books, 1999).

13. Michael McWilliams, *TV Sirens* (New York: Perigee, 1987), p. 56.

14. Fidelman, p. 147.

15. Bart Andrews and Thomas J. Watson, *Loving Lucy* (New York: St. Martin's, 1980), p. 138.

16. Warren G. Harris, *Lucy & Desi* (New York: Simon & Schuster, 1991), p. 269.

17. Andrews and Watson, p. 179.

18. *Ibid.*, p. 201.

19. I am indebted to Ric Wyman of the Lucy-Desi Museum in Jamestown, NY, for obtaining the exact wording of Lucy's end-of-episode speech.

20. Fidelman, p. 157.

21. Jim Brochu, *Lucy in the Afternoon* (New York: Pocket Books, 1990), p. 185.

22. Andrews and Watson, p. 184.

23. Lee R. Schreiber, "TV's Fifty Greatest Characters Ever!" *TV Guide* October 16 1999: 52.

24. Gale Storm with Bill Libby, *I Ain't Down Yet* (Indianapolis: Bobbs-Merrill, 1981).

25. Rick Mitz, *The Great TV Sitcom Book* (New York: Perigee, 1983), p. 52.

26. Mary Ann Watson, "Women's Lives on the Small Screen," *TV Quarterly* Vol. XXVII, No. 2 (1994): 4.

27. "More Liberated Than You Remember?" *TV Guide* Dec. 4–10, 1993: 45+.

28. Ephraim Katz, *The Film Encyclopedia* (New York: Perigee, 1979), p. 311.

29. *Ibid.*, p. 70.

30. Betty White, *Here We Go Again: My Life in Television* (New York: Scribner, 2001).

31. Debbie Reynolds, *Debbie: My Life* (New York: Simon & Schuster, 1988).

32 *Ibid.*, p. 322.

33. Dawn Michelle Nill, "Laverne and Shirley," *Encyclopedia of Television*, edited by Horace Newcomb (Chicago: Fitzroy-Dearborn, 1997), pp. 932–933.

34. *Ibid.*, p. 932.

35. *Ibid.*

36. Steven D. Stark, *Glued to the Set* (New York: Free Press, 1997), p. 26.

37. *Ibid.*, p. 264.

38. Nill, pp. 932–933.

39. Mitz, p. 437.

Chapter 4

1. Mary Ann Watson, "Women's Lives on the Small Screen," *TV Quarterly* Vol. XXVII, No. 2 (1994): 7.

2. David Marc, *Comic Visions: Television Culture and American Culture* (Malden, MA: Blackwell, 1989), p. x.

3. Gerald Jones, *Honey, I'm Home!: Sitcoms, Selling the American Dream* (New York: Grove Weidenfeld, 1992), p. 177.

4. Ronald Smith, *Sweethearts of '60's TV* (New York: SPI Books, 1993), p. 90.

5. Steve Cox with Howard Frank, *Dreaming of Jeannie: TV's Prime Time in a Bottle* (New York: St. Martin's Griffin, 2000), p. 270.

6. Marc, p. 116.

7. Cox, p. 269.

8. Michael McCall, *The Best of 60s TV* (New York: Mallard Press, 1992), p. 75.

9. Marc, p. x.

10. William Kuhns, *Why We Watch Them: Interpreting TV Shows* (New York: Benziger, 1970), p. 69.

11. Marc, p. 111.

12. Herbie Pilato, *"Bewitched" Forever* (Irving, TX: Summit, 1996), pp. 34–35.

13. Smith, p. 89.

14. Pilato, p. 30.

15. Smith, p. 90.

16. Michael McWilliams, *TV Sirens* (New York: Perigee, 1987), p. 30.

17. Vincent Terrace, *Sitcom Factfinder, 1948–1984* (Jefferson, NC: McFarland, 2002), p. 14.

18. Smith, p. 94.

19. www.TVDVDreviews.com

20. Smith, p. 176.

21. Cox, p. 3.

22. *Ibid.*, p. 4.

23. Smith, p. 179.

24. Marc, p. 116.

25. Cox, p. 27.

26. Once Jeannie and Tony are husband and wife, it is Tony who calls into question his wife's continued use of "master." In their discussion, Jeannie says she sees "master" as a term of endearment and, while she won't use it publicly, she will continue to use it privately.

27. Not only does Jeannie regularly turn the military on its ear, she has a similar effect on other disciplines as well. Though Tony often found himself befuddled by Jeannie's magic, no one was more confused more often than Tony's colleague, psychologist Dr. Bellows. Bellows is especially dumbfounded by the goings-on around him since, as a psychiatrist with his training steeped in Freudian penis envy, he can't quite conceive of Jeannie's power or feminine mystique.

28. *Ibid.*, p. 58.

29. Smith, p. 160.

30. David Krell, "Julie Newmar! From Sexy Robotrix to Catwoman & Beyond," *Outre* (No. 15): 77.

Chapter 5

1. Sally Steenland, "Where women stand in television entertainment today," *AFTRA Magazine* Vol. 18, No. 1 (Winter 1985): 13.

2. Laura Morice, "Anything But Work," *Working Woman* (May 1991): 74+.

3. Lisa Schwarzbaum, "We're Gonna Make It After All," *Working Woman* Oct. 1995: 31+.

4. These statistics were supplied by the U.S. Department of Labor. www.dol.gov

5. This figure was proved by the National Center for Education Information. www.NCEI.com

6. United States Department of Labor. www.dol.gov

7. The alleged *Ella Miss* is a mystery. I can find no record of this show. Ms. Faludi cites her source as Diana M. Meehan's 1986 *Ladies of the Evening* but a review of that book's index makes no mention of any such series.

8. Susan Faludi, *Backlash: The Undeclared War Against American Women* (New York: Crown, 1991), p. 156.

9. Eve Arden, *Three Phases of Eve* (New York: St. Martin's Press, 1985), p. 79.

10. Rick Mitz, *The Great TV Sitcom Book* (New York: Perigee, 1983), p. 78.

11. Erica McWilliam, "Seductress or Schoolmarm: On the Improbability of the Great Female Teacher," AARE (Australian Association for Research in Education) Conference, Newcastle (Nov. 1994).

12. Innumerable books and articles over the years have perpetuated the husband-hunter myth, most echoing sentiments like this one from *Working Woman* magazine in October 1995: "Single working women especially found a kindred spirit in Mary [Richards] because, single herself and over 30, she was the first female sitcom lead not using the workplace as a hunting ground or a stopgap to marriage."

13. Michael McWilliams, *TV Sirens* (New York: Perigee, 1987), p. 46.

14. Sam Frank, *Buyer's Guide to Fifty Years of TV on Video* (Amherst, NY: Prometheus Books, 1999), p. 940.

15. Gerard Jones, *Honey, I'm Home!: Sitcoms, Selling the American Dream* (New York: Grove Weidenfeld, 1992), p. 85.

16. Irwyn Applebaum, *The World According to Beaver* (New York: Bantam, 1984), p. 230.

17. Donna McCrohan, *Prime Time, Our Time* (Rocklin, CA: Prima, 1990), p. 167.

18. Tim Brooks and Earle Marsh, *The Complete Directory to Prime Time Network TV Shows* (New York: Ballantine, 1988), p. 41.

19. Richard West, *Television Westerns: Major and Minor Series, 1946–1978* (Jefferson, NC: McFarland, 1987), p. 87.

20. Harris M. Lentz, *Television Western Episode Guide* (Jefferson, NC: McFarland, 1997), p. 370.

21. John O'Connor, "TV Review: 'Sara' Starring Brenda Vaccaro, on CBS," *New York Times* Feb. 12, 1976: 59.

22. Jannette L. Dates and William Barlow, eds., *Split Image: African Americans in the Mass Media* (Washington, DC: Howard University Press, 1990), p. 279.

23. John Stark, "Screen: Feisty, Funny Ann Sothern Rides in From Her Snowy Mountain Home to Score a 'Whale' of a Film Comeback," *People* Feb. 29, 1988: 97+.

24. Michael Logan, "Tribute: Ann Sothern," *TV Guide* April 28, 2001: 5.

25. Frank, p. 995.

26. TVtome.com

27. Mitz, p. 83.

28. Frank, p. 995.

29. McWilliams, p. 46.

30. Mitz, p. 81.

31. *Ibid.*, p. 114.

32. Alex McNeil, *Total Television* (New York: Penguin, 1991), p. 595.

33. Horace Newcomb, *TV: The Most Popular Art* (Garden City, NY: Anchor Press, 1974), p. 96.

34. Max Allan Collins and John Javna, *The Critics' Choice: The Best of Crime & Detective TV* (New York: Harmony Books, 1988), p. 31.

35. McCrohan, *Prime Time*, p. 134.

36. David Marc, *Demographic Vistas* (Philadelphia: University of Pennsylvania Press, 1984), p. 53.

37. Marc, *Demographic Vistas*, p. 53.

38. McCrohan, *Prime Time*, p. 134.

39. McWilliams, p. 83.

40. Dates and Barlow, p. 255.

41. Ron Wynn, "Blacks in Cinema excelled despite race resistance," *City Paper* (Nashville) Dec. 22, 2004. www.nashvillecitypaper.com

42. McNeil, p. 225.

43. Joey Green, *Hi Bob! A Self-Help Guide to "The Bob Newhart Show"* (New York: St. Martin's Press, 1996), p. 69.

44. Hal Himmelstein, *Television Myth and the American Mind* (Westport, CT: Praeger, 1994), p. 155.

45. Tom Hill, *TV Land to Go* (New York: Fireside, 2001), p. 220.

46. McWilliams, p. 161.

47. On October 23, 1993, Erin Gray participated in the panel discussion "Feminine Wiles: Images of Super Heroines" at the Museum of Broadcast Communications (MBC) in Chicago as part of its exhibition "From 'My Little Margie' to 'Murphy Brown': Images of Women on Television." Ms. Gray's comments are taken from this session.

48. Vincent Terrace, *Sitcom Factfinder, 1948–1984* (Jefferson, NC: McFarland, 2002), p. 42.

49. On December 16, 1993, Esther Rolle participated in the panel discussion "Range & Shade: Images of African American Women on TV" at the Museum of Broadcast Communications (MBC) in Chicago as part of its exhibition "From 'My Little Margie' to 'Murphy Brown': Images of Women on Television." Ms. Rolle's comments are taken from this session.

50. McDaniel was hired to play the TV role and did film some episodes, but when she became ill, the role was recast. The McDaniel episodes were never aired though some are now on home video.

51. Donald Bogle, *Primetime Blues* (New York: Farrar, Straus, Giroux, 2001), pp. 32–35.

52. www.tvparty.com/50beulah.2.html.

53. Dates and Barlow, p. 262.

54. Graham Russell Hodges, ed., *Studies in African American History and Culture* (New York: Garland, 1998), p. 64.

55. Dates and Barlow, p. 293.

56. McNeil, p. 192.

57. www.timvp.com/hazel.html

58. Lahn S. Kim, "Hazel," *Encyclopedia of Television*, edited by Horace Newcomb (Chicago: Fitzroy-Dearborn, 1997), p. 745.

59. Susan Sackett, *Prime-Time Hits* (New York: Billboard, 1993), p. 111.

60. In 1954, Coca appeared in NBC's *The Imogene Coca Show*. The show went through various formats during its lifespan, from variety to standard sitcom. It never quite found an identity or audience. It lasted nine months.

61. McWilliams, p. 53.

62. www.tvacres.com/char_nelson_alice.htm

63. Edward Durham Taylor, *The Great TV Book: 21 Years of LWT* (London: Sidgwick & Jackson, 1989), p. 22.

64. McWilliams, p. 62.

65. "More Liberated Than You Remember?" *TV Guide* Dec. 4, 1993: 43.

66. What does it say when our first impulse for describing almost every black female TV character is to call them "sassy"?

67. McWilliams, p. 61.

68. Joe Garner, *Made You Laugh: The Funniest Moments in Comedy* (Kansas City: Andrews McMeel, 2004), p. 45.

69. Dates and Barlow, p. 276.

70. Linda Martin and Kerry Segrave, *Women in Comedy* (Secaucus, NJ: Citadel, 1986), p. 223.

71. Jay Allison, "Studs Terkel's Topic: Interviewing the World's Greatest Interviewer," *The Transom Review* Vol. 1, Issue 10. www.transom.org

72. Mitz, p. 384.

73. Jones, p. 247.

74. Mitz, p. 383.

75. Polly Holliday spun off into *Flo* in 1980; she was replaced by Diane Ladd as Belle for one season and then by Celia Weston as Jolene for the remainder of the series.

76. Sackett, p. 248.

77. Carol Kruqcoff, "Leisure: Monitoring TV's Image," *Washington Post* Jan. 25, 1980: D5.

78. Philip A. Kalisch and Beatrice J. Kalisch, *The Changing Image of the Nurse* (Menlo Park, CA: Addison-Wesley, 1987), p. 148.

79. *Ibid.*

80. *Ibid.*

81. Kalisch and Kalisch, p. 150.

82. *Ibid.*

83. Philip A. Kalisch, Beatrice J. Kalisch, and Margaret Scobey, *Images of Nurses on Television* (New York: Springer, 1983), p. 13.

84. Kalisch and Kalisch, p. 153.

85. *Ibid.*

86. Bob Lamm, "'The Nurses': Television's Forgotten Gems," *Journal of Popular Film & Television* Vol. 23, No. 2 (Summer 1995): 77.

87. *Ibid.*, p. 74.

88. *Ibid.*, p. 73.

89. Another notable episode, "Nurse Is a Feminine Noun," follows the plight of a male nurse recently arrived at Alden.

90. Kalisch, Kalisch, and Scobey, p. 28.

91. Brooks and Marsh, p. 407.

92. Diahann Carroll with Ross Firestone, *Diahann!* (Boston: Little, Brown, 1986), p. 144.

93. Aniko Bodroghkozy, "Is This What You Mean by Color TV? Race, Gender and Contested Meanings in NBC's 'Julia,'" *Private Screenings*, edited by Lynn Spigel and Denise Mann (Minneapolis: University of Minnesota Press, 1992), p. 150.

94. *Ibid.*, p. 151.

95. Brooks, p. 864.

96. One interesting detail about *Julia* in regard to gender concerns the show's fashion doll tie-in. The Julia doll was marketed by Mattel and, while most other dolls of the era arrived dressed in ball gowns, Julia arrived in her nurses' uniform, ready to work.

97. Kalisch, Kalisch, and Scobey, p. 54.

98. Elena Verdugo, interview with author, Feb. 20, 2004.

99. McCrohan, *Prime Time*, p. 192.

100. Verdugo interview.

101. Jack Condon and David Hofstede, "*Charlie's Angels" Casebook* (Beverly Hills: Pomegranate, 2000), p. 9.

102. Marvin Kitman, *I Am a VCR* (New York: Random House, 1988), p. 249.

103. David S. Reiss, "'*M*A*S*H': The Exclusive Inside Story of TV's Most Popular Show*" (Indianapolis: Bobbs-Merrill, 1980), pp. 96–97.

104. Himmelstein, p. 175.

105. Joseph Turow *Playing Doctor* (New York: Oxford University Press, 1989), p. 225.

106. Kalisch, Kalisch, and Scobey, p. 153.

107. McWilliams, p. 76.

108. Sackett, p. 325.

109. Park Overall, e-mail communication with author, Aug. 28, 2005.

110. John L. Wasserman, "Now they allow her a kiss or two," *TV Guide* July 26–Aug. 1, 1969. http://petticoat.topcities.com

111. Turow, p. 178.

112. *Ibid.*, p. 260.

113. Andy Meisler, "Opulence Yields to Stethoscopes," *New York Times* March 27, 1988, pp. 37+.

114. Cary O'Dell, *Women Pioneers in Television: Biographies of Fifteen Industry Leaders* (Jefferson, NC: McFarland, 1997), pp. 119–134.

115. Gary Grossman, *Superman: Serial to Cereal* (New York: Popular Library, 1977), p. 145.

116. Grossman, p. 145.

117. Donald F. Glut and Jim Harmon, *The Great Television Heroes* (Garden City, NY: Doubleday, 1975), p. 26.

118. Grossman, p. 192.

119. *Ibid.*

120. Glut and Harmon, p. 33.

121. Information and insight into how the Lois Lane character addressed her boss, Perry White, during the run

of *The Adventures of Superman* was supplied to the author by Shane McNichols, webmaster for the site www.supermanmegasite.com, and by actress Noel Neill, both via e-mail communication, Jan. 18, 2007.

122. Ephraim Katz, *The Film Encyclopedia* (New York: Perigee), p. 748.

123. Shirley MacLaine, *You Can Get There from Here* (New York: Bantam, 1975), p. 26.

124. *Shirley's World* was an ambitious series and episodes were shot in Japan, England, and Hong Kong, among other places.

125. On November 20, 1993, Linda Kelsey participated in the panel discussion "She Works Hard for the Money: Images of Working Women on TV" at the Museum of Broadcast Communications (MBC) in Chicago as part of its exhibition "From 'My Little Margie' to 'Murphy Brown': Images of Women on Television." Ms. Kelsey's comments are taken from this session.

126. *Ibid.*

127. McNeil, p. 408.

128. Brooks and Marsh, p. 412.

129. Thomas Schatz, "Hill Street Blues," *Encyclopedia of Television*, edited by Horace Newcomb (Chicago: Fitzroy-Dearborn, 1997), p. 465.

130. Tom Stempel, *Storytellers to the Nation: A History of American Television Writing* (Syracuse: Syracuse University Press, 1996), p. 253.

131. Cary O'Dell, "Traveling Thru Space & Time with 'Star Trek's' Diana Muldaur," *Outre* No. 23: 82.

132. On November 20, 1993, Diana Muldaur participated in the panel discussion "She Works Hard for the Money: Images of Working Women on TV" at the Museum of Broadcast Communications (MBC) in Chicago as part of its exhibition "From 'My Little Margie' to 'Murphy Brown': Images of Women on Television." Ms. Muldaur's comments are taken from this session.

133. Robert M. Jarvis and Paul R. Joseph, eds., *Prime Time Law* (Durham: Carolina Academic Press, 1998), p. 239.

134. Brooks and Marsh, p. 260.

135. Cary O'Dell, "'Decoy' ... and Other Grand Dames," *TV Quarterly* Vol. XXXI, No. 2 & 3 (Summer/Fall 2000): 75.

136. *Ibid.*, p. 77.

137. Beretta E. Smith-Shomade, *Shaded Lives: African-American Women and Television* (New Brunswick, NJ: Rutgers, 2002), p. 15.

138. Bart Andrews with Brad Dunning, *The Worst TV Shows Ever* (New York: E.P. Dutton, 1980), p. 32.

139. Craig Nelson, *Bad TV* (New York: Delta, 1995), p. 27.

140. "In Memoriam 2002," *Entertainment Weekly* Jan. 3, 2003: 28.

141. McWilliams, p. 26.

142. Richard Meyers, *TV Detectives* (San Diego: A.S. Barnes, 1981), p. 201.

143. Georff Tibballs, *The Boxtree Encyclopedia of TV Detectives* (London: Boxtree, 1992), p. 331.

144. Susan J. Douglas, *Where the Girls Are: Growing Up Female with the Mass Media* (New York: Times Books, 1994), p. 209.

145. *Ibid.*

146. "50 Sexiest Stars of All Time," *TV Guide* Sept. 28, 2002: 20.

147. "TV's Super Women," *Time* Nov. 2, 1976: 68.

148. Kay Gardella, "Hunter, McCall Are Good Friends," *Miami Herald* Aug. 20, 1987. www.Stepfaniekramer.com

149. "'Hunter' Star Resolves Creative Dispute with Producers," Associated Press, August 21, 1987.

150. *Ibid.*

151. Dave Rogers, *The ITV Encyclopedia of Adventure* (London: Boxtree, 1988), p. 179.

152. Hal Erickson, *Syndicated Television: The First Forty Years, 1947–1987* (Jefferson, NC: McFarland, 1989), p. 285.

153. Brandon and Barber eventually married in real life.

154. *Ibid.*

155. John J. O'Connor, "TV Reviews: ABC Series 'Lady Blue' Switches to Saturdays," *New York Times* Nov. 18, 1985. http://query.nytimes.com

156. McNeil, p. 422.

157. Graham Russell Hodges, *Anna May Wong: From Laundryman's Daughter to Hollywood Legend* (New York: Palgrave Macmillan, 2004), pp. 216–217.

158. In some recaps of the series, the Bakers are described as secret agents. But in no episode I've seen do the Bakers make any reference to working for the government. In fact, in one episode, Mrs. Baker states, "Espionage! Boy, I don't want to get mixed up in it."

159. David Thorburn, "Detective Programs," *Encyclopedia of Television*, edited by Horace Newcomb (Chicago: Fitzroy-Dearborn, 1997), p. 482.

160. Meyers, p. 185.

161. Douglas, p. 214.

162. *Ibid.*, p. 212.

163. *Ibid.*

164. Condon and Hofstede, p. 22.

165. Nelson, p. 22.

166. Many of the details the series is often attacked for were actually created by actress Kate Jackson. As related in Charlie's Angels *Casebook* (Pomegranate Press, 2000), at a pre-production meeting with Aaron Spelling, Jackson stated, "I saw a squawk box on Aaron's desk and suggested that the girls work for a guy they never see; he only talks to them on the phone.... Then I noticed a picture of three angels on Aaron's wall; so I said, "Let's call the girls 'angels.'"

167. Douglas, p. 214.

168. Condon and Hofstede, p. 37.

169. Diana M. Meehan, *Ladies of the Evening: Women Characters of Prime-Time Television* (Metuchen, NJ: Scarecrow Press, 1983), p. 80.

170. *Merriam Webster's Collegiate Dictionary*, 10th ed. (Springfield, MA: Merriam-Webster, 1995), p. 300.

171. Condon and Hofstede, pp. 158, 181, 232.

172. *Ibid.*, p. 46.

173. *Ibid.*, p. 151.

174. *Ibid.*, p. 49.

175. *Ibid.*, p. 47.

176. *Ibid.*, p. 119.

177. Condon and Hofstede, p. 149.

178. Larry Good, "Major film reprises womens liberation," *Aspen Daily News* Sept. 25, 2002. aspendailynews.com

179. Condon and Hofstede, p. 120.

180. Chris Matthew Sciabarra, "The Dialectical Meaning of 'Charlie's Angels,'" *Daily Objectivist* Nov. 7, 1999. www.dailyobjectivist.com

181. *Ibid.*

182. Alan McKee, "Miss Marple," *Encyclopedia of Television*, edited by Horace Newcomb (Chicago: Fitzroy-Dearborn, 1997), p. 1061.

183. Faludi, p. 142.

184. Tibballs, p. 236.

185. http://thrillingdetective.com/mccarron.html.

186. Donna McCrohan, *The Life & Times of Maxwell Smart* (New York: St. Martin's, 1988), p. 154.

187. *Ibid.*, p. 65.
188. McWilliams, p. 54.
189. Michael McCall, *The Best of '60s TV* (New York: Mallard Press, 1992), p. 85.
190. McCrohan, *Life & Times of Maxwell Smart*, p. 64.
191. *Ibid.*, p. 66.
192. Ronald L. Smith, *Sweethearts of '60's TV* (New York: SPI, 1993), p. 131.
193. McCrohan, *Life & Times of Maxwell Smart*, p. 67.
194. Though the Protectors were actually detectives rather than government agents, the team's regular involvement in international intrigue makes the difference moot.
195. Brooks and Marsh, p. 156.
196. J. Fred MacDonald, *Who Shot the Sheriff? The Rise and Fall of the Television Western* (New York: Praeger, 1987), p. 32.
197. Candace Savage, *Cowgirls* (Berkley: Ten Speed Press, 1996), p. 116.
198. *Ibid.*, p. 118.
199. MacDonald, p. 65.
200. McCrohan, *Prime Time*, p. 106.
201. McWilliams, p. 80.
202. Dave Stein, "Spotlight on 'Petticoat Junction,'" MortysTV.com Nov. 1998. www.mortystv.com
203. Al DiOrio, *Barbara Stanwyck: A Biography* (New York: Berkley, 1983), p. 191.
204. Torey L. King, "Spiritual Ancestors to Xena: Barbara Stanwyck: Warrior Woman in Hollywood's Gender Wars," 1997, p. 3. www.Whoosh.org
205. McWilliams, p. 71.
206. Douglass K. Daniel, *"Lou Grant": The Making of TV's Top Newspaper Drama* (New York: Syracuse University Press, 1996), p. 42.
207. McWilliams, p. 60.
208. *Ibid.*, p. 25.
209. McCrohan, *Prime Time*, p. 316.
210. Carroll, p. 237
211. Nelson, p. 300.
212. McWilliams, p. 32.
213. Camille Paglia, *Interview* Nov. 2002. www.Knots landing.net
214. Douglas, p. 137.
215. *Ibid.*
216. Elizabeth Kuhns, *The Habit: A History of the Clothing of Catholic Nuns* (New York: Doubleday, 2003).
217. Douglas, p. 137.

Chapter 6

1. "Saturday Viewing," *Radio-TV Mirror* Aug. 1951: 60–61.
2. Vincent Terrace, *Sitcom Factfinder, 1948–1984* (Jefferson, NC: McFarland, 2002), p. 205.
3. Stephen Cole, *That Book About "That Girl"* (Los Angeles: Renaissance Books, 1999), p. 40.
4. Moya Luckett, "That Girl," *Encyclopedia of Television*, edited by Horace Newcomb (Chicago: Fitzroy-Dearborn, 1997), p. 1655.
5. Cole, p. 142.
6. Gerald Jones, *Honey, I'm Home!: Sitcoms, Selling the American Dream* (New York: Grove Weidenfeld, 1992), p. 195.
7. Cole, p. 46.
8. *Ibid.*
9. Michael McWilliams, *TV Sirens* (New York: Perigee, 1987), p. 48.
10. A.E. Hotchner, *Doris Day: Her Own Story* (New York: Morrow, 1975), p. 259.
11. Today that age hovers around 27.
12. U.S. Census Bureau. www.census.gov
13. Susan Sackett, *Prime-Time Hits: Television's Most Popular Network Programs* (New York: Billboard, 1983), p. 191.
14. Ronald L. Smith, *Sweethearts of '60's TV* (New York: SPI, 1993), p. 218.
15. Rick Mitz, *The Great TV Sitcom Book* (New York: Perigee, 1983), p. 350.
16. McWilliams, p. 92

Chapter 7

1. On October 21, 1993, as part of its exhibition "From 'My Little Margie' to 'Murphy Brown': Images of Women on Television," the Museum of Broadcast Communications (MBC) in Chicago held the panel discussion "Feminine Wiles: Images of Super Heroines." Among those taking part were actresses Yvonne Craig, Erin Gray, and Julie Newmar. The panel was moderated by Dr. Kate Kane of DePaul University. Dr. Kane's comments were taken from this discussion.
2. Julie D'Acci, "Nobody's Woman: 'Honey West' and the New Sexuality," *The Revolution Wasn't Televised*, edited by Lynn Spigel and Michael Curtain (New York: Routledge, 1997), p. 81.
3. John Heitland, *The "Man from UNCLE" Book* (New York: St. Martin's Press, 1987), p. 178.
4. Dave Rogers, *The Complete Avengers* (New York: St. Martin's Press, 1989), p. 87.
5. Many books detail the unique, symbiotic relationship between women's dress and women's social and economic progress. One of the best: Alison Lurie's *The Language of Clothes* (New York: Henry Holt and Company, 1981).
6. Candice Savage, *Cowgirls* (Berkeley, CA: Ten Speed Press, 1996), p. 118.
7. Ibid.
8. Tim Brooks, *The Complete Directory to Prime Time TV Stars* (New York: Ballantine, 1987), p. 232.
9. "Good Lives," *Ms.* Dec. 1997–Jan. 1998: 17.
10. Hal Erickson, *Syndicated Television: The First Forty Years, 1947–1987* (Jefferson, NC: McFarland, 1989), p. 42.
11. David B. Broad, "Sheena, Queen of the Jungle: White Goddess of the Dumont Era" *Studies in Popular Culture* XIX: 3–19.3 (1997). www.pcasacas.org
12. Ibid.
13. Richard Lamparski, *Whatever Became Of...? (8th series)* (New York: Crown, 1982), p. 193.
14. Ronald L. Smith, *Sweethearts of '60s TV* (New York: SPI Books, 1993), pp. 184–195.
15. Michael McWilliams, *TV Sirens* (New York: Perigee, 1987), p. 111.
16. D'Acci, pp. 83–84.
17. Cary O'Dell, "Anne Francis' Radio and TV Days," *Nostalgia Digest* Oct.-Nov. 1996: 18.
18. D'Acci, p. 81.
19. *Model & Toy Collector* Spring, 1986: 27.
20. D'Acci, p. 86.
21. O'Dell, p. 18.
22. "Where Are They Now?: Anne Francis," *Biography Magazine* Sept. 2002: 28.
23. *Honey West* usually won its timeslot but when ABC discovered it could import from England *The Avengers* more cheaply than it could produce *Honey West*, they axed the Francis series.
24. "50 Sexiest Stars of All Time," *TV Guide* Sept. 28, 2002: 19.

25. Toby Miller, *The Avengers* (London: BFI, 1997), p. 154.

26. The Blackman episodes were not seen in America until the 1980s when A&E imported and aired them.

27. Dave Rogers, *The Complete Avengers* (New York: St. Martin's Press, 1989), p. 88.

28. Ibid., p. 87.

29. Ibid., p. 88.

30. Macnee, Patrick. *Blind in One Ear: The Avenger Returns* (London: Mercury House, 1992), p. 30.

31. Miller, p. 49.

32. Moya Luckett, "Sensuous Women and Single Girls: Reclaiming the Female Body on 1960s Television." *Swinging Single: Representing Sexuality in the 1960s*, edited by Hilary Radner and Moya Luckett (Minneapolis: University of Minnesota Press, 1999), p. 276.

33. Smith, p. 212.

34. Miller, p. 73.

35. Ibid.

36. Smith, p. 214.

37. Miller, p. 71.

38. Wesley Britton, *Spy Television* (Westport, CT: Praeger, 2004), p. 74.

39. John G. Nettles, "The New Avengers: Season One" (DVD review) Aug 11, 2003. www.PopMatters.com

40. Patrick J. White, *The Complete "Mission: Impossible" Dossier* (New York: Avon Books, 1991), p. 35.

41. "More Liberated Than You Remember?," *TV Guide* Dec. 4–10 1993: 45+.

42. *Intimate Portrait: Female Spies* (Astoria, NY: Lifetime Home Video, 1996).

43. White, p. 72.

44. Ibid., p. 86.

45. Heitland, p. 178.

46. Ibid., p. 180.

47. Smith, p. 199.

48. Britton, p. 48.

49. Heitland, pp. 250–257.

50. Yvonne Craig, *From Ballet to the Batcave and Beyond* (Venice, CA: Kudo Press, 2000), p. 131.

51. Actually, a character named Batwoman did (and does) exist in the comics. She was introduced in 1956 and appeared on and off until 1964. After a few cameo appearances in the 1970s, the character was dormant until a revised Batwoman was resurrected in 2005.

52. Gina Misiroglu, ed., *The Superhero Book* (Detroit: Visible Ink, 2004), p. 54.

53. Kyle Counts, "Some Call Her 'Batgirl,'" *Starlog* Dec. 1989: 29+.

54. "Feminine Wiles: Images of Super Heroines," Oct. 21 1993. Ms. Craig's comments were taken from this discussion.

55. Marion Purcelli, "Yvonne Craig: TV's Bat Girl [sic]," *TV Guide* Nov. 25-Dec. 1, 1967: 3.

56. "Feminine Wiles: Images of Super Heroines," Oct. 21, 1993. Ms. Craig's statements were taken from this discussion.

57. Ibid.

58. Kyle Counts, "Batgirl Casebook," *Comics Scene #10*, p. 75.

59. Craig, p. 142.

60. In 1974, the blond (!) Cathy Lee Crosby starred in a TV movie titled *Wonder Woman* which bore little resemblance to the comic book heroine, even dispensing with the heroine's classic costume.

61. Susan J. Douglas, *Where The Girls Are: Growing Up Female with the Mass Media* (New York: Random House, 1994), p. 217.

62. Ibid.

63. Les Daniels, *DC Comics: A Celebration of the World's Favorite Comic Book Heroes* (London: Virgin Books, 2004), p. 171.

64. David Houston, *Science Fiction Heroes* (New York: Starlog Press Publications, 1980), p. 15.

65. Gary Gerani and Paul H. Schulman, *Fantastic Television* (New York: Harmony Books, 1977), p. 166.

66. "50 Greatest Cartoon Characters of All Time," *TV Guide* Aug. 3, 2002: 31.

67. Douglas, p. 193.

68. Donna Minkowitz, "Xena: She's Big, Tall, Strong — and Popular," *Ms.* July-Aug. 1996: 74–77.

69. Varla Ventura, *Sheroes* (Berkley, CA: Conari, 1998), p. 297.

70. Douglas, p. 218.

71. "The Bionic Woman." www.TV1.com

72. Houston, p. 8.

73. Gerani and Schulman, p. 156.

74. Mark Phillips and Frank Garcia, *Science Fiction Television Series* (Jefferson, NC: McFarland, 1996), p. 45.

75. Ibid.

76. Douglas, p. 218.

77. Susanna Paasonen, "Thinking through the cybernetic body: popular cybernetics and feminism," *Cultural Studies in Emerging Knowledge*. Vol. 4 (Spring 2002): 5. www.Rhizomes.net.

78. Ventura, p. 296.

79. Joe Sarno, "Inside Tom Corbett, Space Cadet!," *Space Academy Newsletter #7* July-Dec. 1979. www.slicknet.com/space/corbett

80. After her days as Tonga on "Space Patrol" came to an end, actress Nina Bara wrote two autobiographical monographs, "Space Patrol Memories" by "Tonga" (Nina Bara) in 1976 and "America's Great Space Drama: 'Space Patrol'" in 1980. Each was "published" as limited edition collector's items. The Library of American Broadcasting at the University of Maryland holds copies of each.

81. Ibid.

82. Patrick Lucanio and Gary Coville, *American Science Fiction Television Series of the 1950s* (Jefferson, NC: McFarland, 1998), pp. 113–121.

83. The original *Star Trek* pilot, which featured Jeffrey Hunter in the lead, was never aired in full but was later cannibalized for "The Cage," a two-part episode of the Shatner-led series.

84. Herbert F. Solow, *Inside 'Star Trek': The Real Story* (New York: Pocket, 1996), p. 60.

85. "Lewis." "Uhura as the Barbie Doll Moesha of the 1960s." Online posting. July 2005. www.Allscifi.com

86. Nichelle Nichols, *Beyond Uhura* (New York: G.P. Putnam's, 1994).

87. Stephen E. Whitfield with Gene Roddenberry, *The Making of "Star Trek"* (New York: Ballantine Books, 1968), p. 253.

88. Asherman, p. 82.

89. Nichols, p. 164.

90. Ibid.

91. "Unsung Heroes: Nyota Uhura." Online posting. July 29, 1999. www.scifi.about.com

92. Nichols, pp. 297–298, 309–310.

93. Jessica R. Levine. "A portrait of the future: Women in 'Star Trek: The Next Generation,'" Brandeis University: Dept. of Sociology, unpublished paper, 1994.

94. Garcia and Phillips, p. 419

95. Amongst others, Jessica R. Levine makes note of how the female characters of *Star Trek: The Next Generation* fulfill professional yet quasi-maternal roles in her paper "A portrait of the future: Women in *Star Trek: The Next Generation* as did Dr. Kate Kane at the Museum of

Broadcast Communications' "Super Heroines" seminar in October 1993.

96. Levine.

97. Houston, p. 13.

98. Anonymous. Nitcentral's Bulletin Brash Reflections: "Space: 1999": The Characters: Helena Russell. Online posting. 12 Nov. 2002. http://nitcentral.philfarrand.com/discus/messages/3728/20121.html?10891559 28

99. Robert Graves, *The White Goddess* (New York: Farrar, Straus, & Giroux, 1966).

100. Over the years many have likened Catherine Schell's Maya make-up to "sideburns." Most fans of the series believe it was first suggested by *Washington Post* TV critic Tom Shales. www.space1999.org

101. Actually, this was TV's second *Buck*. In 1950 and 1951, ABC aired an incarnation with Lou Prentis in the role of Lt. Wilma Deering. It's believed that no copies of this earlier series have survived.

102. "Feminine Wiles: Images of Super Heroines," October 21, 1993. Ms. Gray's comments were taken from this discussion.

103. Ibid.

104. Ibid.

105. Ibid.

106. "Buck Rogers Comes of Age — Science Fiction to Science Fact: The Uncut New Mexico Space Journal Erin Gray Interview!," *New Mexico Space Journal* No. 5 (May 2003).

107. *Merriam-Webster's Collegiate Dictionary (Tenth Edition)* (Springfield, MA: Merriam-Webster, Inc., 1995), p. 351.

108. Tim Brooks and Earle Marsh, *The Complete Directory to Prime Time Network TV Shows* (New York: Random House, 1988), p. 149.

109. David Krell, "Julie Newmar!: From Sexy Robotrix to Catwoman & Beyond," *Outre* No. 15: 40.

110. Bob Garcia, "Catwoman: Julie Newmar set the standard as the slinky seductress of Gotham City," *Cinefantastique* 24/25 N6/N1 (1994): 18.

111. Krell, p. 40.

112. Ibid., p. 41.

113. Kyle Counts, "The Many Lives of the Catwoman," *Starlog* Nov. 1989: 29.

114. Ibid.

115. Elisabeth Fies, "Batmedia: Catwoman — The Creation of a Twentieth-Century Goddess," 1999. www.aboutcatwoman.com

116. Mark Phillips and Frank Garcia, *Science Fiction Television Series* (Jefferson, NC: McFarland, 1996), pp. 521–530.

117. John Javna, *The Best of Science Fiction TV: The Critics' Choice: From "Captain Video" to "Star Trek," from "The Jetsons" to "Robotech"* (New York: Harmony, 1987), pp. 44–45.

Conclusion

1. As part of its exhibition "From 'My Little Margie' to 'Murphy Brown': Images of Women on Television," the Museum of Broadcast Communications (MBC) in Chicago presented the panel discussion "Leading Ladies: A Luncheon Salute to Television's Pioneering Women" on September 11, 1993. The panel consisted of actresses Gale Storm, Betty White and Jane Wyatt. Ms. White's comments were taken from this discussion.

Bibliography

Abernathy, Michael. "Male Bashing on TV." PopMatters.com 9 Jan. 2003. www.PopMatters.com

Adams, Edie, and Robert Windeler. *Sing a Pretty Song....* New York: William Morrow, 1990.

Alley, Robert S. *Women Television Producers.* Rochester: University of Rochester Press, 2001.

Allison, Jay. "Studs Terkel's Topic: Interviewing the World's Greatest Interviewer." *The Transom Review* Vol. 1, Issue 10. www.transom.org

American Masters: Finding Lucy. PBS, 2005.

American Masters: The Quiz Show Scandals. PBS, 2002.

Andrews, Bart. *Lucy & Ricky & Fred & Ethel: The Story of "I Love Lucy."* New York: Fawcett, 1976.

_____, and Brad Dunning. *The Worst TV Shows Ever.* New York: E.P. Dutton, 1980.

_____, and Ahrgus Juiliard. *Holy Mackerel! The "Amos 'n' Andy" Story.* New York: E.P. Dutton, 1986.

_____, and Thomas J. Watson. *Loving Lucy.* New York: St. Martin's, 1980.

Applebaum, Irwyn. *The World According to Beaver.* New York: Bantam, 1984.

Arden, Eve. *Three Phases of Eve.* New York: St. Martin's Press, 1985.

Bara, Nina. *"Space Patrol" Memories.* Self-published, 1976.

_____. *America's Great Space Drama: "Space Patrol."* Self-published, 1980.

Barnow, Erik. *Tube of Plenty.* New York: Oxford University Press, 1990.

Bellafante, Ginia. "Feminism: It's all about me!" *Time* 29 June 1998.

Berg, Gertrude. *Molly & Me.* New York: McGraw-Hill, 1961.

Bliss, Edward. *Now the News: The Story of Broadcast Journalism.* New York: Columbia University Press, 1991.

Bodroghkozy, Aniko. "Is This What You Mean by Color TV? Race, Gender and Contested Meanings in NBC's 'Julia.'" Spigel, Lynn, and Denise Mann, eds. *Private Screenings.* Minneapolis: University of Minnesota Press, 1992.

Bogle, Donald. *Primetime Blues.* New York: Farrar, Straus, Giroux, 2001.

Brady, Kathleen. *Lucille: The Life of Lucille Ball.* New York: Hyperion, 1994.

Britton, Wesley. *Spy Television.* Westport, CT: Praeger, 2004.

Broad, David B. "Sheena, Queen of the Jungle: White Goddess of the Dumont Era." *Studies in Popular Culture* XIX: 3 19.3 (1997). www.pcasacas.org

Brochu, Jim. *Lucy in the Afternoon.* New York: Pocket Books, 1990.

Brooks, Tim. *The Complete Directory to Prime Time TV Stars.* New York: Ballantine, 1987.

_____, and Earle Marsh. *The Complete Directory to Prime Time Network TV Shows.* New York: Random House, 1988.

Brown, Les. *Les Brown's Encyclopedia of Television.* Detroit: Gale Research, 1992.

"Buck Rogers Comes of Age — Science Fiction to Science Fact: The Uncut New Mexico Space Journal Erin Gray Interview!" *New Mexico Space Journal* No. 5 (May 2003).

Carroll, Diahann, with Ross Firestone. *Diahann!* Boston: Little, Brown, 1986, p. 144.

Cole, Stephen. *That Book About "That Girl."* Los Angeles: Renaissance Books, 1999.

Collins, Ace. *Lassie: A Dog's Life.* New York: Cader Books, 1993.

Collins, Max Allan, and John Javna. *The Critics' Choice: The Best of Crime & Detective TV.* New York: Harmony Books, 1988.

Condon, Jack, and David Hofstede. *Charlie's Angels Casebook.* Beverly Hills: Pomegranate, 2000.

Coontz, Stephanie. *The Way We Never Were.* New York: Basic Books, 2000.

Counts, Kyle. "Batgirl Casebook." *Comics Scene #10.*

_____. "The Many Lives of the Catwoman." *Starlog* Nov. 1989.

_____. "Some Call Her 'Batgirl.'" *Starlog* Dec. 1989.

Cox, Stephen. *The Addams Chronicles.* New York: HarperPerennial, 1991.

_____, with Howard Frank. *Dreaming of Jeannie: TV's Prime Time in a Bottle.* New York: St. Martin's Griffin, 2000.

Craig, Yvonne. *From Ballet to the Batcave and Beyond.* Venice, CA: Kudo Press, 2000.

D'Acci, Julie. "Nobody's Woman: 'Honey West' and the New Sexuality." Spigel, Lynn, and Michael Curtain, eds. *The Revolution Wasn't Televised.* New York: Routledge, 1997.

Dabney, Dick. "How Men Sold Out Their Manhood." *Washington Post* 6 Dec. 1981.

Daniel, Douglass K. *"Lou Grant": The Making of TV's Top Newspaper Drama.* New York: Syracuse University Press, 1996.

Daniels, Les. *DC Comics: A Celebration of the World's Favorite Comic Book Heroes*. London: Virgin Books, 2004.

Dates, Jannette L., and William Barlow, eds. *Split Image: African Americans in the Mass Media*. Washington, DC: Howard University Press, 1990.

_____, and _____. *Split Image: African Americans in the Mass Media*. Washington, DC: Howard University Press, 1993.

DiOrio, Al. *Barbara Stanwyck: A Biography*. New York: Berkley Books, 1983.

Douglas, Susan J. *Where the Girls Are: Growing Up Female with the Mass Media*. New York: Times Books, 1994.

Dufoe, Terry, and Becky. "June Lockhart: TV's Favorite Earth Heart Space Mother." *Filmfax* No. 80.

Ely, Melvin Patrick. *The Adventures of "Amos 'n' Andy": A Social History of an American Phenomenon*. New York: Maxwell Macmillan, 1991.

Erickson, Hal. *Syndicated Television: The First Forty Years, 1947–1987*. Jefferson, NC: McFarland, 1989.

Faludi, Susan. *Backlash: The Undeclared War Against American Women*. New York: Crown, 1991.

Feldman, Ruth Duskin. *Whatever Happened to the Quiz Kids?* Chicago: Chicago Review Press, 1992.

Fidelman, Geoffrey Mark. *The Lucy Book*. Los Angeles: Renaissance Books, 1999.

Fies, Elisabeth. "Batmedia: Catwoman — The Creation of a Twentieth-Century Goddess." aboutcatwoman.com. 1999. www.aboutcatwoman.com

"50 Greatest Cartoon Characters of All Time." *TV Guide* 3 Aug. 2002.

"50 Sexiest Stars of All Time." *TV Guide* 28 Sept. 2002.

Flynn, Joan King. "How Faye Emerson Got Into Television." *Los Angeles Examiner* 1 April 1951.

Fonseca, Nicholas. "Guilty Pleasures: 'Mama.'" *Entertainment Weekly* 23 July 2004.

Frank, Sam. *Buyer's Guide to Fifty Years of TV on Video*. Amherst, NY: Prometheus Books, 1999.

"Frannie's Turn." *TV Guide* 12 Sept. 1992.

Friedan, Betty. "Television and the Feminine Mystique." *TV Guide: The First 25 Years*. New York: Simon & Schuster, 1978.

Futz, Jay. *In Search of Donna Reed*. Iowa City: University of Iowa, 1998.

Garcia, Bob. "Catwoman: Julie Newmar set the standard as the slinky seductress of Gotham City." *Cinefantastique* 24/25 N6/N1, 1994.

Gardella, Kay. "Hunter, McCall Are Good Friends." *Miami Herald* 20 Aug. 1987. www.Stepfaniekramer.com

Garner, Joe. *And the Crowd Goes Wild*. Naperville, IL: Sourcebooks, 1999.

_____. *And the Fans Roared*. Naperville, IL: Sourcebooks, 2000.

_____. *Made You Laugh: The Funniest Moments in Comedy*. Kansas City: Andrews McMeel, 2004.

Gelfman, Judith. *Women in Television News*. New York: Columbia University Press, 1976.

Gerani, Gary, and Paul H. Schulman. *Fantastic Television*. New York: Harmony Books, 1977.

Glut, Donald F., and Jim Harmon. *The Great Television Heroes*. Garden City, NY: Doubleday, 1975.

Good, Larry. "Major film reprises women's liberation." *Aspen Daily News* 25 Sept. 2002.

"Good Lives." *Ms*. Dec. 1997–Jan. 1998.

Gorney, Cynthia. "Good Night, Olivia: Michael Learned Comes Down From the Mountain." *Washington Post* 18 Jan. 1979.

Graham, Jefferson. *Come on Down!!! The TV Game Show Book*. New York: Abbeville Press, 1988.

Graves, Robert. *The White Goddess*. New York: Farrar, Straus, & Giroux, 1966.

Green, Joey. *Hi Bob! A Self-Help Guide to "The Bob Newhart Show."* New York: St. Martin's Press, 1996.

_____. *The Partridge Family Album*. New York: HarperPerennial, 1994.

Green, Jonathon. *The Cassell Dictionary of Slang*. London: Cassell, 1998.

Grossman, Gary. *Superman: Serial to Cereal*. New York: Popular Library, 1977.

Guthrie, Bruce. "Rolle Model." *People* 7 Dec. 1998.

"Hallmark Hall of Fame: The First 40 Years." UCLA Film and Television Archive, 1991.

Harris, Warren G. *Lucy & Desi*. New York: Simon & Schuster, 1991.

Heitland, John. *The "Man from UNCLE" Book*. New York: St. Martin's Press, 1987.

Henry, William A. *The Great One: The Life and Legend of Jackie Gleason*. New York: Doubleday, 1992.

Higham, Charles. *Lucy: The Life of Lucille Ball*. New York: St. Martin's, 1986.

Hill, Tom. *TV Land to Go*. New York: Fireside, 2001.

Himmelstein, Hal. *Television Myth and the American Mind*. New York: Praeger, 1984.

Hodges, Graham Russell. *Anna May Wong: From Laundryman's Daughter to Hollywood Legend*. New York: Palgrave Macmillan, 2004.

_____, ed. *Studies in African American History and Culture*. New York: Garland, 1998.

Holms, John P., and Ernest Wood. *The TV Game Show Almanac*. Radnor, Pa: Chilton Book, 1995.

Hornick, Karen. "Overrated/Underrated: Sitcom." *American Heritage* Oct. 2003.

Hotchner, A.E. *Doris Day: Her Own Story*. New York: Morrow, 1975.

Houston, David. *Science Fiction Heroes*. New York: Starlog Press Publications, 1980.

Humphrey, Hal. "So What's New with Molly?" *Los Angeles Mirror* 9 Sept. 1961.

"'Hunter' Star Resolves Creative Dispute with Producers." Associated Press, Aug. 21, 1987.

"In Memoriam 2002." *Entertainment Weekly* 3 Jan. 2003.

Ingram, Billy. *TV Party*. Chicago: Bonus Books, 2002.

Intimate Portrait: Female Spies. Astoria, NY: Lifetime Home Video, 1996.

Jarvis, Robert M., and Paul R. Joseph, eds. *Prime Time Law*. Durham: Carolina Academic Press, 1998.

Javna, John. *The Best of Science Fiction TV: The Critics' Choice: From "Captain Video" to "Star Trek," from "The Jetsons" to "Robotech."* New York: Harmony Books, 1987.

_____. *The Best of TV Sitcoms*. New York: Harmony Books, 1988.

Jones, Gerald. *Honey, I'm Home! Sitcoms, Selling the American Dream*. New York: Grove Weidenfeld, 1992.

Kalisch, Philip A., and Beatrice J. Kalisch. *The Changing Image of the Nurse*. Menlo Park, CA: Addison-Wesley, 1987.

_____, _____, and Margaret Scobey. *Images of Nurses on Television*. New York: Springer, 1983.

Katz, Ephraim. *The Film Encyclopedia*. New York: Perigee, 1979.

Kaufman, Joanne. "Learned Lessons." *TV Guide* 21–27 Sept. 2002.

King, Torey L. "Spiritual Ancestors to Xena: Barbara Stanwyck: Warrior Woman in Hollywood's Gender Wars." www.Whoosh.org. Nov. 1997.

Kiska, Tim. "Bundys Diagnosed as the Most Dysfunctional TV Family Ever." *Chicago Sun-Times* 27 July 1983.

Kitman, Marvin. *I Am a VCR*. New York: Random House, 1988.

Klugman, Ellen B. "Tribute: Hope Lange, 1933–2003." *TV Guide* 24 Jan. 2004.

Krell, David. "Julie Newmar! From Sexy Robotrix to Catwoman & Beyond." *Outre* No. 15.

Kruqcoff, Carol. "Leisure: Monitoring TV's Image." *Washington Post* 25 Jan. 1980.

Kuhns, Elizabeth. *The Habit: A History of the Clothing of Catholic Nuns*. New York: Doubleday, 2003.

Kuhns, William. *Why We Watch Them: Interpreting TV Shows*. New York: Benziger, 1970.

LaGuardia, Robert. *Soap World*. New York: Arbor House, 1983.

Lamm, Bob. "'The Nurses': Television's Forgotten Gems." *Journal of Popular Film & Television* Vol. 23, No. 2, Summer 1995.

Lamparski, Richard. *Whatever Became of...?* 8th series. New York: Crown, 1982.

Lasswell, Mark. *TV Guide: Fifty Years of Television*. New York: Crown, 2002.

"Legacy: Isabel Sanford." *People* 27 Dec. 2004.

Lentz, Harris M. *Television Westerns Episode Guide: All United States Series, 1949–1996*. Jefferson, NC: McFarland, 1997.

Levine, Jessica R. "A portrait of the future: Women in 'Star Trek: The Next Generation.'" Unpublished paper, Brandeis University, Dept. of Sociology, 1994.

Lewis, Judy. *Uncommon Knowledge*. New York: Pocket, 1994.

Logan, Michael. "Tribute: Ann Sothern." *TV Guide* 28 April 2001.

Lucanio, Patrick, and Gary Coville. *American Science Fiction Television Series of the 1950s: Episode Guides and Casts and Credits for Twenty Shows*. Jefferson, NC: McFarland, 1998.

Luckett, Moya. "Sensuous Women and Single Girls: Reclaiming the Female Body on 1960s Television." Radner, Hilary, and Moya Luckett, eds. *Swinging Single: Representing Sexuality in the 1960s*. Minneapolis: University of Minnesota Press, 1999.

Lurie, Alison. *The Language of Clothes*. New York: Henry Holt, 1981.

MacDonald, J. Fred. *Blacks and White TV*. Chicago: Nelson-Hall, 1992.

_____. *Who Shot the Sheriff? The Rise and Fall of the Television Western*. New York: Praeger, 1987.

MacLaine, Shirley. *You Can Get There from Here*. New York: Bantam, 1975.

Macnee, Patrick. *Blind in One Ear: The Avenger Returns*. London: Mercury House, 1992.

Marc, David. *Comic Visions: Television Culture and American Culture*. Malden, MA: Blackwell, 1989.

_____. *Demographic Vistas*. Philadelphia: University of Pennsylvania Press, 1984.

Marill, Alvin H. *Movies Made for Television*. New York: Zoetrope, 1987.

Martin, Linda, and Kerry Segrave. *Women in Comedy*. Secaucus, NJ: Citadel, 1986.

McCall, Michael. *The Best of '60s TV*. New York: Mallard Press, 1992.

McCrohan, Donna. *The Life & Times of Maxwell Smart*. New York: St. Martin's, 1988.

_____. *Prime Time, Our Time*. Rocklin, CA: Prima, 1990.

McLaughlin, Lisa. "Paint by Numbers: Back to Donna Reed." *Time* 10 Mar. 2003.

McNeil, Alex. *Total Television*. New York: Penguin, 1991.

McWilliam, Erica. "Seductress or Schoolmarm: On the Improbability of the Great Female Teacher." AARE (Australian Association for Research in Education) Conference, Newcastle, Nov. 1994.

McWilliams, Michael. *TV Sirens*. New York: Perigee, 1987.

Meadows, Audrey. *Love, Alice: My Life as a Honeymooner*. New York: Crown, 1994.

Meehan, Diana M. *Ladies of the Evening: Women Characters of Prime-Time Television*. Metuchen, NJ: Scarecrow Press, 1983.

"Meet Margaret Matlin." Lucyfan.com. www.lucyfan.com/margaretmatlin.html

Meisler, Andy. "Opulence Yields to Stethoscopes." *New York Times* 27 Mar. 1988.

Meyerowitz, Joanne. *Not June Cleaver*. Philadelphia: Temple University Press, 1994.

Meyers, Richard. *TV Detectives*. San Diego: A.S. Barnes, 1981.

Miedzien, Myriam. *Boys Will Be Boys: Breaking the Link Between Masculinity and Violence*. New York: Doubleday, 1991.

Miller, Lisa. "Tribute: Joanie Weston." *TV Guide* 7 June 1997.

Miller, Mark Crispin. "Dads Through the Decades: Thirty Years of TV Fathers." *Media & Values* #48, Fall 1989. www.medialit.org

Miller, Toby. *The Avengers*. London: BFI, 1997.

Miller, Will. *Why We Watch*. New York: Fireside, 1996.

Minkowitz, Donna. "Xena: She's Big, Tall, Strong — and Popular." *Ms.* July–Aug. 1996.

Misiroglu, Gina, ed. *The Superhero Book*. Detroit: Visible Ink, 2004.

Missing in Action: The Women Behind Television's Golden Age. 2003. www.womenbehindtv.com

Mitz, Rick. *The Great TV Sitcom Book.* New York: Perigee, 1983.

Model & Toy Collector. Spring 1986.

"More Liberated Than You Remember?" *TV Guide* 4 Dec. 1993.

Morella, Joe, and Edward Z. Epstein. *Forever Lucy: The Life of Lucille Ball.* New York: Berkely, 1990.

_____, and _____. *Jane Wyman: A Biography.* New York: Delacorte Press, 1985.

Morgan, Robin. *Saturday's Child: A Memoir.* New York: W.W. Norton, 2000.

Morice, Laura. "Anything But Work." *Working Woman* May 1991.

Myers, Deb. "Faye Emerson." *Cosmopolitan* Aug. 1950.

Nelson, Craig. *Bad TV.* New York: Delta, 1995.

Nettles, John G. "The New Avengers: Season One" (DVD review). PopMatters.com. 11 Aug. 2003. www.PopMatters.com

Newcomb, Horace. *TV: The Most Popular Art.* Garden City, NY: Anchor, 1974.

_____, ed. *The Encyclopedia of Television.* Chicago: Fitzroy-Dearborn, 1997.

Nichols, Nichelle. *Beyond Uhura.* New York: G.P. Putnam's, 1994.

O'Connor, John J. "TV Review: ABC Series 'Lady Blue' Switches to Saturdays." *New York Times* 18 Nov. 1985. http://query.nytimes.com

_____. "TV Review: 'Sara' Starring Brenda Vaccaro, on CBS." *New York Times* 12 Feb. 1976.

O'Dell, Cary. "Anne Francis' Radio and TV Days." *Nostalgia Digest* Oct.–Nov. 1996.

_____. "'Decoy' ... and Other Grand Dames." *TV Quarterly* Vol. XXXI, No. 2 & 3, Summer/Fall 2000.

_____. "A Station of Their Own: The Story of the Women's Auxiliary Television Technical Staff (WATTS) in World War II Chicago." *Television Quarterly* Vol. XXX, No. 3, Winter 2000.

_____. "Traveling Thru Space & Time with 'Star Trek's' Diana Muldaur." *Outre* No. 23.

_____. *Women Pioneers in Television: Biographies of Fifteen Industry Leaders.* Jefferson, NC: McFarland, 1997.

O'Reilly, Jane. "At Last! Women Worth Watching." *TV Guide* 27 May 1989.

Overall, Park. E-mail communication with authur. 28 Aug. 2005.

Paasonen, Susanna. "Thinking through the cybernetic body: popular cybernetics and feminism." *Cultural Studies in Emerging Knowledge.* Spring 2002, #4. www.Rhizomes.net.

Paglia, Camille. *Interview* Nov. 2002.

_____. *Sexual Personae: Art and Decadence from Nefertiti to Emily Dickinson.* New York: Vintage Books, 1990.

Phillips, Mark, and Frank Garcia. *Science Fiction Television Series: Episode Guides, Histories and Casts and Credits for 62 Prime-Time Shows, 1959 through 1989.* Jefferson, NC: McFarland, 1996.

Pilato, Herbie. *"Bewitched" Forever.* Irving, TX: Summit Publishing Group, 1996.

Powers, Ron. *The Beast, the Eunuch, and the Glass-Eyed Child: Television in the '80s and Beyond.* New York: Anchor/Doubleday, 1990.

"Primetime Pioneer." *People* 3 Nov. 1997.

Purcelli, Marion. "The Gals Take Over." *Chicago Sun-Times* 7–13 April 1962.

_____. "Yvonne Craig: Tv's Bat Girl [sic]." *TV Guide* Nov. 25–Dec. 1, 1967.

Queenan, Joe. "Boobs on the Tube: How sitcom dads make all men look bad." *Men's Health* Sept. 2003.

Ralphedwards.net, www.Ralphedwards.net

A Really Big Show: A Visual History of "The Ed Sullivan Show." New York: Viking, 1992.

Reed, J.D. "Diamond in the Rough." *People* 19 Feb. 1996.

Reed, Jennifer. "Beleaguered Husbands and Demanding Wives: The New Domestic Sitcom." Americanpopularculture.com. Oct. 2003. www.Americanpopularculture.com

Reiss, David S. *"M*A*S*H": The Exclusive Inside Story of TV's Most Popular Show."* Indianapolis: Bobbs-Merrill, 1980.

Reynolds, Debbie. *Debbie: My Life.* New York: Simon & Schuster, 1988.

Ritchie, Michael. *Please Stand By: A Prehistory of Television.* Woodstock, NY: Overlook Press, 1994.

Robinson, Marc. *Brought to You in Living Color: 75 Years of Great Moments in Television & Radio from NBC.* New York: Wiley, 2002.

Rogers, Dave. *The Complete Avengers.* New York: St. Martin's Press, 1989.

_____. *The ITV Encyclopedia of Adventure.* London: Boxtree, 1988.

Sackett, Susan. *Prime-Time Hits: Television's Most Popular Network Programs.* New York: Billboard, 1993.

Sanders, Marlene, and Marcia Rock. *Waiting for Primetime.* Chicago: University of Chicago Press, 1988.

Sarno, Joe. "Inside Tom Corbett, Space Cadet!" *Space Academy Newsletter #7* July–Dec. 1979. www.slicknet.com/space/corbett

"Saturday Viewing." *Radio-TV Mirror* Aug. 1951.

Savage, Candice. *Cowgirls.* Berkeley: Ten Speed Press, 1996.

Schreiber, Lee R. "TV's Fifty Greatest Characters Ever!" *TV Guide* 16 Oct. 1999.

Schwarzbaum, Lisa. "The Sketch Artist." *Entertainment Weekly* 15 June 2001.

_____. "We're Gonna Make It After All." *Working Woman* Oct. 1995.

Sciabarra, Chris Matthew. "The Dialectical Meaning of 'Charlie's Angels.'" *Daily Objectivist* 7 Nov. 1999. www.dailyobjectivist.com

Scifi.about.com, www.scifi.about.com

Settel, Irving. *A Pictorial History of Television.* New York: F. Ungar, 1983.

Shales, Tom. "Comedy with Class." *Washington Post* 19 Mar. 1984.

Smith, Ronald. *Sweethearts of '60s TV.* New York: SPI Books, 1993.

Smith-Shomade, Beretta E. *Shaded Lives: African-American Women and Television.* New Brunswick, NJ: Rutgers, 2002.

Soloman, Michael. "The 50 Greatest Game Shows of All Time." *TV Guide* 27 Jan. 2001.

Solow, Herbert F. *Inside "Star Trek": The Real Story.* New York: Pocket, 1996.

Sommers, Christina Hoff. *Who Stole Feminism?* New York: Touchstone, 1994.

Space1999.org, www.space1999.org

Spangler, Lynn. *Television Women from Lucy to Friends: Fifty Years of Sitcoms and Feminism.* Westport, CT: Praeger, 2004.

Spiegel, Lynn. *Make Room for TV.* Chicago: University of Chicago Press, 1992.

Stamberg, Susan. "Manipulation 101." *Electronic Media* 1 Oct. 2001.

Stark, John. "Screen: Feisty, Funny Ann Sothern Rides in From Her Snowy Mountain Home to Score a 'Whale' of a Film Comeback." *People* 29 Feb. 1988.

Stark, Steven D. *Glued to the Set.* New York: Free Press, 1997.

Steenland, Sally. "Where women stand in television entertainment today." *AFTRA Magazine* Vol. 18, No. 1, Winter 1985.

Stein, Dave. "Spotlight on 'Petticoat Junction.'" Mortystv.com. Nov. 1998. www.mortystv.com

Stempel, Tom. *Storytellers to the Nation: A History of American Television Writing.* Syracuse: Syracuse University Press, 1996.

Stern, Jane, and Michael. *The Encyclopedia of Bad Taste.* New York: HarperCollins, 1990.

Storm, Gale, with Bill Libby. *I Ain't Down Yet.* Indianapolis: Bobbs-Merrill, 1981.

Taylor, Edward Durham. *The Great TV Book: 21 Years of LWT.* London: Sidgwick & Jackson, 1989.

Taylor, Ella. *Prime-Time Families: Television Culture in Postwar America.* Berkeley: University of California Press, 1989.

Terrace, Vincent. *Sitcom Factfinder, 1948–1984: Over 9,700 Details from 168 Television Shows.* Jefferson, NC: McFarland, 2002.

_____. *Television Specials: 3,201 Entertainment Spectaculars, 1939–1993.* Jefferson, NC: McFarland, 1995.

Thrillingdetective.com, www.thrillingdetective.com

Tibballs, Geoff. *The Boxtree Encyclopedia of TV Detectives.* London: Boxtree, 1992.

Timberg, Bernard. *Television Talk: A History of the TV Talk Show.* Austin: University of Texas Press, 2002.

Timstv.com, www.timstv.com

Tomashoff, Craig. "Tribute: Isabel Sanford, 1917–2004." *TV Guide* 1 Aug. 2004.

"Tribute: The Television Generation Mourns Its Favorite Surrogate Mother, Tough But Tender Donna Reed." *People* 3 Aug. 1992.

Turow, Joseph. *Playing Doctor.* New York: Oxford, 1989.

TV1.com, www.TV1.com

"TV's Super Women." *Time* 2 Nov. 1976.

U.S. Census, www.census.gov

U.S. Department of Labor, www.dol.gov

Ventura, Varla. *Sheroes.* Berkley: Conari, 1998.

Verdugo, Elena. Interview with author. 20 Feb. 2004.

Waits, Kathleen. "Battered Women and Their Children: Lessons from One Woman's Story." *Houston Law Review* 35, Rev. 29, 1998. www.omsys.com

Wander, Philip. "Was Anyone Afraid of Maude Finlay?" Adler, Richard P., ed. *Understanding Television.* New York: Praeger, 1981, p. 225.

Wasserman, John L. "Now they allow her a kiss or two." *TV Guide* July 26–Aug. 1, 1969, http://petticoat.topcities.com

Waters, Harry F., and Janet Huck. "Networking Women." *Newsweek* 13 Mar. 1989: 48–54.

Waters, John. "A career colored by Lucy." *Electronic Media* 1 Oct. 2001.

Watson, Mary Ann. *Defining Visions.* Fort Worth: Harcourt Brace, 1998.

_____. *The Expanding Vista.* Durham: Duke University Press.

_____. "From 'My Little Margie' to 'Murphy Brown': Women's Lives on the Small Screen." *Television Quarterly* Vol. XXVII, No. 2 1994.

Weissman, Ginny, and Coyne Steven Sanders. *The Dick Van Dyke Show.* New York: St. Martin's, 1983.

Werksman, Deborah, ed. *I Killed June Cleaver: Modern Moms Shatter the Myth of Perfect Parenting.* Bridgeport, CT: Hysteria Publications, 1999.

West, Richard. *Television Westerns: Major and Minor Series, 1946–1978.* Jefferson, NC: McFarland, 1987.

"Where Are They Now? Anne Francis." *Biography Magazine* Sept. 2002.

Whitburn, Joel. *The Billboard Book of Top 40 Hits.* New York: Billboard, 1996.

White, Betty. *Here We Go Again: My Life in Television.* New York: Scribner, 1995.

White, Patrick J. *The Complete* Mission: Impossible *Dossier.* New York: Avon Books, 1991.

Whitfield, Stephen E., with Gene Roddenberry. *The Making of* Star Trek. New York: Ballantine, 1968.

Wynn, Ron. "Blacks in Cinema excelled despite race resistance." *City Paper* (Nashville) 22 Dec. 2004. www.nashvillecitypaper.com

Index

Numbers in **bold italics** indicate pages with photographs.

The A-Team 141, 204
Abatemarco, Frank 150
Abbott and Costello 163
ABC 18, 93, 111, 117, 122, 135, 138, 143, 187
ABC Stage '67 17
Abernethy, Michael 37
abortion 59
Absolutely Fabulous 7, 77, 87, 184
Academy Awards 35, 45, 55, 107, 109, 131
Ackerman, Bettye 126
Adam-12 147
Adams, Don 151
Adams, Edie 19, 56
Adams, Maud 127
Adam's Rib 134, 174
Adam's Rib (film) 8
The Addams Family 54–56
The Adventures of Fu Manchu 200
The Adventures of Ozzie and Harriet 4–5, 20, 23, 29–**31**, 32, 37, 86, 94, 128–129, 159, 165
The Adventures of Superman 14, 86, 94, 128–129, 176, 205
The Adventures of Tugboat Annie 160
advertising 21, 26, 85, 181
The Affairs of China Smith 200
African Americans 61–64, 67–69, 70, 105–108, 113–115, 121–122, 138, 157, 195, 202
ageism 56, 79, 116–117
AIDS 14
Airplane! 39
Alberg, Mildred Freed 20
Albert, Eddie 45
Albertson, Mabel 164
Alexander, Jane 14
Alfred Hitchcock Presents 20
Alias 147, 186
Alias Smith and Jones 20
Alice 8, 115–116
Alice Doesn't Live Here Anymore 115
Alice in Wonderland 8
All About Eve 8
All in the Family 57–59, 63, 89, 114, 159–160, 169, 171–172, 205
All Is Forgiven 21
All the King's Men 131
Allen, Debbie 102
Allen, Gracie 6–7, 46, 68–69, 80
Allen, Vera 47

Allen, Woody 15
Allison, Fran 20
All's Fair 132
Ally McBeal 3, 7, 101, 114, 162, 175
Allyson, June 13
Amanda's 157
The American Girls 132
American Masters 75
American Medical Association 36
American Society of Medical Assistants 122
AmericanPopularCulture.com 37
Amini, Ali 135
Amish 90
Amos, John 63
Amos 'n' Andy 32, 69, 70, 108
Amy Prentiss 134, 140, 175
Anderson, Barbara 143
Anderson, Gerry 196
Anderson, Judith 15, 17
Anderson, Loni 106
Anderson, Marian 17
Andrews, Bart 77
Andrews, Julie 17, 111
The Andy Griffith Show 45, 54, 101, 160
Andy Hardy (films) 25
Angie 157
Anholt, Tony 152
The Ann Jillian Story 14
Ann-Margret 14, 17
The Ann Sothern Show 160
Anna and the King 101–102
Annie Get Your Gun 15, 17
Annie Oakley 177–**178**, 180, 182–183, 203, 205
Another Mother for Peace 35
Another World 21
anthologies 13–14, 19, 155
Anthony Adverse 28
Anton, Susan 132
Anything But Love 132
Applebaum, Irwyn 34
Archer, Beverly 160
Arden, Eve 45, 47, 99–101, 114, 162, 175
Are You Smarter Than a Fifth Grader? 13
Armen, Margaret 20
Armstrong, Bess 157, 160, 169
Armstrong Circle Theatre 20
Arnaz, Desi 19, 44, 47, 75–76, 166

Arnaz, Lucie 76, 132
Arnold, Judy 18
Arthur, Beatrice **58**, 113, 157
Arthur, Jean 133
As the World Turns 21
Asher, William 91
Asherman, Alan 194
Asian-Americans 143
Asner, Ed 131
The Associates 135
Astin, John 55
Atkins, Eileen 112
Auntie Mame 8
Austin, Steve 191
Australian Association for Research in Education 99
Author Meets the Critics 20
Autobiography of Miss Jane Pittman 14, 106
Autry, Gene 179
Avedon, Barbara 20, 35
The Avengers 142, 152, 172, 176, 182–185, 202, 205

Babbin, Jacqueline 20
Babe 14
Baby boom 23
Baby Boom 4
Bacall, Lauren 14
The Bachelor 5, 100
Bachelor Father 3, 38, 20, 162
Backlash (book) 3–5, 61, 98–99
backlash myth 8, 66, 68, 142, 157, 175
Backus, Jim 82, 132
Badler, Jane 202
Baer, John 200
Bain, Barbara 184, 196, **197**
Baldwin, Alec 175
Ball, Lucille 7, 14, 19–20, 42, 44, 73, **75**–80, 83, 85, 102, 115
Bankhead, Tallulah 14, 200
Bara, Nina 192, 201
The Barbara Stanwyck Show 155
Barber, Glynis 142
Barbie 181–182
Baretta 138, 143
Bari, Lynn 152
Barnaby Jones 151
Barnard College 33
Barnes, Priscilla 132
Barney Miller 119

Barnow, Erik 54
Barnum, P.T. 168
Barrett, Majel 193–194
Barrie, Wendy 11
Barry, Gene 100
Barrymore, Ethel 15
Barrymore, John 110
Bartlett, Juanita 20
Batman 170, 176–177, 185–188, 200–202, 205
Batman Returns 202
Bavier, Frances 45
Baxter, Anne 157
Baxter, Meredith 102
Beacham, Stephanie 157, 159
Beat the Clock 20
The Beatles 26
Beauty and the Beast 205
Beavers, Louise 108
Bel Geddes, Barbara 72, 157
The Bell Telephone Hour 17
Ben Casey 20, 126
Benaderet, Bea 126, 155
Bendix, William 38
Beniot, Patricia 117
Benjamin, Richard 162
Benny, Jack 7
Berg, Gertrude 19, 27, 29
Bergman, Ingrid *13*, 14
Berringer's 157
Bertinelli, Valerie 60
Bessell, Ted 166
Bethune, Zina 119–120
The Betty White Show 160
Betz, Carl 35–36
Beulah 107–108, 114
The Beverly Hillbillies 45, 53–54, 95, 104–105, 155, 170, 205
Bewitched 8, 20, 37, 88–*89*, 90–96, 128, 159, 205
Bewitched *Forever* 91
The Bickersons 15, 55
Biff Baker, USA 144–145
Big Town 127
The Big Valley 8, *155*–156, 205
Billingsley, Barbara *3*, 25, 33, 39
The Bionic Woman 4, 8, 176, 190–191, 205
Bishop, Joan 13
Blackman, Honor 182
Blackmore, Brenda 20
Blake, Amanda 153
Blake, Whitney 59–60, 160
blended families 61, 65, 78–79, 112
Blind Date 12
Bloodworth-Thomason, Linda 19
Bloom, Claire 14
Bloomingdale's 27
Bluebeard 91
Bly, Nellie 127
Bly, Robert 171
The Bob Cummings Show 9, 104
The Bob Newhart Show 37, 71–72, 102, 106, 205
Bobbin, Jacqueline 20
Bochco, Steven 134, 141
Bombeck, Erma 66–67
Bonanza 20
Bones 185, 197

Bonino 115
Bono, Sonny 15
Bonsignori, Mili 21
Boone, Pat 49
Booth, Shirley *109*–110
Born Free 160
Bosley, Tom 159
Bosom Buddies 157
Boss Lady 152
Boyle, Peter 37
Bracken's World 107
The Brady Bunch 6, 24–25, 65–66, 71, 104, 112, 124, 148
Brandon, Michael 142
Breakfast at Tiffany's (book) 8
Brenda Starr 132, 176
Brennan, Eileen 160
Brent, George 131
The Brian Keith Show 127
Bridge Loves Bernie 102
Bridges, Lloyd 148
Bridges to Cross 132
Britton, Barbara *144*
Broadside 160
Broadway *see* theater and plays
Brolin, James 122
Bronco 148
Brooklyn Bridge 28
Brooks, Mel 15
Brooks, Tim 33, 152
Brosnan, Pierce 204
Brothers, Joyce 12
Brotman, Joyce 149
Brown, Ben 148
Brown, Charlotte 20
Brown, Vanessa 13
Bryn Mawr 163
Buch, Frances Buss 20
Buck Rogers in the 25th Century 198–199
Buddism 56
Buffalo Bill 160
The Buffy Vampire Slayer 3, 176
Burke, Lynn 18
Burke, Mildred 19
Burke's Law 180
Burnett, Carol 14–15, 17, 76
Burns, George 68
Burns and Allen 7, 68–69
Burr, Ann 126
Burr, Raymond 104
Burstyn, Ellen 160
Byington, Spring 70–71
Byline 127
Byron, Jean 101

Cabaret 8
Caesar, Sid 15
Caesar's Hour 20
Cagle, Jess 89
Cagney & Lacey 8, 35, 77, 119, 135–136, 141, 146–149
Callas, Maria 15
Calvinism 54
Camacho, Corinne 127
Cameo Theatre 20
Cameron, Kirk 148
Cannell, Stephen J. 141
Capote, Truman 17

Captain Video and His Video Ranger 20
The Cara Williams Show 107
careers, traditional for women 23, 79, 98, 184–185, 188, 190–191
Carlisle, Kitty 12
Carney, Art 40–41
The Carol Burnett Show 15, 56
Caroline in the City 162, 172
Carrey, Jim 62
Carroll, Diahann 14, 121, 157
Carroll, Francine 140
Carroll, Jean 17
Carson, Jeannie 169
Carter, Jimmy 61
Carter, Lynda 18, 151, *177*, 189
Carter, Nell 114–115
A Case of Rape 14
Cass, Peggy 12
Cassidy, David 49
Cassidy, Joanna 143, 152, 160
Cassidy, Shaun 150
Castro, Fidel 18
CBS 11, 17, 22, 126–127, 132, 172
CBS Playhouse 20
The CBS Television Quiz 20
Champlin, Irene 193
The Changing Image of the Nurse 118
Channing, Stockard 132
Chantler, Peggy 20
Charlie's Angels 115, 123, 146–149, 183, 189, 205
Charlie's Angels *Casebook* 148
Chase, Ilka 11
Chastain, Don 84
Chatterton, Ruth 14, 17
Cheers 100, 105, 169
Cheever, John 25
Chenoweth, Kristin 175
Cher 15
Cher (show) 15
Chicago Story 127
Chicago Sun-Times 106
Child, Julia 21
child support 60, 77
Children's Television Workshop 21
CHiPs 148
Christie, Agatha 150
Christie, Julie 14
City Hospital 126
civil rights 122
Civil War 71
Clark, Dane 131
Clark, Susan 14, 67–68
Clayton, Jan 47, 51
Clemens, Brian 182–183
Cliff Hangers 132
Clinger, Debra 132
Clooney, Rosemary 15
clothing 25, 43, 46, 55, 60, 117, 134, 154, 177, 180–183, 189, 194, 199, 202, 204
Coates, Phyllis 128
Coca, Imogene 15, 110
Codename: Foxfire 152
Colbert, Claudette 14
The Colbys 157
Cold War 26, 92, 110, 185
Colin, Margaret 150

Collins, Ace 51
Collins, Joan 8, 154, 157, 200
Collyer, June 38
Columbia University 135
Columbo 67
Comic Visions 90
Commenici, Nadia 18
commercials *see* advertising
The Complete Directory to Prime Time TV Shows 121
The Complete Mission: Impossible *Dossier* 185
Conners, Chuck 154
Conway, Shirl 119–120
Cooney, Joan Ganz 21
Cooper, Jackie 119
Corbett, Gretchen 135
Cornell, Katharine 14
Correll, Charles 69
Corsaut, Aneta 101
Cosby, Bill 17
The Cosby Show 66
Coville, Gary 193
Cowgirls 178
Cox, Vivian 20
Cox, Wally 19, 117
Craig, Yvonne 187–188
Crane, Norma 101
Crawford, Cindy 181
Crawford, Joan 14
Crenna, Richard 99, 135
Crisis at Central High 14
Crosby, Denise 195–196
Crowley, Pat 64, 147, 160
CSI 185
Cue (magazine) 12
Cummings, Bob 96, 104, 163
Curtis, Jamie Lee 132
Cuthbert, David 104
Cutter to Houston 127
Cynthia Lindsay 20

Dabney, Dick 37
D'Acci, Julie 181–182
Dadaism 151
Dadda Is Death 14
Dagmar 148
Dalí, Salvador 9, 46
Dallas 72, 157
Dalton, Abby 119
Dancing with the Stars 66
Danner, Blythe 134
The Danny Thomas Show see Make *Room for Daddy*
Danson, Ted 169
Danza, Tony 169
Darcel, Denise 12
A Date with Judy 20
A Date with the Angels 19
Dateline: Europe see Foreign Intrigue
Dates, Jannette 64, 108, 114
Dave's World 148
Davis, Ann B. 104, 112
Davis, Bette 14, 157
Davis, Gail *178*, 179
Davis, Geena 175
Davis, Joan 19, 82–83
Davis, Madeline 9, 20
Davis, Sammy, Jr. 94

Day, Doris 52, 121, 169, 170
Days of Our Lives 21
deadbeat dads *see* child support
Deal or No Deal 11
Dean, James 85
Deane, Pamela S. 70
Dear Detective 134, 140–141, 175
Dear John 100
Dear Phoebe 129, 131
Death of a Salesman 39
Death Valley Days 20
The Debbie Reynolds Show 84–85
DeCarlo, Yvonne 43–44
December Bride 54, 70–71, 205
Decoy 135–*136*, 137–138, 161, 205
The Defenders 20
The Defiant Ones 148
Delaney, Pat 53
Dell, Myrna 200
Demographic Vistas 54
demographics 134, 171, 181
Dempsey and Makepeace 142
Denning, Richard **144**
The Dennis O'Keefe Show 109
Dennis the Menace 20, 60
Denoff, Sam 166
Designing Women 6, 8, 19
Desilu Productions 47, 132, 164
Desjardins, Mary 29
Desperate Housewives 5
Dey, Susan 49, 135
Dharma & Greg 89, 96
The Diahann Carroll Show 15
Diamond, Selma 20
Diana (show) 60, **172**–173
Diana! (special) 17
Diaz, Cameron 149
The Dick Van Dyke Show 4, 7, 42–43, 100, 160, 167
Dickerson, Nancy 18
Dickinson, Angie 138–139
Didrickson, Babe 14, 67
Dietrich, Marlene 17
Diller, Phyllis 17
Ding Dong School 21
Dinsdale, Shirley 21
Dior, Christian 45
displaced homemakers 60
divorce 39, 47, 49, 58, 60, 72, 77, 122–124, 140, 172, 174
The Dobie Gillis Show see *The Many Loves of Dobie Gillis*
Doc 125
Dr. Hudson's Secret Journal 118–119
Dr. Kildare 120
Dr. Quinn, Medicine Woman 127
Doctor's Hospital 127
The Doctors and the Nurses 120
domestic violence 40, 44
Don Quixote 152
Donahue, Elinor 32, 160
The Donna Reed Show 4–8, 11, 20–21, 24–30, 35–37, 43–44, 65
The Doris Day Show 4, 20, 52, 169–171, 175, 205
Douglas, Susan J. 4, 55, 61, 147, 158, 191
Dragnet 119, 135–137, 147, 205
Drake, Christian 180

Drescher, Fran 115
Dressed to Kill 139
Druce, Olga 20
Dryer, Fred 141
DuBois, Ja'net 63
Duff, Howard 44, 45
Duke, Patty 135, 160
The Dukes of Hazard 148, 204
Dumont 19
Dunaway, Faye 14
Duncan, Sandy 171–172
Duncan, Wanda 20
Dunne, Steve 39
The DuPont Show of the Month 14, 20
Duryea, Dan 200
Dynasty 8, 154, 157

Earhart, Amelia 14, 67
An Early Frost 14
East Side/West Side 105–106
Eastwood, Clint 143
Eaton, Evelyn 14
The Ed Sullivan Show 15–17
Eden, Barbara **93**
Edwards, Anthony 135
Edwards, Joan 15
Edwards, Ralph 22
Edwards, Vince 126
Eggar, Samantha 101
Eleanor & Franklin 14
Electronic Media (magazine) 73
Elizabeth the Queen (play) 15
The Ellen Burstyn Show 160
Elvira 55
Ely, Melvin Patrick 70
Ely, Ron 148, 179
Emergency! 125
Emerson, Faye 11–*12*, 21, 26, 56, 117, 148
Emerson, Hope 109
Emmy Awards 21, 33, 52, 64, 67, 101, 108, 140, 156, 191
Empty Nest 125
The Encyclopedia of Television 5
English, Diane 19
Entertainment Weekly (magazine) 15, 89, 138
Equal Right Amendment (ERA) 58, 116, 124
E/R 125
Erickson, Hal 179
Ericson, John 181
Erwin, Stu 38
Ethel and Albert 19
Evans, Dale 152–153
Eve 175
The Eve Arden Show 45, 47
An Evening with Julie Andrews and Harry Belafonte 17
Everybody Loves Raymond 37, 39, 162
Evita Peron 14
The Exorcist 131

F Troop 20, 47, 157
Fabares, Shelley 35, 127, 157
Fabio 205
Fabray, Nanette 60
The Facts of Life 4, 157
Faithfull, Marianne 16

Falcon Crest 117, 119, 157
Faludi, Susan 3–5, 61, 98–99
Fame 102
Fame (film) 102
Family 72
Family Affair 38, 108
The Family Holvak 53
Family Matters 15
Family Ties 48
family values 53
Fantastic Television 189–190
The Farmer's Daughter 110–111
Farnsworth, Elma "Pem" 21
Farnsworth, Philo T. 21
Farrell, Charles **80**–81
The Father Dowling Mysteries 159
Father Knows Best 4, 6, 10, 20, 24–
    26, 28–30, 32–33, 36–37, 39,
    43, 76, 89, 122, 205
fathers 30, 33, 37–39, 121, 162
Faust 182
Fawcett, Farrah 147, 148
Fay 174
The Feather and Father Gang 135
Federal Communications Commis-
    sion (FCC) 21
Feldon, Barbara 12, 151
Felton, Norman 186
Felton, Verna 71
The Feminine Mystique 88, 174
feminism 3, 5, 28, 42, 49, 58–60,
    62, 74–75, 87–88, 122, 130, 134,
    146, 149, 166–167,
    170–171, 174–175, 180, 201, 204, 205
Ferrell, Conchata 115, 125
Fey, Tina 175
Fibber McGee and Molly (radio show)
    107
Fickling, G.G. 176, 180
Fidelman, Geoffrey Mark 79
Field, Sally 14, 158
Fies, Elisabeth 202
film 6, 8, 26, 44, 102, 110, 123, 134,
    144, 148–149, 155, 176
First Amendment 49
Fisher, Gail 151
Fitzgerald, Ella 15
Flash Gordon 192–193
Flippen, Ruth Brooks 20
Flipper 148, 160
Flo 157
Flockhart, Calista 3
The Flying Nun 158–159, 205
Flynn, Miriam 66–67
Foley, Ellen 135
Follies 44
Fontana, D.C. *see* Fontana, Dorothy
Fontana, Dorothy 20
Fonteyn, Margot 15
Ford, Betty 22
Ford, Glenn 53
*The Ford Lucille Ball-Desi Arnaz
    Show* 76
Foreign Intrigue/Dateline: Europe
    127
Foster, Jodie 121
Four Freedoms Awards 22
Four Star Jubilee 14
FOX 15

Francis, Anne **180**, 182
Francis, Arlene 11–12, 20–22
Francis, Connie 16
Frank, Sam 100
Franklin, Aretha 16
Franklin, Bonnie 60
Frannie's Turn 28
Frederick, Pauline 18, 127
Freeman, Cathy 177
French, Peggy 163
The French Chef 21
Freudianism 56, 92
Friedan, Betty 24, 88, 174
Friendly Fire 14
From Here to Eternity (film) 35
The Front Page 131
Full House 3, 38, 162
Funny Face 171–172
Furness, Betty 21, 127

Gabor, Eva 46
The Gale Storm Show 4, 160, 162
The Gallery of Madame Liu-Tsong
    143
Gamble on Love 12
game shows 11–12
Gardner, Ava 157
Garland, Beverly 72, 135–137, **136**
Garland, Judy 15
Garner, James 135
Garner, Joe 114
Garner, Peggy Ann 163
Garrett, Jimmy **78**
Garson, Greer 17, 26
Gautier, Dick 188
gay families 61
Gaynor, Gloria 16
Gaynor, Mitzi 18
GE Theater 14
gender switch episodes 24
*The George Burns and Gracie Allen
    Show* 68–69
Gerber, David 39
Get Christie Love! 138, 140, 205
Get Smart 12, 151–152, 205
Ghost and Mrs. Muir 48, 95, 121,
    160, 205
GI bill 23
Gibbs, Marla 70, 114
Gibson, Virginia 163
Gidget 20
Gilbert, Melissa 53
Gilbert Toys 181
Gilligan's Island 6, 20, 56, 74, 82,
    132, 144, 193, 205
Gilmore Girls 141
Gimme a Break 114–115
The Girl from UNCLE 6, 176, 185–
    187, 205
The Girls 163
Girls Clubs of America 27
Girls Gone Wild 5
Gleason, Jackie 20, 38, **40**–41
Gleason, Joanna 132
Glee 102, 163
Glut, Donald F. 128–129
Glynis 145–146
The Goldbergs 19, 26–29, 35, 205
The Golden Girls 54, 70, 83, 157, 167

Goldfinger 182
Gomer Pyle, USMC 7, 205
Gone with the Wind 26
Good Times 61–63, 205
Gordon, Dorothy 11
Gordon, Gale 87, 99
Gordon, Glen 200
Gordon, Ruth 17
Gore, Lesley 16
Gorgeous George 19
Gosden, Freeman 69
Gossett, Lou 125
Grace Under Fire 4, 47
Graham, Katherine 156
Graham, Virginia 11
Grandma Moses 22
Grant, Fay 174
The Grapes of Wrath (book) 70
Grassle, Karen 53
Graves, Peter 111
Graves, Teresa 138
Gray, Erin 106–107, 199
Great Depression 52–53
The Great TV Sitcom Book 104
Green, Mitzi 163
Green Acres 37, 45–46, 49, 55, 87,
    95, 160, 170
The Green Hornet 185
Greene, Lynnie 157
Greene, Marge 19
Grey's Anatomy 125
Grier, Pam 138
Griffin, Merv 17
Griffith, Andy 160
Grindl 110
Grindl (literature) 110
Grossman, Gary 129
Growing Pains 39, 148
Guiding Light 21
Gunsmoke 6, 153–154, 178, 205

Hack, Shelley 127, 147
Hagen, Jean 38–39
Hagman, Larry 93, 95
Hail to the Chief 160
Haines, Lloyd 101
Hale, Alan 144
Hale, Barbara 104
Hall, Tom T. 87
Hallmark Hall of Fame 17, 20
Halop, Florence 167
Hamel, Veronica 134
Hamill, Dorothy 18, 184
Hamilton, Linda 205
Hamlet 31
Hamner, Earl 53
Hampton, James 52, 66
Hanks, Tom 157
Happy Days 85, 204–205
Hardin, Ty 148
The Hardy Boys/Nancy Drew Mysteries
    149–150, 205
Harmon, Jim 128–129
Harper, Valerie **173**
Harper Valley PTA 87
Harper Valley PTA (song) 87
Harriet, Nelson 159
Harrington, Pat, Jr. 61
Harris, Julie 17, 53

Harris, Rosemary 17
Harris, Warren G. 77
Harrison, Joan 20, 118
Harrison, Noel 186
Harrison, Rex 186
Harry and Lena 17
Harry's Law 132
Hart, Ralph **78**
Hart to Hart 135, 144, 186
Hartley, Mariette 17, 132
Hartman, Phil 125
Harvard Medical School 127
Having Babies 126
Having Babies II 126
Havoc, June 132–133
Hayes, Helen 14, 17, 146
Hays, Kathryn 127, 194
Hayworth, Rita 56
Hazel 20, 59, 107–**109**, 110, 113, 205
He & She 162
Heartbeat 127
Hedda Gabler 139
Hello, Larry 132
Hemphill, Shirley 157
Hemsley, Sherman 63–64
Henderson, Florence 17, 66
Henderson, Marcia 129, 163
Hendry, Ian 182
Henner, Marilu 160
Hennesey 119
Henning, Paul 45
Hennock, Frieda 21
Hensley, Pamela 143
Hepburn, Katharine 8, 187
Here's Edie 15, 19
Here's Lucy 78, 79
Hervey, Irene 181
Hewitt, Virginia 192
Hey, Jeannie 169
Heyn, Dalma 37
Hickson, Joan 150
Higgins, Joel 106
High Chaparral 20
High School of the Performing Arts 102
Hill, Steven 185
Hill Street Blues 119, 124, 134
Hiller, Wendy 17
Hilton, Paris 46
hippies 54, 92, 96, 171
Hispanic Americans *see* Latin Americans
Holland, Steve 193
Hollander, Jean 20
Holliday, Polly 116
Holliman, Earl 139
Holm, Celeste 132, 160
Home Improvement 3, 30, 39
The Home Show 20–21
homosexuality 61, 105, 126
Honestly, Celeste 132
Honey West 8, 176, 180–**181**, 182–183, 186, 203, 205
The Honeymooners 4–5, 22, 29–30, 32, 37–**40**, 41–42, 58, 62, 64, 83, 89, 106
Hope, Bob 7
Hopkins, Telma 15, 114–115
Horne, Lena 15, 17

Horwich, Frances 21
Horwitz, Howie 187
Hotel 157
Hour Glass 14
House Calls 160
Houseman, John 191
How to Marry a Millionaire (film) 8
Howard, Anne Bailey 20
Howard, Ken 134
Howard, Lisa 18
Howdy Doody 21
Howland, Beth 116
Hunt, Gareth 184
Hunt, Helen 53, 135, 140
Hunter 141–142
Hunter, Ann 18
Hunter, Holly 14
Hunter, Kim 14
husband hunter myth 7, 81, 98, 100, 102, 129–130, 179, 187, 205
Hutchinson, Anne 17
Hutton, Ina Ray 15

I Am a Camera 8
I Dream of Jeannie 8, 87–88, **93**–96
I Killed June Cleaver 30
I Love Lucy 4–9, 11, 19, 20, 22–24, 39–40, 42, 44, 47, 58, 65, 73–**75**, 76, 79, 82, 84–87, 91, 108, 158, 163, 166
I Married Dora 115
I Married Joan 19, 40, 83
I Remember Mama 28
I Spy 185
idealism 25, 37, 33
I'm a Big Girl Now 157
In the Beginning 159
The Ina Ray Hutton Show 15
The Incredible Hulk 94, 127
Inherit the Wind 172
Inside Star Trek: *The Real Story* 193–194
The Interns 127
The Invisible Man 20
Ironside 20, 140–143
Irwin, Carol 19
It Takes Two 135
It's a Living 117
It's a Wonderful Life 35
It's Always Jan 47–48

The Jack Benny Program 39
The Jack Paar Show 17, 66
Jackson, Gail Patrick 20
Jackson, Janet 63
Jackson, Kate 122–123, 147, 148
Jackson, Mahalia 15
Jackson, Wanda 16
James Bond (character) 182, 184–185, 191, 204
Jamieson, Mai 195
Janet Dean, Registered Nurse 205
Jarvis, Lucy 20
Javna, John 75
The Jean Arthur Show 133
The Jeffersons 63–64, 114
Jeffreys, Anne 44, 154
Jenkins, Carol Mayo 102
Jenkins, Phyllis Adam 20

Jenner, Bruce 37
Jeopardy! 56
The Jerry Springer Show 89
Jessica Novak 132
"Jiggle" TV 146, 148–149, 158
Jillian, Ann 14, 117
The Jim Backus Show 132
Joan of Arc 17, 87, 187
The Johnny Cash Show 16
Johns, Glynis 145
Johnson, Brad 179
Johnson, Robin 152
Johnsons, Janet Louise 150
Jolie, Angelina 55
Jones, Carolyn 55, 202
Jones, Shirley 49
Joplin, Janis 15
Joyner, Florence Griffith **177**
Judge Judy 3, 135
Julia 8, 61, 121–122, 205
Julie and Carol at Carnegie Hall 17
Julie Farr, MD 126–127
Justman, Robert H. 194

Kahn, Madeline 84
Kalisch, Beatrice J. 118–119, 122, 124
Kalisch, Philip A. 118–119, 122, 124
Kalish, Irma 20
Kallen, Lucille 20
Kane, Kate 176
Kanter, Hal 121
Karen 175
Karloff, Boris 186
Karras, Alex 67
Kassel, Michael B. 32
Kate and Allie 72, 77
Kate Loves a Mystery 151
Kate McShane 134
The Kate Smith Show 15
Kavner, Julie 173
Keenan, Staci 135
Keeping Up with the Kardashians 37
Kellems, Vivien 11
Kelly, Grace 102
Kelly, Paula 135
Kelly, Roz 204
Kelsey, Linda 131–132
Kennedy, Jacqueline 22, 43
Kennedy, Jean 20
Kennedy, John F. 43
Kennedy, Yvonne Files 22
Kent, Mona 20
Khrushchev, Nikita 18
Kilgallen, Dorothy 12
King, Billie Jean 18
King, Mabel 72
King, Martin Luther, Jr. 195
King, Torey L. 156
The King and I 101
King Henry VIII 91
Kirk, Phyllis 145
Kitman, Marvin 123
Kitt, Eartha 14, 200, 202
Klein, Leotine 20
Knots Landing 157
Kojak 138
Kove, Martin 148
The Kraft Mystery Theatre 20
Kraft Television Theatre 20

Krakowski, Jane 175
Kramer, Stepfanie 141
Kreitzer, Catherine 13
The Kremlin 20
Kristin 175
Kuhn, William 90
Kukla, Fran and Ollie 20
Kulp, Nancy 104–105
Kurtz, Swoosie 160

LA Law 8, 107, 134–135, 196
LaBelle, Patti 17
Ladd, Cheryl 147
Ladies of the Evening 4
Lady Blue 142–143
LaGallienne, Eva 14, 17
Lamparski, Richard 180
Lampert, Zohra 127
Land of the Giants 20
Landau, Martin 187, 196, **197**
Landon, Michael 53
Lange, Hope 48, 121, 160
Lassie 20, 45, 47, 51–52
Laszlo, Marge 19
Latin Americans 76, 122, 158, 167
Laugh-In see *Rowan & Martin's Laugh-In*
Laurel and Hardy 76, 163
Laverne & Shirley 77, 85–**86**, 87, 163, 165
Lavin, Linda 116
Lawford, Peter 145, 171
Lawless, Lucy 182
Lawrence, Vicki 56
Leachman, Cloris 51, 70
Lear, Norman 6, 57, 59, 63, 87, 159
Learned, Michael 10, 52–53, 124
Leave It to Beaver **3**–8, 23, 25–26, 29–30, 33–36, 39, 61, 65, 101, 204
Leave It to Joanie 82
Lee, Joanna 20
Lee, Michele 157
Lee, Peggy 16
Leg Work 150–151
Leigh, Vivien 26
Leighton, Margaret 14
Leonard, Sheldon 166
Leslie, Elaine 20
The Leslie Uggams Show 15
Less Than Perfect 175
Levy, Ralph 126
Lewis, Emmanuel 67–68
Lewis, Judy 19
Liberty Belles 11
The Life & Times of Maxwell Smart 151
Life Goes On 33
The Life of Riley 30, 37–38
Life with Elizabeth 19–20, 83–84
Life with Lucy 87
Light, Judith 169
Lil' Abner 184
Lincoln, Abraham 34
Linville, Joanne 194
Lipton, Peggy 137
Liston, Sonny 44
literature 6, 8
The Little Foxes 59
Little House on the Prairie 20, 53

Little Women 8
Live Aid 17
Liza with a "Z" 17
Lockerman, Gloria 13
Lockhart, June 51, 126, 204
Loeb, Phillip 27
Loillobrigida, Gina 157
London, Julie 15, 125
The Lone Ranger 178
Long, Shelley 169
Lopez, Pricilla 159
Lord, Marjorie 39
The Loretta Young Show 19
Lorne, Marion 101
Los Angeles Times 147
Lost in Space 20, 191, 126, 204
Lou Grant 131–132, 156, 205
The Louvre 20
The Love Boat 131, 160
Love, Sidney 160
Love That Bob see *The Bob Cummings Show*
Love That Jill 154
Lovsky, Celia 194
Loy, Myrna 145
Lucanio, Patrick 193
Luce, Clare Booth 22
The Lucie Arnaz Show 132
Lucky Louie 36
The Lucy Book 79
The Lucy-Desi Comedy Hour 76
The Lucy Show 60, 72, 76–**78**, 79, 87, 122
Luez, Laurette 200
Lumley, Joanna 184
Lupino, Ida 20, 44–45
Lux Video Theatre 20
Lyman, Dorothy 57
Lynch, Peg 19

Mabley, "Moms" 17
MacDonald, J. Fred 153
MacKenzie, Gisele 15
MacLaine, Shirley 18, 131
MacLeod, Gavin 131
Macnee, Patrick 182–183
macro vs. micro analysis 5
Macy's 28
Mad About You 3
made-for-TV movies 14
Madigan, Amy 14
Madonna 17, 149
Maggie 66–67
Magnum, PI 146–147, 150, 205
Magnuson, Ann 132
Major Dad 160
Make Room for Daddy 38–39, 115
Makeba, Miriam 15
Making a Living 117
Malcolm in the Middle 37, 57
Malone, Dorothy 156
Mama 19, 28–**29**, 35, 44, 62
Mama Malone 28
Mama's Family 56–57
Mame 80
The Man from UNCLE 152, 181, 185–186, 205
"The Man Question" 7, 205

Mandrell, Barbara 15
Manimal 198
Mann-Winkler, Rhoda 21
Mannix 151
Mansfield, Sally 193
The Many Loves of Dobie Gillis 101
Maples, Joan 20
Marc, David 6, 25, 46, 76, 89, 90, 105
March, Hal 133
March, Peggy 16
Marchand, Nancy 156
Marcus Welby, MD 122
Marge and Jeff 19
Marie, Rose 7, 160
Marlo Thomas and Friends in Free to Be ... You and Me 17
Marmaduke, Virginia 22
Marquis de Sade 92–93
Married ... with Children 36, 67
Marsh, Earle 33, 152
Marsh, Jean 112
Marshall, Penny 85–**86**
Martin, Anne Marie 143
Martin, Dick 77
Martin, Mary 17
Martin, Pamela Sue 150
Mary Hartman, Mary Hartman 117
Mary Kay and Johnny 23
Mary Poppins 111
Mary Tyler Moore 4, 6, 8, 43, 58–59, 71, 83, 98, 103, 112, 115–116, 129, 131–132, 134, 141, 146, 150, 161–162, 166–168, 170–173, 175
MASH 123–124
MASH (film) 123
Masquerade Party 12
Masterpiece Theatre 112
Mata Hari 184
Matt Houston 147
Maude 8, 57–**58**, 59, 61, 107, 109, 113–114, 134
Maxim (magazine) 149
McBride, Mary Margaret 11
McCalla, Irish 179–180
McCallum, David 185–186
McCambridge, Mercedes 131, 153
McCarthy, Joe 33
McCarthy, Mary 125
McCloud 141, 160
McCormack, Patty 14
McCrohan, Donna 7, 23, 41, 151
McDaniel, Hattie 69, 107–108
McDonough, Mary 53
McFadden, Gates 195–196
McKee, Alan 150
McMillian and Wife 115
McNeil, Alex 109
McNellis, Maggie 11
McQuade, Arlene 27
McQueen, Butterfly 108
McWilliams, Michael 15, 33–34, 41, 44, 46, 59, 77, 100, 103, 105–106, 111, 113, 139, 155–157, 174, 199
Mead, Margaret 22
Meadows, Audrey **40**–42
Meara, Anne 17, 134
Medical Center 127

Meehan, Linda 4
Meet Millie 122, **167**–169
Meet the Press 21
Meir, Golda 22
Men's Health (magazine) 37
Mercer, Frances 118
Meriweather, Lee 151, 160
Merman, Ethel 15, 17
Meyers, Richard 146
MGM 102
Miami Vice 137
The Middle 67
Midler, Bette 18
Mike and Buff 20
Mildred Pierce 101
Milland, Ray 102
Miller, Ann 15
Miller, Will 30
Mills, Alley 135
Mills, Donna 157
Mills, Juliet 111
Mimieux, Yvette 157, 160
Minnelli, Liza 17
Mirren, Helen 3, 140
Miss America pageant 171, 189
Mission: Impossible 176, 184–186, 196, 200, 203, 205
Mr. Adams and Eve 44–45
Mr. and Mrs. North 20, **144**
Mr. Belvedere 108
Mr. Mom 3
Mr. Peepers 101, 117–118, 163, 181
Mr. T 135
Mitchell, George 136
Mitchell, Joni 16
Mitz, Rick 38, 70, 81, 87, 102, 104, 116
The Mod Squad 137–138
Modern Family 37
Mona McCluskey 160
Mondrian, Piet 49
The Monkees 20
Monroe, Marilyn 139, 148, 176
Montalban, Ricardo 194
Montgomery, Elizabeth 14, 88–**89**, 111
Moonlighting 131, 154
Moore, Candy **78**
Moore, Del 83
Moore, Mary Tyler 42–43, 167
Moorhead, Agnes 91
Morgan, Robin 19–20, 29
Morgan, Tracy 175
The Morning Program 132
Morse, Barry 196, 198
Morse, Hayward **13**
Mosner, Marianne 20
Most Deadly Game 160
Mother Teresa 179
The Mothers-In-Law 20, 47
Mrs. Columbo 151
Mrs. Miniver 26
Ms. (magazine) 29, 60, 179, 190
Muldaur, Diana 135, 160, 194, 196
Mulgrew, Kate 151
Mulligan, Richard 125
The Munsters 7, 37, 43–44, 54–55, 64, 205
Murder, She Wrote 145–146, 150

Murphy Brown 4, 6, 19, 59, 61, 71, 75, 82, 106, 132, 146, 171
music 15–17, 49
music shows 15
My Friend Irma 99
My Hero 104
My Little Margie **80**–82, 160, 205
My Living Doll 96, 191
My Mother the Car 56
My Sister Eileen 165, 175
My Sister Sam 4
My Three Sons 20, 61, 72
My Two Dads 4, 135
myths 3–5, 9, 11, 19, 24, 30, 161, 205

Nancy 160
The Nancy Walker Show 157
The Nanny 110, 115
Nanny and the Professor 20, 111–112
NASA 93–94
Nash, Joe 193
National Association for the Advancement of Colored People (NAACP) 108, 195
National Center for Education 98
National Coalition on Television Violence 143
National Commission on Working Woman 98
National Conference on Christian and Jews 27
National Education Association (NEA) 99
Natwick, Mildred 146
NBC 14, 17, 20, 85, 93, 132, 152, 162, 185, 198
Neill, Noel 128
Nelson, David 5
Nelson, Gene 95
Nelson, Harriet 5, 30–**31**, 32, 34
Nelson, Ozzie 5, 30–**31**, 32, 37, 159
Nelson, Ricky 5, 32
Nelson, Tracy 159
Nesbitt, Cathleen 111
The New Avengers 184
The New Loretta Young Show 160
New York Times 33, 49, 143
New York Times Youth Forums 11
The New Yorker 144
Newcomb, Horace 59, 74, 104
Newhart, Bob 71
Newmar, Julie 96, 184, 200–202
news, broadcast 18
News Gal see *Byline*
Newsweek 19
Nichols, Denise 101
Nichols, Nichelle 194–195
Nigh, Jane 127
Night Court 20, 135, 167
Nightingale, Florence 36
Nill, Dawn Michelle 85
Nilsson, Birgit 17
Nimoy, Leonard 195
Nine to Five 103, 107
Nixon, Richard 21
Nolan, Kathy 160
North, Sheree 157
Norton-Taylor, Judy 125
Not June Cleaver 30

nuclear families 23
Nurse 124, 126
Nurse Jackie 117
The Nurses 4, 8, 119–**120**, 124, 127
Nuyen, France 194

O'Brien, Margaret 17
occupations 79, 86, 196
O'Connor, Carroll 58
The Odd Couple 20
Odetta 15
An Officer and a Gentleman 125
Oh, Madeline 80, 84
O'Hara, Maureen 17
O'Keefe, Dennis 109
O'Keefe, Georgia 22
Olympics 14, 18, 20, 177
On Our Own 157, 175
One Day at a Time 8, 59–61, 116, 157, 205
One in a Million 157
One Upon a Mattress 17
The O'Neills 47
Open End 20
Oppenheimer, Jess 84
Orr, Mary 20
Osbourne, Sharon 57
The Osbournes 37, 57
Our Miss Brooks 4, 45, 47, 59, 98–**99**, 100–101, 103, 105, 107, 161–162, 205
Overall, Park 125
Overton, Frank 136
Owen, Tony 37

Paar, Jack 17
Paasonen, Susanna 191
Pack, Betty 184–185
Page, Bettie 56
Page, Geraldine 17
Page, Patti 15
Paglia, Camille 6
Paige, Janis 47, 147
The Pajama Game 48
Palmer, Betsy 12
Palmer, Lilli 17
Parents-Teacher Association (PTA) 24, 87
Paris, Jerry **164**
Parker, Eleanor 107
Parrish, Helen 14
Partners in Crime 151
Parton, Dolly 15
The Partridge Family 49, 61, 163
PBS 8, 75, 112, 150
Peace Corps 17
Pearl, Minnie 17
The Pearl Bailey Show 15
Pena, Elizabeth 115
Penton, Edward 93
People (magazine) 41
Perils of Pauline 176
Perlman, Ron 205
Perrin, Nat 55
Perry Mason 104, 119, 205
Person to Person 22
Peter Lawford 129
Peter Pan 17, 39
Peters, Bernadette 132
Peters, Roberta 15

Petersen, Paul 36
Peterson, Patty 36
Petticoat Junction 45, 54, 126, 154–155
Peyser, Lois 20
Peyton Place 156
Peyton Place (book) 8
Pfeiffer, Michelle 202
Philco Television Playhouse 14
Phillips, Irna 20–21
Picasso, Pablo 96
Pickles, Christina 125
Pilato, Herbie J. 91
Pinza, Ezio 115
Playhouse 90 14
Playing for Time 14
Please Don't Eat the Daises 64–65, 160, 205
Pleshette, Suzanne 71, 102, 132
Police Story 135, 138–140
political correctness 7, 114
Pollyanna 36
Poltrack, David 4
PopMatters.com 37
Porter, Dawn Nyree 152
Porter, Don *103*
Post, Markie 135
Powell, William 145
Power of Women 11
Powers, Ron 41
Powers, Stefanie 135, 186
Presley, Elvis 15
Price, Leontyne 15, 17
Prime Suspect 3, 140
Prime Time, Our Time 8, 26
Princess Diana 179
Prisoner: Cell Block H 143
Private Benjamin 160
Private Secretary 4, 98–100, 102–*103*, 104, 106, 160–162, 205
Professional Father 39
Profiler 3
Profiles in Courage 17
The Protectors 152, 196
Prowse, Juliet 160
Prudential Family Theater 14
Public Service Announcements (PSA) 188
Pyle, Denver 52

Queen Elizabeth II 22
Queenan, Joe 37
Quick as a Flash 12
The Quiz Kids 13, 20
quiz programs 12–13

racism 26, 92
radio 29, 32, 38, 69, 82, 99, 107, 131, 144, 153
Radio-TV Mirror (magazine) 163
Rains, Ella 118
Raising Hope 70
Ralph, Sheryl Lee 152
Rand, Ayn 149
Randall, Sue 101
Randolph, Amanda 69, 115
Randolph, Lillian 14
ratings 6, 27, 36, 120, 134, 150, 155, 172, 187, 199

Raye, Martha 15
Reagan, Nancy 22
reality TV 12, 37
The Red Skelton Show 17
Reddy, Helen 16
Redgrave, Lynn 102, 160
Redgrave, Vanessa 14
Reed, Donna 8–9, 21, 35–37, 44, 157
Reed, Robert 124
Reese, Della 15
Reiner, Carl 15, 41, 166
Remington Steele 204–205
Revere, Paul 169
Reynolds, Debbie 84–85
Reynolds, Marjorie 38
Rhoda *173*–175
Rich Man, Poor Man 127
Richards, Michael 62
Richards, Renee 14
Richardson, Patricia 3
The Rifleman 20
Rigg, Diana 60, *172*, 174, 182, 184
Riggs, Bobby 18
Riley, Jeannie C. 87
Rio Bravo 139
The Rise of the Goldbergs (radio show) 28
Ritter, John 62
Rivers, Joan 17, 66
The Road West 127
Robert Montgomery Presents 20
Roberts, Doris 67
Roberts, Rachel 17
Robinson, Larry 27
Roble, Chet 115
The Rockford Files 135, 140
Rockne, Knute 85
Rockwell, Robert 99
Rocky Jones, Space Ranger 20, 192–193
Roddenberry, Gene 193–194
Roe v. Wade 120
Roe vs. Wade (TV movie) 14
Rogers, Roy 153
Rolle, Esther 61–63, 107, 113
Roller Derby 18–19
Romeo and Juliet 47
Ronstadt, Linda 16
The Rookies 122–123, 205
Room 222 20, 101, 175
Rooney, Mickey 35
Roosevelt, Eleanor 22
Roosevelt, Elliott 12
Roosevelt, Franklin D. 12
Roots 14, 106
Rose, Jamie 142
Roseanne 5, 47, 54, 56–57, 65, 67, 87, 109
Rosenzweig, Barney 147, 149
Ross, Diana 17
Ross, Marion 28, 204
Rountree, Martha *21*
Rowan & Martin's Laugh-In 138
Rowlands, Gena 14, 160
The Roy Rogers Show 152–153
Rudolph, Wilma 18
Rush, Barbara 132
Ruskin, Bud 137

Russell, Jane 148
Russell, Rosiland 8
Rutan, Susan 107
Ryan, Irene 54

Saint, Eva Marie 14
St. Elsewhere 124–125
Saints and Sinners 132
Salvage 1 160
Sanders, Marlene 18
The Sandy Duncan Show 172
Sanford, Isabel 63–64
Sanka 26
Sara (drama) 102
Sara (sitcom) 175
Sargent, Dick 88–89
Saturday Night Live 16, 100
Saunders, Gloria 200–201
Savage, Candace 152, 178–179
Scarecrow and Mrs. King 107
Schell, Catherine *197*–198
Schell, Maria 14
The Schlitz Playhouse of Stars 14
Schneider, John 148
Schroeder, Ricky 106
Schultz, Barbara 20
Sciabarra, Chris Matthew 149
science fiction 176, 190–199
Scolari, Peter 157
Scott, George C. 105
Scott, Sydna *128*
Sea Hunt 148
Second Serve 14
See It Now 21
Seinfeld 62, 165
Sellecca, Connie 135
Selleck, Tom 148
Sesame Street 21
Sesame Workshop 21
Seven Year Itch 176
Sex and the City 100, 162
Sex and the Single Girl 184
sexism 4, 66, 68, 74, 88, 97, 180, 196, 204, 205
Sexual Personae 6
Shades Lives 138
Shakespeare, William 12, 55
Shane 91
Shangri-Las 16
Shatner, William 195
Shaver, Helen 132
Shayon, Robert Lewis 121
Sheena 176, 179–180, 182, 203, 205
Sheena (comic book) 179
Sheldon, Sidney 93, 95
Shepherd, Cybill 4, 98
Sherwood, Madeline 159
Shindig 15
The Shirelles 16
Shirley's World 131
Shore, Dinah 15, 17
Sidaris, Arlen 149
Siegel, Lionel 190
Sills, Beverly 15
Silver Spoons 106–107
Silverman, Fred 149
Silverman, Treva 20
Simon, Neil 15
Simon and Simon 148

Sinatra, Nancy 16
Sinclair, Madge 125
Singin' in the Rain 84
single fathers 38, 81, 111, 114, 162
The Single Guy 162
single mothers 4, 47–49, 51–52, 72, 76–78, 101, 117, 121–122, 134, 140, 160, 169, 179
single women 3–4, 65, 86, 98, 130, 150, 153, 162–176
Sioussat, Helen 11
Siouxsie Sioux 55
Sirtis, Marina 195
Sister Kate 159
Sister, Sister 14
Sit or Miss 12
The Six Million Dollar Man 190–191
The $64,000 Question 12
60 Minutes 22, 132
Sledge Hammer! 143
Smith, Alexis 157
Smith, Jaclyn 147
Smith, Kate 15
Smith, Margaret Chase 22
Smith, Patti 16
Smith, Ronald L. 46, 91, 96, 151, 201
Smith, Sandra 127
Smith, Shelley 135
The Smothers Brothers 17
The Snoop Sisters 146
So This Is Hollywood 160, 163
Solow, Herbert F. 194
The Sonny & Cher Show 15
The Sopranos 156
Sorbo, Kevin 189
Sothern, Ann 56, 76, 98, 102–**103**, 104, 106, 111, 160–162, 175
Space: 1999 152, 196–**197**, 198, 205
Space Patrol 192, 199, 205
Spangler, Lynn 76
specials 17–18
spectaculars *see* specials
Spelling, Aaron 123, 137, 147
Spielberg, Steven 25
spinoffs 58, 149, 173, 185
sponsors *see* advertising
sports programming 18–19
Spy TV 186
Stafford, Jo 15
Stahl, Lesley 18
staid wives-wacky husband genre 39–44
Stanley, Florence 135
Stanley, Kim 14
Stanwyck, Barbara 8, 13, 19, 148, **155**–157
Stapleton, Jean 57
Star Trek 20, 184, 192–195, 197, 199, 205
Star Trek (films) 194
The Star Trek *Compendium* 194
Star Trek: The Next Generation 192–193, 195, 196–197
Star Trek: Voyager 3, 198
Starlog (magazine) 138, 142, 148, 189, 190, 197
statistics 23, 98, 167, 171
Stearns, Christopher 23
Stearns, Johnny 23

Stearns, Mary Kay 23
Steel Magnolias 67
The Stepford Wives 5, 191–192
Stephen J. Cannell Productions 141
Sterling, Robert 44, 154
Stevens, Inger 110–111
Stevens, Julie 127
Stevens, Mark 127
Stevenson, McLean 159, 170
Stevenson, Rachel 20
Stewart, Jimmy 35
Stiller, Jerry 17, 134
Stone, Pauline 20
Stone Pillow 14
Storch, Larry 47
Storm, Gale 9, 15, **80**–82, 160, 162
Stracke, Win 115
Streisand, Barbra 17
Stritch, Elaine 165
Stromstedt, Ulla 160
Struthers, Sally 57
Stuart, Randy 144
Studio One 20
Suddenly Susan 162, 175
Sullivan, Susan 117, 127
Sunset Blvd. 8
superheroines 106, 107–203
Supernanny 111
The Supremes 15–**16**, 17
The Survivors 157
Sutherland, Joan 15, 17
Suzanne Pleshette Is Maggie Briggs 132
Swanson, Gloria 11
Sweet Bird of Youth 8
Swift, Lela 20
Swiss Family Robinson 53
Swit, Loretta 123–124
Sybil 14
Syndicated Television (book) 142, 179
syndication 22, 29, 65, 83, 135–136, 142, 152, 177, 179

T and T 135
T, Mr. 135
Talbot, Nita 132
Talent Patrol 12
talk shows 11
The Tall Man 20
Tallchief, Maria 15
Tammy 84
Tandy, Jessica 14
Tarzan 148, 179
Taxi 160
Taylor, Ella 61
Taylor, Holland 157
Teachers Only 102
Tebaldi, Renata 17
Television Women from Lucy to Friends 76
Terkel, Studs 115
Terry and the Pirates 200–**201**, 203
That Girl 59, 74, 160, 162, 165–167
That '70s Show 37
theater and plays 8, 47, 144, 165
Thelma and Louise 77, 143, 175, 198, 201
The Thin Man 145, 152, 183, 204
30 Rock 175
Thirtysomething 3

This Is Your Life 22
Thomas, Danny 38, 115
Thomas, Marlo 17, 160, 166
Thomas, Richard 52
Thompson, Dorothy 127
Thompson, Sada 72
Thor, Jerome 128
The Thorn Birds 159
Those Whiting Girls 163–**164**, 175
Three's Company 62, 108, 117, 173
Thrillingdetective.com 150
Tillstrom, Burr 20
Time (magazine) 3, 7, 35, 37, 121
The Time Tunnel 160
TimsTV.com 109
Title IX 189
Titus 37
To Kill a Mockingbird (book) 8
To Tell the Truth 12, 20
Today Show 66
TODON Productions 37
Tom Corbett, Space Cadet 192
The Tom Ewell Show 39
Tomlin, Lily 15, 17
Tonight Show 11, 26
Tony awards 109, 114
Tony Orlando & Dawn 15
The Tony Randall Show 135
Toohey, Geraldine 20
Top Secret, USA 160
Topper 44, 154
Trapper John, MD 125, 148
A Tree Grows in Brooklyn (film) 163
Trotta, Liz 18
Trouble with Father 37–38
Tucker, Ken 89
Tucker, Sophie 15
Turbiville, Betty 20
Turner, Lana 56, 157
Turner, Tina 15, 17–18
Turney, Catherine 20
TV Guide (magazine) 4, 12, 19, 28, 35, 37, 73, 80, 82, 93, 120, 139, 203
TV Sirens 33, 103, 151
TVAcres.com 112
Twenty-One 13
Twilight Zone 20, 200
Two and a Half Men 115
2 Broke Girls 87, 175
240-Robert 143
Two Girls Named Smith 160, 163, 165
The Two Mrs. Greenvilles 14
227 6
Tyler, Beverly 127
Tyson, Cicely 14, 105–106

UFO 196
Ugly Betty 103
Ullman, Tracey 15
Uncommon Knowledge 19
US Census 23
US Department of Labor 23, 98
US military 92, 160, 200
US Park Service 51
The United States Steel Hour 14, 20
United States Supreme Court 68
The Unsinkable Molly Brown 84
The Untouchables 20

Upstairs, Downstairs 112–113
Urecal, Minerva 160

V 202–203
Vaccaro, Brenda 102, 140
Valentine, Karen 175
Valley of the Dolls (book) 8
Vampira 44
Van Ark, Joan 157
Vance, Vivian 60, 76–*78*
Van Dyke, Dick 42
Variety 15, 35
variety shows 14–17
Vaughn, Robert 152, 185
Verdugo, Elena 122, *167*
Versace 182
Victor, David 122, 186
Vietnam War 18
villainesses 199–203
Violett, Ellen M. 20
Von Nardroff, Elfrida 13
Von Saltza, Chris 18

"Wacky Wife" sitcoms 39, 42, 63, 69, 73–87
WACs 9, 169
Wade, Ernestine 69–70
Waggoner, Lyle 189
Wagner, Lindsay 190
Waits, Kathleen 40
Walker, Clint 77
Walker, Jimmy 62
Walker, Nancy 115, 157, 173, 174
Wallace, Marcia 106
Wallace, Mike 20
Waller, Judith Cary 21
Walter, Jessica 140
Walters, Barbara 3
The Waltons 8, 52–53, 61, 112, 124–125
Wander, Philip 59
War & Peace 6
Ward, Burt 188
Washington Post 37, 136
Waters, John 75
Watson, Mary Ann 9, 82
Watson, Thomas J. 77
WAVES 160
The Way We Never Were 25
WBKB *see* WLS
Webster 67–68
Weeds 5
Weisblat, Dakota 5

Welles, Orson 131
Wells, H.G. 176
Wells, Mary K. 127
West, Adam 188
West, Mae 17
Westfall, Kay 12
Westinghouse 21, 26
Westinghouse Desilu Playhouse Presents the Lucille Ball-Desi Arnaz Show 76
Weston, Joanie *18*–19, 22
What's Happening! 72, 157
What's My Line? 12
What's the Problem? 20
Where the Girls Are 4, 55, 61, 147, 158
White, Anne 177
White, Betty 9, 19, 83–84, 160, 205
White, Patrick J. 185
White, Vanna 12
White Goddess 79, 179, 198
Whiting, Barbara 164
Whiting, Margaret *164*
Whitney 6
Whitney, Grace Lee 194
Who Said That? 12
Who Will Love My Children? 14
Who's Afraid of Virginia Woolf? (play) 8
Who's the Boss? 4, 107, 169
Who's There? 12
Wickes, Mary 115, 125
Wild, Wild West 185
Wilkerson, Martha 185
Williams, Barry 66, 148
Williams, Cara 107
Williams, Cindy 85–*86*
Williams, Erica 99
Williams, Esther 180
Willy 132–133, 205
Wilson, Elizabeth 105
Wilson, Flip 17
Wimbledon 177
Windom, William 77, 110
Winfrey, Oprah 3
Winters, Jonathan 17
Winters, Shelley 200
WIOU 132
Wire Service 131
witchcraft 88, 90
WKRP in Cincinnati 106, 135
WLS 18
WMAQ 21

A Woman Called Golda 14
Wonder Woman 8, *177*, 188–190, 205
The Wonder Years 135
Wong, Anna May 143
Wood, Peggy 14, *28*–29, 35
Woodman, Ruth 20
Woodstock 49
Woodward, Bob 131
Woodward, Joanne 14
Woolf, Virginia 96
Woolworth's 27
Wopat, Tom 148
Working (book) 115
working mothers 45, 48–49, 65, 67, 86, 116–117, 122, 125, 166, 169, 170–171, 179, 185, 187, 190; *see also* working women
Working Woman (magazine) 4, 98–99
working women 4, 23, 42, 44–45, 48, 52, 62, 64, 67, 71, 76, 88, 98, 175; *see also* working mothers
World War II 9, 14, 23, 25–26, 30, 184, 188–189, 202
World Wrestling Entertainment (WWE) 19
Wrather, Bonita Granville 20
wrestling 19
Wright, Teresa 14
Wright Brothers 158
Wroe, Trudy 127
Wyatt, Jane 33–34, 194
Wyler, Gretchen 157
Wyman, Jane 13, 19, 157

The X-Files 3, 160, 197
Xena, Warrior Princess 3, 5, 176, 182, 195, 203, 205

York, Dick 88–89
Young, Loretta 13, 19, 26, 160
Younger, Beverly 115
Youngfellow, Barrie 117
Your Hit Parade 15
Your Show of Shows 15, 20, 110
Youth Forums see New York Times Youth Forums

Zachary, Beulah 20
Zane Grey Theater 14
Zenith 9
Zimbalist, Stephanie 204